46 AND COUNTING

A Family Journey

46 AND COUNTING

A Family Journey

IAN BUNTON

CHARLOTTE BUNTON

THOMAS BUNTON

SUZY BUNTON (aka 'the football widow')

And guest contributors

© Ian Bunton, 2016

Published by Ian Bunton

A CIP catalogue record for this book is available from the British Library.

ISBN 978-0-9955628-0-6

Book layout and cover design by Clare Brayshaw

Front cover images:
Top: Photo by Zemanek/BPI/REX/Shutterstock
Bottom: Getty Images *(Tom knows it's in)*

Prepared and printed by:

York Publishing Services Ltd
64 Hallfield Road
Layerthorpe
York YO31 7ZQ

Tel: 01904 431213

Website: www.yps-publishing.co.uk

ACKNOWLEDGEMENTS

All Football Supporters
For the terrace whit and humour. Football without supporters is nothing. You are the heartbeat of your club, no matter how big or small.

Guest Contributors
For all your words and contributions, thank you. Made my job a lot easier.

Pictures and Images
Thanks to PA Images, Getty Images, REX Shutterstock for use of their images. And to Hallyink and Janine Lees for the time and patience on their artwork.

 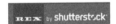

York Publishing Services
For guiding this non writer through the process.

Amber Nectar
For the consistent insight into what it is to be a City fan. Somehow, they have the uncanny habit to *"Think the Things that we think we think"*

Hull City Supporters Trust
I only came on board late. However, the absurdity of the membership scheme compelled me to join. Dare to say the phrase, a 'united front'. Geoff Bielby is as eloquent as I can never be.

Advertisers and Sponsors

For your contributions. Saved me having to dig to deep my into my own pockets, so hopefully raising more for Alzheimer's.

Next Door Sue

For making time to read and correct my grammatical errors. And the lucky pants.

Nick Patrick William Walker

A sad start to the season, but always in our minds at every game, and will continue to be so, win, lose or draw.

Bri Lee

No words required, just songs! And never a derogative one, always in support behind the eleven out there. Every team needs a few of you. Glad you are in the City end. Proud to be associated.

Steve Bruce

For apparently "*having a dream…*" and letting us share it.

The Players of Hull City

For achieving what should have always been, which once felt impossible, but eventually came reality.

The Mother In Law

What really this book should be about. Nothing to do with football, but about doing 'the right thing' and thank you for 'being with us' along the way, especially at the end. "*Up the Tigers*"

Charlotte

Simply for being the eternal optimist and great daughter. Oh, and for putting up with a grumpy old dad.

The Football Widow

For understanding my mood swings. For ever getting involved with me in the first place. For your continued support, you will never know. For trying to comprehend what it all means, but actually admitting that you don't. And lastly, for just being you. Not quite on page three, but not far off!

Thomas

My beloved son, the new football casual. Please continue to take your designer labels around the football globe. It's been a pleasure to share it all with you, the pain, the endurance, the ecstasy.

My job now feels done. You entered the season a football boy, you finished it a football man.

Take defeat on the chin, enjoy the victories.

"WE ARE HULL CITY, SINCE 1904...."

INTRODUCTION

If you've flicked open to this page in a book store, go on, get your hand in your pocket and spend a tenner. If you've already bought it, I'd personally like to say thank you.

Not only have you decided to share in our journey following Hull City, but you have also contributed funds to an extremely worthwhile cause, the Alzheimer's Society. More of this in a short while, but rest assured, all profits from this book will be donated towards those suffering from dementia, a disease close to my family's hearts.

Just in case you were mistaken, this book is most certainly about football, predominantly Hull City. Our team.

It will attempt to portray the feelings and emotions of following them throughout an entire season. It will no doubt, tip toe back into days gone by, back to Boothferry Park and The Kempton, recollecting events that I am still unable to erase. Mood swings will no doubt change, there will be highs and lows but that is all part of being a football fan.

I offer no apologies for constant references to my family and fellow Hull City supporters. They are what makes following our team even better, whether to share the pain or enjoy the highs.

I believe I'm a relatively uncomplicated bloke. The simple things in life are what give me the greatest pleasure, the things that I love.

So put into the mix a few pints, Hull City and my beloved family and what more could a man want?!

Hope you enjoy the read.

I give you…..

"46 AND COUNTING ; A FAMILY JOURNEY"

'THE PERSON I MISS MOST IS ME' – LIVING WITH DEMENTIA

The picture on this page includes my mother in law, Christine Mary Walters. This very phrase 'mother in law' might be enough for many married men to groan and wince. Not me.

She used to be the life and soul of the party, skipping around like a ballerina, making sure every family member and friend was being looked after, always considering herself last. Full of song and dance, life was lived to the full. Always wearing a glowing and warming smile, her very presence and effervescence for life was infectious. To put it simply, you couldn't help but enjoy yourself in her company.

Sadly, Christine was diagnosed with early onset dementia back in 2008.

It's gradually taken its toll in the ensuing years, and today, she is a shadow of the person we all know and love.

But every now and then, flashes of her old self will jump to the fore. In amongst stringing a sentence together in three unfathomable newly invented languages, impossible to comprehend, she can burst into one of her favourite songs, word for word. Incredible.

It is those flashes that we all cling to, to see the old Christine.

I know for a fact that my wife, the football widow, would swap anything to have her mum back, even if just for a day. We all would.

She can now often be seen and heard, walking around her care home, saying *"Up The Tigers"*, much to our amusement.

So we could think of no better cause to donate any profits from this book to, than to the Alzheimer's Society. It may well be too late to help Christine, but if, in some small way, it helps to assist someone else coping with this disease, then it is money well spent.

Since the start of this journey, the football widow has now become the Dementia Lead Nurse for Hull and East Yorkshire Hospitals NHS Trust. It's a disease that according to recent statistics, someone in the UK is diagnosed with every three minutes. So please continue to donate and help the fight.

Thank you.

"I have dementia
My eyes do see, my ears do hear
I am still me, so lets be clear
My memory may fade, my walk may slow
I am me inside, don't let me go."

ALZHEIMER'S SOCIETY

Alzheimer's Research UK is the UK's leading dementia research charity. The charity powers world class studies that give us the best chance of beating dementia sooner. Its scientists' ground breaking work focuses on prevention, treatment and cure.

In the UK more than 850,000 people are currently living with dementia. Worldwide the figure stands at more than 44 million. Whilst it's true that the majority of people with dementia are over 65, the condition is not a normal part of getting older. Nor is the condition only linked with later life; in the UK over 40,000 people under 65 have dementia.

There are currently no treatments to stop the diseases that cause dementia, most commonly known as Alzheimer's.

While some treatments can help some people to live with their symptoms a little better, there are no treatments that slow or stop diseases like Alzheimer's. This means that the diseases will continue to get worse over time unless new treatments can be found. Alzheimer's Research UK is leading the charge to find these treatments and preventions.

Because Alzheimer's Research UK receives no government funding, the charity is completely dependent on the generosity of supporters to fund its research programme.

In support of

Alzheimer's
Research
UK
The Power to Defeat Dementia

FOREWORD

As a football fan, or indeed any passionate sports fan, I, like many others have often thought "*What if …?*"

What if we could visit all League Football Grounds for example?

What if I could go to an FA Cup Final or a Champions League Final?

We should all have goals and set ourselves challenges in life.

For Hull City fans of my generation, for decades it was, what if City could compete in the top league? A dream finally achieved of course on 28th May 2008. That following season I made a pledge to visit as many Premier League grounds as possible with my eldest son Matt. We only managed ten when finance, work and family commitments prevented more. At least we witnessed City's first Premier League away win at Newcastle and that magnificent North London double in eight days, with wins at Arsenal and Spurs, still one of my personal favourite times as a City fan.

So to Ian, he asked himself "What if he and his son Thomas could go to all Hull City's games last season? Now unlike my pledge and many fans great intentions, Ian and Thomas achieved it, fantastic effort!

To mark their quest rather than leave it there he decided to document it. Mates suggested "*Why not write a book?* "

Ian wasn't convinced "*It'd be rubbish, I'm no writer*". The reply was "*So what if it's rubbish, it will be your own rubbish!*"

So this book was born and having committed to write it, as an accountant, so to the numbers, costing and finances, obviously. Now as an accountant that was easy but what about marketing and promotion? Ian contacted the club for support and advice. Perhaps they'd stock the book in the club shop? The advice was don't criticise the owners, management, players and when it's written we'll consider it.

So the season begins, optimism is high that Steve Bruce can lead the club back to the Premier League at the first attempt. On the field all's well initially. Off the field yet again it's what's sadly become the norm for City fans under the owners regime. Fans disgruntled, lack of meaningful dialogue, still no promised sale and the continued refusal of the club to use the clubs correct playing name, many felt simply due to vindictiveness. As the season moves on these feelings increasingly creep into the narrative.

Once the Membership Scheme is announced in March, there's a major shift in many fans views when concessions are abolished for 2016/17. This book isn't now going to make it to the shelves of the club shop!

At this point Ian contacts me to ask if Hull City Supporters Trust can help, not financially I add, just promotional support. Having read a few chapters the HCST Board agree and here I am!

Now like me, Ian admits he's no literary master. This may not be a great written work but what he's created is a very personal and accurate view of the 2015/16 season from a fans perspective. A view many City fans will relate to.

Call it luck, good or bad, the season, Ian calls *"46 and Counting"* just kept growing, on and off the field. City enjoyed a record breaking League Cup run ending at an Ethiad quarter final. On the way we enjoyed Accrington Stanley, what a fantastic evening that was!

City also enjoyed an FA Cup run too, until our now inevitable annual failure against Arsenal. In addition of course, despite a barren run in February, we still made the playoffs with a "Typical City" two legged performance to Wembley and victory to gain a third promotion into the Premier League in just eight years.

So *"46 and Counting"* became *"58 and Writing...."*

It may not win any literary prizes but as Ian's mates said *"So what, it's Yours."* Read it and perhaps it will resonate with you too, as it certainly did with me. Enjoy!

Geoff Bielby – *Chairman, Hull City Supporters Trust*

—

CHAPTER 1

"NOT FOR THE FIRST TIME, BLOODY BURNLEY"

This book starts at a typical City match. One that meant so much but you almost kind of expected the outcome long before the two teams had done their bit (or lack of it)!

To remind you, City had gone into the game after good results and performances against Palace and Liverpool. Renewed optimism was in the air. Three more points would have been a massive stride towards Premiership safety, and all that this brings with it.

However, this was Burnley at home. We'd played them away earlier in the season, or should I say we turned up (we lost 1-0). On more cases than not, Burnley bring out the worst in City, the proverbial bogey team. Barring what ended up being a 9 a-side game a few years ago at home, and a last minute Michael Turner winner in our promotion year, I can't recall many matches against them being good for us.

Before I mention the actual match it's maybe worth discussing why I never really understand people leaving early at games. You see loads leave at matches when the scoreline is close, one goal either way or even drawing. So no matter how you are playing, you could always snatch a late equaliser or winner. If you are winning, surely you want to see your team get over the line?! How much of a rush must all those people be in? Where have they got to go so quickly? (Maybe they are all parked in that nightmare called Walton Street match day car park?).

I can maybe understand it though if you're playing rubbish and getting trounced, it simply doesn't make for easy viewing.

I can probably count on one hand the number of times I've left early.

One involves an away visit to Chester. We lost three nil. The first goal was scored after about two or three minutes, we missed it as we were just paying at the turnstiles. Chester scored again after about five minutes, I missed it as I was having a pee. And to make matters worse, Chester scored again after about ten minutes. I missed that too as I was queuing for a pie! The pie was shit too! I can't recall a City shot and having suffered until about sixty or seventy minutes, we called it a day.

At least two other early leaving incidents involve bloody Burnley.

I recall leaving a game at Turf Moor a few seasons back, only just after half time when Burnley had put their fourth passed the City keeper. We had not troubled the scoreboard. Our entourage was well down the M62 that night on our way home, way before the man in black blew his final whistle.

I also remember leaving early when losing to Burnley 4-1 at home, which just about condemned us to relegation in the Premier league first time around.

So, back at the KC on Saturday 9th May 2015.

Yep, we already know the inevitable happened. City lost 1-0.

We were left to think of the remaining fixtures, just Spurs away and the Mancs at home. Maybe we were really actually looking at other team's fixtures, rather than ours? Between 3pm when we had all taken our seats and just before 5ish, City pretty much summed up most of my memories, *if only...............................!*

We huffed and puffed without getting up much of a head of steam, and even actually struck the woodwork a couple of times. In-between Burnley scored a scruffy goal and went one up. At that moment the penny really dropped for me. We weren't going to score and we would be relegated.

The pre-season had been great.

We were basking in the glory of reaching the FA Cup Final. Yes, that's right, Hull City in the FA Cup Final. For a long time, we even almost had our hands on the trophy, leading Arsenal 2-0 early on, only to be ousted in extra time. More of that soon.

But we 'nearly' won it. Again, pretty much City for me........'nearly'.

But to be honest, I'm quite happy with that. Certainly at the moment and certainly considering the umpteen years I've experienced watching them in the lower leagues in a ground that was in a state of disrepair. Dubious owners followed dubious owners, gates were locked, 'last games ever' 'nearly' played and yet we are still here.

And then something happened. Why I didn't know? Why I didn't care? City, like a phoenix from the flames, actually became quite good. They won more than they lost, and they began rising through the leagues. My usual pessimistic score predictions of a 1- 0 defeat at home, and 2-0 defeat away were wildly wrong. And then we got into the Premier League.

What's happening?!

This was the Holy Grail. The tag of being one of the largest Cities in England never to have been in the top flight was gone. We were there (although I'm convinced most people probably wished we weren't.)

But for me, watching City then became a very different experience.

You had to buy tickets in advance for a game. You had to travel much further to see away games. Pre-match pubs were home fans only. There was a whole array of new faces in the away ends. You weren't allowed to stand up, or you faced the wrath of over-officious stewards. It was still watching football, but not quite as I knew it.

For the majority of the time, I still enjoyed it though. As a football fan, most of the time we pretty much put up with anything. Beating Arsenal at the Emirates and listening to Arsene Wenger saying 'he felt sick', beating West Brom at the Hawthorns to go joint top, or watching 'Super' Paul McShane rise like a salmon to head in against Liverpool. You can't write things like that, or make them up.

They actually happened.

But punctuated between all the moments, were many more 'nearly' moments. We 'nearly' equalised, we 'nearly' beat them but for a last minute goal, we 'nearly' scored.............

Being in the Premier league is tough. Unless you have a rich Sugar Daddy, you're going to struggle. The money is ridiculous. As good as Sky is, the game has gone mad? They have obviously got a vested interest in maintaining their product, despite showering it with us. There is so much difference to watching a game sat in an armchair, to those who have to travel and pay. I'm not always sure Sky totally understand this.

So once City were there, we reverted back to type, a '*nearly*' team. The challenge became just to finish one place above the drop zone, to just survive. And we have hovered around there ever since, and below, and back, and below again.

So when Mr Atkinson, blew his full time whistle against Burnley back in May 2015, and we had almost predictably lost 1-0 at home, I knew the writing was on the wall.

A season that started with a fantastic away trip to Lokeren in the Europa League, and with what I firmly believed was the best City squad in my lifetime, was ultimately going to end in failure; we were not going to '*nearly*' stay up. We all trudged down the corridors and stairs and filtered out of the ground. You could almost smell it in the air. I looked at my son and daughter and could see their disappointment. Thomas, now twelve has known nothing really but City success; Charlotte, aged fourteen, the eternal optimist – the exact opposite of me!

We talked on the way back down Anlaby Road to our car about what would happen if we were relegated, which players would stay, who would go. Charlotte's optimism said '*surely we will just go up again?*' I wasn't too sure. Inevitably players would leave thinking they were better than those playing in the Championship (not sure why as they were about to contribute towards a relegation season). For me, I wanted most to stay with just a few changes. I wanted to see some loyalty in the squad, just like most of the fans show, season on season, year after year.

I told the kids that we would still renew our season tickets and that we will be able to aspire to achieving something more than finish one place above the relegation trap door. And then I told them that they would be loads more local games in the championship. In fact, I said 'why don't we try and go to all 46 games?'

I had always wanted to do it for some reason.

And then I added........................ '*Let's write a book about it!*'

Not just a book about each game with statistics in it. No, a book which tries to portray OUR emotions about OUR team. Words to try and depict the feelings through the eyes of a forty six year old Dad, seeing the games through the backdrop of many years of underachievement (albeit disappointment does really helps you to appreciate the good times, you almost need to go through the suffering to feel the pleasure), but also through the eyes of a fourteen and a twelve year old, the next generation of Hull City fans.

And so the embryonic stages of this book were born.

We weren't even relegated yet, but from a season that started with such high expectations, and that was going to end in failure, I felt <u>we</u> had rescued something.

A new adventure that we had started together with <u>OUR</u> team.

After all as the song goes,

'NO SILVERWARE, WE DON'T CARE,
....*'*

You know the rest!

UTT!

CHAPTER 2

"WHAT DOES BEING A FOOTBALL FAN MEAN...?"

Now there is a question!

Maybe this chapter might help to try and rationalise the irrational hold that a football team can have on us.

It probably means a whole myriad of different things to different people, and there will be those that are not that interested in football who simply just don't get it.

As I once read somebody saying – "I understand football, I understand there are fans of football teams, but I do not understand what it means to be a football fan." – you either get it or you don't.

Here are the thoughts and opinions of a Hull City supporter, me!

When you think about it, it's a strange thing. Up and down the country, in fact across the whole world every weekend millions of people will travel along to watch their team, not quite knowing what to expect. And the vast majority of us will go home disappointed.

Why do we put ourselves through it? And what keeps us going?

Probably that little word again.....if.....

If we were asked would you accept three or four seasons of mediocre dross, for every one good and successful season, most of us would snap your hands off. Unless you are a fan of one of the now elite top teams, who have such a stranglehold of English domestic football; in fact probably most leagues around the world, then you've got no chance of breaking through.

My thirty years or so of watching City has until recently, suffered many more lows than highs. It's easy to jump in a car and drive hundreds of miles to watch your team if you are playing well, not so, if you're not, and defeat is inevitably on the cards before the game even kicked off.

For many seasons I was watching City in the lower leagues, as we were looking downwards not upwards. Sometimes what drove me onto watch say a potential eighth away defeat on the trot was the pure thought that today we might win. I can't miss it! The thought of how good it would be if we won and I'm there, to how bad I might feel, if we win and I'm not.

I will never forget an away day at Bradford when we won our first game of the season at about the seventeenth or eighteenth attempt. The pure joy, but we were still bottom!

To me though football is like an extended family. When you support a smaller, less glamorous team (which City definitely are), you feel part of it all. I cannot envisage that to be the case with your Manchester United's or Liverpool's.

I'm sure one City win is worth about twenty of Man United's – what would an away win at Rochdale mean to them? What pleasure can be derived from one win after another, all in consummate ease? The majority of their fans simply won't understand why we support 'little old Hull' – we can't understand why anyone would support Man United – 'glory hunters'!

You generally see the same faces at City matches. If playing at home and you have sat in the same seat for a while, you tend to talk to people who sit near you; you probably don't even know their names. No small talk, it's all about City. During away games, you meet up with friends that in the hurly burly of life, you simply do not have the time to regularly socialise with. It really does feel like a community, and as such you feel part of it, part of the success, as if you have contributed to it, and hence also the pain of failure. There is a real sense of tribalism as you head to an away game, the oppressed minority.

At a club like City, the players also feel close to you. By that I mean they are approachable and human! At the end of the day they are no different to you or me, they have just been given a different skill set in life, which fortunately for them, pays them handsomely in this Sky driven era. However, at times they can still display their human fragility and ability to royally fuck things up!

Ask them to put together a set of accounts like I can, or treat a patient like my wife, or service a car etc etc, they probably wouldn't have a clue! And once you have met a few of the players and conversed, you feel even more part of it. The pleasure you have taking your children to matches and when they meet players, well to them…… they are like Gods! The whole concept of them being role models is so true. (although some lesser than others!)

When my kids have met City players, and on occasions I have had to force a few more drinks down at the bar to wait for them to come out and sign autographs, they have always been great. The players have been courteous and happy to spend time with you. You could see my kids eyes light up (but why can you never read the signature and why do they insist on putting their squad number next to it?!)

As I write this chapter my son informs me that there might be a riot about to happen, (as the song goes) as Super Paul McShane has just been released. Another has been let go, who was always fantastic was Liam Rosenior. On a few occasions, some members of my family have stalked him for his signature and for a selfie. He was only too happy to oblige, even if out with his own family. I suppose it goes with the territory?

As I get older, I seem to prefer going to the away games. There seems to be more adventure about it, visits to new grounds, another thing that next season in the Championship will bring.

The atmosphere at home games to me, can sometimes be subdued. It probably doesn't help that I currently sit in the 'family section' but regardless, the vocal support seems to be spread out around the ground. This isn't the case at away game. You tend to have more like minded supporters, who want to sing, who are in close proximity with one another and that feeling of being outnumbered and common purpose can really spur you on for ninety minutes.

There is a belief amongst the fans that encouraging your team can improve their performance and get them over the line for victory. You can then really 'lord it over' the home fans at the full time whistle as your return to your car. Its great listening to them moan at how rubbish they were, or you can say how crap they were, just loud enough for them to hear!

The away trip also actually means a visit to a liquid refreshment outlet of some description. The fans tend to congregate in the same place and as soon as you see your own fans, you can't help but smile. *'We are 'Ull, we are 'Ull'.* You are proud to be associated, we are part of this together.

And then you usually bump into the same faces. I am thankful to have met some good friends directly as a result of City. Friends that otherwise probably wouldn't be, they would just be another face in the street. Friends that have stayed loyal to their team through thick and thin and you respect them for that. I'm not going to do a load of name dropping here (that can wait until later chapters), but if you are reading this text, you know who you are.

As I have got older, football has brought about slightly different emotions.

In younger years, you would be thinking about the weekend match all during the week, nervous and excited. If you won, you would go out and celebrate and talk about it incessantly, working the table out, predicting future fixtures and results. If you lost it could feel like your whole world had crumbled, especially if it was a really important game. It would pray on your mind for days.

The words of Bill Shankly are so true.

> *"....Some people think Football is a matter of life and death. I don't like that attitude, I can assure them it is much more serious than that....."*

When your partner/wife/husband/friend says to you as you leave the front door on your way to the next match "enjoy yourself", you know they don't really understand. This is not about enjoyment!

However, as I've got older, these emotions have changed. This predominantly coincided with starting to take my son to watch.

His due date of birth was the 26th December 2002, the first competitive match at the KC, a glamorous home tie against Hartlepool. I fully envisaged a tannoy message a few minutes into the game saying 'Mr Bunton, please make your way to the Maternity Hospital, you are about to become a Father!' Needless to say, much like his more recent years, the lazy git was too late and didn't arrive until January.

City went on to win the game 1-0 thanks to a Stuart Green goal. I remember sitting at the KC, thinking this is a really great stadium. Much as I missed Boothferry Park for memories it gave me, it really felt like a new era. We were the big boys in a new league with a new stadium. The away team really were playing their cup final!

And with that and about time too, City actually started to be quite good. We started rising through the divisions with meteoric success; success was until now, an unheard of concept. The last game at the old ground had ended a predictable damp squid and an anti-climax, a 0-1 reverse to Darlington. This all felt totally alien!

Thomas' first game was at home to WBA. At the time I sat exactly on the half way line in the East Stand and went with my Dad and nephew. My nephew couldn't go to this game, so there was a spare seat. I think Thomas was about three and was decked out in the latest City top with the obligatory number 3 on his back, which next year would be four and five and so on.

I can't recall much about the game, other than Thomas' excitement. He couldn't see a lot, he was barely heavy enough to stop himself from falling through his seat when it tipped up and down, his little legs dangling but not long enough to touch the floor. A certain Welshman and compatriot were immediately in front of us, constantly standing and encouraging the crowd to sing. One is fondly known as Taffy, but Thomas thought his name was Toffee – and that has stuck to this day!

But it didn't matter, they were enjoying themselves, as was Thomas. He didn't stay in his own seat for long and ended up sitting on my knee. By half time, the excitement had clearly got too much and he fell fast asleep until the full time whistle. This happened on more than one occasion, and I do recall City scoring against Wolves, Thomas on my knee fast asleep. I'm sure only Thomas and the away fans remained seated. He didn't blink an eye! The same happened when his favourite player, Sam Ricketts scored his (I think) one and only home goal for City v Southend.

Almost from this moment on, I started to watch City both through my own eyes and my son's. The two perceptions are not necessarily always the same. My father stopped going soon afterwards; it was almost as if his work had been done. The next generation of City fan was here!

More recently, my daughter has joined the Saturday afternoon visits to the KC. I can see the same excitement in her as both Thomas and I had. She is a great contrast to me, I am the eternal pessimist, and she is the eternal optimist and is convinced if you will the ball into the net it will happen, her Mum calls this cosmic ordering. I have tried this concept without too much success. I often say to them both, I hope you are enjoying this. They have known little but success, certainly when you compare to the previous twenty or thirty years.

And that is what makes football great, be that a follower of Hull City (or god forbid anyone else). City is one real thing that brings us all together, something we do collectively, we win together, we lose together; we feel the elation of scoring and the pain of conceding a goal; we go through the bad times and enjoy the good.

It has divided opinions, but ultimately you have one common goal, to help and see your team win. Whether it's a goal that secures promotion, a cup success, a win against a team you hate or a win that ends a hopeless losing streak, it can unite us all. Next time City score, close your eyes and soak it all in. Trust me, try it! That unbridled joy of scoring a goal. When Geovanni and then Daniel Cousin scored at the Emirates, I seriously thought I was going to have a heart attack.

You feel part of it and that in some way you have contributed to it.

And once you are in, you are in, and it is very difficult to break.

On the rare occasions that you cannot attend a match, you are there in spirit, your attention removed from whatever else you should be doing. You may as well have gone; you are no use to anyone else! Be that, glued to the TV watching for score updates, listening to the radio or updating your phone every ten seconds.

Watching another team can't retain the same interest, you simply just don't belong.

Players will come and go, owners will come and go, but those genuine supporters stay. They do keep coming back for more, you just can't help it!

"CITY TILL I DIE"

CHAPTER 3

"HALF TIME DESPAIR, IMMENSE PRIDE AND BELGIUM BEER – HOPE AND EXPECTATION"

Before I start to talk about the impending 15/16 season and the challenge of *'doing all 46'*, I feel that I must go back in time slightly, firstly to the latter part of the 13/14 season and then to early 14/15.

Why?

Because for me, at this time there seemed to be a seismic shift in the expectation of many City fans. Gone were the thoughts of struggle, blind faith and hope. These seemed to have been replaced with a new air of expectation. A romantic optimism that we were going to win every game.

For us fans of umpteen years, this is a hard concept to understand!

At this time, certain meteoric things happened for long standing City supporters. And in typical City style, they didn't last long, but god how they affected me.

If you were at any or all of the games below, I think you'll understand. If you weren't just try to imagine.

I'll first go back to just gone four pm on Sunday 9th March 2014.

Charlotte, Thomas and I have just left the KC Stadium and are walking through West Park back to our car.

We are all ecstatic as a ten minute second half spell has seen City totally blow away Sunderland in an FA Cup Quarter Final. We romped to a three nil victory (Sunderland were lucky to get nil!) and we even had the luxury of missing a penalty.

I particularly enjoyed David Meyler leaving Lee Cattermole for dust for the second goal.

City are in an FA Cup semi-final at Wembley, the first semi-final in about eighty years and certainly something I never thought I'd see. Yes, we maybe got lucky with some of the draws, but I'd say after lots of crap years in the cup, eventually your time and luck with the draw must come your way.

That being said, there has been many a year when we think we've maybe got a decent draw, only to cock it up and get dumped out by a lower ranked team, through a combination of not performing on the day and / or not putting out a full strength team and taking it seriously.

Anyway, be it right or wrong, the Cup semi-finals are now at Wembley, and no longer at a neutral ground.

We already knew most of the other teams left in the draw; it was Sheffield United, Arsenal and Man City or Wigan (who were playing later).

God we didn't want Arsenal or Man City!

As we were walking out, the news soon spread that we'd got Sheffield United. They were two leagues below us.

It couldn't be better could it?

Well for me, maybe it could.

Being the eternal pessimist, I'm already shitting myself.

If all the years watching City has taught me anything, it's never to let City get your expectation level up too much. More often than not, they'll let you down and shatter your dreams. Some of us have become pre-conditioned to expect the worst.

It doesn't stop you supporting them, but it's more of hope than expectation, and at times it's bloody painful and soul destroying!

So, in my own mind, I knew that City will never have a better chance of getting to an FA Cup Final, and then who knows what could happen on a final day. But it would be 'typical City' to lose and balls up such a great opportunity.

The problem is that there's still over a month to go until the semi-final.

I've decided that the whole family is going to attend and we are going to make a weekend of it.

In hindsight I was a little disappointed that the City end seemed to have some spare seats. Rumour was that many 'fans' were saving themselves for the final (ridiculous I know).

Not us Bunton's, never guarantee anything. City had only been to Wembley once in over one hundred years, this was not to be missed.

So I treat us all to a fantastic hotel in Chelsea (partly because I was too slow to book something and all the cheap ones had gone) and we travelled down the day before the semi-final. I was going to try and enjoy it, albeit I knew that unless we were three up in the first ten minutes, it would be unlikely.

We had a great night out in Covent Garden the night before and you could hear City chants coming out from all the pubs, there was 'Cod' everywhere!

This all changed for me on the day of the game. It was going to be a long day as kick off was not until just gone four pm.

I woke up at stupid o'clock am, dry mouth, knots in my stomach, the whole works. I couldn't eat, drink or anything, I felt sick.

The rest of the family found it highly amusing and I couldn't explain or articulate to them quite why I felt this way. This was going to either be one of my best City days, or one of the worst, nothing in between.

Minutes, hours, seemed to drag by.

Eventually we got to the stadium, and without repeating it all, we all know how shit that first half felt. I, like many others, felt so deflated.

There were disturbances between City supporters and the whole atmosphere where we were sat, was not how it should have been. My worst nightmare was coming true, a team from two leagues below were outplaying us, we simply hadn't turned up.

I turned to Thomas and I could see his angst. Water filled eyes said it all, I could see how much it meant to him.

My god I said to myself, what have I done to my poor son, what have I inflicted on him!

And then you remember why you are a football fan.

'Never give up hope,' 'it's only a game' and all that, and whilst *'tomorrow never comes'* and *'utopia doesn't exist'*, the dreaming and hoping is what we have to stick to.

If we don't have that, then many of us would stop coming altogether.

So I gave Thomas a hug, told him to 'man up' and stop acting like a twelve year old kid ("oh, you are a twelve year old!"). I told him that a game can soon change and predicted that whoever scored the next goal would probably go on and win (honestly I did!)

As we now know, half time probably came just at the right time for us.

Captain Curtis Davies gave them all a rollicking in the changing room and the team came out all guns blazing.

In twenty blistering minutes, we turned a 2-1 deficit into a 4-2 lead. All the goals were at our end, and we were sat right behind the goal on the front row.

I won't forget Huddlestone's goal ever. The minute it went in, I knew we'd win. How quick things can change, an FA Cup final awaited.

Moral of the story I suppose, is never give up that hope. One minute you can feel utter despair, soon after, unbridled joy.

The rest of the league season was a bit of an anti-climax. Focus seemed to be off the league games and we limped to Premier league safety – fortunately we had won enough points early in the season.

And so the 17th May 2014 came.

The cup semi-final win meant we were playing Arsenal. By that very fact, City had qualified for Europe next season.

City in Europe; not a pre-season friendly, a competitive match in a proper European competition.

It was also fun singing to Man United fans at Old Trafford in our last away league match, *'We're all going on a European tour'* City had achieved something that season which Man United hadn't.

On the night Man United strolled to a 3-1 win.

On the day of the final, just Thomas and I drove down and back on the day – the semi-final had cost enough already.

The 'football widow' had done her duties well. As we set off, she'd put a key ring on my car keys, denoting that City were in an FA Cup final and scarves and flags were on display. This was our day and we were proud, so happy to let everyone know that *We are 'Ull, We are 'Ull.'*

In complete contrast to the semi-final, I wasn't nervous for this game at all. We were up against Arsenal and I didn't expect us to win, just so long as we kept ourselves in the game long enough to make it a contest.

I'll never forget that feeling when the teams lined up and Abide with Me played. This felt even bigger than the Championship Play-Off Final; we were in a major Final being screened all over the world against one of the big boys.

A real lump in your throat moment and I'm not ashamed to admit feeling very emotional, perhaps *'we had arrived'?*

It had been worth visiting all those crappy little grounds, the Deva Stadium, the McCain Stadium the list is endless. In that moment they all came flashing back. For this moment, the wait had been worth it.

And how City played their part. Two up within the first ten minutes. If only Alex Bruce's header had not been cleared off the line, three up would surely have been game over.

But it was not quite enough. Arsenal are a good team, which was summed up in extra time. They brought on Rosicky and Wilshire, probably about £30-£40 million of talent; we brought on Boyd (no disrespect) –*'he's only got one eye!'*

So Arsenal snatched a victory from defeat.

It's often said that no-one remembers the FA Cup final losers. As I drove home, Thomas fast asleep providing no company whatsoever, I had never felt prouder of **my** Hull City. It had been a great game full of incident and even though we'd lost, I couldn't fault a single City player. They had run their socks off and unfortunately had simply run out of gas, nothing else could have been done.

No sore losers here, just immense pride.

And we had the added bonus of a European tour to look forward to.

The season was over and you could sense that something had changed amongst some City fans.

For many, it was no longer hope, but one of expectation and those expectation levels had risen drastically. The talk was of who we would be buying with unheard of transfer fees being offered. Pre-season filled with wasted time on pointless pornographic football transfer speculation.

I remember Boothferry Park days when people were chucking coins into plastic buckets emblazoned with *'Put A Tiger In Your Team'*. If I'm right, I'm sure those buckets contributed towards the wages of fan's favourite, *'Knees Up Linton Brown'*.

And so a squad was assembled that we all thought quite capable of Premiership survival, and who knows maybe a Europa League run. With a bit of luck we might get into a group with an Inter Milan? Great times to be a City fan.

City were drawn away to Trencin first.

I made my first mistake.

Both due to family holidays and over confidence, assuming we'd easily go through, not to mention the possible cost, I didn't book up for the away leg. Also there was no way I wasn't going without Thomas and the 'football widow' was yet to be convinced he should be going all that way.

We sneaked through the tie although not without a scare after they scored a very early goal at the KC.

The next round draw, and last before a possible group stage, brought us up against Lokeren in Belgium – an ideal trip, and we were away first.

The plan was to go there and back without too many nights stopover if possible. This was due both to work commitments, (football on a Thursday night in a foreign country, my hat goes off to fans who travel all those miles spending all their money and using all their holidays in the name of their team), and also it would hardly be fair to take Thomas on a three or four day bender!

I cocked up again!

By the time I rang the organised trip which flew out and back in the same day (which ticked all my requirements), it was already full.

Shit!

So I crossed my fingers hoping that City would qualify for the group stages where other opportunities might arise for an overseas trip. Even if it was a trip to Kazahkstan, we'd be going.

And then about a week before the game, a stroke of luck. I'd left my name with the tour operator and they rang me up to say somebody had cancelled and there were two spare places.

I took about a nano-second to decide, the credit card took a £600 or so dent and we were booked on. Get in!

Very much like the FA Cup final, as we arrived at Humberside Airport, I felt proud to be a City fan, and so proud that I was there with my favourite pal Thomas.

I could tell he was excited. He'd even gone to bed early, and set his alarm clock for about four am without any prompting. This hadn't happened in any of the preceeding three hundred and sixty four days of the year, and anyone who has a twelve year old boy might appreciate how difficult it can be.

At Humberside Airport, most were tucking into a fry up, washed down with a pint, all before seven am. The tone was set for the day.

We arrived in Lokeren after a short coach ride just around mid to late morning. As we disembarked the coach, it was like an army of ants, all following in a line like follow the leader, heading for the town square, before descending into the first bar we saw.

Immediately we bumped into an old pal, Dave Waters. Dave used to frequent the Cross Keys pub in Cottingham when we were all a lot younger, but had since moved to Holland. He'd jumped on a train from Holland and turned up on the off chance of getting a ticket for the game, saying he wasn't going to miss this. (Bri and James Lee (more of those two later) ultimately produced the goods and got Dave a ticket). City does that. Sometimes you lose touch with people but City brings you back together.

And so the day started.

The atmosphere in the square was fantastic. There were City flags everywhere and the hosts had put on a great set up. A marquee beer tent had been erected, even though there were many small bars to frequent. The weather was great, and the beer and songs flowed.

As the time went by, more and more City fans turned up, coming from whichever town they'd been staying in, each with a story about the previous night's escapades. Ultimately filling the square and large games of footy took place, much to Thomas' amusement.

With one shot, Thomas probably hit the best volley of his life, which clean took my full pint of beer (in a plastic glass I add) out of my hand. He immediately started laughing as the glass, beer et al, almost in slow motion, spiralled through the air. He soon stopped laughing when it fell on his rucksack containing his IPad!

This was basically a twelve year old watching loads of grown men drinking beer all afternoon in the sun, getting dafter as the day goes on. He loved it. I'm sure I'll be doing some worrying about him when he's old enough to drink the amber nectar.

Later, when Lokeren fans turned up, the atmosphere was still great, with songs being sung back and forth, beers purchased for each other and tops swapped.

This was great, this was what we'd been waiting for all those years. We'll have more of this thank you.

As kick off time approached, we all 'en masse' then meandered our way down through the streets to the ground, accompanied by the police. It was still at this time a great atmosphere with locals hanging out their windows clapping and applauding all the City fans – it felt like we were a big team, our time had come.

And then we got to the game, and things started going downhill.

First of all, you know that feeling you get, when you've been drinking for several hours and suddenly stop. Really quickly you realise that you are quite drunk. You've 'broken the seal' and can't seem to stop going to the toilet. I can really remember saying to myself, God I need my bed, and I'm at least six or seven hours from being in it.

The game was pretty unmemorable. Lokeren were organised if not dynamic and I wasn't sure we'd break them down. Then a McGregor howler, and they had a one nil lead to protect.

Meyler had a great chance near the end but it wasn't to be, and so it stayed one nil. Maybe we could overturn it in the home leg.

For many, the night got worse.

Thomas and I were very fortunate, as our coach was immediately outside the ground and before we knew it, we were on our way back to the airport.

At the same time, and unbeknown to us, the City fans were being frogmarched by the Belgium Police Riot Squad into a crowd of Lokeren yobs, who choose to hurl bottles and anything else they could get their hands on at the City fans.

Not being there (thankfully), I can't portray what this must have been like. All I can say is that, particularly having Thomas with me on that trip, he could have been mentally (if not physically) scarred. It could certainly have put him off going to future football matches.

I've got no problem with football hooligans knocking ten bells out of like minded hooligans of other teams, if they both choose to, so long as that doesn't involve or effect anybody else, certainly not young kids or pensioners.

In a few hours, the fantastic atmosphere, hope and expectation, had all come crashing down.

The inevitable happened in the return leg.

It was somewhat disappointing that no real welcome was put on for the visiting Lokeren fans (I obviously refer to the good natured ones, not the bottle throwing ones) and whilst we won the game 2-1, we went out on the away goals rule.

Going out at this early stage was a blow, but I am grateful that I'd had the chance to both watch and take my son to watch City play in Europe. Not many people can say that and I'm proud to be in that select group. I fear it may never happen again in my lifetime.

So the European adventure was over almost before it had begun – one hundred and eleven years in waiting and over in a flash.

And for me, that set the tone for the rest of the season. We'd not got into a stride in Europe, and never really did in the League either.

Which, with a press of the fast forward button, unfortunately takes us back to bloody Burnley at home!

"...WE ALL WENT ON A EUROPEAN TOUR, A EUROPEAN TOUR, A EUROPEAN TOUR..."

CHAPTER 4

"SPURS AWAY AND THE MANCS AT HOME"

In the words of AC/DC, *'..and so it came to pass..'* – the relegation trap door opened and we duly fell in.

Only a win away at Spurs would leave our fate in our own hands. I wasn't expecting that to happen.

As we'd enjoyed previous visits to White Hart Lane, albeit with mixed results, we were definitely going. My first visit had been many years ago, for an FA Cup game, which City battled hard but eventually lost two nil to late goals. We travelled there and back in a car that cost £1 and for much of the journey home, followed a City supporter's coach that had had its back window smashed. They must have been freezing.

As a football fan, you never quite know what is around the corner, *'it's a funny old game'* and all that. And this could be our last Premier league away game, we should be taking up every opportunity we get – the sort of excuses you make up to convince yourself that you have to be going.

Added to that was that my next door neighbour Sue had agreed that if I drove down, she'd drive back. This clearly meant I could have a few pre match beers. As a father whose children cannot yet drive, this means a lot of time is spent behind the wheel.

Sometimes football can look better through rose tinted spectacles, much like the girl near closing time (not that I can remember any of that mind!)

So we drove down to Enfield, met up with the Clines and jumped on the train into White Hart Lane. Several beers later in an Irish club and we were on our way.

City passed it about nicely but never really threatened to score and a few bad moments just after half time meant we were two down with a mountain to climb. The rest was predictable.

A loss always makes the drive home seem longer. Particularly when you are trying to stop yourself nodding off after a few lunch time sherberts in an attempt to keep the driver company. It's even longer when you're in the relegation places with just one game to go.

So it was all down to the last game – the Mancs at home.

We had to win and rely on other results going our way. This was unlikely as in about twenty attempts Steve Bruce had never achieved it. But hope kicked in again and until that fat lady starts warbling, it might happen?

Unfortunately, we had already planned a week away in Spain, so we were going to miss this game. I wasn't sure if I was happy or not. Our record against the Mancs is rubbish and it would be hard for us all, particularly Thomas and Charlotte to experience confirmed relegation first hand. Maybe it would be easier to watch from a distance in a bar in the sun?

By the time the game came around, we felt like we had betrayed our team. Anyway nothing could be done now.

A few days prior to the game we located a bar (full of English!) that had Sky and duly rolled up ready to pray inside.

The prayers weren't answered.

The bar concerned had a number of TV's, and was going to show the City match and the Newcastle match (the only other team we could change our relegation place with). We duly found a table just in front of the largest TV and ordered some beers.

Then just before kick-off, a dozen or so Geordies rolled in and the Newcastle game including commentary was put on the large TV. We were outnumbered!

And so we squinted at the City game on a much smaller TV whilst also watching and listening to the commentary of Newcastle. I'm not sure if you've tried watching two matches at once? It's not easy, you're senses naturally take you to the one emanating the sound.

At half time I was relatively content. Forty five minutes left and one goal would still swing it in our favour. City had played well and even had a couple of goals disallowed. The Mancs didn't look like scoring and under normal circumstances, a point against them would be credible. Not today though and we had still not scored. This sounds obvious, but clearly this was basically our downfall for the season. I think we didn't score in about half our games – it doesn't take a mathematician to work out that makes the job of securing enough points to stay up even harder.

And then Newcastle scored and it was over.

They scored again just to confirm it and we were down.

To be fair the Geordies in the bar were okay, but they would be wouldn't they? We should have never dropped two points against them away when we threw a two goal lead away. That phrase again, *if only….!*

The simple fact was that we had lacked a cutting edge.

The underlying thing that I remember from the game though, and texts that we got from people that were actually there, wasn't one of despair and utter disappointment. In fact, the reaction the team got from the City supporters was great – everyone was still extremely proud of City and the feeling was strong, this is OUR team.

I looked at the family and said, *"right, that's it, the book is definitely on, no backing out now!"*

The highs of football can more than make up for the many lows we experience. It is extremely difficult to explain the feelings that run through your veins when things are going well, it just seems to make all of life feel that much better.

Today obviously felt the opposite initially. Would we ever get back into the top league?

As a supporter of a small team, whilst we all know that utopia may never exist, it is the dream and what makes us come back for more. Whilst this dream may have been temporary for City, it can never be erased or taken away.

After all, we are not supporters of The Premier League, we are supporters of Hull City.

We just now need to rebuild and come back.

"THERE'S ONLY ONE HULL CITY, ONE HULL CITY…………"

CHAPTER 5

"WHO ARE YA - ABOUT THE FAMILY"

Ian (Dad – 46)

First of all, there is myself, Ian.

I am a 46 year old father of two, a veteran of some thirty plus City years. From that first game against Tottenham way back in 1977, I eventually got my first season pass when I was about fourteen. This was in the years when if you played for your school football team, you got a free season pass. I'm not quite sure how I got into the school team. I was always small for my age and never the fittest (a virtue I hold to this day!), but unlike most kids (and without blowing my own trumpet), I could actually use both feet and know how to play the game, well in my head at least.

My own football career eventually peaked at the dizzy heights of Division 14 of the Hull Sunday League playing for a pub team where actually having eleven players on the pitch was seen as a result! Pre match preparations on a Saturday consisting of a night out at Waterfront were probably not the best, and when you saw your goalkeeper smoking a fag and wretching in his net, it didn't fill you full of confidence!

So watching City turned out to be my football route; getting your first pass was almost like a rite of passage, like your first pint or losing your virginity!

So Mum allowed me to catch the bus from Cottingham where we lived at the time, down Priory Road, and I started going regularly. At that age, the result wasn't always the most important thing. It was the freedom, and that feeling of being a bit more grown up, part of a crowd with a common purpose. It felt like a gamble each week, as you are not in control, the result and performance is, to all intents, beyond your control. I suppose supporting say Man United is an odds on gamble, City, at best a double carpet, 33-1 ride!

Initially I went in The Kempton. Being quite small, this meant either sitting or standing right at the fence at the bottom, or balancing on the rusty metalwork right at the back of the stand so you could see over the sea of heads, the rust almost holding the thing together.

I remember one particular match against Derby in 1985. City were two down but a typical brutish Billy Whitehurst display roused City to come back to a 3-2 win. The Kempton was certainly rocking that day, the number of times I fell off the stanchion at the back of the stand.

As years went by and with Boothferry Park in a state of disrepair with no money to make any improvements, the Kempton was eventually shut. I recall Warren Joyce 'ironically' celebrating a goal in front of it, arms aloft, to receive the accolades of, err, no-one!

And so positions were moved. After brief spells in the Well (always dangerous for getting out of the way of a centre half's clearance) and then onto to the South Stand terraces, and ultimately to the South Stand seats.

On the odd occasion, Simon Cawkhill, the then Marketing Manager, would ring one of us on the Friday before a home game, to say he had some spare hospitality tickets, only a tenner each! And so we'd go in, and ultimately blag our way into the Sponsors Lounge and Players Bar under the West stand after the game.

After a memorable (and once in a lifetime) 7-1 home win against Crewe, and after too many celebratory drinks in the said bar, we found ourselves the last people in the ground.

So with no further thought, we went onto the pitch and re-inacted each of 'Knees Up Linton Brown's' goals (he scored a hat trick that day) very much in the style that Baddiel and Skinner used to do at the time.

Memorable days of Boothferry Park.

Or maybe my memories are fading, or I am just choosing to forget the numerous poor performances and defeats, or maybe I'm just sounding cynical when I say that the match day experience at Boothferry Park seemed to be more magical. Or maybe I was just more drunk?!

Fiveways and Three Tuns were regular haunts. There were not as many new supporters in those days, you could still be ordering your last pint at ten to three, and still have time to make kick off! Hell the Weaver brothers often ordered two each!

I'm sure with proper planning, some sort of beer tent in West Park, like the one in Lokeren, could be organised, even if only during the warmer months. Just a simple offering like they have at the cricket, lager or bitter with a four pint limit, with last orders say at two pm? Only an idea, albeit no doubt Health and Safety would have something to say about it nowadays.

I used to also enjoy the half time giants racing across to the theme of Stuart Hall and Eddie Waring's 'It's a Knockout'. We'd all put a few quid into a pot and choose a separate contestant, winner takes all.

On the eve of the FA Cup Final with Arsenal, I sent out a text to various people I have become acquainted to over the years, as to what was there favourite City game and why.

The response was varied, obviously dependent upon their age.

Some predictably selected City v Bristol City at Wembley thinking they'd never see the day, some Yeovil away (*'where it all started'*), the older ones picked Chelsea in the FA Cup.

I remember my dad also telling me about City playing Stoke at home in the FA Cup. Stoke were a great team at the time and City took a two nil lead. My Dad threw his hat in the air in jubilation, never to see it again! City lost 2-3, but I think of that story with fondness and can almost picture him. No matter how old you get, you always hold your father in high esteem (even when you become a parent yourself), hopefully Thomas and Charlotte will feel the same in years to come.

My most memorable game though was Rochdale away in May 1983 in the old Division 4.

This was my first away game on a coach.

I recall me and some school mates being booked on the 'world famous' Simon Gray Travel, not always the most organised, but usually entertaining.

I must have been about fourteen, about eight stone wet through, but remember sipping cider on the coach. Then the bus stopped somewhere near a pub and most got off and went in. Needless to say, I didn't look anywhere near old enough and stood outside waiting.

City won the match 3-1 and were promoted, and I remember the euphoria, there were even a couple of light hearted pitch invasions, and I got on the pitch and just into the penalty box at our end before quickly running back!

We felt like kings of the world, at fourteen!

Anyone remember who won the league that year?

I'll give you a clue. They have a different name now and we'll be playing them this season, albeit they have since moved many miles away.

I've probably clocked up about sixty to seventy grounds with City now, but Spotland will always hold a special place in my heart (not many will say that!)

From that moment, I think City had me for good. I was in!

I've tried dalliances with other teams from time to time. My work as an Accountant took me up to Glasgow many years ago and I remember watching midweek games at Rangers in the Gazza era. But even an Old Firm game, as tense and exciting as it may be, it couldn't quite compare. If the outcome of the match doesn't mean as much, or you don't find yourself adopting the 'football fans foetal position' (sat forward on the edge of your seat, head in hands, biting your nails etc), it's simply not the same.

Subsequent moves to the KC have to date seen us move around the ground, currently residing in the South Stand since Charlotte and Thomas have started going (it's cheaper!).

A few times I've been in the Corporate section, but like many of us, that's not for me. Football is and should be a great social leveller. Judges, solicitors, bin collectors etc etc can all discuss the same topic. And everyone can have a view. No-one's is correct or incorrect. We may not always agree, but in a way we all respect each other.

And anyway, I'm prone to using the odd bit of 'language' and that is certainly frowned upon in the West Stand! Football can be that release of energy, a way out of the daily grind, and in some ways can allow you to act differently than you might in normal life, a release. Everything else in life being placed on temporary hold for the duration of the game at least, as we cling onto something more important.

Who are ya...?

For some, it can be a benign form of escapism, or for some it can help give them some sort of notoriety, stop them just being a Mr Average, even if just for a moment in time.

This is certainly the case at away games. Away fans constantly standing (Thomas simply stands on his seat and has now just accepted it), offering numerous hand gestures to the home supporters. I do have some reservations how Charlotte might take all this in the ensuing season, spending time hanging around with predominantly sad middle aged men!

One of her few away experiences to date was Liverpool away on New Year's Day where there was a vile atmosphere, in my view instigated by jobsworth stewards insisting that all away fans remain seated. This being whilst the Kop remain stood, double standards!

Previous seasons at Anfield even ended in three of my colleagues being ejected for doing nothing wrong. Mind you at that point City were level at

1-1 and so in my mind we drew. (We actually lost 6-1 but we weren't there to witness the last five Liverpool goals!) I vowed not to go back again.

Football fans pay a lot of money to follow their team, and unless they are acting in an unruly manner, they should be treated like a paying customer. Without fans, yes there may still be Sky, but the grounds would be soul less and interest would soon wane.

So, all in all, I'm now in for the duration at City, no matter what gets thrown at us. I'll look forward to the day when Thomas or Charlotte can drive so that they can take me to away games.

This will continue no matter what division we are in.

The impending season will be a test and once the fixtures are out, a midweek away game at Brighton may test my sanity, not to mention the logistics. However, I'm confident it can be done.

I won't be the first or last to do it. Surely all I've got to do is just turn up?

Good results mind will make it easier!

Thomas (Son – 12)

I've already touched upon when Thomas first started attending at the tender age of three. He got his first season pass a couple of years later I think and has been going ever since, starting to attend away games also.

He's a bit of a 'statto' and can usually remember the scores of all City games, who scored etc etc. I could envisage him as a sports journalist at some point in the future, so this book might be a good experience for him. Imagine a 'Hull City' Jeff Stelling beaming into the living rooms and pubs up and down the country; we'd almost become a popular team.

I can see a lot of me when I was younger in Thomas, when he's watching City.

He is very passionate about it and can become extremely annoyed and frustrated if things aren't going well on the pitch – you can just see it in his face.

He'll grow out of it in time, just like I eventually did, somehow you become better at controlling your emotions, and more realistic – this is Hull City we are talking about after all.

None of us like losing, but sometimes you just have to hold your hands up and say the best team won.

I think I've tried to educate Thomas that in my view, I'd always rather have eleven players who try for the shirt, and always try their hardest, even if they aren't the most technically gifted, than some prima donna.

He's a fantastic and caring person and I'm very proud of him, as you would expect. City just brings us even closer, a bond.

At times, we don't need to communicate with each other, we just know how each other are feeling whilst watching City.

Sometimes I think I have maybe brainwashed him into liking football and watching City. But I'm sure I haven't; he'd say so surely?!

One day, when he starts taking his own offspring, he'll understand. Then, just like my own dad, my work will be done.

Charlotte (Daughter – 14)

Now there is no reason for football to be a male dominated environment. I never expected Charlotte to get interested in football or City, so it never really crossed my mind to consider if she wanted to go, and nor did she ask.

That was until a couple of seasons ago when, whilst in The Championship, she asked if she could come. I was delighted.

She soon got a liking for it, and we did well in that first year, culminating in an exciting, if not nail biting, end to the season with that game against Cardiff, and ultimately promotion back to the Premier League. And so season tickets were purchased.

Whatever you may think about City's current ticket prices, those for kids are great value (post script : obviously this was originally written pre Membership scheme). This year, Thomas' is £32 (that's £1.40 per game); Charlotte's £95 (£4.13 per game). Tell me something else I can do with kids nowadays that takes up the best part of a Saturday afternoon for under £6!

Charlotte is the eternal optimist, constantly telling me off for being too pessimistic, so she's a good person to watch a game with. Maybe she simply hasn't watched long enough yet?!

Whether she'll be as keen on sitting in a car for several hours up and down the motorway remains to be seen – there are away games as well as home fixtures I tell her.

Just like Thomas, I'm very proud of Charlotte and delighted that she has taken an interest in City. There's not a lot else I can tell Thomas, so Charlotte is my new disciple!

Suzy (Mum -44 aka 'The Football Widow')

From our family, this just leaves the final, but possibly most important piece of the jigsaw, Mum.

For the purposes of this book, she is to be referred to as *'the football widow.'*

Suzy's normal attendance at City games rarely exceed two or three per season, not that anyone stops her from coming. To be honest, I think she is quite happy to have a bit of peace and quiet at home whilst the rest of us are out.

She was always brought up with football having an older brother, Des. He 'used' to support Liverpool and had a team photo on his wall. Suzy tells us that he would cover the player's names up, and make her learn and recite their names, from left to right, row by row. If she got one wrong, she'd have to start again from the beginning until she got them all right.

This was back in the 80's / early 90's, and Barry Venison was her favourite player – oh the tight rolled up shorts and mullet, every teenage girls dream. I think City's equivalent at the time was Gareth Roberts.

Now when I first suggested the book idea, she first kind of rolled her eyes, thinking it would never come to fruition.

However, having given it more consideration, she is now warming to the idea, which kind of worries me! I have this feeling she is envisaging endless hours of visa card shopping and / or girly afternoons drinking Prosecco! Either way, 46 days / evenings out could end up costing a whole lot more!

However she is part of the team. In fact she is probably the non playing club captain. She makes sure we are all organised, the planner. And as such, it is only right that she has her input, and what she is having to put up with (or getting away with!)

Oh, and no she doesn't understand the offside rule, but then again who does anymore!

Guests

During the course of the season, I also envisage inviting the odd guest along to games, who can hopefully articulate their feelings and experiences on the day.

Apologies but these may be supporters of the opposition – it may be interesting to hear their take on the same game, or maybe just non football followers who may just think, *'what's all the fuss about?'*

We now just need the fixture release date to come round, so that we can start the 'masterplan' and journey.

"WE'LL SUPPORT YOU EVER MORE, WE'LL SUPPORT YOU EVER MORE, HULL CITY, HULL CITY....."

CHAPTER 6

"FIXTURE RELEASE DATE"

The day before the official fixtures are released (well before TV and Sky set about changing them all anyway), the first round of the draw of the League Cup, or whatever it is called nowadays, is made.

Last year, City were afforded the luxury of a bye until the third round. This came about as a reward for Europa league qualification, in an attempt to assist our fixture programme, ensuring we qualified for the league stages, and thereby helping to enhance the English co-efficient.

Some luck there then, sorry FA!

This year, we have been drawn away to Accrington Stanley. How the mighty have fallen! Any team that is more famous for a milk advert (*Accrington Stanley? Who are they? Exactly*), can't be that glamorous.

However we have decided that, it being school holiday time, a visit will be made. Clearly this is an extra curricular match, it is not part of the 46. However, I am swayed by the fact that I have never been there previously, and a friend, Ady Day, a lifelong Liverpool supporter, also wants to come with us. He's a bit of a 'groundticker' too!

I also decide that it will be an education for the kids, and help them to appreciate the facilities we have at the KC. They'll have to stand on a terrace, which may help them to think of what it used to be like in the old days when Dad was younger.

We'll no doubt field a 'weakened' team albeit judging by the mini exodus from the squad (so far Rosenior, Quinn, McShane, Harper and Ince have all left, with Brady looking likely to join them) we may not have sufficient players to do so! If we do lose, no doubt the old cliché of *'we can now concentrate on the league'* will be rolled out. I don't quite understand all of this. Surely the squads are big enough and players are fit enough to take every game seriously, and to progress as far as possible. They should just think back to that FA Cup final day.

City have never done very well in the League Cup. I think the 13/14 season equalled our best ever run, and that was only to the fourth round when we got knocked out by Spurs on penalties.

The more I think about that 13/14 season, how good it was for a City fan. A record equalling League Cup run, an FA Cup final, Premier League survival and qualification for Europe. Kind of made 14/15 a real anti climax, and the problems already discussed of expectation, as opposed to hope and blind faith.

So nine o'clock on Wednesday 17th June 2015 comes along.

I'm sat in a queue of traffic listening to Alan Brazil on Talksport.

The first few fixtures are quoted. Needless to say, these all relate to Premier League teams, the big boys, and there is no mention of Hull City.

We are back in the pack, in the Championship with the also rans.

I'm not quite sure how some people measure success. I don't really like to see it as just survival in a league. This is all we can ever hope for in the Premier League. So for me, the best we can ever achieve is a promotion. And to achieve that, we had to get relegated first!

Having said that, it will be difficult for us to get out of the Championship. Don't forget I am a pessimist, I'm sure I've told you that already. Firstly, it's littered with good teams, once 'big names' – Derby have to be up there and are already making some good signings. I always feel that Nottingham Forest should be there or thereabouts, but seem to be perennial underachievers.

For us though, we will have a depleted squad and whilst some people will just expect us to do well, football isn't that easy, ask recent fans of say Leeds, Wigan, Blackpool etc.

So there is no mention of City and I have to wait until I'm sat at my PC. To be honest I'm more interested in if they are going to be kind to us from a logistical point of view, than who we are playing first, last etc. I'm particularly concerned about Brighton away.

They could have been kinder. I'm never quite sure what goes through the heads of whoever organises the fixtures sometimes – do they ever bear the considerations of a football fan into it?

This year we've got away games in midweek against:

Cardiff (which immediately follows Brighton away)
Brentford
Ipswich and;
Reading.

Oh joy! Thomas is already worried about these, none of which are during the school holidays, and thinking of numerous dentist appointments!

Rolled in is a delightful Boxing Day fixture at home to 'Bloody Burnley', that'll be sure to bring some festive joy, at least to the Burnley supporters anyway.

Oh well, I suppose we have to play everybody twice at some point, it just adds to the challenge.

We have decided against the recently re-instated Away Direct scheme, guaranteeing you a ticket for every away game. This is based on the thought process that many 'recent' fans may not be as interested in games in the Championship, so it's unlikely we'll sell out our allocations. Plus by buying as each game comes around, you can choose who you sit near, and Thomas and Charlotte may not attend all matches anyway (even though Thomas think's he is going to!)

So the cast is dyed. We roughly know where we need to be and when.

Roll on the 8th August and kick off.

" ...COME ON YOU 'ULL..."

A season awaits. 'Come on you Ull'

CHAPTER 7

"THE BERNABEU AND EARLY SEASON LOSS"

City have just started playing the first few pre-season friendlies. Normally we would probably have attended, certainly the annual North Ferriby fixture which Thomas always likes to go to. I think it's something about being even closer to the action.

He thoroughly enjoyed last season's FA Trophy semi-final there against Bath City. The occasion was great with fans of both teams mingling together in the packed bar beforehand and terraces thereafter. The kids, Thomas and his mate Matthew, went for a burger and to occupy a spot immediately next to the goal; the dads in the bar – real old school.

From the bar at Ferriby you can actually see part of the pitch so you could stay in there most of the match. However we chose not to. The match was blood and guts, with several challenges going unpunished; challenges that would have seen many a Premier league player rolling around as if they'd been shot. Eventually it was extra time, a sending off and penalties which were all taken at 'our' end. Thomas loved this, filming them on his phone, and Ferriby were triumphant and a Wembley date awaited them.

For me the game was really refreshing compared to the usual Premier league stuff. City were away at Stoke that day; a ground we hate visiting. They say it has the best atmosphere – it can't be when City are visiting because I'm yet to experience it. City predicatably lost one nil.

The semi-final victory for Ferriby tempted us all to travel to Wembley to watch the final against Wrexham. The day was slightly surreal with only about 16,000 fans occupying about a sixth of a partly opened Wembley, and the Ferriby contingent were heavily outnumbered – but memories of City at Wembley always come back when you revisit the place. A goose bump just as you picture in your mind *that* Deano volley – history in the making.

I remember the day being very cold and when Ferriby went two down, we started to contemplate an early exit. But a rousing fightback led to three all after extra time, with first Ferriby equalising near the end of normal time, to then take the lead, only for Wrexham to equalise themselves right near the end of extra time. So umpteen penalties were taken and Ferriby eventually sneaked through. Even though for us, the outcome wasn't all important, we all felt nervous during the latter part of extra time and as penalties were being taken. We've never had many experiences, certainly not important ones, of City in penalty shootouts, god knows what we'd be like in such an event.

Again though a great advert for football – no histrionics from the players, no players diving, no swarming the referee over every decision, proper challenges and tackles going unpunished. Basically football as we used to see it. Whilst the football may not have been up to the standards of the Premier League, the endeavours and commitment of both teams certainly was. North Ferriby, a village with a population of about 3,000, and an average home crowd of 250 had won the FA Trophy. For me, it was one of the most memorable games of the whole 14/15 season, and City weren't involved!

Anyway, we've had to miss this year's Ferriby match, as the commitment to attending all 46 games, has meant that our family holiday needed to be taken before the season started.

It's funny but football supporters tend to not refer to specific calendar dates, but instead refer to their fixture list as reference points.

For example, when's dad's birthday? It's just before Bolton away.

Or, what day is New Year's Day on this year? Not sure, but it's QPR away the day after.

So for holiday, we opted for a few days in Madrid, followed by a couple of weeks in Feurteventura, where the 'football widow's' dad now lives.

As soon as we mentioned Madrid, Thomas' eyes lit up and a trip to the Bernabeu was on the cards. Thomas and I have this sort of unwritten rule that I'm reasonably happy to purchase him stuff if it's Hull City related, but be that of any other team, then he needs to either buy it himself, or find some other mug to do it.

At the age of twelve, with Sky thrust down your throats, and endless hours of playing FIFA on Xbox or Playstations, kids tend to be romanced by the

Premier League and world stars of football. Your David Meylers and Alex Bruces don't get much of a mention!

Thomas in particular has seemed to opt for Real Madrid as his 'Spanish team', especially a certain Mr Ronaldo. Personally, whilst I can appreciate his football skills, I have never liked the bloke. He always seems so arrogant and full of his own self importance and appearance, probably the polar opposite to me. Surely it's not natural for someone to look like that?!

I made sure that I wore a City top during our tour, if nothing else just to get a few photo shots. Chances are that we'll never actually see one playing in there. All that really happened was that people squinted at me, trying to work out what team it was, Hull who? Albeit the no name badge didn't help.

Needless to say, Thomas dragged us round the club shop and made a dent in the visa card, albeit the understanding being that he had to pay for it; the items not being of City ilk.

As good as the Bernabeu is, to me it still feels like a bit of a concrete jungle from the outside and not quite as appealing as the KC. I remember also thinking the same about the Nou Camp and various other grounds. Or maybe I'm just looking through my obviously unbiased rose tinted spectacles again, and the KC just feels like home to us?

And so we then moved on to the Canary Islands. Whilst there we ordered our St George's flag which hopefully during the course of the season, we are hoping to display. By the time you are reading this, maybe you remember seeing it?

It was during this stay however, that we received some terrible news.

On the evening of 22nd July 2015, my mobile showed a certain Bri Lee calling. It seemed strange for Bri to be calling at approx. 10.30ish in the evening, and as sometimes happens, in the split second that it takes you to press answer, all sorts of thoughts rush through your head.

Being the eternal pessimist, I assumed the worst, and unfortunately my fears were confirmed.

Bri informed me that one of our dearest City supporters, a certain Mr Nick Patrick William Walker had died during his sleep.

We were all shocked and lost for words.

Nick was only fifty three, and to my knowledge, had no history of illness.

The conversation with Bri was fairly short, as at times like this, words cannot express your inner most feelings. I could tell from Bri's voice that he was devastated – a number of them had been due to imminently set off to Austria to watch a City pre season friendly against Hannover. I'm sure the same feelings will be shared by all of Nick's fellow City supporters, friends and family.

Nick was a top bloke, whom I had the pleasure of knowing for some twenty plus years. I first met him in the Fiveways pub where we used to have a few pre match beers in the Boothferry Park days.

He was always a very unassuming chap, and I can barely recall him ever having a bad word to say about anybody. If he did feel that way, he certainly kept his thoughts to himself – what a great virtue to have, if only the rest of the world was like that.

His friendship, along with that of Rich Hewson, resulted in the three of us following the fortunes of the England cricket team on a tour of South Africa in 1995/96.

After spending about six hours waiting for an internal flight at Capetown on Christmas Day, we took in tests at Port Elizabeth and then back to Capetown. We took the City luck with us; at the latter test in Capetown, England lost inside three days and they even had to hastily re-arrange a one day game to appease the supporters who'd already bought tickets for all five days.

Many years of watching City with Nick followed, and I am indebted to both him and Rich for the countless number of times they talked me into, and drove me to the likes of Crewe, Witton Albion and Bristol Rovers, to name but a few – cheers Nick!

Nick was always a bit of a statto deep down. He once went to every pub in Beverley in the same day (there used to be fifty two) and whilst the 'rules' were that you obviously didn't have to have a full pint in each, you had to at least intake some alcohol in each. So with military precision, he got his street map out, organised and executed the mission! He also liked to do the same with all the pubs in the Hull boundary, and from time to time would ring you to see if you fancied a beer in the 'so and so' pub which had just opened.

Pre season tour of the grounds. Valencia, The Bernabeau anyone? One day maybe?

He also loved the football fans idea of 'ground ticking' – basically going to as many grounds as you can (they only count mind if it's whilst watching your own team). This is clearly made harder with the advent of so many new grounds these days. Recently, he took great pleasure in taking his daughter, Emma, to all of the Premier league grounds, something that re-assured me that I wasn't the only one dragging my kids up and down the country – they all do actually want to go!

And so I recall that Nick was one of the first people I broached the idea of this book and 46 game experience to. I vividly recall the discussion in that Irish bar at Spurs away. Nick liked the idea, and was happy to partake, if not for all the journey, certainly most of it, with us. He actually encouraged us to try and see it through.

We also talked about going to watch the Darts – on the TV, it always looked like a great idea. What better way to spend a night than watching two blokes throw arrows at a dart board that you can't even see, whilst getting pissed in fancy dress as say, a pencil crayon! So I have earmarked QPR away in early January when I think the World darts championship may still be on in London. Not sure about the pencil crayon bit mind!

Nick was the first to text when the fixtures were announced, stating that Cardiff away on a Tuesday night in September would be our first big challenge. He added that he was definitely 'up for' Brentford away on a Tuesday night; a beer in each of the pubs on all four corners of the ground and memories of a Rob Dewhurst winner many years ago. We hadn't got round to who might have been driving yet!

Alas, Brentford away will not quite now be the same, but we will ensure we raise a glass to you Nick.

Times and events like these, in a weird sort of way, remind you that life can be extremely fragile. We all shouldn't stress about stuff too much, but should embrace life to the best of our ability, doing things we enjoy.

I am an emotional person, and am not ashamed to have shed a tear or two since Bri's call. The funeral will be a very emotional day and I hope that during the season, a chant will be raised in the name of Nick. It may not mean anything to most, but it certainly would to those that knew him – I can see himself laughing at the thought of it.

The news of Nick's passing have made me even more determined to complete this journey, and whilst he may not be with us in person, he certainly will in spirit.

As I write these words, it's about ten in the morning. We are still on holiday so it's clearly 'Beer O'Clock!' So with a heavy heart, the ring pull of the Estrella can is opened, *'Here's to you Nick, RIP'*

"...HE'S ONE OF OUR OWN, HE'S ONE OF OUR OWN, NICK WALKER, HE'S ONE OF OUR OWN..."

CHAPTER 8

HUDDERSFIELD TOWN (H) – SATURDAY 8TH AUGUST 2015

"OPENING DAY SUCCESS"

And so 76 days of non competitive football action have come to an end – the football starvation is over. The screaming at missed fouls, inept refereeing decisions, players lacking effort, the tears of joy as unlikely draws or victories are snatched from the jaws of defeat, can all begin again.

Life without football has ended!

The opening fixture had pitted us up against Huddersfield at home and I reckoned this was fairly kind to us, as they were more than beatable, although I have never really liked them much. This is for a number of reasons.

Firstly, I've usually witnessed rubbish City results at the McCalpine Stadium, having endured endless traffic queues to get there, and then struggling to find anywhere to park.

Secondly, they were the team involved when I think I have probably only ever, close up, witnessed any sort of fisticuffs at the KC, as we walked our way back through Walton Street car park.

And thirdly, and definitely worst of all, was something that I can only recall and describe as an assault by their goalkeeper Paul Rachubka on City's then forward Ben Burgess, causing him to miss practically a full season thereafter. Ben happened to be a neighbour of ours at the time so was always one of our favourite players, and such a likeable chap to. He's now a school teacher I think.

And if the attack on Ben Burgess was not sufficient, another assault took place on the *'God'* that was Stuart Elliott, by Huddersfield's Efe Sodje. An elbow late into injury time during one fixture, as Efe, took the interpretation just too far. I don't think Stuart ever quite came back the same player after that.

It's probably worth time just to discuss Stuart Elliott. In my opinion he was a great player for City. To score that many goals ghosting in on the back stick was incredible. Remember he wasn't a striker and in my time watching City, we've hardly been blessed with loads of players hitting twenty plus league goals a season. Since the days of Chillo and Wagstaff (pre my days), we've only had six players score twenty or more league goals a season. All of Keith Edwards, Les Mutrie, Big Billy Whitehurst, Andy Payton and Deano were strikers.

In those seasons when City got promotion and started being successful following the move to the KC, it felt like everything that Stu touched seemed to go in the net. I particularly loved his header against Swansea at a night match at home in September 2003. Both teams were near the top of the league, there were over 20,000 in the KC, the kick off was even delayed due to crowd congestion. I'm sure I later read that people were locked out – people locked out at a City match in the bottom tier of English league football!

A bullet like Stuart header sent City to victory and to the top of the league, the first time we'd been top of any league since the mid nineties. You don't get a much better feeling than that – winning under lights to go top of the league against another leading team, I don't care what league it's in.

You'll have to excuse the pun, but Stuart certainly was a 'gift from god'.

So back to the opening game of the season.

To be fair, there were lots of factors building up to this game to suggest it might feel like a bit of an anti-climax.

City had just been relegated from the alleged Holy Grail, the Big League that is the Premier League. The player exodus had started, both to reduce the wage bill and because some players just do not want to play in anything other than the Premier League. Rumours were circulating that many more may follow out of the KC, including but not necessarily limited to Huddlestone, Jelavic, N'Doye, Hernandez and Elmo. Not many faces were yet incoming, it was a case of shift some out before new ones come in. As such, the squad is in real danger of looking fairly threadbare with a lack of quality in depth, several youngsters were included in the squad for today and in line to make their City debuts.

England had just absolutely annihilated Australia in the Ashes at cricket – how could City top that?

And just two days before, myself along with others, had carried the coffin of our close friend Nick at his funeral. Football for once, felt a little less important.

But life does go on, and so our Saturday rituals of lucky pants and clothing, habitual routines and superstitions began again.

We arrived relatively early (maybe I had been expecting a bigger crowd?), and Charlotte had brought along her friend Faye (her dad is a Sheffield Wednesday supporter so I'm kind of hoping he'll drive us to the away game there). I'm not sure if they actually both enjoyed the game. They actually moved seats in the second half and sat away from us. This may have simply been to move away from me, the *annoying dad*, or because they had seen some City squad players sat watching in the end hospitality box. They didn't answer, but teenage girls being teenage girls, I'm sure most of the second half was occupied by the taking of 'selfies' trying to get Alex Bruce and Mo Diame in the background. Oh the stardom!

There was a strange feeling to the day. Disappointingly there were many empty seats on display, the attendance was some four to five thousand below last seasons, clearly emphasizing how the Premier League can brainwash fans, particularly the younger ones, the alleged next generation.

In addition to the empty seats, the bookies were not open to put our usual score / first scorer predictions on. To be fair, this is probably a blessing in disguise as we rarely trouble them to payout, and wouldn't have today as we would have plumped for a 2-1 City win. The only time I can remember winning anything decent was when I put money on Liam Rosenior to be first goalscorer against WBA at home. Not sure what made me pick him, he very rarely scored, the long odds of 80-1 maybe? Anyway, cue a bigger than normal celebration when after a penalty miss, Liam promptly put the rebound in. Immediately Thomas 'told' me that I was splitting the winnings four ways.

However on more occasions than not, money is handed to the bookies, rather than taken from them. I'm sure it is not my success rate that has seen them closed for today's game.

So after remembering how gassy the lager is at the food outlets on the concourse (and I had two just to make sure!), we took our seats to watch in a bit of a 'half hearted' mood.

There were also some new faces sat around us today. In particular an extremely annoying bloke sat on the row behind us (let's call him Mr DD), who insisted on giving us a running commentary during the entire game, littering it with as many footballing cliché's as you could think of. Now I'm sure I talk shite some of the time, but this bloke was full of it. I'm sure he'd only ever watched football from his armchair before. Both Thomas and Charlotte mentioned it almost straight away, and on a few occasions, I was sorely tempted to take up a discussion with him about his commentary. Either that or simply tell him to shut up. I refrained from this, Charlotte not wanting to cause a scene, but will take note to see (or hear) if he is still sat that in a few games time. Hopefully not.

And after that build up, yes the game did feel like a bit of an anti-climax.

City strolled to a 2-0 win without really getting out of second gear. It will be difficult to assess how we might do this season until that stupid thing called the transfer window closes at the end of August (why it doesn't close before the season actually starts, god only knows). Then we'll be able to see what squad we've got. On paper it currently looks good, but players are bound to leave in August, then they'll be another transfer window in January when even more might leave. And on paper, we shouldn't have gone down last season, although we know that football isn't played on paper.

We played some okay stuff in the first half without looking really dangerous, Huddersfield were even less of a threat. City played lot of sideways passes and at times just lacked that bit of impetus and drive forwards. On one of the few occasions we did, we scored the opening goal just before half time, through new boy Sam Clucas. A bit of fortune as a good save from his first shot came straight back at him to allow him to put away the rebound.

Scoring first for City this season will be important I feel as it has been in many of our promotion seasons. The defence looked very solid, although maybe lacks a bit of pace. It's up top that I'm a bit more worried as to where, and who is going to score the goals.

Another new boy Chuba Apkom, on loan from Arsenal, looked lively although I sense he may get a bit of rough treatment, you're allowed to tackle and foul outside the Premier League.

So after Huddersfield enjoyed a reasonable spell in the second half, without really looking like scoring, it was pleasing to see Chuba thump home a second late on. This allowed the remaining minutes to be watched in relative comfort, unlike the usual nail biting and constant clock watching, too many times have I seen us let in late equalisers or winners to ever be overly confident. Today was a welcome exception.

All in all, whilst the day was nothing spectacular, three points were earnt and City are in the play off places! Just forty five games to go and at this point I'll hand you over to Thomas.

Right, dad's been pestering me, so here is my first contribution to this book. I can assure you that these are my words and will be shorter than dad's – he tends to go on a bit.

I quiet enjoyed today watching the new players. I got a bit worried when Huddersfield missed a sitter in the second half but we won, and we didn't do that too much last year. I'd almost forgotten how to celebrate a goal. I hope that Andre Gray will sign from Brentford, someone who might be able to score twenty plus goals a season. Hopefully he'll join his team mate Moses Odubajo.

I'm not too bothered about us being in the Championship this season. We should win a few more games and have more possession. I quite fancy us to go up (Dad is not so sure, but he always predicts us to lose). It clearly won't be the same as in the Premier. When the teams get read out before a Premier League game, you've heard of nearly every player. You hardly know any in the Championship, but I'm more bothered about our players anyway.

I'm glad the season has started again. Until it did, I couldn't stop thinking of missed chances and late goals conceded from last year thinking, if only we'd scored or they hadn't, then we'd have two points more there, an extra point there and hey, we'd have stayed up. Anyway I am looking forward to the away games in particular, visiting new grounds and places. The atmosphere also feels better at away games and Dad has set me a challenge to see if I can start a chant. I said can I start one with swear words in it, he said no, to which I replied there wasn't any then.

Bad bits about today were no potato wedges on sale!

Good bits about today, with Mum ('the football widow') being at work tonight, I got to watch all of the new football show on Channel 5 and then Match of the Day afterwards. You can never get enough football. Funniest bit about the show was watching the Scunthorpe goalie get sent off, type in Scunthorpe's goalie Luke Daniels sent off into You Tube, hilarious.

Oh, and it's always a good day if City win!

"CAN WE PLAY YOU EVERY WEEK, CAN WE PLAY YOU EVERY WEEK……"

CHAPTER 9

ACCRINGTON STANLEY (A) LEAGUE CUP – TUESDAY 11TH AUGUST 2015

"YOU'RE ONLY HERE TO SEE THE STANLEY, HERE TO SEE THE STAAAAANLEY.."

I'm not really sure how we ended up at this game and including it in this book. The plan was only to go to all 46 league games, going to all the cup games as well – surely that's just ridiculous. However we went, so it's now 47 (kind of makes the title of the book look a bit daft now).

This was a cup game in the Milk / Littlewoods / Rumbelows / Coca Cola / Worthingtons / Carling / Capital One / League Cup. City have never been good in this, so I was expecting a reserve team to be fielded, if in fact we have got a full one at the moment, followed by a defeat and cliché's of *concentrating on the league.'* How teams are allowed to field weakened teams is just wrong. It's like saying to the fans, *'We'll take your money, but basically, we won't be trying that hard.'*

Initially it was Thomas and Charlotte who were the keenest to go, school holidays and all that. In addition, our first guest of the season, Ady Day, had spoken about being interested in joining us. So off we were going.

As it turned out, Charlotte got cold feet at the eleventh hour, preferring instead to opt for an evening at the beach feasting on fish and chips with the football widow and family dog. Had I not been the driver, I may have been tempted myself. Thomas was however delighted that his sister wasn't going as this meant that there was a spare ticket and he got to take his mate Jaden along. Jaden must have enjoyed it as he ended up having a sleepover and didn't go home until Thursday teatime, a full two days later.

During our drive across the M62, we discussed Ady's footballing exploits. Ady is an ex work colleague of mine and is a massive Liverpool fan, living in Hull. For many, this is abhorrent and I've had various discussions where certain people are of the opinion that all football supporters should support their home town team.

I don't quite agree.

To me, as long as a supporter gets off their backsides and actually goes to watch their team, and sticks by them through good times and bad, then as far as I'm concerned, they can support who they want. It's those that claim to support a team, but basically only ever watch from their armchair that I have less time for.

In my humble opinion, Ady certainly falls into the dedicated supporter category. Obviously, I'm sure it's easier to support Liverpool than smaller teams like City, but read these notes below and I'll let you decide. If anything, he's gone too far, he makes this 46 game season seem a walk in the park.

Ady first went to watch Liverpool aged nine, going on the train to Anfield, due to the fact that his mum wouldn't drive on the motorway. Once he started going consistently, you could say he got hooked.

Bear in mind that for Ady, every home game is approximately a two hundred and sixty mile round trip.

In the last sixteen seasons, he has missed just three games in England home and away. One of those was shortly after the death of his father; the other two both involved road traffic accidents on the way to a game preventing him actually attending – that's three games missed out of just over six hundred.

We roughly calculated that including trips to European games, he's probably spent around £90,000 watching Liverpool. Needless to say, Ady still lives at home and has no children!

When quizzed by Thomas what was his favourite game, the obvious answer was the Champions League Final against AC Milan in Istanbul in May 2005. However his attendance at the game had an interesting story to it. In the January of that year with the final way off, his family and friends were trying to organise a holiday. Normally Ady doesn't go on holiday, as he uses up all his work holiday entitlement (and money) taking time off to go and watch Liverpool.

Despite the fact there was only a remote chance that Liverpool would get to the final, Ady insisted that he would only attend the one week holiday, the very week in which the final was due to take place, if it was booked somewhere in Turkey, just on the off chance.

So it was booked in Marmaris, Turkey. We now know that Liverpool did in fact get to the Final. So no sooner had he landed, he informed the holiday party that he would be leaving, and promptly boarded a rickety old bus driving fifteen hours on pot holed roads, and fifteen hours back. In all he left for three days to watch two hours of football, but is bloody glad he did.

And last but by no means least, and much to Thomas' interest, Ady has got an impressive collection of memorabilia.

From time to time we collect things that help us remind us of our team and the memorable occasions. Thomas has the City shirt he wore at the Bristol City play-off game (he was only five), signed by Deano, framed with his programme and match ticket.

Programmes are the usual though. I've never quite understood these as most of them never contain anything of great interest. The home ones, other than the manager's notes have the same things in match after match; the away ones full of pages about the other team which we don't want to read. However I can see them being a point to refer back to.

Ady has gone a step further! He has currently got every programme of every Liverpool game going back to 1966 – that's about 3,300 programmes – bloody geek! I agreed that Thomas could collect all 23 (and cup) away fixtures for this season, but that's all.

So if Ady is that mad about Liverpool, why on earth did he want to go to Accrington Stanley?

The same reason as most of us football anoraks – it's another ground 'tick'. Now this is serious business – to see if you can get to as many football league grounds as possible and there are a whole set of rules to play by, everyone seeming to be playing by different rules. My rules are that you have to watch City (or whoever your team is) at the ground and if a team moves ground you have to then go to the new one or the 'tick' is lost. Not sure Ady agreed with these rules, as this would mean he wouldn't get a 'tick' from tonight's visit as Liverpool were not playing.

After we got home, I checked how Thomas and I were doing on the 'tick' front; I'm up to sixty two, Thomas twenty eight – not bad for a twelve year old. His tally will increase come the end of this season.

Being a ground 'tick' night, it was no surprise when in The Crown pre match, having a couple of pints, many familiar City faces were there to get their 'tick'. The terraces were awash with Adidas trainers worn by middle aged men that should know better – we don't!

This was a real old school football ground.

I was mildly amused that it was called The Wham Stadium. *'The drinks weren't free but there was sunshine!'* They even played *'Wake Me Up Before You Go Go'* at the end of the game. The stadium name surprisingly does not have anything to do with George Michael and Andrew Ridgeley, but a local company called What More UK Limited, a plastics company.

The ground only holds about 5,000 and tonight just over 2,000 were in presence. Quick predictions were made of how many balls would be kicked over the miniscule stands – think it ended at ten, even a couple of late penalty misses came close. The fact that there was a basin in the toilets just about doubled the urinal capacity and I wasn't sure if the music being played was actually on a PA system or just someone playing their stereo loud in one of the nearby houses.

Thomas and pal, sporting their *'casual'* Fred Perry tops promptly took their place leaning against the crush barrier on the open terrace right at the front near the goal. They then told me I could go and stand somewhere else with my mates! All part of growing up I suppose, and took me back to my early days at away games with City.

To my amazement, City put out a full strength team, but really struggled to break down Accrington. In fact the vast majority of the game was boring, neither team really looking like scoring, but City being an ex Premier league team, should really have been capable of breezing through such a fixture.

Talk on the terrace turned to trying to remember equally crap games in the League Cup, the obvious consensus was Lincoln away, absolutely hated going there.

Many yawns took place as the end of ninety minutes approached and when one person yawns, it becomes infectious, and was soon spreading across the

terrace. As the referee blew for full time, you could hear the audible groans –
"Bollocks, we're going to have to watch another thirty minutes of this!"

Extra time was a bit better. Akpom had come on as a sub for a very disinterested Jelavic, and sparked a bit of life into the game from a City point of view. He scored to put us one up, we soon managed to let them equalise. We then went 2-1 ahead, but determined to make the night last even longer, Jakupovic decided to punch a shot onto an Accrington player and the ball bounced into the net to make it 2-2.

And so penalties it was, and at our end.

Thomas loved this, recording it all on his phone.

A penalty shoot-out, assuming you win, helps you to forget the previous one hundred and twenty minutes of abject football, far too much sideways and backwards passes had taken place, with a lack of cutting edge. I hope City can address this soon or it could be a long season.

Penalties ebbed and flowed. Maguire blazed over the bar (centre half's shouldn't take penalties) and Meyler horribly screwed one wide, but Jakupovic redeemed himself with a couple of saves and City were through.

Despite the football not being great, I enjoyed our visit to Accrington. It is so far removed from the Premier League, albeit now we've got our 'tick', not sure I want to be rushing back.

Thomas certainly enjoyed his night, he even got on TV when the goals and penalties were shown. I had also challenged him the previous Saturday to start a chant and he claimed he did this tonight. Not standing next to him, I cannot verify this, but whilst the game was crap, the City fans were distracting themselves, having a bit of banter with the Accrington goalie, a chap called Mooney.

Thomas claimed he started a chant singing, *"What a waste of Mooney..."* and that others joined in. Well done son, and not one swear word!

And with ground 'ticks' a plenty, we all trundled off home thinking of the draw on Thursday. God I hope it's not something like Plymouth away (mind you, there's a 'tick' in there!).

On the way home, I asked Ady if this recent City experience had tempted him to break his allegiances with Liverpool. It was a rhetorical question!

"QUE SERA SERA, WE'RE GOING TO WEMBLEY..."
(YEAH, RIGHTO!)

CHAPTER 10

WOLVES (A) – SUNDAY 16TH AUGUST 2015

"HI HO WOLVERHAMPTON"

And so the first away game of the 'proper 46' arrives – Accrington was almost just a dry run (although I could just see City going on a cup run, and us feeling compelled to attend all these games as well, clocking up even more miles and expense).

Thomas was buzzing about his trip to Stanley and despite the fact that the football was relatively abject, he loved standing on the terraces with a bit more atmosphere. The onset of all seater stadiums, whilst obviously for all the right reasons following Hillsborough, seems to have taken away some of the atmosphere at grounds. Maybe one day it will come back a bit in certain areas of grounds, they are already trialling standing areas at Cardiff and Celtic. It certainly seems to improve atmosphere. After all, if you are sitting, what is the first thing you tend to do if you're team is about to score? Get to your feet, and I don't think that's just because people are in front of you do. It's almost an involuntary reaction to do so, maybe we are just trying to put the ball in the net ourselves. I've often found myself *'doing a header'* as a cross goes in.

So whilst we are talking atmosphere, I can categorically say that there was very little in the away section at Molineux for this fixture.

A general air of apathy seems to be in place amongst City fans, I know of several who haven't renewed their passes this year. Combine this with the power of Sky, moving the kick off to midday on a Sunday, meant an early start for City fans. We set off at just gone 8.30 ish. Factor in the ticket prices and you can understand why some fans would be prepared to watch from the comfort of their living room or local pub, rather than drive for a total of about five hours there and back. As I type this, I can maybe see their point!

So, with a shove of Thomas in his pit, he rolled out of bed and quickly got dressed. As is the want of a twelve year old he wore his City top. For some reason I very rarely wear any colours, maybe the home shirt clashes with me being a ginner.

Thomas immediately said, *'I'm hungry and what was for breakfast?'* Being the culinary whizz that I am I said *'A McDonalds.'* And so almost before we'd even started, we stopped off at Goole at The Golden Arches. In my view, McDonalds is a strange phenomenon. It must be great marketing because I'm certainly *'not loving it'* as the slogan says. Every time I'm persuaded to go, I say to myself that I'm not going to have anything, but then I do. And then after having eaten whatever processed rubbish it is, approximately ten minutes later you are hungry again.

If you haven't watched it before, I advise you to watch a film documentary called *'Super Size Me'*.

In it, some American challenged himself, as part of some research for increasing levels of obesity, to see if for thirty consecutive days he could eat nothing but McDonalds. So he ate it for breakfast, lunch and tea, day after day, week after week. If at any point he was asked *'if he'd like to go large',* (or Super Size as I think they call it in the States), he had to say yes. He also had to eat and drink only things included on the McDonalds menu and had to eat everything on the menu at least once. Along the way he had regular doctors' check-ups and monitored what effect this *'diet'* was having on him. Obviously the results weren't great, on average he ate an equivalent of nine Big Macs per day, put on loads of weight, experienced mood swings, started getting depressed and lost his sex drive. Remember that next time you're tucking into one.

I'm not going to have anything next time, I told myself.

One of the benefits of an early kick off is that there is less traffic on the road, but today we still have to go through those bloody roadworks on the M1, which both seem to have been there forever, and go on for miles and miles. I'm sure I've never actually seen any road workers there. Having said that, it's probably a blessing this week as I've had to attend a speeding course after getting caught down Beeford straight. Having accumulated six points on my licence at the moment, all these away games may test my ability to actually keep a licence.

Thomas was actually quite chatty today and did pose a testing question as to who was City's first ever coloured player. The earliest I could remember were Ray Daniel and Charlie Palmer. Not sure if they are correct but answers on a postcard please.

However, Thomas soon reverted to type and put on his headphones, turning up the volume just to that annoying level when all anyone else can hear is that tinny noise without quite being able to decipher what the song is. He then fell asleep and started snoring making the possible song recognition absolutely impossible.

Once arrived we parted with the usual £5 to a dodgy looking geezer of dubious origin to park our car along with umpteen others on a postage stamp sized car park.

Being a football fan, and at the start of a new season, the lucky superstitions have started already. Having been undefeated so far, I'm wearing the new lucky t-shirt and must have at least one pint before the game (as that was the case in the previous two undefeated games). Why I do these things I don't know. But if I don't, maybe it will be my fault if City then go on to lose. Maybe the players run out, see that I'm wearing my lucky t-shirt, smell my breath and then decide to play well?

Anyway at some point, the lucky t-shirt won't work and I'll have to change my superstition to something else. I've already decided that if the 'at least one pint before the game' superstition doesn't work, then I'll have to change it to 'at least two pints before the game', and then at least three, etc etc.

Hell, a relegation season might cause damage to my liver.

So today we sneak a pint in before the game in the Lounge 107 pub just opposite the ground. We are the only City fans in there and Thomas does lots of deliberating about whether to use the amenities on offer in there. I offered to check these out and soon told him not to. If you are ever in need of a number two, those on offer at a public house or football ground are not to be used. Better to hold on until you get home when you can take some reading material – it used to be a newspaper, nowadays it's an IPhone or IPad. Thomas can be in there ages!

I was mildly amused by the selection of Wolves tops on display. It looked like their third kit or maybe training kit is purple. This always reminds me of

Sunday morning pub football when the shout at a corner or cross would be, *"Come on lads, get a purple head on it"*.

Molineux has never been my favourite ground. The last promotion season visit was particularly disappointing ending in a 1-0 defeat.

However I do recall an enjoyable evening back in September 2007. It was a 1-0 win courtesy of a Deano penalty, but was inspired by a sublime JJ Okocha, making his City debut. When substituted near the end, all four stands, home fans included, gave him a rapturous ovation.

Today's visit was not going to, and did not live up to that night.

We knew the turnout was poor when the section housing our seat ticket numbers wasn't even opened. *"Sit where you like"* the steward said, *"you've hardly sold any tickets"*, and so we did, bang on the half way line. I reckon about only six hundred had made the journey.

City did not start well at all. A crap back pass after about ten seconds nearly saw us go behind, but fortunately Davies cleared off the line. The resultant corner saw us give the ball away again, Elmo this time, but our luck was in as the striker blazed it high and wide.

This did remind me of when Nick Barmby scored for City after only seven seconds at the KC against Walsall.

City continued to look sluggish and it was somewhat against the run of play when a clumsy push on Davies saw us win a penalty. Jelavic put it right down the middle but beyond the keeper. One up and a quiet ironic round of *'We are top of the league, we are top of the league'* rang out.

Overall Wolves looked lively, but I still felt comfortable that we could keep a clean sheet. And so we did until half time.

McGregor had been doing his usual slowing up play at goal kicks and alike, much to the annoyance of the home fans. They got their own back early in the second half. An innocuous cross went straight to him unchallenged, a routine catch. Not this time. Like the proverbial bar of soap, McGregor spilled it, even pushing it towards our goal as opposed to away from it, and it was a gift for Henry, the Wolves midfielder to equalise.

Fuck. Ing. Hell. What a cock up.

Needless to say McGregor then got lots of hand gestures and ironic applause whenever the ball went remotely near him. Apparently, McGregor was wearing new gloves and his sponsors had shown clips of him wearing them making a first half save. Needless to say they didn't show the clips of him punching himself on the head after his mistake. Maybe he should change his gloves and wear some mittens with string down his sleeves. Thomas could have done better.

City actually finished the game quite lively as Wolves seemed to run out of steam. Akpom hit the post late on, but overall, despite gifting them a goal, we were both reasonably happy with a draw. It's a cardinal sin to gift the other team a goal. If they score a 'worldy' so be it, you just hold your hands up and accept it. But McGregor's mistake would not have been out of place on Costello pitch number 16 on a Sunday morning.

However, a point was earned. Wolves only just missed out on the play offs last year on goal difference and are likely to be there or thereabouts this season, so maybe this game was a good yardstick. So far, it hasn't been an overly exciting or dynamic start to the season, all a bit *after the Lord Mayors parade*. But we are still undefeated, despite not playing that well.

We returned home and Thomas finally got to sit and read his IPad in familiar surroundings. We later watched the match again on Sky, albeit much of it on x 16.

"IS THAT ALL WE BRING AWAY, IS THAT ALL WE BRING AWAY...."

CHAPTER 11

"2-1 TO THE NORTHERNERS"

The games are coming thick and fast now. Hell footballers are being asked to play two or three games a week, how will they survive? Stuff them, what about our wallets.

Never seemed to stop me when I was a kid. We used to play out kicking a ball about for hour after hour, and we didn't get paid for doing it. Mind you the games were sometimes about twenty-a-side so you could go absent for a while. It was always even better if you actually had real goalposts rather than jumpers. If the goals actually had nets on, well it was like playing at Wembley.

For tonight's game, we'd talked the football widow's brother Des into re-attending a City game. Des has a tendency to change his mind about which team he supports from one week to another, depending on how they are playing. For years he supported Liverpool, mainly from his armchair. Then when City starting being quite good, he supported them, and attended the KC. Like many of us, I think he partly saw it as a bit of an excuse for a few beers on a Saturday, but once he started going he quite enjoyed it. It's always easier to watch a winning team after all.

Then they got relegated and I think he stopped. He isn't the only one mind, this applies to a number of City fans at the moment, the seven or eight thousand empty seats tonight are testament to that.

So we've decided to make it our mission to see if we can persuade him to come back to the KC. It is helped tonight mind that we've acquired a free spare pass. It's also his birthday soon, so instead of buying the usual crappy gift voucher or something, may well buy him a ticket for an away game, see if he likes the experience.

The football widow herself is also making her first appearance of the season. Partly because she has become a bit nosey about what we are all up to. She's read a few chapters of the book so far and maybe wants a piece of the action.

However I think the real reason is more to do with her sense of duty and goodwill. Her day, or should I say night job, is a nurse both at Hull Royal and Castle Hill Hospitals. I know from her nature that she is a very caring person, she'd have to be to work at 'Hell Royal' on a Friday or Saturday night full of pissed up people clogging up the system. Anyone who can come through our front door at about eight in the morning after a thirteen hour shift, explaining that in any one single evening they have had to encounter patients who have been stabbed to death, hung themselves or come in accompanied by riot police because they are off their tits on Ketamine, has to have a fairly understanding nature.

So when our next door neighbour asked if we'd take their elderly mother to the game because they were on holiday, it was not in the football widow's make up to even consider declining. She was happy to be of help and oblige.

This actually meant that, due to having a wheelchair, we got a prime parking spot at the ground and free use of a pass, even if it was in the West Stand.

A 'lucky pint' was had again in hopeful preparation and we took our seats.

The football widow was genuinely excited, albeit I'm sure I must already be boring her with this whole book thing. During the game, and in an attempt to get involved and contribute, she started making a few notes in her phone to assist her submitting a written contribution. This actually resulted in her missing one of the goals, although it was only Fulham's goal.

City actually played quite well in the first half, again though without really creating loads of clear cut chances. In the end we had very few shots on target. We probably just about deserved to go in one nil up, thanks to an Elmo header at the far post from a good Robertson cross.

We were helped slightly by a bizarre incident which saw two Fulham players, one of which was their goalkeeper, collide late in the first half. Both were taken off, which did prompt the football widow to wonder whether they were going to be treated at Hull Royal. If that were the case there would be no chance of them even making the team coach home, let alone coming out for the second half.

We can still play a lot better though and at half time I made some notes about what I've seen so far this season.

Hernandez is still struggling to shine and merit the extortionate £10million fee. Jelavic doesn't look too interested about being here anymore. We desperately need something else up front, albeit I appreciate that these don't come cheap. Hell, Ross McCormack was up front for Fulham, he cost £11 million and tonight he was crap. Mind you he did come from L**ds so that's understandable.

We could also do with a box to box midfielder who drives forward and chips in with a few goals. Hopefully the Jake Livermore situation might get resolved sooner or later, we'll at least know if we can play him or not, it should have been resolved by now really.

Hopefully the return of Mo Diame and Snodgrass might help there as well. We might even score from shots outside the box and free kicks. We never seem to score many goals in either of these ways, people seem to either be afraid of shooting from distance or just simply can't get a shot on target.

Tom Huddlestone also seems to be struggling. His pass completions stats are probably great but the vast majority are backwards and sideways, very few at the moment are incisive and goal threatening. A Tom Huddlestone in the right frame should be able to walk (no let's say run) through this division. Whilst it's competitive, the standard is nowhere near the Premier League.

Michael Dawson is probably playing the most incisive crossfield passes at the moment, and looking the ever assured centre back. Hope nobody takes a punt at him in the transfer window.

We can't help thinking of Fulham without remembering our 6-0 win, it's definitely the only time I've seen a footballer get his hair cut on the pitch during a game, when Huddlestone scored.

But that is exactly the type of thing that lulls you into thinking you're going to win easily. Go into a game thinking you've already won usually only means one thing, you won't.

And to confirm my thoughts, the second half starts and it's almost a mirror copy of the Huddersfield game. City don't really come out at all and Fulham enjoy the majority of the possession. Add to the mix, that an ex player is up against you and one thing is a certainty, they are bound to score.

Tonight was Tom Cairney's turn to score and he certainly enjoyed it. He did have a great deal of help mind both from another questionable piece of McGregor goalkeeping, followed by a bit of Aluko shimmering on the edge of our own box before being dispossessed. I'm sure my old coaches and PE teachers always said, *"If in doubt, boot it out"*.

Another goal gifted in my opinion and one that could have been avoided.

And so from almost coasting in the first half, we were now level, 1-1.

Fortunately City carved out another chance. Jelavic had come on as a sub and unlike recent performances, did actually look lively. I even saw Steve Bruce give him a bear hug at the end of the game. And so with four minutes of normal time left, Jelavic set up Aluko (who only five minutes earlier I had suggested to Thomas should be substituted, what do I know?) to hit the ball into the ground and past the keeper.

In total we'd had two shots on target, scored twice and now sat second in the league.

Never being content though, something still feels not right. We should easily be beating teams like Fulham and Huddersfield, they were nothing special and I'd be amazed if either were challenging the top half of the league. If only we could play for a full ninety minutes instead of just one half, or patches. One wonders what happens to them at half time.

But let's not complain too much. As the cliché goes, if you can still win whilst not playing that well, surely that bodes well. And whatever the performance is like, there is nothing quite like scoring a late winner.

There were smiles on the Bunton's faces.

The football widow was even talking about coming again.

Des commented *"It's good to be back"* – it remains to be seen if he'll come again if free passes are not up for grabs.

"CHAMPIONSHIP, WE'RE HAVING A LAUGH..."
(WELL SORT OF)

CHAPTER 12

"INTO THE VALLEY – THE SKIDS ARE PUT ON"

This was not the most successful away visit we ever made. In fact that was something of an understatement.

Firstly, we could persuade no-one to join us again, it was too far. Tony Cline *'ummed and erred'* but declined the opportunity of spending six or hour seven hours in a car to see some dross disguised as a football match.

So Thomas and I set off early doors, match tickets in hand, lucky t-shirt on, heading for the A1 so as to avoid those bloody roadworks. The plan was to park up at High Barnet tube station and travel to the ground via The Underground and then overground train. In usual Thomas style, he had been out of bed for all of five minutes before we set off, so no sooner had we passed through North Cave, he again uttered his usual words, *"I'm hungry, when are we stopping?"*.

Now especially if I'm driving, I prefer to get my foot down, get to the end destination and ditch the car as soon as possible.

He had his eye, or should I say stomach, on a services stop. Oh the joy of being fleeced for everything on offer and paying £50 for a Ginsters pasty. Today he declared his desire for a Costa Coffee stop. I reluctantly agreed; he then promptly nodded off.

I kept quiet until well down the A1, where there are fewer services. He was a bit gutted, so we made a deal. If City won, we'd have a slap up tea at say a Carluccios or something in Barnet on the way back. A draw meant a Costa Coffee, a defeat meant thrashing it all the way home and a homemade cheese sandwich.

We were also planning to meet Tony Weaver, who is currently working down in London for a construction firm. This would certainly involve a couple of pints before the game, so it was best to get there as soon as possible.

So we parked up at High Barnet station and boarded the tube. As we approached London Bridge, the first crap part of the day unfolded. On a packed and sweltering tube, I let out a fairly loud *"Bollocks"*. A few eyes turned on me. Thomas asked *"What's up?* I asked him if he had the match tickets, to which his obvious answer was no, he thought I had them. They were still in the car. Dumwits!

Rather than get off the tube and travel back (there may not have been enough time anyway), a quick check on the phone told us we could pay on the day fortunately (or should I say unfortunately). And so upon final arrival at Charlton, we headed for the ground, The Valley, and proceeded to buy a second set of tickets for the same game.

Now I've bought a match ticket before and not actually turned up to the game, but never before have I paid twice to get into the same game. And so having paid a second set of £35, tickets now firmly in my pocket, we headed for the pub.

Ian Puckering, a good friend had already left a message saying he was in a pub called The Antigallican which was just near the train station.

Second crap part of the day happened. A call from Tony Weaver meant he couldn't make it – he was stuck at work overseeing the laying of umpteen tonnes of concrete.

The pub also turned out to be, shall we say, less than attractive. It was one of those pubs that you only imagine opens on match days, as it was close to the ground. It was hardly an establishment where you'd want to spend your Friday night out. The *indoor* furniture mainly consisted of *outdoor* picnic tables, and many of the drinks were not draught, but simply poured straight out of a bottle.

Needless to say, a couple of Guinness were supped (in a plastic glass obviously), and as ever, Ian proved good company, and soon kick off time approached.

Whilst the weather was scorcheo, being from 'up north', we were prepared for all eventualities, and had jumpers and cap.

Next crap thing of the day, I left my cap in the pub. *"Oh stuff it Thomas, let's go in, I'll just buy another one."*

And so in we went. This was a new ground for us both. I'd seen City play Charlton away before, but at that time The Valley was closed and they were ground sharing with Crystal Palace. I've already explained the rules here, so a new 'tick' for us both today.

There was a much better City following today, maybe a 1,000 or so. Taffy, Bruce, John and Co were already in the ground and were staying overnight in London, the capital of the country and home to umpteen million. They informed us that they were not catching their train home until about six pm the following day, and then asked what could they do all day that didn't involve drinking. No answers were forthcoming.

Seats were taken and the match started.

This was the next crap thing of the day.

City were woeful for the most. Again lots of sideways, backwards, sideways, backwards possession with very little penetration or goal threat. The Charlton goalkeeper, a certain Mr Pope, at the far end, had not a single save to make in the first half.

Charlton were not much better. They did have some big target man, a Dane called Simon Makienok, who was keeping us busy and on our toes. By the look of him, he had also been keeping the tattoo parlour busy as well with, not just the mere fashionable one 'sleeve', but two 'sleeves'. He'll regret it when he's an old man with wrinkly skin. He had not though, been keeping the hairdressers very busy, sporting a ridiculous ponytail. Cue the inevitable, *"Where's your caravan"*, *"The wheels on your house go round and round"* and *"Gypo, Gypo"* chants.

With little football to cheer, The City contingent were being mildly amused and entertained by some of their own chants, including:

"You're soft, you're a Southerner" – as endless Charlton players kept going down injured, which would surely lead to stupid amounts of injury time (see the consequences of this below)

"You're so Southern, you must be from France"

"If you can't bang a bird, bang a drum" – aimed at the idiot constantly banging a drum in the Charlton "Covered End", in a vain attempt to create an atmosphere, as if playing in Europe at the San Siro.

And always thinking on their feet, a quick shout of *"Fuck The Pope"* aimed at the Charlton goalkeeper in the second half when taking a goal kick at our end (well it makes a change from *"You're shit, ahhhhh"*)

Whatever people say or think about football supporters, there can be some quick thinking and light hearted humour and banter, none of which is really done with any malice.

One of my all time favourites was at Liverpool, directed at the then Liverpool manager Rafa Benitez, being *"You're just a fat Spanish waiter, fat Spanish waiter.."*

Even L**ds fans have one I like from last season, being to the tune of Only Fools and Horses along the lines of, *"No income tax, no VAT, he hides his yachts in Italy, Cellino, Cellino.."*

Recent Sunderland chants have also amused me. Their current manager, is / was a fairly rotund Dutch chap called Dick Advocaat. And so you now have many grown men stood together chanting *"We want Big Dick"*.

So chants aside, half time arrived with little to entertain us, a big fat nil – nil.

We were fortunately in the shade, as it was a sweltering day. It always seems to be sunny at the beginning of every season. I know it's still summer and all that, but this is England, yet I can barely remember early season games ever being played out on a cold, wet afternoon.

Thomas was now getting hungry. I reminded him of our deal, so as not to fill himself up, albeit the first half performance had not suggested his stomach was going to be overfed too soon.

In addition, I persuaded him *not* to try the local cuisine at The Valley. Most food in and around football grounds is not of a great standard. I can't recall seeing many '5' grade stickers on display. More often than not, you know you shouldn't eat it, but you talk yourself into believing that you are hungry.

Somehow, you convince yourself that the burger sizzling away on the griddle plate at the back of the burger van looks quite appetising, so you order one.

Only to see the spotty overweight attendant promptly grab a pair of tongs and pluck an already cooked burger that is being kept warm in a water trough. It may have been in there for weeks. It is then placed in a 'Crappy Shopper Breadcake' and you are directed to the sauces. These either don't dispense at all due to the great big congealed clog on the nozzle, or it comes out at strange angles and at 100mph, threatening to cover your clothing.

The only other options you are given is, *"You want onions with that?"* This always reminds me of that old haunt, Bun In The Oven in Hull City Centre. Many a time after a night out in Hull, you'd end up there and I'm sure the only words (and only thing on the menu) the server would say was *"Cheeseburger Chips"*. Like the proverbial kebab, you wouldn't eat it sober.

I also recall a rumour about Boothferry Park, that the 'Billy Boy' meat pies were allegedly stored in the ladies toilets, as this was the coldest part of the ground.

So I think you have gathered that nowadays I usually stay clear of football food. Instead I'd much prefer to pay an extortionate price for a gassy pint of lager served in a plastic glass or bottle, after having queued in a rugby style scrum, never quite knowing which is the beginning or the end of the queue.

And so today Thomas agreed, clearly thinking of that Carluccios. The teams then re-appeared.

The half time team talk had achieved little, we were still playing crap.

And then the Gypo scored, one nil Charlton.

We nearly went two down, a long ball forward saw Robertson, for some reason slip over, and a Charlton player was through on goal. To his credit, McGregor made a good save, slightly making amends for errors in previous games.

It took until late in the second half after Huddlestone was subbed for Hayden, and Akpom went off for Hernandez, that City finally came to life.

Hayden at last drove forward and not sideways, and Hernandez looked interested and lively holding the ball up. Not quite sure why this is, but the subs in recent games have livened up our overall performance. Why don't they do this when they are given a starting berth – you'd think they would be playing for a place, or a transfer perhaps, putting themselves in the shop window by showing the football world their talents.

With about five minutes to go Jelavic missed a sitter, when instead of burying a Hayden cross and celebrating right in front of us, he instead chose to 'shoulder' the ball harmlessly wide. Jelavic flung his arms in the air as if it was someone else's fault. He's frustrating the hell out of me at the moment. Today he was caught offside about four times in quick succession. At the moment both him and Huddlestone, (both of whom I would add clearly do have lots of talent – millions of pounds of transfer fees and wages suggest so) just don't seem to be putting the effort in that is required in The Championship. Do they think they are above playing at this level?

Soon after the Jelavic miss though, we equalise in the 89th minute. Hayden drives forward and thumps a low shot from just outside the box, against the post and the ball bounces out.

Bollocks. That's it we think, our chance of nicking a point is gone.

No wait, Clucas retrieves the ball and passes back to Hayden again. He shoots again.

'The Pope' spills it and Hernandez is *Abel* to bundle it in.

There is no question that this means something to Hernandez. He promptly goes into the crowd and celebrates with the City fans, getting a yellow card for good measure.

Meanwhile, 'The Pope' is getting treatment for a bloody nose and looks a bit stupid when the game restarts with tissue paper sticking out of both nostrils to stop the bleeding.

The endless injury breaks see the fourth official put up eight minutes.

The delirium in the away end has just died down. *"Bloody hell, we could win this yet"*. The previous abject seventy five minutes or so are forgotten.

"Come on City, Come on City" is roared.

Another cross, up rises Hernandez to head past the keeper into the net.

2-1!

No, some twat on the left hand side touchline is pointing a yellow and orange flag. Offside. Disallowed.

Oh well a draw is a good result anyway. We are still unbeaten, despite playing badly for most of the game. Imagine what might happen if we actually play for say sixty or seventy minutes.

But no.

In the 98th minute, Charlton throw a high ball forwards towards the big Dane. He beats both *"He's magic you know, Moses Odubajo"* and Michael Dawson, and heads the ball down for some midfield Charlton midget to race unchallenged and head past McGregor. 2-1 Charlton, and soon after the referee puts us out of our misery. Cue lots of kicking plastic seats and pent up frustration. Stupid bloody game.

The day is just getting crapper.

To be fair, Charlton probably deserved to win. At the moment, the opposition seem to pick up most second balls. That's not just luck or co-incidence. That is about attitude and desire.

So we trundle off to get on a packed train, which is absolutely roasting. There is sweat pouring off us, standing room only. Being in London, nobody but City fans speak or make eye contact. The tube stations and service stations are packed with supporters of other teams. Thomas is keen to check what their scores were. Do they all look as glum as us because they've lost too?

We get back to the car about 6.45 ish and, a deal is a deal.

We drive past a Carluccios, Thomas waving goodbye with a sad face. His stomach is now making noises.

To be fair, Thomas is on good form on the way home.

Despite reflecting on the fact that we personally, have now not seen City win away in the league since QPR back on the first day of the 14/15 season, over a year ago (we didn't go to Sunderland or Crystal Palace) and being very hungry, he is still smiling.

He stayed awake all the way, acting as DJ using Spotify on my phone (something that is way too technical for me) playing lots of loud music. This helped us to drive that bit faster (the recent speed awareness course being something of a distant memory) and thus shortening the journey time, and beating the Sat Nav.

He again mournfully looked at each service station as we sped past. We got as far as Doncaster before I relented to stop at one, namely one with a Costa Coffee. Thomas had his heart set on a Cheese and Ham Toastie.

They had sold out. What a crap day! I am already beginning to question our sanity.

The last leg of the journey saw us pass the Hull City team bus. A few rasps on the horn got them looking our way. Thomas waved. I felt like giving them two fingers but didn't.

We rolled in about ten pm.

The football widow had done us proud. She knew we may be disappointed, tired and maybe hungry, always thinking of us. An Indian takeway awaited us on the table. Our stomachs were replenished, and I reflected on the day. Are we glad we went?

Of course we were. This is all part of football's rich tapestry and experience. Next time we might win, after all, we've only got Rochdale at home to look forward to in three days time.

A loss in the capital. We paid twice to get in as we left our tickets in the car.
Not a good day.

"WHAT A WASTE OF MONEY...." (TWICE!)

CHAPTER 13

ROCHDALE (H) LEAGUE CUP– TUESDAY 25TH AUGUST 2015

"MORE CUP SUCCESS"

Following the disappointment of the Charlton game the previous Saturday, we all hoped that a home cup match against Rochdale would be a stroll in the park and allow us to score a few goals. This was not the case and this may well be a short chapter. In the attempt to try and forget the match, it has taken me a couple of weeks or so to get round to typing this up.

Now the football widow and I sometimes disagree. She says that love makes the world go round. In an attempt to wind her up, I say no it doesn't, money does. If I'm right, then there could also be some truth in the sentiment that *'you get what you pay for.'*

This particular fixture was free admission to season ticket holders who had renewed before a particular date – some sort of 'reward' for getting relegated.

So basically most of us paid nothing tonight.

Therefore if my sentiment is correct, as we paid nothing, we certainly got nothing, or at least very little.

The fact that it was free probably explained why there was a crowd of just over 10,000. Had it not been free, I'm sure there would have been even less. I do feel sorry for those that did actually pay money to watch this.

I should have known it wasn't going to be an enjoyable night, when from the start, our usual pre match ritual were put out of joint by one of those over efficient stewards. Some are great, others seem to think that putting a fluorescent jacket on gives then the right to turn into dictators, little Hitlers.

Tonight there was a new steward at the entrance nearest our regular seats, which leads us to the concourse running under the West Stand. For some reason, we have always used this concourse rather than the South Stand one. Most of us football supporters do like to keep our rituals, we are a bit like homing pigeons.

So tonight when this steward refused us entry down to our usual concourse, our noses were put out of joint. This was a fixture with about 15,000 empty seats, did it really matter?

So a quick pint under the South stand, although this felt uncomfortable – our ritual felt like it was in tatters.

Clearly the steward was a 'new boy' and the donning of his yellow bib, was an initial attempt to impress his superiors in the orange bibs.

Having annoyed me and with little to watch on the pitch, I even noticed him part way through the first half ask someone to sit down – the guy was stood on the back row with no-one behind him and thousands of empty seats everywhere. Do they use any common sense?

Before the match, a minutes 'silence' was held in respect of the Shoreham Air Disaster which had recently taken place. This is not meant as any disrespect at all, but I'm not quite sure why this particular match warranted it. The disaster wasn't local to us, nor did it have any direct link to Hull City, other than that some of the casualties were in essence, part of the football community. A proper and more fitting tribute certainly took place at our next away game against Brighton, as I'll touch on later.

That being said, and as there is in these modern days, there is always the deliberation of whether it should be a minutes silence or a minutes applause. Tonight it started as a silence, one or two people started clapping, and so it turned into a part minutes silence, part minutes applause.

No worries, the events on the pitch, and lack of atmosphere in a two thirds empty KC, soon turned it into a ninety minute silence.

This evening, we were sat with Rich Hewson, who I have spent many a match with in yesteryear – poor games in the bottom divisions and with no disrespect meant, against teams the like of Rochdale. The surroundings aside, tonight's game felt like going back in time.

There was also a terrible smell of piss engulfing the KC tonight!

In these circumstances, you can't help looking round at people to try and ascertain if it is them that have pissed themselves. In reality it wasn't, something to do with some blocked toilets, although it certainly did resemble something of an old folk's home.

A few brief words then about the match.

City made a few changes, and whilst the team may have been a bit unfamiliar, the lackadaisical performance wasn't.

Ryan Taylor was back in, although at the moment, I can't see what he adds to the team. He looks very slow, wanting too much time on the ball. I'm sure he gave the ball away three times in succession in a small patch of play called, *'I don't want it, so you have it. No I don't want it either, have it back, etc etc etc.'* He also seems to be the chosen one for set pieces. I haven't seen him take a decent one yet, but that being said, neither has anybody else. When was the last time we scored from a direct free kick?

There was the welcome return of Mo Diame though, and he certainly showed signs of forward momentum and drive, instead of the backwards, sideways stuff we've been demonstrating. We did all hold our breath every time he went down injured though as I feel he could be a very important player for us this season, assuming he stays injury free.

City stroked it about reasonably well and took the lead after ten minutes, Hernandez and Diame linked up well, creating space for Gregg Luer to place a shot neatly beyond the keeper for 1-0.

Little else was created in the first half and you kind of got the belief that we thought the job was already done. The game was played at a slow tempo with a lack of urgency, reminiscent of a pre- season friendly when, with a quiet crowd, you can actually hear the players shouting at each other.

We looked fairly unambitious with no-one showing much determination to actually have a shot, more a desire to try and walk the ball into the net. The speed of our play didn't allow too many spaces to be created.

The second half saw an early chance for Hernandez, but after he was played in by Robertson, he somehow spooned the ball over from about four yards. Maguire nearly gave a penalty away when trying a diving header in his own box when the ball was about a foot off the floor. He then later found the top section of the West Stand with a good old fashioned centre half's clearance. Wouldn't it be good if one day, somebody could clear the full stand?!

Rochdale then enjoyed a reasonable spell of possession without ever looking really dangerous and City just about hung on. A Rochdale equaliser would have subjected us to an extra thirty minutes which would have been hard viewing, and the smell of piss was by now becoming annoying.

Fortunately they didn't and a third round place was secured. The subsequent draw pitted us against Swansea at home, another freebie. Hopefully it will be a bit better than this fare, although I don't think the Swans will be too scared of The Tigers.

As we walked out, I asked the football widow (who had once again accompanied our neighbour's mother) if she'd enjoyed it and would be coming again soon?

She said she'd give it a miss for a while!

"BORING, BORING CITY..!"

CHAPTER 14

"PARTY TIME"

Another home game soon followed, the matches in The Championship really do come round very quick, especially when you've still got previous games to write and type up. The timing of this game is just before the closing of the first transfer window of the season – this really should close before the season starts rather than a month or so into it.

For the first time of the season, I was genuinely feeling guilty about us all going to City. Following Nick's funeral a few weeks earlier, the football widow had decided to have a 'City BBQ' at the Bunton house after today's game. So Bri, Tony C, Tony W, Shaun and Rich and partners were all to descend on us early evening.

So whilst we were sat watching City, the football widow was busy preparing enough food to feed a small African nation, and scurrying around the house cleaning. My sole contribution pretty much was to make sure the dog was taken for a very long walk (or did she just want me out of the way?) and put together a quick City quiz.

If I do say so myself, I was actually quite impressed by my quiz. So at seven am in the morning, with the help of an IPad, Google and Wikipedia, I scrawled a host of questions. Each question commenced with the opening lines of a City terrace chant that all guests had to sing along with, and then Thomas read the questions. The guests did say it was 'rock hard'. The idea of the quiz really just came from those that are carried out in The Malt Shovel before a Saturday home game. Since Nick's passing, this has taken on a slightly changed version.

Prior to the Huddersfield home game, Bri Lee brought the pub to a hush and spoke a few heartfelt words about Nick – absolutely everyone was held captive and then he asked for a minutes applause, to which everyone joined in, even those that didn't know him – a fitting tribute. And then a new tankard was put in place, bedecked with Black and Amber ribbons. This is now referred to as 'Nick's tankard' and the winner of the quiz gets to drink a pint from it, it to be then retained behind the bar.

Rumour is that Jelavic is leaving to join his ex Croatia manager Slaven Bilic at West Ham. Personally, I don't think this will be a massive loss, his heart doesn't look in it anymore and his knees look shot. I can't believe he will get many chances at West Ham, a mere squad player until Andy Caroll is fit again. But hey ho, not a bad job if you can get thirty grand a week or so for the pleasure. As a result, he was dropped for this game, and likely we won't see him in a City shirt again. He'll no doubt be paraded in front of the Sky cameras on transfer deadline day, holding up the hastily printed shirt of his new club, totally forgetting his old one. If you can tell, it totally disappoints me that there is so much lack of loyalty by the majority of football players nowadays. They are too happy to jump ship when things aren't going well, or a better offer comes along – us football supporters don't get this choice.

Speaking of letters and shirt printing though, it does remind me of the day when Thomas wanted a new City shirt to be printed, only to be told he could have anything he wanted, but they had no vowels left!

So Jelavic out, but after his midweek cup turnout, Diame was back and on the bench was new signing Shaun Maloney, he of ex Villa, Wigan and Celtic. Huddlestone was also dropped after some indifferent performances.

There were empty seats on show again, the number of which may have been enhanced by the fact that Hull KR were playing in the Challenge Cup Final against Leeds. Despite the fact that some call this a 'rugby town', this was their first appearance in a final for over twenty years, an eternity in a league which constitutes only twelve teams. They managed to achieve an Hawaii 5-0 result; Leeds 50 Hull KR 0, so not a great day for them.

Preston started lively and were the better team and their travelling contingent were being fairly vocal singing things like " *I wanna go home, I wanna go home, Hull is a shithole, I wanna go home*". Dawson put in a great old fashioned tackle, perfectly okay (in the Championship anyway), and a combination of the two, seemed to fire up the City supporters as well.

Robertson let the Preston winger cut inside and McGregor was forced into an early save. Robertson is certainly not at the levels he was last season, he never seems to cut out crosses at the moment and is certainly not the attacking force he has been.

Bruce moved Clucas inside to provide more support in the middle. Although this did little to provide support in front of Robertson.

Preston's goalkeeper was looking a bit iffy on crosses, dropping a couple and this provided encouragement to City. After Odubajo had won a corner, Thomas and I exchanged our usual *"We never score from corners"* routine (in the vain attempt that we actually might). Bloody hell, this time we did after a good stroke of fortune.

Clucas crossed, Akpom headed, Hernandez poked it goalwards and a Preston defender cleared it off the line, only for it to hit Hernandez and bounce back into the net. He knew little about it, but who cares, Hernandez wheeled away and celebrated, 1-0 City.

We'll make a point now of changing the *"We never score from corners"* to *"We never score from free kicks"*, maybe that will do the trick.

City one up usually is a good thing. Certainly at this level with this squad, we very rarely lose after taking the lead. Mind you, conversely, we very rarely win either after having gone one down.

We should have gone further ahead when a shot from Dawson fell into the path of Hernandez, but he shot straight at the keeper, and Diame blazed the rebound way over.

Preston continued to look lively and had some half chances, but we were never too concerned about them scoring.

Diame was now tiring and he was eventually replaced by Maloney (although it must have taken some three or four minutes to get him on). His cameo appearance looked encouraging and late on he swung over a great corner for Curtis Davies to thump home to make it two nil. Who says we never score from corners? Two in one game. Cue the City fans responding to the earlier Preston chants with *"You're going back to your shithole, back to your shithole"*

This book has seen me constantly typing notes into my phone whilst at games. That stupid invention called predictive text and my 'sausage fingers'

We never score from corners. (PA Images)

caused Thomas great amusement as my notes for the goal appeared as *'Davies thumping **shit** into the back of the net'.*

At two nil, it was certainly game over, although there was still time for Preston to miss a gilt edged chance when they headed over unmarked from about six yards, their effort probably deserved a goal at least.

Overall, a reasonable performance, a bit more convincing than previous ones, and another welcome three points. There is definitely more to come and we are now up to second. Dawson and Davies look very solid, but there will be tougher tests to come.

And so later in the evening, several beers were supped, they always taste better after a win.

"WE ARE GOING UP, WE ARE GOING UP..!"
(DON'T COUNT YOUR CHICKENS JUST YET)

CHAPTER 15

BRIGHTON (A) – SATURDAY 12TH SEPTEMBER 2015

"YOU'RE SO SOUTHERN, YOU'RE PRACTICALLY FRENCH"

The win over Preston was followed by a blank weekend, an international weekend with England playing against the mighty San Marino. This was bad news for me and a chance for a bit of payback from the football widow.

That's right, no football meant I was in for what most of the UK do when they've got nothing else planned, a spot of DIY. This is certainly not my area of expertise, most shelves in my house have very little on them, just in case. However Thomas had a bedroom wall that was in need of a lick of paint. So we both set about the task, whilst at the same time having a few beers (me that is, not Thomas). This resulted in us stopping whilst the football was on and then falling asleep. The painting was finished quite late.

Fortunately the next weekend came round quick and this brought along the next fixture, an away top of the table clash against Brighton. A first away win of the season would see City go top, something that doesn't happen too often.

Originally we had planned to all go down to this one on the train and make a weekend of it. Unfortunately the football widow's shift pattern meant she was working on the Saturday night so it was just me and the kids. Charlotte wanted to come to this one. Apparently, Brighton is a hot spot for 'You Tubers' and a certain Alfie Day who is one of her favourites. Naturally she assumed she might bump into him – it's only a town with a population of 150,000 people.

And by the time, I got round to looking at hotels, any within our price range were all booked up. Those that were still free, were about the same price as a seven day break abroad. The plan therefore was to go there and back on the day, on the train from Doncaster, so tickets and seats were booked. That was until Bri Lee rang a few days before, asking if there was room in our car for him and his son James.

And so eager to please, train tickets were 'unbooked' shall we say, and the car it was. The deal made was that I'd add Bri to my car insurance. Being an old bugger this was the princely sum of about a tenner for a year! I would drive down, he would drive back. This also allowed me to have a few sherberts.

This also worked well for us, as the organisational stress was completely removed. This is because Bri excels in organising all things City related, like a military manoeuvre. Every move is thought and planned ahead, from route planners, ground details, park and ride schemes, through to which pub we were visiting.

So it was no surprise when they both pitched up on our driveway at 7.20am, a full ten minutes before his estimated time of departure. We would have no doubt been late had the roles been reversed. Not Bri. Needless to say, I was still getting dressed when he arrived.

In addition they had brought packed lunches (very cool for a football fan!), although I'm sure they had been done by female hands. A bloke's would consist of about eight packs of crisps or a family size pack of sausage rolls, not the selection on show today in their nice Tupperware boxes.

And you've guessed it. As we left the door, the football widow had done exactly the same for us. Clearly this was all to Thomas' dismay, although he did manage to sneak a quick Costa stop in, at the obligatory toilet stop on the way down.

In advance of this trip, I was a bit concerned. The round trip from our front door to the Amex Stadium is five hundred and forty two miles. That's a long distance with five people sat in a car.

Just for good measure, the fixture list had thrown up Cardiff away the following Tuesday. In total, just over one thousand miles travelling to two football matches within four days.

I needn't have been concerned about the trip at all. In total we probably spent about nine or ten hours travelling, but there was no more than a few minutes of silence in the car. The conversations simply flowed, and the fact that James, sixteen, was a bit younger meant that Charlotte and Thomas had someone they could relate to a bit more, rather than the usual old buggers.

In fact the conversation was flowing so much that we totally missed the A1 turn off resulting in 'those roadworks' and ultimately, more time on the 'car park' that is the M25.

Even now in my forties, I still get excited about certain away trips. The fact that it was a new ground for us, a chance to go top of the league, and having good company along the way meant we were excited. Sometimes this can be spoilt by the return journey, especially if you've lost. But even though our day was punctuated by a very abject City performance, this did not happen today.

We set off in typical 'Ull weather, it was raining. But by the time we got to our park and ride bus system, the weather was sunny.

The Amex, at a cost of £93million, is a lovely stadium, padded seats, the lot. Access to and away from it though is not great, with very little parking.

A ticket cock up (mine simply did not turn up in the post, and nor did my Cardiff ones) meant collecting them before the game and as such, much of the pre match pub time was reduced. A couple of pints were had in The Swan, a nice old farmhouse converted into a pub, with one barn house acting as a bar. We also met up with Johnny Harrison, who in good old Yorkshire fashion, moaned about the prices of, well, everything, and Ed Faulkner (he of Tribfest and Beautiful Couch fame) who was at a weekend music festival on the Isle Of Wight.

And then we decamped to the ground, there being a pre match tribute to the victims of the Shoreham Air Disaster. This was a much more fitting tribute to the minutes silence / applause at the Rochdale home fixture.

It was also the first show of our City flag and the Brighton stewards were extremely helpful fastening it to the mesh segregating the City away seats. For those of you that haven't purchased a flag and tried to display it at a football ground, you wouldn't believe how many rules there are. You need fire retardant certificates, you can't cover advertising boards (and nearly every square inch within football grounds have now all been sold to the devil), they are not supposed to be above a certain size, they can't display offensive words, the list goes on. Not only that, you need to go into the ground earlier to beat any other 'flag displayers' from nicking the few available spots. You are supposed to get permission from the home team as well, although in practice I don't think this happens. I can't believe all those flags at England games do. There are loads and if you notice, they are usually of lower level teams, probably all wanting a bit of success – they won't get it with England.

A debut outing for our flag at Brighton away.

Needless to say, I can see why people don't bother.

Anyway, this was our little thing and so once up, I felt quite proud (sad git that I am). Then the slightest gust of wind and it blew up. A few more alterations, and a tight knot soon saw to that and pride again.

And then a few minutes later, a couple of lads put next to ours, their '*Goole Tigers*' / '*Charleston Club*' flag and it made ours look like a postage stamp, dwarfing it. And to make matters worse, when I watched the highlights later on TV, it wasn't quite low enough to catch the camera angle and get shown. Bloody amateurs!

The Shoreham tribute was well put together. Some City fans on the concourse, possibly unaware it was taking place, were making a bit of a noise, but Bri soon told them to shut up.

And then the game started.

Well, Brighton did and City didn't.

After only four minutes, Meyler was caught in possession, and after a further couple of failed clearance attempts, a Brigton player stroked it into the net. One down and already Brighton had something to defend.

Not that they had to defend too hard for much of the game mind. Some strange selections saw Clucas at left back (Robertson was on the bench though) and we were all at sea for the first twenty or thirty minutes. Brighton could easily have got another.

Meyler got his usual booking and Mr Bruce Senior decided it was time for a change already. Meyler started limping as if injured, to explain to us fans the reason for him being taken off. The reality was with still sixty minutes or so to go, he was walking a tightrope, and we simply needed to change something, so on came Huddlestone.

We did improve slightly, although the best we had to show in the first half was an Akpom free kick which went into about row twenty five.

The second half was marginally better. We had loads of possession, but little goal threat, as is worryingly the case at the moment, and it took us until about seventy minutes to actually have a shot on target, when both Elmo and Huddlestone actually managed to make ex City loanee Stockdale in the Brighton goal, use his gloves.

The modern way of football seems to be very much about scoring the first goal, and then defending the lead. In days gone by, the team having the majority of ball possession usually went on to win. This doesn't seem to be the case anymore, when invariably, those having, say only 40-45% possession go on to win. Today we had 60%, but had only three shots on target.

To be fair, they only had three, but simply did a job on us having been gifted an early goal.

As ever, there were some amusing chants during the day. Being in Brighton, a notorious popular destination for those who like same sex relationships, the usual:-

"We can see you holding hands"

"Does your boyfriend know you're here" and;

"We saw your boyfriend on Jeremy Kyle" (a twist on the usual 'sister' version)

We obviously got the Rosenior tribute,

"His nanna's from Hull, his nanna's from Hull, Liam Rosenior, his nanna's from Hull".

The man himself put in his usual seven or eight out of ten performance – we should never have got rid and he would have been perfectly capable cover for us at either right or left back.

The favourite shout of the day though had to go to Johnny Harrison.

A small group of younger City supporters who were sat just in front of us, were obviously determined to adopt the Bri chant leading approach. A Bri of yesteryear would not have stood for this and would easily have out done them, he has one of the loudest singing voices I've ever heard at a football match, and I swear you can often hear him chant even in a different stand. However today he was not playing. Maybe it was because my kids were with us and he felt he needed to be a bit more reserved, or maybe he is getting a bit older, or maybe he just couldn't be arsed, let the younger foot soldiers get on with it.

Anyway these lads thought it would add to the atmosphere, by taking their tops off. You see this regularly at football matches, god knows why. It's not like they are Adonis' with six packs.

This was certainly the case today as these lads had clearly not done too much sunbathing.

And at exactly the same time as there was a hush in the crowd, Johnny H shouted,

"And that reminds me, I need a pint of milk"

I'll give it to him, perfect timing.

So the game finished in a one nil defeat and we collected our flag (of course I tied the bloody knot too tight so needed young sixteen year old James to untie it rather than me and my sausage fingers) and descended to the park and ride queues.

A quick fill up at the petrol station and we were on our way straight home. Bit cheeky I know, but having had the pre match pub time curtailed, I bought a four pack to entertain myself on the way home. The conversation flowed constantly with City related stories being exchanged, even the kids joined in and refrained from going to sleep or putting their headphones in. Thomas was slightly alarmed mind when his IPhone was down to only 1% charge, they do become like a fifth limb.

For me the best two stories (of those that can be printed) both had to go to James.

The first involves Roary the Tiger, Hull City's mascot and happened a number of years ago. The Lee's are quite a tall family and when James was about seven or eight years old, being taller than most kids at that age, he enjoyed considerable success at catching sweets from Roary at home games, when he does his usual 'chucking sweets at the kiddies from a bucket' routine. Apparently this carried on for a few games until at one particular game, with pockets already bulging, Roary grabbed James by the lapel and lifted him off his feet and whispered,

"Don't you think you've had enough sonny?"

Needless to say, James scuttled back to his seat not to return. In reality, I fear he may now be a bit scared of Roary.

The second story involved something that Thomas has always wanted to achieve, the catching of a sweaty footballers shirt when they throw it into the crowd. Now this is usually only done at the end of the season or when a glorious achievement has been carried out. So the chances of catching anything are fairly remote.

Thomas came close when we drew away at Fulham 2-2, after a late Shane Long equaliser more or less kept us up. The latter 'passing' his shirt to a city fan just three places away from Thomas.

James has gone one better.

This took place at West Ham away on the last game of the 2011/12 season, so some three years or so ago. West Ham had got promoted to the Premiership and duly beat us 2-1. It being the last game, some City players threw their shirts into the City section of the crowd, which obviously sets off the usual scrabble to try and catch it. One of these players was goalkeeper, Vito Mannone, who as only being a loan player, was playing his last game for City.

As he threw his shirt into the crowd, James managed to get his hand onto it.

But almost immediately, some 'old' lady, about sixty years old snatched it from his grasp. There were groans and shouts of, "*Give it to the bairn*", but this old lady was having none of it. She quickly passed it to her husband rugby style, and they were away out of The Boleyn Ground like Linford Christie.

James was crestfallen.

And to rub salt into the wounds, every now and then, he still sees that old lady walking around Hull, wearing that very same top (probably still unwashed).

Shame on you old girl!

So before we knew it, we were about home. In the blink of an eye, the short two hundred and seventy mile return trip was almost done. Still time for me (not the kids) to act like a nine year old and ask for a piss stop at North Cave. Having drained the tinnies, I was bursting and could wait no longer and had no desire to wet myself in the back of my own car. I'm sure more than four cans came out and as I was stood on the grass verge, it did remind me of the time years ago, when being slightly worse for wear, I rang a mate asking him to come and pick me up from the pub and give me a lift home. He duly did, only for me to then be sick in the passenger seat. It was only the next morning, that I realised he'd picked me up in my own car!

So all in all, we got home just before ten pm.

Pretty good going I reckon and the whole trip had not been as daunting as first thought, albeit the City performance was left wanting.

In fact next time, maybe we'll just give the football a miss, and just turn straight back when we get there.

Only another four hundred and eighty four miles to clock up on Tuesday, Cardiff awaits.

"...I'D WALK A MILLION MILES FOR ONE OF YOU'RE GOALS, WHOAH CITY, WHOAH CITY..."

(WELL, DRIVE ABOUT A THOUSAND ANYWAY !)

CHAPTER 16

CARDIFF (A) – TUESDAY 15TH SEPTEMBER 2015

"A LONG WAY HOME, BUT THREE POINTS"

After the long and unsuccessful footballing trip to Brighton, the 'short' trip to Cardiff followed just four days later. This is not actually a short trip, just a round four hundred and eighty four mile round trip from our front door.

This is not an easy trip to make in midweek, what with the balancing of work commitments and schooling. Those clowns at the FA who set the fixtures really do not think of what the normal fan has to go through to try and attend games, particularly straight on the back of an equally long away fixture at Brighton. I sometimes also wonder if players appreciate the fan's efforts. When they walk over to the away section to applaud the travelling army, is this really in a show of appreciation and do they comprehend what they have been through to attend? Or do they only really come over if they've actually won the game?

Now we could have taken the easy option here as City decided to screen a 'beam back' at the KC for this one. But that would have felt like cheating and people might have spotted us! And deep in our hearts and minds, we would have known that we didn't actually attend every game.

So along with the 350 or so other Hull City fans, we all made the trip down to another country to watch our team.

In reality, for us, we were *'killing two birds with one stone'* here. Back in April 2015, my mother (Thomas' grandma) moved to Cardiff, just four miles from the ground. They had relocated from the metropolis that is Barton Upon Humber, (a sleepy old town still stuck in the Seventies littered with charity shops) into a retirement home to be nearer to other family relatives, who are now clearly higher up the pecking order than us!

We'd not visited them since this move, so as soon as we decided to take up the 46 game challenge, both this fixture and Bristol City away, were a natural. Pity this one was bloody midweek though.

Thomas was feeling 'unwell' the night before, so was highly unlikely to be able to go to school so, in the end, we decided to travel down the evening before, spend the day in Cardiff, and then head straight back after the match.

I questioned the football widow whether she was okay with this. Her response was immediate. *"Yes"*, she said, *"You'll never get this time back again with your son, go for it, enjoy it."* Such immediate affirmation from the football widow was great to hear, as pangs of guilt do kick in from time to time, when so much time is being pre-occupied with football.

Her commitment to the cause has also made us even more determined to savour the experience. Hopefully, City will pay their part and make the experience even sweeter.

On our way down, we were a little apprehensive in case our room for the night in the retirement home was going to smell of piss, but fortunately this was not the case. Massive brownie points were scored with my mum, and Thomas was on his best behaviour; he even used his p's and q's, and cleared the dishes. Well hey, Christmas is just around the corner.

A relatively early rise on the morning of the game, and with the Rugby World Cup due to start imminently, we decided a tour of The Millenium Stadium would be a good idea. This would also be relatively educational to Thomas as well, much more use than double algebra or whatever he was missing.

If you haven't done this tour or visited the ground, I would strongly recommend it. It's not a Wembley (as no memories of Hull City actually playing there come flooding back), but it is still very impressive.

In particular when in the changing rooms, an extremely motivating pre match speech is played to you, with references to the honour of wearing the Welsh shirt, *"it's not just a shirt, it's a symbol, an honour."*

Do you get that feeling when you put on a bit of Hull City clothing, be that a replica top or anything else. I still do, sad as it may sound. Proud to be 'Ull!

As I type these notes up, Wales have just beaten England in the Rugby World Cup in a passion fuelled backs to the wall performance; it looks like the

England RFU will follow the England FA in getting your hopes up, only to let you down.

Not even being Welsh, you could feel how it would inspire a player. It also made me think what the pre match and half time team talks in the City dressing room are like currently. I'd love to be a fly on the wall for one.

Other nice touches in the ground are that the back of one of the new stands, butts onto one of the old remaining stands of the old Cardiff Arms Park. The Arms Park ground still exists and is literally next door, where Cardiff Blues now play.

Also, I'm sure if you've ever noticed at most football stadia, many of the seats are usually covered in bird shit. Thomas always notices this and gets me to swap seats so he can occupy the least covered one. At The Millenium, there is hardly any bird shit at all. This is because they actually house a bird of prey within the stadium. This bird of prey then wards off and keeps away all pigeons, other birds, pests and rodents from the ground.

On a Rugby match day, the ground can often be full of tanked up Welshmen drinking beer at silly o'clock. Basically if Wales are playing away, say in Australia or New Zealand, they sometimes open the ground up, so that spectators can watch on a large screen. They are allowed to take beers into the ground and drink and watch from their seat. Imagine that, 74,500 pissed up Welshmen at eight am in the morning.

The '*having a beer in your seat*' thing at a stadium has always amazed me. Somebody could sit in the very same seat watching Rugby Union or Rugby League and have a beer, but not if they are kicking a round ball. And this seems a special rule just for the UK. We've been to watch Barcelona at the Nou Camp and you can quite happily have a drink at your seat whilst the game is being played. Definitely something to do with somebody high up? I have got a feeling that it could get quite messy here mind if they ever did change the rules.

So after the Millenium Stadium tour, I thought we'd give Thomas a bit more 'home education', namely language and history, by taking in an open top bus tour of Cardiff.

First of all the language, which the tour guide did use a bit. It is ridiculous. Hardly anybody speaks it unless they live in the hills with the sheep, so why they insist on displaying all signs in both languages, god only knows.

The history part of the tour was fairly enlightening and it did get me thinking if we'll do any of this in 2017 when Hull is the City of Culture ("...*We know what we are...*"). Where in Hull would an open top bus tour take you and what would it tell you?

So enough of all that. A quick bite to eat and it was time for the match to see what part of history City could write into the 15/16 season.

And bugger me, it was quite good; a much improved display to that in Brighton. In my mind, this was helped by us reverting back to a 3-5-2 formation. Elmo had been dropped after one hundred consecutive appearances, replaced by Bruce Jnr.

Alex Bruce does have his critics. It can't help him being the manager's son, but for me, you know what you get and he doesn't often let you down. I'm not expecting him to get man of the match but I usually think of him being extremely steady (even if he always seems to go down injured or unable to complete a full ninety minutes). Don't forget that Liverpool home game where he totally out marked Luis Suarez, keeping him quiet all game. Not many Premiership defenders could say the same during that particular season.

The performance tonight was very encouraging, and was as close to a perfect away display as you can get. We started with positive intent, scored early, defended stoutly, and then nicked a late goal on the break.

Cardiff were second before the game, so are no mugs, but as the game went on, you did kind of feel that they played into our hands, pumping high balls into the box. The strength of our three centre backs is certainly in the air.

We only just made it into the game for kick off. As both our Brighton and Cardiff tickets (ordered together) simply didn't arrive in the post, we had to collect some reprints. They hadn't been reprinted, so we had to wait for some eighteen stone steward to amble all the way from the away end, to the home ticket office, print them off, and amble back again. Olympics she won't be entering, and they re-appeared at about 7.44pm.

Due to this delay, there was no time for the flag tonight, or no pre match beer (which was probably a blessing as I still had to drive the two hundred and forty two miles home). As we took our seats we noticed Tony Cline and Annerley (his Welsh 'bird') just below us. He'd somehow managed to arrange a work meeting in Cardiff for exactly the same day as the fixture. That way he could watch the game and claim his expense, never one to like parting with money Tony.

Kenwyne Jones was looking lively early on as a target man for Cardiff, winning several headers and holding the ball up well, and there was a couple of scary moments in the first few minutes. City recovered and a good run by Sone Aluko (who looked sprightly all night) led to a cross that was only half cleared. The ball fell straight in the path of Mo Diame who said '*thank you very much*' and fired home. 1-0 City.

As the half drew on, Cardiff piled on the pressure with numerous corners being won but the City defence held solid, without too many saves being made by McGregor. Fabio (ex of Man United) was also looking lively, if not a bit hot headed. This was all leading to the Cardiff fans getting a bit restless.

Half time came and all was reasonably okay, albeit a one goal lead is never enough. One error and points can be dropped. I exchanged texts with a friend who was listening to Burnsey and Swanny on the radio, who had been discussing the meat pie offering at the ground. The text suggested we shouldn't partake in one (clearly not that I would anyway). Swanny had eaten one and was complaining of feeling unwell and even had to momentarily leave the commentary box to relieve himself of said pie. With that, and impeccable timing, three City supporters returned from the concourse and sat right next to us, each one of them tucking into a pie. I had a quick laugh to myself, being thankful I wasn't giving them a lift home. I've told you about football food already.

The second half resumed and the home crowd was certainly getting restless. McGregor was already doing his usual time wasting antics (it's so annoying when the opposition does this to you, but funny the other way round) and Aluko did a couple of shocking dives to actually win us free kicks. This didn't help the home crowd's feelings.

The half full Cardiff stadium let out a chant of;

"*Same old English, always cheating*"

As Cardiff put more and more balls into the box, the home contingent also started shouting for anything that remotely looked like a handball, and some that didn't. So it was hilarious when after about six failed appeals in quick succession, the referee immediately awarded a handball in City's favour.

The City fans returned with the chant

"One nil to the referee" and *"The referee is English"*

The pressure was mounting, and City were having difficulty keeping possession and holding the ball up. Akpom was stripped and ready to come on.

I actually had a brief conversation with the chap sat next to me bemoaning Hernandez. *"He doesn't jump for headers at all, and can't hold the ball up. Get him off and get Akpom on"* I said. *"I know"* said the bloke, *"How he thought he was going to get a transfer to Inter Milan, god only knows"* came the reply. What the fuck did we both know.

With that Diame played a delightful scooped pass over the Cardiff back line. Hernandez brought it down really well and drove the ball low and hard past Marshall.

The travelling fans (and probably those at the KC beamback) went into delirium.

"He came from Italy, to play for Hull City. Hernandez, whoah, Hernandez, whoah…."

Hernandez was then subbed before the game even kicked off again. His last contribution had effectively secured the points, and for once with a now two goal cushion, this meant the last few minutes could be watched in more comfort than is the norm with City.

The City fans led a chorus of,

"..If you're watching on the beam back, you're a c**t.."

Needless to say, Thomas didn't join in, and it was only afterwards, did we learn that the beamback had failed a couple of times and had no sound commentary.

Being two up, and with only ten minutes or so to go, City quite easily saw the reminder of the game out. The home fans streamed out to *"Is there a fire drill?"*, and there was still time for Meyler, who had just come on, to get his customary yellow card. Akpom also rolled about like he'd been shot by a sniper right in front of the Cardiff fans. I'm sure he was laughing. The Cardiff boys weren't and a few hand gestures were proffered to him. McGregor caught one final cross, collapsed to the ground amid rapturous applause and the referee blew full time.

A great trip. Not a vintage performance, but very effective all the same, and back up to fourth in the league.

A win always make the next two hundred and forty two miles miles seem quicker and by 1.45am we were safely tucked up in our own beds. This was the first away win we had witnessed since the opening day of the 14/15 season at QPR, it had been three hundred and ninety five days in the waiting.

The football widow had listened to it all and had awaited our safe arrival. She'd even texted into Radio Humberside.

We had reason to feel positive about City again and felt privileged to be one of the few who were there first hand to witness it.

"TWO NIL, TO THE ENG-ER-LAND, TWO NIL...."

CHAPTER 17

QPR (H) – SATURDAY 19TH SEPTEMBER 2015

"A VISIT FROM THE JOCKS"

After an encouraging three points against Cardiff in midweek, a run of three home games followed. First up was QPR.

I've never liked QPR really. This stems back to an opening day home Championship game against them back in the 2005/06 season. City were on the crest of a wave having just secured back to back promotions. The question was how would we apply ourselves in The Championship.

QPR, whilst they didn't beat us, were extremely physical in a 0-0 draw. City's full back, Mark Lynch, was absolutely smashed by Paul Furlong, after about a minute. Not sure he ever wore a City shirt again. My dislike for QPR was born at that minute.

We did get our revenge a few years later at home though, when after trailing 1-0, two late Stuart Elliott goals, one in the last minute, saw us run out victorious on a cold January day in 2007, much to their fan's dismay.

QPR had come down with us last year, but I always felt that we were a much better team than them. That said, we have still ended up playing in the same division.

Today's game also had a special guest and visitor for us, a certain Mr Allen Ferrier. Allen is now officially the founder member of the Renfrew Hull City Supporters Club; current membership one!

This was to be Allen's first visit to the KC, one which was many years overdue.

I first met Allen over twenty years ago, through his best pal, James Alexander Nutt, or Jim as we still refer to him. At that time, I had just started a new job which entailed me travelling up to Glasgow and spending time up there during the week, Monday to Friday.

I was a scrawny youngster in those days and had barely been out of Yorkshire. So spending time in Glasgow, holed up in hotel rooms, could have been daunting. It wasn't, and this was solely down to the warm hospitality that Jim and his team, Allen included, offered me.

Jim was a *'great wee man'*. He was small in stature, but massive in heart and leadership, certainly the sort of man you'd want on your team, and not lining up for the opposition.

Me being a youngster, and Jim as my boss at the time, he was something of a role model and when I look back now, I do believe he was a very influential character on me. He certainly helped me to understand the virtue of hard work, but to also make sure that you enjoy yourself doing the things in life that give you pleasure, things you really want to do, and with the people that mean the most to you.

Now being in Glasgow all those years ago, football was bound to come into things. Football really is a religion up there and has to be witnessed first hand to truly understand it. You simply are a blue nose or a Celt, nothing in between.

This is football rivalry at its best, and certainly was in those years (things have changed slightly in recent years due to the demotion of Rangers). As a Hull City fan, this sort of rivalry is not the easiest thing to relate to. We don't really have, what I would refer to as real rivals. Yes we may think that L**ds are our rivals, but that feeling is not mutual I'm sure. They don't really see City as anything, and still consider Man United to be their rivals, even if they are currently on a different football planet to them. I don't class L**ds as our rivals, we simply don't like them.

The Rangers – Celtic thing really is a hatred of each other. Pubs are either blue or green (even including the colour of the baize on the pool tables), no mixture, nothing in between. Simple as.

As fate would have it, Jim and Allen happened to be on the blue side – Rangers.

So, if there were any matches on during the week, they would take me along. Some of these were Champions League games, albeit they never seemed to do that well, some were league or cup games. In essence, the league pretty much boiled down to the four fixtures against each other every season.

This was the era of Gascoigne, Laudrup and McCoist for Rangers; the likes of Larssen, Jorge Cadette (hair like spaghetti!) and Van Hooijdonk for Celtic. So I joined Jim and Allen for a few Old Firm games, which were usually a sight to behold. One in particular that I remember was at Celtic Park back in November 1996.

The pre match lubrication was held in what was clearly and normally a Celtic designated pub, somewhere near the ground. For this night only, the local constabulary had earmarked it for the Rangers fans, in a vain attempt to keep them together, and apart from the Celtic fans. How the landlord must have been delighted. It really didn't work as it was nowhere near big enough. I can recall my feet standing outside the threshold of the pub, my hands and beer on the inside (it being apparently illegal to drink on the streets, if you can believe that in Glasgow).The Rangers fans had no respect for the establishment. As soon as drinks were finished, you could hear the smashing of glasses and bottles, the place was certainly in a state by the time the patrons departed for the stadium.

The game itself had everything, even if only one goal (a 1-0 win for Rangers). Two missed penalties (one by Gazza, one by Van Hooijdonk), endless one on ones, umpteen yellow cards, and even a fox invading the pitch. If you have a few spare minutes, type in Celtic 0 Rangers 1 in You Tube, and play the clip entitled 'Laudrup outfoxes Rivals'.

Ever since those days, we have both looked out for each others' results. No-one could have predicted how our fortunes would have changed. City climbed from the basement of the bottom league to the Premier; Rangers entered financial meltdown and ended up playing the likes of East Stirling.

Long before this happened, my career resulted in a job move back to Hull. We still kept in touch, but with life being busy and as the years passed by, the regularity became further apart.

Then back in November 2014, the news came to me that Jim had sadly passed away. He had been struggling with prostate cancer and one day had a massive heart attack. Poor Allen, watched his best mate take his last breath. At the relatively young age of sixty five, Jim's days had gone. Sometimes in life, adversity helps us put thing into perspective. It had been fifteen years or so since we'd last met up. I could have kicked myself for it being so long. Allen was clearly hit hard, so we made a vow at Jim's funeral, that we would make sure that we would each attend at least one of the other's teams fixtures each year; Allen coming down to Hull, us up to Ibrox.

Allen made the first running, and had picked QPR at home. Quite when we will get to go to Ibrox this season, I'm not sure, but hopefully the fixtures will allow us to at some point, if not this season, definitely next.

I was desperate for City to perform and win, for Allen's sake as much as ours. We wanted to be proud of our team, to show them off if you like.

An early Saturday morning trip to collect Allen from York train station, a quick beer, and already it was time to head to the KC.

Like a true test of friendship, and even after fifteen years, we dropped into conversation as if we'd been down the pub the night before, and after a first home airing of our flag, the game was underway.

City started well and both Aluko and Robertson were looking lively going forward. The cross field balls from Dawson were also creating space, particularly for Robertson to run into. However, considering the quality within both teams on display, the game never quite got going. City had one 'nearly' moment, not quite getting on the end of crosses, and then, just as we thought City were making all of the running, QPR scored. And you could have predicted who scored.

Yep, that's right, Charlie Austin. A player, who apparently City could have signed from Burnley for £5million a few years ago, but we decided against it as we thought he had a dodgy knee. Clearly the memory of Jimmy 'glass knees' Bullard still fresh in the memory.

Charlie Austin went on to sign for QPR, who were quite happy to take a gamble on him. He played most games for them, so the dodgy knee was maybe not so dodgy after all? He scored a hatful of goals in The Premier league and even got a call up to the England squad. He is just the type of centre forward, I would love City to have, a real focal point. Someone to hold the ball up, but also an outlet for a long ball to relieve defensive pressures, not to mention the ability to score twenty goals a season. This point was clearly made by Steve Bruce in his post match interviews describing the failure to sign Austin as his biggest regret during his time at City. Not so much the 'one that got away', but 'one that we pushed away'.

The transfer u-turn had not been lost on Charlie. His celebration when he scored against us last season at the KC said just as much, as he 'limped' away pointing to his knee in front of the South Stand. So today when he nodded in a corner (always disappointing to concede at set pieces), to put QPR one up, I was a bit apprehensive.

No such 'knee' celebration from Charlie today though.

However, credit to City who fought back well. The energy and drive of Diame and Robertson in particular, won us several corners and free kicks. From one of these, Huddlestone crossed to the near post and Michael Dawson's run met it, left Rob Green stood still, and the net bulged to make it 1-1.

The second half pretty much fizzled out. It looked like QPR were happy with a point and were fairly unadventurous, although they did miss a glorious chance right at the death. City 'huffed and puffed' but it was all a bit pedestrian and we failed to break down the QPR defence.

Much of the second half was spent looking on our phones, checking the Rangers and other scores to see how Allen's betting coupon was doing. For the record, Allen did not trouble the bookies, and Rangers beat the mighty Dumbarton.

So we had to settle for a point. Neither side had really done enough to justify a win. Nobody had a bad game, but nobody had an outstanding one either. The school report might read, *'Could do better'*. We have the players to do it.

Allen and I decided that the best thing to do was have a few jars, to celebrate, if you can, a 1-1 home draw. Hopefully City will do us prouder next time, and encourage new membership of the Renfrew Hull City Supporters Club. Next time, there might even be a car full!

"...D..D..D..D, MICHAEL DAWSON, ...D..D..D..D, MICHAEL DAWSON..."

CHAPTER 18

SWANSEA (H) LEAGUE CUP– TUESDAY 22ND SEPTEMBER 2015

"MORE 'SHEEP SHAGGERS' – THEIR WORDS NOT MINE"

Back to the League cup tonight with a home game against Swansea.

I've always quite liked Swansea. I remember playing them years ago on the last day of the season. Had they lost, they would have gone into the non league. They ended up beating us 4-2 to ensure their league status, some bloke scoring a hat trick, and it kind of felt like we'd played our part in helping them!

Then, a bit like our meteoric rise from the bottom division to the Premier League in only a decade, they achieved something very similar. So lots of similarities, albeit they've done a much better job of staying in the Premier League than we have.

However, before we talk about this particular match and it's events, it's worthwhile referring to a noteable football event of the evening.

Bayern Munich were at home tonight against Wolfsberg, no mugs in German football and participants in this year's Champions League. For some reason, as can be the desire of a team as big as Bayern Munich, they had decided to leave a certain Mr Robert Lewandowski on the bench. A disappointing first half for Bayern, saw them losing at half time and Lewandowski was told to take his tracksuit off and warm up (or whatever the German equivalent for that is – I never did it at school).

Within, to be precise, five minutes and forty five seconds of coming on, Lewandowski had equalised. By the time a further three minutes and eighteen seconds had elapsed, he'd scored a hat trick (and still had the audacity to hit the post in between).

A further five minutes and thirty nine seconds later, he'd scored a further two goals, taking his tally to five goals in just under nine minutes.

Now that's what I call a substitution.

Could you imagine your reaction if a City player achieved such a feat. For me, I think it would just about be heart attack time.

Mr Lewandowski wasn't content with just his five goal feat tonight. At the time of typing he then went on to score a hat trick in the following game, three braces, and then just a single goal thereafter; a total of fifteen goals in just six consecutive games. And he's probably not finished. Hell, we'd be happy if a City player could score that many in a whole season.

So Lewandowski's feat kind of got me racking my brain, trying to recall if City had ever had something similar. Yes we had Duane Darby score six in a bizarre 8 – 4 extra time FA Cup win, but with all due respect that was only against the might Whitby Town.

And then it came to me. Of course it had to be City's favourite son, Dean Windass. Long before he scored 'that' goal at Wembley against Bristol City, he had a week to remember back in the early part of the 1993/94 season.

Okay so we weren't quite up against the same quality of opposition but let's get this into some sort of perspective. City were in the old League Division 2 and had made a good start to the season, and an early away fixture at Cambridge United loomed. A topsy turvy game saw City come out victorious, with our favourite Deano scoring a hat trick in a 4-3 away win.

The following Tuesday night saw a 1-0 home win against Brentford, yours truly Deano netting a penalty. This was followed on the Saturday with a home 3-0 win over Bristol Rovers, Deano scoring another hat trick. So seven goals in a week for Deano. Amongst his other current football commitments, he's now turning out for Walkington FC, who play their home games no more than about three hundred steps from our front door.

Needless to say, I'm not sure Deano's seven goal feat made as many column inches as Lewandowski's. But then we are just little old Hull City aren't we.

City's early 1993/94 form continued. Another 4-3 away win at Cardiff soon followed and everything was looking good for promotion. That was until we visited Port Vale away in October. We were top of the league, they weren't far behind. I'd organised a mini bus for this game (the first and last time I've done so), although when we collected it, the fuel gauge was dodgy to say the least. So we put some fuel in and kind of kept our fingers crossed that there was enough fuel in it to get us there and back.

With about five minutes of the match remaining, City were looking likely to stay top of the league and as the Port Vale fans started leaving the stadium to the tunes of "*We can see you sneaking out*", they promptly scored. We looked and sounded daft. How dare we assume we would not let any late goals in. The Vale fans all started coming back in, as if the players were going to carry out a replay of the goal (this was well before the days of TV screens inside football grounds).

We left the ground dejected having lost, and the fingers crossed trick failed, as the mini bus ran out of petrol and ground to a halt on the hard shoulder on the M18. This was pre any services on the M18. We all got out, shrugged our shoulders as if to say what shall we do now, then started laughing and then obviously all lined up to relieve ourselves on the grass verge, all twelve or thirteen of us.

Fortunately a tow truck soon stopped and took us to the nearest petrol station and we all bunged him a couple of quid; he'd probably seen it all a hundred times before. A bit like our minibus, the wheels soon came off City's promotion charge and we ended up finishing just above halfway.

That season I did also witness something that not many City fans will ever have done. We had been drawn away at Runcorn in the FA Cup. The first game was abandoned after a wall collapsed and the rescheduled match was at the mighty Witton Albion's ground. It was on a foggy and absolutely freezing November night. I remember wearing a pair of tracksuit bottoms as well as jeans and about five layers up top, but was still 'niddered'. The trip ended in a 2-0 win and yes, a Chris Hargreaves goal! Remember this was when the Premier league was but a dream.

Still no matter what the results, travelling and following City usually throws up some memorable stories and recollections.

Tonight's match in itself was fairly entertaining, and after what the recently departed Cilla Black would describe as a City enjoying a *"lorra, lorra luck"*, especially in the first half, we managed to progress to the fourth round of the League Cup with a 1-0 win.

A combination of free entrance again and reduced prices swelled the crowd for this one to more like a league attendance. This however is still currently only at about 16-17,000 so well down on full capacity, although there were still ridiculous queues for this new automated turnstile system. Not quite sure if it is actually quicker or not, or whether it's just too complicated for most supporters.

There was only a smattering of Swansea fans, but they were humorous in ensuring they got in the first chant of *"We know what we are, we know what we are, sheep shagging bastards, we know what we are." (to the obvious tune of City of Culture, we know what we are).*

Despite a slightly weakened team, make no mistake, Swansea are a good team. They kept possession well, making quick and incisive passing, with good movement both with and without the ball. City were struggling to keep up and actually get the ball off them. To say our goal was having a charmed life was something of an understatement. However, and I'm not quite sure how, they couldn't put the ball in the net.

There was one particular moment when Jakupovic took an eternity to kick the ball out. As a result, his attempted clearance was charged down and the ball ricocheted onto the post. Seconds later it was crossed to Siggurdson who simply had to tap it into our empty net. It felt like the match went into slow motion as somehow his 'pass' into the net, was cleared off the line by Curtis Davies.

Routledge then missed a good one on one chance, Jakupovic redeemed himself with a point blank save from a Rangel header, and we felt like it was only a matter of time before we conceded.

City did enjoy a few promising moments mind, and with half time approaching, Swansea were made to pay for missing numerous chances as City put together a neat piece of play. An Elmo cross was headed goalwards by Maloney, the keeper parried and Meyler was on hand to tuck it away from about a yard. One up at half time, albeit well against the run of play. So what, who cares.

At half time, I think the entire row behind us were all eating Cheese and Onion crisps (no exaggeration), a particular dislike of mine, and the smell was unbearable. A quick trip to the little boys room, and with the crisp smell fading, the teams re-appeared.

Having taken the lead, the half time team talk must have been to try and nullify Swansea's forward attacking, and it certainly worked. They had much fewer chances, albeit you felt like they would still score at some point and then probably go on to win it. I'd already started clock watching at about forty six minutes.

They brought on a few more of the regular first teamers, Jonjo Shelvey, Kyle Naughton and Gomis, but so did we. Odubajo came on for Ryan Taylor who continues to look well off the pace. Livermore, who was making his first appearance since April following a failed drugs test, also went off to a standing ovation. Understandably, he was blowing a bit, but hopefully, he'll soon be fully match fit again and add something to our midfield – his early form for us certainly showed he has the ability.

Our defence just about managed to hold on. We retreated into our own half at times but with a number of well timed and last ditch tackles, a goal line clearance by Robertson, and an excellent man of the match display by Curtis Davies, we somehow saw our way into the next round.

The following evenings draw, fortunately for us, saw us avoid either Southampton or Bournemouth away, but pitted us against Leicester at home.

Hopefully we haven't quite used up all our luck in one game.

"...SHEEP SHAGGING BASTARDS, WE KNOW WHAT WE ARE..."

CHAPTER 19

BLACKBURN (H) – SATURDAY 26TH SEPTEMBER 2015

"TWO POINTS DROPPED"

Now don't get me wrong, City haven't made a bad start to the season. They have done okay, we are in the upper reaches of the league and have not yet been outside the top six, but somehow given the quality (on paper at least) within our squad, I still believe that we are under achieving.

Today, we should have put this game to bed. Blackburn are nothing special, they've just got a striker in Jordan Rhodes who knows how to put the ball in the net and has a strikers uncanny habit of being in the right place at the right time.

So I, like many others, was extremely pissed off when in the 94th minute, we let him ghost in at the near post unmarked to nod past McGregor from within the six yard box. His goal made it 1-1. Yes, we'd not lost, but it was certainly a case of two points dropped.

We knew all about Rhodes before the game, so if there was one player you needed to mark it was him. I think Odubajo was given the job, but lost him, although I'm not sure why Davies or Dawson weren't assigned to him. Likewise, the fashion nowadays seems to be for goalkeepers not to come for crosses as much, instead choosing to stay on their line. Maybe I'm a bit old school, but I was always led to believe that the six yard box belonged to the keeper. Hell, half the time, the referee will give a free kick in the goalies favour anyway.

To be fair, McGregor did still have time to make a great save even after their equaliser, reacting quickly to stop a thunderous volley from only seven or eight yards out. And then we could have still won it.

The sense of disappointment was confounded when, as the reality of letting in a 94th minute equaliser was still sinking in, a launched City free kick fell to Meyler, who nodded to an unmarked Davies. It was all very reminiscent to the Charlton winner a few weeks ago. Only this time the header went about five yards wide, rather than nestle in the net.

It might be me, but we seem to concede many more goals in the dying minutes of games than we score ourselves. This all results in dropped points. I can understand it a bit more in say the Premier League, when you've been 'under the cosh' and legs are getting weary. The same excuse shouldn't apply in the Championship where the quality is nowhere near the same. We should be imposing ourselves much more on some of these teams, and playing with much more tempo, rather than sitting back and trying to preserve a slender lead. We are capable of beating some of these teams by two or three goals, and we need to believe in this quality. With the squad we currently have at our disposal after the first transfer window (yes we may lose some more in January), and from the teams I've seen so far, there is nothing to be afraid of. The other teams should be afraid of us. We'll never have a better chance of going straight back up. We just need to play for a full ninety minutes, rather than just patches in a game.

I should have known this game wouldn't go our way. We were all away for the weekend in Filey and the previous night had involved a few beers. The football widow and I went out to share a few jars in The John Paul Jones pub. Whilst there we bumped into some Glaswegian chaps who had been sent out by their wives to get some ice. So after a quick 'three and a half hour session' they finished their last drinks, and returned to deliver said bucket of ice. We stayed a bit longer but were soon joined by some Glaswegian girls, who told us this story of how they'd just thrown a full bucket of ice over their partners for staying out too long!

So Saturday morning, I awoke with a bit of a sore head. There was no welching out of going today though as I'd already agreed to take my old man for his 'once a season' appearance at the KC. If I come across as a bit pessimistic, you should hear him! Talk about a nervous spectator, it's full of "*Get a tackle in*", "*Close him down*" and sharp intakes of breath as he constantly withdraws into his seat expecting the worst.

So as we took our seats, we were welcomed by a clip on the screens showing City goals (you never tire of watching them over and over again), to the tune of AC/DC's Back In Black.

City got off to an edgy start. Davies got booked after about thirty seconds for pulling his opponent back, and the heady heights he had reached against Swansea were not to be repeated. Robertson cleared a header from a corner off the line (that is why they stand there after all) and the crowds was becoming tetchy, my old man definitely included.

We slowly grew into the match, but most attempts on goal were shots from distance. City don't do scoring from outside the box very often – most of our shots today were wide of the mark. Do we not practice this in training. If we ever arrive early for home games, Thomas and I are often amused at the pre match shooting practice. Probably only about one in three are on target and standing just to one side of the goal is not advisable.

The referee was awarding lots of free kicks and it became a battle of half chances. Then after about seventy minutes, after having given numerous free kicks for innocuous challenges, the referee decided not to give anything against Davies, after he lunged at Rhodes on the edge of our box. Davies could have got a second yellow card, but whilst the Blackburn players were flaying their arms in dismay, City raced up the other end and Elmo swept in a lovely low inch perfect cross for Hernandez to tap in from about four yards.

Hernandez is still a bit of an enigma for me.

At times he annoys me as he rarely seems to jump for headers, and sometimes his hold up play could be better. Maybe he's not that type of player. However he seems to have started the habit of scoring a few goals. Every one mind seems to be from within the six yard box.

As the clock ticked by, the substitutions came around. You could hear the crowd playing the 'who is coming off' guessing game. One of these was so obvious today.

In that good old fashioned practice of time wasting, Hernandez actually started walking over to the East Stand for no reason other than to be as far away from the bench as possible. His number was duly flashed up on the fourth official's board and he duly trudged all the way back towards the West Stand, slowly, with just a light trot at the end so as to avoid a yellow card, all in the name of winding the clock down. Maybe we do practice that in training?

Unfortunately, thanks to a combination of Jordan Rhodes and some crap marking, it didn't work today and two points were dropped. Steve Bruce has some work to do to lift spirits.

Mind you, if you think he's got a hard job, spare some thought for our friend Rich Hewson. He has just taken his first coaching role, helping out his daughters football team. Two games in and he has so far masterminded them to a 16-0 defeat, followed by a 16-1 defeat. You can almost hear the calls of 'Hewson out, Hewson out'.

As we walked down Anlaby Road for our drive back to Filey, for some reason I thought of the phrase, 'It's never Dull in 'Ull'. It felt like it today and I could feel my headache returning.

Having had a trip down memory lane in the last chapter, I'm now going to try and lighten today's mood a bit by taking another.

I was flicking through the results of the day on my phone, when I stumbled across the story involving Ricky Drury, the goalkeeper of Holbeach. They were today playing an FA Cup second qualifying round tie against Worcester City. Trailing 1-0 in the dying minutes, the goalie went up for a free kick. The ball gets launched into the box and he scores a dramatic overhead kick to earn his team a replay. The pictures aren't great but it's there to see on You Tube or the BBC Football website.

This all reminded me of the 1994/95 season when one of our goalkeepers, Allen Fettis actually scored two goals in one season. These weren't the usual 'goalkeeper makes a long kick out of his hands, wind gets behind it, and opposition goalkeeper looks stupid being caught all out of position' moments. No, to make his story even more remarkable, he actually scored both goals whilst playing as an outfield player.

Remember this was in the days when City didn't have a pot to piss in, and were playing in that ridiculous tiger print top (not out of place on a Ford Capri car seat cover). Mind you I quite liked the away kit that year which was green as it always made me laugh when we sang "We all follow a black and amber team, a black and amber team, that sometimes play in green" (to the tune of "we all live in a yellow submarine" by The Beatles).

Anyway Fettis' first goal came in a home game against Oxford. The squad was small as it was, due to financial constraints, (this was Boothferry Park days, we simply didn't have any money) injuries and suspensions. This meant Fettis was named on the bench, not as a sub goalkeeper but as an outfield player. He ultimately came on during the second half to play up front and scored right near the end, causing delirium and a mini pitch invasion.

Just to prove it wasn't a fluke, he was then picked to start a game, playing the entire ninety minutes up front against Blackpool away on the last day of the season. This was a Bank Holiday weekend, and a group of us had chosen to spend the weekend at the Las Vegas of the North.

Basically I can't recall Fettis getting a kick all game (albeit we'd had a few before kick off anyway) until the last minute of the season when he poked home to score the winner in a 2-1 win. You couldn't have scripted it. Honestly, it really did happen.

Obviously this meant we had to drink even more to celebrate, including emptying of most of the beer in the 'honesty bar' at our B&B.

Recollection of the events did cheer up my mood momentarily, but I hope that today is the last time this season, I need to talk of dropping points.

"..BOLLOCKS, BOLLOCKS AND MORE BOLLOCKS.."

CHAPTER 20

NOTTINGHAM FOREST (A) – SATURDAY 3RD OCTOBER 2015

"A WIN TO MAKE ME FEEL BETTER"

There are some away grounds you hate to visit, there are some you love.

For those that you love, there are reasons why you love visiting. It might be because it's not too far to travel, because of a great pub pre match, or simply because your team has achieved great results there.

For me, the trip to Nottingham Forest ticks many boxes.

Firstly, it obviously has a great name, The City Ground! So, surely it was inevitable that it was going to end up being a happy hunting ground for us. It took years for us to actually play there mind.

Whilst during the late 70's and 80's, Forest were enjoying playing and winning the top league in England, not to mention winning the European Cup twice, and signing the first million pound player in Trevor Francis, we were heading down the leagues. And so our paths never crossed.

Then our meteoric rise to the top coincided with Forest's decline and we once again avoided each other. Eventually after thirty three years, we ended up in the same division, the Championship. I've loved our visits ever since.

Certainly compared to the distance of our away visits so far, it's a relatively short trip. It also has a great spot for a pre match drink. The River Trent is all that separates the grounds of Nottingham Forest and Notts County. Obviously when one is playing at home, the other is away. So, Notts County usually open up their supporters bar for the away fans visiting Forest. This always makes good sense to me. Why be open for business only twenty three days of the year, when you can be open for forty six. It also avoids the 'No Away Supporters' pub shenanigans which many grounds have nowadays. Basically the Notts County bar is full of away fans singing their songs and supping beer.

Today was no different. Beer being swilled, one fan even in fancy dress as Popeye, and lots of City chants being sung. In particular today, chants being sung with reference to the recent You Tube hit of Hull's very own road rage Ronnie Pickering.

"There's only one Ronnie Pickering, one Ronnie Pickering, he don't like motorbikes, bare knuckle fights, walking in a Pickering wonderland"

For some reason, I couldn't bring myself to join in.

Our results have been good at The City Ground. Three successive away wins, courtesy of Matty Fryatt, Aaron McClean, Robert Koren and even a Paul McShane handball. So despite the late disappointment of the Blackburn game, confidence is high today.

We were joined today by our neighbours, Sue and David. This was a blessing as I felt absolutely shit. The night before I was seriously contemplating not going (at which point this book would already have been incomplete). I had suggested to Thomas that he could just go on his own. He knows Sue and David, that way he could write up the day's events. He declined the offer and so I felt compelled to go.

The reason for me considering non attendance? Those reading of female persuasion will not for one minute understand. This ailment is enough to kill a female. The male readers will fully understand – I had man flu! This is a disease worse than an epidemic of bubonic plague.

Having decided to make the journey, I can honestly say that there is never a dull moment with Sue. This week's escapade involved one of her overnight work trips to London, which have a funny habit of usually working quite well for Sue, and co-inciding with City fixtures. This wasn't the case this week but her trip still involved an amusing tale.

Sue had experienced an arduous day looking at highly complicated and convoluted spreadsheets, and then attended meetings trying to explain them to people who clearly didn't understand. She therefore decided that she'd have a quiet night in her hotel room watching TV before doing it all again the following day.

She checked in to her room at the Premier Inn, threw her laptop into the corner, kicked off her shoes and climbed into her pyjamas – her 'comfies'.

However, upon trying the TV set, no picture was received. The usual method of turning it off at the wall and back on again produced no success either. She then also noticed that the waste bin was full of tissues and other assorted items, once purchased from the local barber, now from the chemists. Someone had been enjoying themselves in the room! Sue immediately rang down to reception and they promised to send somebody up.

The Lithuanian bellboy duly attended, tried the same tactics with the TV (still no success) and agreed in broken English about the 'rubbish' that had been left. He spoke with the reception desk who suggested that either room 116 or 616 was free and suggested that the customer, Sue, move room. Sue thought they had said room 116, about two doors away, but the bellboy said it was room 616.

Sue quickly gathered her belongings and followed Mr Lithuania up to room 616. She felt slightly uncomfortable walking through the hotel corridors in her nightwear, but at least she would have a clean room with fully functioning TV.

Upon arrival at room 616, the bellboy slid the room card into the door and entered.

Unfortunately the room was occupied. A middle aged man was lying on the bed, shall we say, semi dressed also watching TV. What he was doing, Sue wasn't totally sure, but she wasn't staying to find out. Exactly what the middle aged man thought, she was not sure either. As he glanced in her direction, maybe he thought she was being brought as his evenings entertainment, already dressed in bed attire!

A hasty exit was made with many apologies being proffered and they went all the way back to room 116, just metres from Sue's original room.

Fortunately this one was empty, with TV working, and the ordeal was over.

The 'happy ever after' for Sue was that the manager gave the night's stay for free, although knowing Sue, I bet she claimed it on her expenses.

We took up our seats in the ground and whilst I was actually present at the game, I'm not sure I was in mind. So as the Trent End were joining in to the chorus of *"Mull of Kintyre, Mist rolling in from the sea..."*, I could barely sum up the energy to respond with any City chants.

There was a good following from City today though, the away allocation had sold out so my dulcet tones were not missed. In fact the City contingent were in good voice, standing for the whole game (the one day I didn't want them to!).

Now this will also not have pleased Sue.

Sue likes to get value for money in life, never liking to waste it away. This probably originates from her father's upbringing. Apparently, he used to turn his car engine off when travelling downhill so as to save fuel!

So when Sue has paid for a seat ticket, she wants to sit on it, not to have to stand. I have yet to hear her burst into song at a City game, even when they are winning. Hopefully there is time for that yet this season.

For this lack of singing and preference to be seated, there are some which do not know Sue, who might consider her to be referred to as a 'plastic' – a term which she categorically disagrees with. Not only is she a season ticket holder (and has been so for a number of years even when we were in the bottom division), attends many away games, and generally knows 'all things City.'

This thought did get me wondering though exactly what is the term 'plastic fan' defined as? I'll give this some thought and research and report back during a future chapter.

Sue also likes to be in control and be organised. Her mixture of this and her chattiness does from time to time, lead her to speak on behalf of her son David. Many a time, we've been stood at the bar, and as I turn to David to ask him what he'd like to drink, as his mouth has just opened to utter his answer, you'll hear Sue answer for him. This probably explains the quiet nature of David. Either he can't get a word in edgeways, or he just lets his mum organise him. Hell, all of us males play that game, I know I do. Anything for an easy life. I'm sure I have noticed him singing at City games though, although no noise actually comes out, a bit like when you're forced to sing at church or when you mime along to a song.

I reckoned we must have travelled thousands of miles in the car watching City with Sue and David, and at least seventy per cent of the time is taken up with Sue talking. The conversation between David and Thomas, must be about one word every thousand miles.

In addition, Sue never drinks at football. I'm not sure why this is, as I know she likes a drink, I have witnessed it first hand on many occasions, but never at football. For me, a drink often makes the football look slightly better.

So today, Thomas and I were indebted to Sue as she happily drove. I had a couple of pints but overall my company was rubbish. I was just feeling sorry for myself, so sorry Sue, I'll make it up to you later in the season.

As we finally took our seats, or should I say stood in front of them, I still felt confident of a City success.

City didn't let us down.

Forest had lots of pressure early on and played with lots of tempo (something I'd like us to do a bit more) but their end product was lacking. Their shooting on target was on a par with ours, not very accurate.

As a result, at no point did I really feel that they were going to score.

Steve Bruce had decided to put a few 'square pegs in round holes' and Odubajo was being given a tough start at left back by Forest's winger, Mendes. Clucas mind, playing on the right hand side put in a good shift.

A familiar pose and one we'll get used to. Abel nets the winner at Forest away.

(PA Images)

With City giving away possession, the initial impetus was handed to Forest, and the quasi modo of a midfielder, David Vaughan, was dictating play for Forest.

However, City slowly started to grow into the game, and after Diame had smacked a twenty yarder against the woodwork, we won a penalty when Mills, the Forest centre back, tripped Maloney. Despite screams of "*Off, Off, Off, Off*", he only received a yellow.

Hernandez duly grabbed the ball to take the penalty, but twelve yards is way too far out for him to score at the moment. His spot kick pretty much went straight down the middle, hit the keeper's legs and went out for a corner. Shit!

However, Hernandez didn't let his head drop, and just before half time, a quickly taken Maloney corner was headed goalwards by Clucas. His header hit the keeper and Hernandez was there to put it in from his preferred distance, about thirty centimetres. All the same mind, whether it's bundled in from two yards or volleyed in from thirty yards, it only counts for one (be nice to score an absolute 'howitzer' though).

We kept the ball really well at the start of the second half, without really testing their keeper, other than a Dawson shot from a corner being tipped round the post. And so as the minutes ticked by, and as the City fans started wishing the next twenty minutes of our lives away, we did what we usually do. We retreated into our own half and tried to hold on to what we had, a one goal lead.

Fortunately, unlike the Blackburn game, Forest haven't got a natural goalscorer. They had chances, but there shots became even more erratic, high and wide. They made a few subs, even subbing the sub, but it didn't change much.

Mills got sent off for them late on, after a crude challenge on Akpom but this didn't change much either. He even got a round of applause from the Forest fans for getting a red card.

And so we gained another three points and kept our little unbeaten run going. It still feels like we are only in second gear, and there 'should' be much more to come. Who knows if it will or not?

Hell, we might even get Sue to sing?

"*..SHALL WE SING A SONG FOR SUE.."*

CHAPTER 21

"HE'S GOT AN ALIEN ON HIS HEAD..."

A trip to Hillsborough is always one to look out for on the fixture list for City. A big old ground, not too far to travel and one that brings back a number of memories and thoughts, some good and some bad.

Clearly you cannot mention the word Hillsborough without thinking back to that tragic day in April 1989 when 96 Liverpool fans died. People who just went to a football match, never to come home again. Being a football supporter and having visited a number of grounds of varying standards, you cannot imagine what it must have been like.

I've stood in the Kop and other packed grounds, pre all seater days, but nothing compared to what that day must have been like. I remember asking Ady Day, our Liverpool supporting friend who joined us at the Accrington game earlier in the season, about it. Basically, there are a number of Liverpool fans that he still goes with, who were present on that day. Apparently none of them talk about it or mention it and haven't done so for years. That's how raw it still is, twenty six years on. They still attend the annual memorium at Anfield.

At times, the beauty of football is that, whilst we all support different teams, and often shout abuse at each other from the terraces, in times of grief and adversity, it can be like one big family; a family that all pull together.

One of my first memories of actually watching City at Hillsborough was in the 90/91 season. It wasn't a great trip. This was in the era of Ken De Mange and *"Kenny's gonna get ya"* chants. On this visit, neither he, nor any of the other City players 'got anybody' as Sheffield Wednesday romped to a 5-1 win. David Hirst scored four, and probably felt a bit unlucky at only scoring that many. It was certainly men against boys. Wednesday went on to get promoted and won the League Cup; City finished bottom and got relegated; needless to say we didn't win any cups either.

In total contrast, it would be an iconic night in December 2004 when Hillsborough became **Hull**sborough. City were doing well in League One, having gained promotion the season before, and it was our first game there for thirteen years.

Wednesday (and probably City) were ill prepared for the Tiger invasion as about seven thousand City supporters made the trip and watched from The Leppings Lane End. Only about half the turnstiles were open (this was still pay on the gate days) and it was slow getting supporters in. The Leppings Lane end was soon clogged up and it was impossible not to think of April 1989. City fans were still only just getting into the ground after half time.

It really was a sight to behold and I doubt if, other than Wembley appearances, we'll see as many City fans present at an away game again. City didn't disappoint on the pitch either as a Nick Barmby inspired performance saw us victorious 4-2.

By the time we'd got to our seats, City were 1-0 down, but we soon saw a Michael Keane penalty equalise, before Barmby stole the show for the travelling City masses. He scored two before half time, the second a sublime

Wednesday away. The boy takes in 'all things City'. Even if nobody else was there.

volley. Danny Alsop scored a fourth and we ultimately marched on to a back to back promotion. After decades of mediocrity, we sent a message to the rest of Yorkshire that we were a force to be reckoned with.

From the ridiculous to the sublime, that can describe watching City over the years.

Today's game had unfortunately been switched by Sky to a 12.30 kick off. The kick off time and the fact that it was on TV limited the City following to about two thousand. In days gone by, you might get excited by the fact that

City were live on the telly. I can recall going down to the Cross Keys pub in Cottingham to watch City play live on TV for the first time. This was back in November 1990, an away fixture at Middlesbrough, at the old Ayresome Park, in the oh so glamorous Zenith Data Systems Cup. Believe it or not, in those years, not many homes had Sky so the pub was as good a place to watch it as any. City lost 3-1 after extra time, which also meant at least thirty minutes extra drinking time, our goal scored by Paul Waites. Ever since, we have, more often than not, been 'shit on TV'. This always disappoints me, as you suspect the TV viewer then assumes that City are always shit, and this is not necessarily the case.

Nowadays, a TV game just means that less people actually attend the game, so reducing the actual 'live match' atmosphere and experience. Today was no exception, although those in presence did their best to enjoy themselves and spur City on.

Bri Lee gave us a lift this week along with son James and daughter Sophie and a pre match 'am' beer was shared in The Railway where we met Tony Cline, Annerley and Taffy.

I suspect the majority of people reading this book will know Paul Williams, aka Taffy. He's probably played for every amateur football team in Hull, and always seems to be on every golf course, coming down the opposite fairway whenever you seem to play, but he certainly bleeds black and amber.

Everybody seems to know him and this was proved today.

As eluded to during the notes from the last game, a certain resident of Hull, Mr Ronnie Pickering has had his 'Andy Warhole famous for fifteen minutes' moment on You Tube, displaying a bit of road rage. This has created the strap line, "Don't you know who I am? I'm Ronnie Fucking Pickering" (Only in Hull eh?). Everybody has seen it.

Well this week, Taffy was approached by someone in the street, "Now then Taffy, how you doing?". Taffy, just back from a fortnight's holiday looked the guy up and down and replied, "You're gonna have to help me here, can't quite picture you"

"It's me, Ronnie, Ronnie Pickering" came the reply.

That just about summed it up for me. Today's internet 'sensation' still knew who Taffy was.

So we made the short walk to the ground and made our way to the upper Leppings Lane End. A quick watch of City practising shots, totally unchallenged from the edge of the box, before kick off (we counted about three shots that went in out of about thirty). This was made even more amusing by a sign warning spectators to watch out for stray shots (must have seen us in action before).

A quick burst of that early Eighties classic, 'Waterfront' by Simple Minds, and the teams appeared. This place really is in a time warp, they even still had cheerleaders. Next they'll be bringing back Tiger Cola!

The home section sang something derogatory about their neighbours Sheffield United and then onto 'Hi Ho Sheffield Wednesday' just before we kicked off. This was all very reminiscent of Wolves a few weeks earlier and in my opinion it's not a patch on the Sheffield United song, which always makes me smile.

Sung to the tune of John Denver, it goes:

You fill up my senses
Like a gallon of magnet
Like a packet of woodbines
Like a good pinch of snuff
Like a night out in Sheffield
Like a greasy chip butty
Like Sheffield United
Come fill me again.
Na Na Na Na Na Oooohhh

If ever there was proof that Sheffield is stuck in a time warp, those lyrics must confirm it.

The ground itself, whilst good and historic, is one of those old ones which still has, wherever you stand or sit, annoying posts in the way of your view. It doesn't matter where you move to, the action is guaranteed to nearly always be behind the post.

City controlled much of the early possession but still looked a bit lethargic and didn't really trouble the Wednesday goal. It's been a while since I can recall City really 'coming out of the blocks' and starting a game with real intent and tempo. Once we start slowly, you just feel we get stuck in a rut, struggling to find ways to change a game.

So after hogging the ball, but lacking any killer pass, we were made to pay for these failings when Wednesday took the lead. A hopeful header into the box found Forestieri in acres of space and he slotted home. The defending was questionable with both Davies and Elmo playing him onside when they should have known better.

This gave Wednesday some encouragement and both Dawson and Davies were being tested. McGregor spilt a shot causing panic and Bannan fired over just before half time.

We expected changes at half time and City did come out much improved. A quick substitution taking off Diame, who had been woeful, for Akpom, meant two up top and his initial lively pace posed a few more problems for the Wednesday defence.

This soon resulted in an equaliser, when after a couple of good saves by the Wednesday keeper, Livermore played a cool pass to Hernandez, who finished smartly; it seems he can't stop scoring.

This, like Wednesday earlier, fired City up and Hernandez came close with a header from an Elmo cross soon after, and Clucas then pulled a shot just wide from the edge of the box.

The game then fizzled out for a period and the crowd had to entertain themselves for a while.

Predictably, Wednesday's was a dated affair, basically some prat banging a drum and grown men taking their tops off (it really wasn't that warm).

City's was far more up to date, even if slightly pinched from Barnsley, (again this is down to Thomas' research here on You Tube). Have a look at a clip entitled "*He's got a plant pot on his head*" – Barnsley fans, on You Tube.

Basically, this involves Barnsley fans at a match against Rochdale. Maybe their game was a bit boring at times as well?

Initially, one of the Barnsley fans, pulls out a plastic plant pot from his bag and puts it on the head of a female steward. This is the cue for the Barnsley fans to all start singing:

> "*She's got a plant pot on her head, she's got a plant pot on her head, she's got a plant pot on her head, she's got a plant pot on her head*"

Said plant pot is then removed from her head and then thrown upwards into the Barnsley contingent. Should a spectator then wish to participate, they then pick up the plant pot and place it on their own head.

Clearly this then entices another chorus *of "She / He's got a plant pot on his head...."* and the whole process is repeated, again and again and again (very much like the Smash Hits ending in *'repeat to fade'*). I found it very amusing anyway – we may try and replicate it at some away game.

City's fans today had a tweaked version of this. Instead of a plant pot, for some reason, someone had taken in an inflatable alien into the match.

So, as above, but basically replace the word plant pot for alien; *"He's got an alien on his head..."* You get the gist.

Bear in mind this is a televised game and in the middle of the upper tier, there was a Sky cameraman on one of those temporary scaffolding erected camera things.

So the inevitable happened. Yes, the alien was placed on the camera man's head and cue another chorus, much to our amusement, and not to the camera man's, who was clearly willing the game to finish. He did temporarily leave his post, fleeing from the alien.

With alien fun dying down, the game by now had reached its latter stages, and we focused back on events on the pitch.

There was enough time left for first McGregor to make a superb save from Robertson, who had inadvertently diverted a free kick towards his own goal.

Then, Akpom accidently barged into the referee who collapsed in a heap and had to hobble off, and finally Davies had a chance to nick it at the death, but he couldn't quite connect properly to a cross and his attempt went either wide or over, or both.

In fairness, a draw was probably about fair. A game of few chances saw us stretch our unbeaten run to six games. At half time, we'd have settled for a point, although you still thought the game was there to be won.

"MONDAY, TUESDAY, WHO THE FUCK ARE WEDNESDAY..?"

CHAPTER 22

LIGHT SWITCH TOWN (H) – TUESDAY 20TH OCTOBER 2015

"KATIE IS DELIGHTED.."

No this isn't a chapter pertaining to a game that you might have missed, this is actually our home game against Ipswich Town. However, from a very early age, Thomas mistakenly called them Light Switch Town, and it's kind of stuck ever since.

So another evening game against one of the higher placed teams, so another test of our credentials.

Before we refer to the actual events on the pitch, I'd been doing some thinking about the term 'plastic'; probably the worst insult in football? I'd used this term in my Nottingham Forest notes.

Now as football fans, we are used to trading cruel taunts with opposition fans. Terms like dirty northern bastards (hurled at us, not by us), sheep shaggers, rent boys etc etc, will be heard up and down the country every weekend. And to be quite honest, we are fairly immune to them. In fact, we almost take them in good humour, it's just like calling each other names in the playground, but for grown ups.

However, if a fan is called a 'plastic', that hurts. No-one would ever confess to being one. Sue was testament to this, when reading her draft chapter of the Forest away game. Just the mention of the term and her name in the same sentence stirred a reaction.

So what is a 'plastic' fan?

I've googled it and there seems to be no definitive answer.

In my opinion though, the term plastic in this context, must mean something fake.

Before you can actually use this analogy for spectators, for me, there are many fake or plastic things that exist within football grounds, and the level of noise or atmosphere created.

Most of this is all part of the ever increasing commercial nature of football nowadays. The prawn sandwich brigade certainly exists!

Most new grounds have numerous executive boxes, charging exorbitant prices, full of suited and booted individuals on corporate days out. It almost seems that the football is just a side event rather than the main event. You only need to take a look at The Emirates, the corporate lot take their seats after kick off, leave early before half time, come back late after it, and then leave before the full time whistle. Most of the game, there are rows and rows of vacated red seats.

For me, I want to try and see every second of action, who knows what you might miss (that old adage of *it only takes a second to score a goal*). The working man is slowly been priced out of the game, which clearly has an effect on the atmosphere generated.

Then we have at some grounds, goal music, as if the fans need a cue to instigate singing. I'm so glad City haven't introduced this. (Maybe I speak too soon?!)

Then there is the use of a drum to orchestrate chanting. No need, we are not on the continent. This should always be met with ridicule.

All of these things should be classed as plastic as they help to create a manufactured atmosphere. Give me the old fashioned British way any day. The use of voice and hands, to clap if necessary, and creativity and wit, and use of spontaneity. There is no better site or sound when you see all sides of the KC in full voice with one common purpose. Clearly it is up to fans to create this atmosphere.

Some fans do not wish to stand up – should this be referred to as plastic?

Maybe, as I've touched on, you certainly get a different atmosphere at away games as there are more like minded individuals in close proximity of one another, rather than being spread out around the ground.

However the worst trait must be to only start watching your team when they are successful. It's easy to follow and sing when you're team is winning (and obviously should take place). However, when your team needs you the most is often when they are losing and underperforming. The term 'The twelfth man' should always apply.

Then there are fans who support more than one team. Eh? Just don't get it.

And last but by no means last, there are those that buy and wear those dreadful 'half and half' scarfs. There should be no place for these, and just an idea of someone trying to make a few quid from the gullible.

Having said all that, I understand that in today's game, there must be a place for all types of fans. There are no written rules, there is no correct way of behaving at football. I'd much rather see a full KC, full of all sorts of fans, than a half full one (just no half and half scarf wearers please).

Tonight was not a full house, but in the end a comfortable 3-0 home win, should hopefully put a few more bums on seats for future home games. We are undefeated at home and now back into the play off places.

Thomas was highly amused at our usual turnstile when the gentleman immediately in front of him, barely a year younger than eighty, gained access on an under sixteen ticket. Nobody questioned this, and as we took our seats, we were to find out why.

Sat a couple of seats from us, is a young man called Richard, who until the last home game, used to work on the away turnstiles as a steward. As a result, he usually arrived in his seat, about ten minutes after kick off. In a weird sort of humour, I always wanted us to score an early goal so that he missed it, although this hasn't happened too often.

So I was slightly taken aback when he was already in his seat. Basically at the previous home game, all the gate stewards were given a letter giving them immediate notice. So from now on, he'll have to get his hand in his pocket and pay for a ticket like the rest of us (even if some are clearly not going in on exactly the right tickets).

Like us, he has also recently started taking his young daughter, Katie, who without fail, every game comes along with painted Tiger face. I can't help thinking of that Peter Kay episode when, as part of a fundraiser, The Phoenix Club offered face painting. Only it was done with permanent face paints, not to disappear or be washed off. Maybe Katie's face paint is permanent too. Mental note to check if her design is different at the next home game. Her favourite player is Alex Bruce. This often causes her distress and on occasion tears, when he is substituted or goes down injured, a common occurrence.

Prior to kick off, we were treated to City's new funky floodlight display, more akin to a dance floor. I'm not sure how much it cost, hopefully not at the expense of some gate stewards, but it was something different.

If the light show was spectacular(ish), the opening exchanges weren't. Ipswich probably edged the opening exchanges, and my pessimistic brain was telling me this had all the signs of a 0-1 home loss, our run has to end at some point?

It felt like we were sitting off, not getting enough tackles in. Then when we did get possession, we were guilty of giving it straight back. Davies went off injured early on to be replaced by Alex Bruce, much to the delight of Katie.

We slowly grew into the game and it was noticeable that we were being slightly more direct from the back. Hernandez missed a header from the edge of the six yard box, and Clucas dragged wide from a good move.

And then Katie was in ecstasy as Alex Bruce got one for the collector's book. Following a half cleared corner, Clucas put in a lovely cross that Bruce looped over the keeper for 1-0. He had played for Ipswich so it was inevitable that he'd score. However, I can't remember him scoring too many before.

I know I've said it before, but that first goal is so important. You can almost see the confidence grow, the crowd is lifted, and with our Scrooge like defence, you kind of feel that we should go on to win the game.

We now counter attacked with pace and after Dawson had been needlessly booked (we'll miss him if and when he gets suspended) we went two up. Odubajo nicked the ball off an Ipswich defender, played a one-two with Hernandez and crossed low for Akpom to fire home.

The second half pretty much saw City in control, and I can't remember McGregor having to dirty his gloves. Elmo had a volley just over, Bruce had a half chance, but Meyler wrapped up a comfortable 3-0 victory with, wait for it, a lovely volley from just <u>outside</u> the box. This capped off a good performance from Meyler, who really looks like creating a partnership with Livermore in central midfield.

The encouraging signs are starting to emerge and the unbeaten run goes on. Long may it continue.

"..3-0 TO THE 'ULL CITY, 3-0 TO THE 'ULL CITY.."

CHAPTER 23

BIRMINGHAM CITY (H) – SATURDAY 24TH OCTOBER 2015

"IT'S ALL LOOKING GOOD SO FAR"

Another trip to the KC this weekend. This was the middle of three home games in a week and after the 3-0 home win against Lightswitch Town, confidence was high. However, Birmingham had started the season very well too, they were currently second in the league, so another good test for us.

We were all spending the weekend up at Filey again, so the football widow's frown was directed towards me when Thomas, Charlotte and I stated that we would be driving back to Hull for the game. Not to worry, we'd made sure we had strength in numbers. The football widow's cousin, Dave (or 'Honest Dave' as we call him due to him being a bookmaker) and family were also joining us at Filey. This meant we weren't leaving the football widow totally on her own.

They arrived on Saturday lunchtime, just as we were about to set off. I quickly asked Honest Dave if he wanted to join us. He is also a Sunderland fan so replied by saying that at the moment he was *'off football'*. He then asked if we had Sky and WiFi. Upon a satisfactory answer of yes to both, he chose to opt for an afternoon in front of the TV and laptop, watching Channel 4 racing and Betfair, to see if he could invest anything for a quick return.

In the end, he got dragged out to take the dog for a walk on the beach and a bag of chips.

He should have joined us, because today was probably City's best performance of the season so far.

During the weeks build up, I had heard that Don Robinson, once of City fame, had been unwell. It's probably worthwhile just recollecting a bit about Don Robinson and his Hull City involvement.

City had just been relegated to the bottom division for the first time in their history, the receivers had been called in over non payment of debts, no local person with any money had expressed an interest in saving the club, and well, the whole outlook was very bleak.

The local media headlines were either about rugby league, or if of football, were headlines about funeral marches depicting 'the death of Hull City', bucket collections to pay players wages, how low attendances had slumped to, the demolishing of the old North Stand to be replaced by, err, a Supermarket, the closure of the Boothferry Park railway line etc etc, The list was endless and basically, represented anything other than any footballing success.

Such was the decline at Boothferry Park, that the club did not have enough money to replace the light bulbs on the Supermarket. So instead of lighting up to read in bright red "BOOTHFERRY PARK", it now read, "-----FER---ARK". And so 'Fer Ark' it became known.

At the same time, Scarborough AFC, then run by Don Robinson, were one of the top non league football clubs in the country. I had always had a soft spot for Scarborough as my grandparents were from there, and often took me to games when I happened to be visiting in my early years. The one game that really stood out for me was an FA Cup fourth qualifying round game against Blyth Spartans. The ground was in chaos and in the end, police alsation dogs were let loose in an attempt to try and control the crowd.

Anyway, Don whilst being a little eccentric, had demonstrated some business acumen. So in 1982, the Needler family asked Don to get involved in Hull City. Don got out his cheque book and City bound he became. He brought with him Colin Appleton as manager.

Don was certainly a character and he brought some fun back into the game, which had sadly been missing for several years prior.

He paid for his own seat, sold raffle tickets to incoming home fans before a game, and introduced Tiger Cola. The latter would be thrown into the crowd, and usually if you were lucky enough to get one, when opened, would just spray it's contents over anyone nearby.

He organised City tours to America. Remember the Arrow Air trophy? It was one of the few things in City's bare trophy cabinet! At the home fixture, Don came onto the pitch riding a white horse and wearing a stetsun. Imagine football club owners doing that nowadays.

At the same time, City started playing quite well. They were promoted and we nearly repeated it the following season. I remember being on a Simon Gray coach in mid winter going to an away game at Burnley. As we got part way across the M62, a snow blizzard started and like us, The City team coach got stranded. The match was postponed and ultimately re-arranged for the last game of the season, every other team had completed all their fixtures. We had to beat Burnley by more than two goals. If we did, we pipped Sheffield United to promotion.

We travelled again by Simon Gray coach, and typically arrived late, by which time City were already one nil up, Brian Marwood had scored. It was a weird crowd as there were three sets of supporters there, a few hundred or so Sheffield United fans in attendance.

Marwood scored again, but despite pressing couldn't get a third goal, so promotion it was not – Bloody Burnley!

Appleton resigned immediately after the game to be replaced by Brian Horton. The good times continued on the pitch and promotion was achieved the following season with players like Richard Jobson and Garry Parker.

In the end, and despite Horton getting City into the upper reaches of the old Second Division, the upward trend eventually stopped. Players were sold and after a bad home defeat against Swindon, Horton was sacked and replaced with Eddie Gray.

This didn't work out and City turned back to Colin Appleton. Being in the old Second Division, Appleton was out of his depth. We started the season by not winning any of the first sixteen league matches. Relegation duly followed. Appleton was sacked and Don left with him.

Whilst it ended in relegation, sandwiched in between two very grim periods of City history, Don had put fun and enjoyment back into watching City.

He once famously said that one day, Hull City would play football on the moon! Whilst City's performance today was not quite 'out of this world', Don would have been proud of it, as it certainly was our best of the season to date.

131

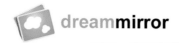

dream**mirror**

The NEW Photo Booth Experience!

dreamMirror is a photobooth hidden behind a magical mirror! Hidden
behind the mirror glass is customisable photobooth technology.
Allow the mirror to talk to guests, operate it by touching the mirror
and even raising their arms.

- You can sign your name on the mirror
- Instant Branded Prints from the Mirror
- A new Photo Booth concept that is unique to your guest experience

For More info call us or email us on our contact details below!

dreambooth supporting Hull City and it's famous author Ian Bunton
Visit: **www.dreambooth.co.uk** - Email us: **info@dreambooth.co.uk** - Call: **0330 660 1300**

TAN EXPRESS

45 MINUTES FOR ONLY £10

Salons Throughout Hull

Over 18s only
www.tanexpress.co.uk

Don't risk scoring an own goal...
call Towergate!

Insurance for you and your business. Professional independent advice.

Tel: **01482 330300**

email: **Hull@towergate.co.uk**

Towergate Insurance, Estuary Business Park, Henry Boot Way,
Priory Park East, Hull HU4 7DY

towergate
insurance

Congratulations to
Ian Bunton
on his amazing journey
through the 2015/16 season

TEDDYS
A M U S E M E N T S
Hull's number 1 for gaming!
Proud to support
Hull City

Good luck for the
Premiership 2016/17!

Jon Mail
Solicitors
&Co

Employment Law

Sports Law

Education Law

Criminal Law

Social Media Crime

Motoring Offences

Jon Mail Solicitors & Co Limited
Station House, Stamford Road,
Altrincham, Cheshire WA14 1EP
Telephone **0161 924 2246**
Facsimile **0161 924 2247**
Mobile **07971 912 385**

Bespoke Picture Framing

- Sports Shirts
- Certificates
- Needlecraft
- Memorabilia

- Prints
- Posters
- Photography
- Watercolours/Oils

HULL'S PREMIER FRAMING SERVICE

Studio and Gallery
5 Wilson Street, Anlaby, HU10 7AN
Tel: 01482 652325 ● studiono1.com

studio
NUMBER ONE

OFFICIAL FRAMING SUPPLIER TO HULL CITY, HULL FC AND HULL KR

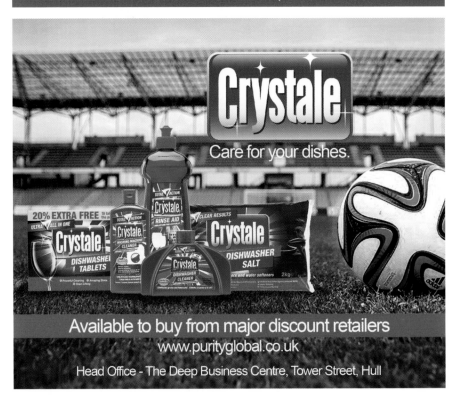

City out worked and out passed Birmingham and came out 2-0 winners. If anything, the scoreline flattered Birmingham.

A same starting eleven to that from the Lightswitch game, and partnerships were formed and consolidated all over the pitch. Moses and Elmo on the right, Robertson and Clucas on the left, but most noticeably, Livermore and Meyler in midfield.

Birmingham had the first chance but McGregor saved well from Gray. Ex City player Clayton Donaldson was up front for Birmingham, but there was none of the 'ex player scores against us' rules today, as he was well marshalled out of the game by Dawson and Alex Bruce.

A step up in tempo, instigated predominantly by Livermore, saw City score two quick goals just before half time.

The first, a good team goal with some slick passing, eventually seeing Elmo slide a pass to the in form Meyler, who swept in off the far post.

Literally a minute later, a marauding run by Robertson, saw him pass to Hernandez, who turned and volleyed past Kuszczak and it was 2-0, and almost game over.

Birmingham tried to change it at half time by bringing on two subs, but in truth, whilst they enjoyed a bit more possession, it never felt like they were going to score. It almost felt like City could, at any time, just go up a gear, and when they did, we had numerous chances, with Hernandez, (handballing it into the net rather than heading it, and getting a yellow card for his efforts) Clucas and Akpom coming close.

Comedy moment for me in the second half was when City were awarded a free kick just outside the box. Out came the shaving foam, and perhaps the referee was struggling to count to ten, as the wall looked very close. So Elmo decided to walk it out himself just to check, and with the crowd counting in unison, got to only seven before the wall was met. No, the referee, never known to be wrong, just waved his arms away and told us to get on with it. He'd seen exactly what we had.

In the end, we won 2-0 at a canter. Livermore even had the audacity to just walk off the pitch in the dying moments, and, having made all our substitutions, we finished the last few moments with ten men. That's how comfortable it was, and this against a team who were second in the league.

Every player put in a performance, no mistakes were made, another clean sheet kept and an ever improving goal difference (all very un-City like), and we moved up to second.

It's funny but somehow when City play well and are winning, it manages to change your whole mood. Somehow, absolutely everything in life seems to be rosy and great.

"..I'M H, A, P, P, Y, I'M H, A, P, P, Y, I KNOW I AM, I'M SURE I AM, I'M H, A, P, P, Y.."

CHAPTER 24

LEICESTER CITY (H) LEAGUE CUP – TUESDAY 27TH OCTOBER 2015

"GREAVESY, GREAVESY..."

Two impressive home displays against Ipswich and then Birmingham, led us into a third home game in a week.

A lengthy league cup run (a what I hear you say!) had taken us to the fourth round. This is the furthest we have ever been in this competition and now pitted us against Leicester City after rather fortuitously going through against Swansea in the last round. I kind of thought we had used up whatever 'cup luck' we deserved in its entirety in that match. So to progress any further, we needed to play well. And bloody well we did!!

Make no mistake, Leicester may not seem like the biggest scalp, but they have started the season off like a house on fire. They currently sit in a Champions league spot in the Premier League, so we had to be at our best.

Yes, they may have rested a few players, but so did we. Which all goes to endorse the fact that despite losing a few big names in the first transfer window of the season, City do still have strength in depth.

The match was an entertaining affair, but even with our rose tinted spectacles on, City definitely deserved to progress, eventually going through 5-4 on penalties when the teams finished 1-1 after extra time.

There will probably have been more important games at the KC, more with a greater level of quality and goal mouth incidents, but for its significance, drama and sheer enjoyment, I can't remember that many.

To listen to Charlotte say that she felt sick and almost wet herself as penalties were being taken, demonstrates the tension and drama towards the end. Obviously, this feels so much better when you came out victorious. Had two spot kicks gone Leicester's way rather than ours, our feelings may not have been the same, such can be the fine margins.

Meyler's final, and winning spot kick, took us into the quarter final of the League Cup, a stage we have never reached previously in our 111 year history.

Approximately four hours or so earlier, we couldn't have dreamt of such high drama and tonight we were privileged to have the company of former City player Mark Greaves.

In the Bunton house, we tend to have jobs around the house designated as 'blue jobs' and 'pink jobs'. Now you would think that the stereotypical thought process would be that I'd do all the blue (male) jobs and the football widow would do the pink (female) jobs. This is not quite the case in our household. One of the usual blue jobs, in particular the gardening, is quite happily carried out by the football widow. Or so I thought! A couple of years ago, it emerged that she had enlisted some outside help.

Thomas spilled the beans one day, saying that he'd been taking penalties in the front garden with our new gardener, an ex Hull City player. I asked him who it was but being much before Thomas' viewing days, he couldn't remember his name, and the football widow just had him stored in her phone as 'Mark Gardener'! They tried to give me his description, but Mark now being a few years older, is no longer sporting that boy band 90's hair cut (a bob?) that must have struck fear into the opposition, so I was still none the wiser. Only when they added the position he used to play and after a few guesses did I deduce who it was.

Mark no longer takes penalties in our front garden or carries out the gardening for us, much to Thomas' disappointment, but we often bump into him at City or North Ferriby. So when this book idea came along, hell we thought, let's ask him if he would like to come to a match with us. Mark was only too happy to oblige, keen to help wherever he can.

Having talked to Mark previously, there are a number of reasons for this.

Firstly, because Mark is a genuinely nice bloke, and I'm not just saying that for the purposes of the book, he really is.

But more importantly, it is very apparent that first and foremost, Mark is a massive Hull City fan. Born just a few minutes from Boothferry Park in Gipsyville, he said he could run there in about two minutes. Way before the notion of him wearing the black and amber, he was a City fan, still is, and continues to be so. In my mind, that makes him just like you and me. I bet there are not many ex-players who are happy to pay their entrance fee, and go and watch just like the rest of us mere mortals.

I often wonder when players come up to their fans and clap them at the end of a game whether there really is any conviction, or are they just going through the motions? Do they fully understand what us fans put ourselves through from time to time, how we trust our emotions in their hands (or feet)? I reckon Mark did mean it.

Little did Mark realise that tonight, we were all about to fire questions at him. He described playing for City as his *dream come true*, a real boyhood dream. Obviously, this was in an era when local talent had a much greater chance to breakthrough into the first team, but Mark certainly took his chance.

Predominantly a centre back, but versatile as a holding midfielder, Mark went onto make 177 appearances for City between 1996 and 2002, so pretty much a starting regular. Without being too sycophantic, I recall him as being very consistent in those Boothferry Park days. Remember, this was not in a golden period like those that City have enjoyed recently.

Mark had opportunities to move to teams in higher divisions. However a combination of badly timed injuries, and his steadfast belief that City *were always a bigger team and that one day it would come good*, kept him at City for a number of seasons.

He recalls that in his early City days, the penny hadn't quite dropped that he was a professional footballer, playing for his hometown club. Once he had got his head around it, his performances continually improved.

His lucky superstition of putting his right boot on first (bloody hell players are as daft as us supporters) was clearly helping, and ultimately he won the Player of the Season award in the 1999/2000 season. In Mark's words, this remains the proudest achievement in his career.

He personally recalls his best City game as a 0-0 draw against Darlington when he won the Man of the Match award, totally outmarking Marco Gabbiadini.

The accolade really gave him confidence as a youngster, and confidence was a word repeatedly emphasised by Mark time and time again.

Confidence was certainly something not lacking in the person chosen as the best City player that Mark ever played with. It took him a nano-second to name Theodore Whitmore as that player. At times he could make the game look so easy, so laid back. On occasions he would still be asleep just twenty minutes before kick-off!

Mark unfortunately was badly injured during the latter stages of his City career, breaking his leg in a home game against Kidderminster Harriers. Whilst in pain and being stretchered off, not quite with it, he could hear cheering, and in his state of semi-consciousness assumed it was for him – it wasn't, City had scored a late winner!

And with that his City days were numbered. He then moved onto Boston United, commuting every day from Hull (now that is a shit drive). As they say '*you can take the man out of 'Ull but you can't take the 'Ull out of the man*'.

In a sad of twist of fate, this was just before City moved to the KC, and his only appearance there was actually for Boston but he still fondly recalls the very warm welcome that the City fans all gave him that day.

Noteable highlights during his time at Boston were actually scoring against City, only for it to be disallowed. Mark said he wasn't even that disappointed, and Stuart Elliot then went on to score the winner.

He also shared some time with Gazza, during his short stint there. This was Gazza in the latter days of his career, now with his demons in the background. However, you could still tell what a gifted player he was. Often Mark gave Gazza a lift back from training with some other team mates, and looking in his rear view mirror, asking himself "*Is that really Gazza in the back seat of my car?*"

Now this wasn't Premiership footballers in a flash BMW or sports car, this was Mark in his Peugeot 306. So clarity was certainly proven that it was Gazza as he often reminded Mark that "*this is the shittest car I have ever been in!!*" in his thick Geordie accent.

Mark later moved onto Burton Albion, York City, Gainsborough Trinity and North Ferriby.

Just as kick-off approached, one last question we asked Mark was whether he had any regrets for his footballing days? Did he wish he could have stayed at City a bit longer, played at the KC, and in a slightly more successful era? The obvious answer would've been yes. It wasn't. It was an emphatic no, he had just been so immensely proud to have played for City, something that not many people can put claim to.

I genuinely don't think he was just saying it for our ears but regardless, it was exactly the answer a supporter wanted to hear. There **are** players, as well as supporters, who bleed black and amber.

So after a bit of a Q&A, we focused our attention on the pitch. It was interesting watching the game with a footballer, and things they see. He was closely observing the City centre half pairing of Dawson and Maguire and was extremely complimentary about the pair. Particularly Dawson whose headers and interceptions are not just clearances but he actually makes them into passes to teammates so retaining and/or setting up attacks. This clearly differentiates him from the more 'old school' centre halves.

City looked very comfortable in possession in the first half without creating a lot of clear cut chances. Leicester, considering their great start to their own Premier league campaign (and end of the previous one, which in turn damaged our chances of survival) were poor.

Hayden had a bright game also, and his play seemed to allows Huddlestone to play much further forward. When on his game, Tom poses a much greater threat further forward, his quick thinking, composure on the ball and eye for a pass, can influence a game much more than umpteen square passes sat on top of our defensive unit.

Tonight, I thought he looked much more like the old Tommy Tommy that we saw a while back, and he just shaded the Man of the Match vote. Odubajo must have been a close second. That being said, the admirable work done by both Livermore and Meyler in recent League games should still mean that Tom will have to settle for a place on the bench for the time being.

Ryan Taylor also looked lively, as did Shaun Maloney. In fact, it would be hard to say any City player struggled. As a team and a unit they all combined well and were much the more impressive team.

The football widow, in attendance tonight, actually chose McGregor as her Man of the Match, until we politely told her that he wasn't playing! She then chose Jakupovic instead.

Luer had City's best chance in the first half, after just three minutes, when he was a little unfortunate to see his goalbound shot blocked, after a fine move involving Diame, Maloney and Magic Moses. I can't recall any Leicester effort that caused us any trouble.

So half time and 0-0. We were quite content with that.

We asked Mark what it was like in the dressing room as half time. Personally he never liked a Manager who came in ranting and raving. Such actions never made him feel any better or more confident, and as such, rarely did it make him play any better. This is a thought I concur with on the terraces as well. When I hear somebody berate a player, or worse still, boo them (well our players anyway, clearly it is fine to do this to the opposition), I'm often close to asking them how they think that will make the player perform better. If somebody came up to me at work and said I was crap, it would hardly motivate me. By all means have a moan and groan once the game is finished. Unfortunately the standard answer nowadays is *"I've paid my money, I'm entitled to voice my opinion"*.

Mark much preferred constructive criticism and words of encouragement.

He also felt it was important to have a leader(s) in the dressing room. He cited Ian Ashbee as a very influential character in his time in the City dressing room. I'm sure many of us City supporters would be in total agreement with this. On occasions, we still sing, *"..Ashbee's gonna get you.."* and he finished playing for us years ago.

His achievement of captaining City in all four divisions of the Football League should never be underestimated. I'd be amazed if any other player has or will achieve the same feat. And, I'll add, that at no point, despite having certain doubters, did Ashbee let City down, even in the first Premier League days. You can also add to that list, Boaz Myhill (love to see him back in the *'middle of our goal'* one day) and Andy Dawson.

The second half restarted and City continued to dominate.

Ryan Taylor headed wide and Ranieri 'The Tinkerman' had seen enough. He threw on Jamie Vardy, the country's current leading goalscorer, in an attempt to spark up his team. Likewise, we replaced Luer who had worked hard, with Akpom and then Hernandez came on for Taylor.

Then came a real moment of contention. Schwarzer in the Foxes goal, fumbled a Maloney corner and Maguire headed goalwards. Schwarzer did a bit more juggling and from our vantage point, it looked like he'd taken it over the goal line. To be fair, the linesman didn't have a great view, with the post and various players in his way.

The referee tonight was Stuart Atwell, who famously and incorrectly awarded a goal when the ball never even went between the posts, now referred to as the 'phantom goal'. I reckon he was never going to 'guess again' so took the safe option and favoured the 'big team'. The doubting Thomas in me suggests that had it been at the other end, a goal would have been awarded.

And obviously this not being a Premier League match, and so not really a match of any importance, no goal line technology was in force. Schwarzer's expression suggested the ball was over the line, and mobile phones in the stands were soon suggesting the same, as spectators received Sky screen shots freezeframed, via text and social media.

The full time whistle blew, still 0-0, but I hoped that decision wasn't going to cost us.

If the potential goal decision wasn't enough, Mr Atwell infuriated us further by instead of awarding City a penalty (we don't seem to get that many) for what looked like a foul on Akpom, he booked him for diving instead.

I was flaying my arms again when another possible penalty appeal, for a barge on Maguire was waved away. To rub salt into the wound, Leicester broke upfield and Vardy, who looked miles offside (my later observation on Sky showed he was just onside), broke clear. Jakupovic saved well but the ball fell into the path of Mahrez who sidefooted home into an empty net and we were 1-0 down in extra time.

Bollocks! Not what we deserved.

Vardy was a prat, fist pumping in the direction of the South Stand. Sorry Jamie but *we* would eventually have the last laugh.

The crowd were incensed by the apparent injustice, and people actually got out of their seats in the lower West Stand to berate the linesman. All very reminiscent of Kempton days. Andy Robertson himself was livid (I think he was actually the last man who had played Vardy onside) and certainly believed the decision was incorrect. He hurtled towards the linesman and somehow stopped within about an inch of his face. For a split second, I actually thought he was going to head-butt him.

A City team of a few weeks ago or last season may have then gone through the motions and lost the match. But renewed confidence of the last couple of games and a resurgent crowd (there was definitely more than the 16,000 plus quoted) encouraged their team on.

This paid dividends as shortly after, and just near the end of the first period of extra time, we equalised. Akpom's low drive was saved by Schwarzer, the rebound hitting Abel 'I can't do anything wrong at the moment' Hernandez and the ball was in the net, 1-1, and no less than City deserved for their efforts.

City continued to be the better team for the remainder of extra time but couldn't force a winner so penalties at the South Stand it was. Mark added that he had never taken a penalty before (confirming my belief that a centre half should never take them) although I did remind him that Thomas beat him in a 'best of five' in our front garden. To be fair, that's probably why he has never taken one in his football career.

We correctly predicted that the penalties taken should basically start from the forwards and work backwards, so Hernandez, Maloney, Huddlestone, Akpom and Meyler were chosen.

Being ever the pessimist, I expected to lose. Charlotte told me off, but as already mentioned, she now felt sick and wanted to wet herself with excitement.

Leicester were first to take and Jakupovic made a great save, pushing Mahrez's spot kick onto the post. He then proceeded not to watch any of our penalties, but just watched and listened to the home crowd's reactions to see if we had scored or not.

Every single City player then dispatched their penalties with aplomb. Watching in real time, I wasn't sure how good they were, but later watching on TV, they really were emphatic. Old man Schwarzer may as well have had mittens on as he wasn't getting anywhere near them.

I did have a sense of trepidation as Meyler stepped up to take the last potential match winning penalty, thoughts of his shocker at Accrington in my mind. No such problem this time, and City history was made. A great team performance, we were into the quarter finals, unchartered territory.

We bid farewell to Mark, thanking him for his company and insight. He asked us for a sneak preview of 'his' chapter and promised to help us in any way to assist this book effort. Top man.

Charlotte asked if she could now go to the toilet and as we waited, we basked in the thought that City were in the last eight of the League Cup, we must be one of the best eight teams in the country!

All we want is to avoid Southampton away for a midweek fixture, then to avoid Manchester City away. Give us anybody at home.

Shit!

We got Manchester City away.

Oh well, we'll just have to turn them over at their place.

"..STEVE BRUCE, BLACK AND AMBER ARMY.."

CHAPTER 25

WIMBLEDON AKA MK DONS (A) – SATURDAY 31ST OCTOBER 2015

"NO SCARES ON HALLOWEEN AT STADIUM MK..."

Following the extremely encouraging performances at home against Ipswich, Birmingham and Leicester, all within the space of a week, it actually felt like City were slowly moving up the gears.

With each performance it really felt like the style of play, tempo and threat going forward was improving and so we headed for our next game, away at Milton Keynes, feeling fairly confident. Hell me, confident, things must be looking up!

With a fully fit squad at our disposal we have very few teams to fear in this league. Basically, if we perform to our abilities, then we should win many more matches than we lose. Where exactly that will take us, this journey will see.

Today's particular trip by Thomas and I, was shared with a friend of many years, Mr Tony Cline, partner Annerley and son Taylor. Tony has been watching City for as many years as I have, if not longer, and so many City trips and tales have been shared together.

He is normally a very laid back, joyful person, but when watching City, he can have a tendency to get very carried away. In the old Boothferry Park days, he particularly enjoyed following the linesman up and down the line, giving him a right volley of abuse, in the vain hope that he'd eventually award City a dubious decision. It rarely worked.

Several away trips spring to mind with Tony. It was he who made us late for the Chester game when I missed all three goals, despite him thrashing his shiny red Xr3i down the motorway. I also vividly remember an away day with him at Stoke, the old Victoria Ground. City were bottom of the league, Stoke top, so whilst sharing a few pre match beers with their fans, they were an expecting an easy win, scoring a hatful in the process. We expected the same. Due to our league position, the City following had dwindled, meaning many empty away seats and lots of room to move around.

Somehow, City pulled off a 3-2 away win, inspired by many Leigh Jenkinson shuffles. I'm not sure what came over me that day, but I can recall manically running up and down the rows of seats, flicking loads of v's at the adjacent Stoke fans. Well, until a friendly tap on the shoulder from the local constabulary, suggesting I calm down, anyway. Bloody party poopers.

We also shared numerous trips to the old Feethams, Darlington, where we'd meet Tony's old man and take him for a few drinks and to the match. Mr Cline senior is a giant of a man, and now sports a large white beard, which makes him look very much like Captain Bird's Eye. He is the only person I've met who will try and hurl abuse at a football match without ever swearing. At one particular trip to Feethams, just after the City contingent had been singing offensive ditty's in the direction of Darlington's long haired midfielder (including the one about, *"..the wheels on your house go round and round.."*) and at the exact time as there was a hush in the crowd, Tony's dad shouted, *"And get your hair cut young man"*. Enough to create laughter in the crowd but embarrassment for Tony.

I also recall sharing an away trip to York City with Tony and many others. We'd decided to all go on the train and have a few beers. There had been a lot of rain during the day, and as we were about to change trains at Selby, news filtered through that the match had been postponed due to a waterlogged pitch. *"Stuff it"* we all said and continued on with our journey to York and decided to make a full day of it, with no football to 'get in the way'.

As the afternoon and early evening descended, the party, all now a bit worse for wear, started drifting off. Tony and I decided we'd had our fill and got a train back to Hull. Tony soon nodded off, the rest of the train full of sober passengers. He then proceeded to dribble from his mouth a long trail of saliva, stretching from his bottom lip to his lap. Each time, just before you thought it was going to drop off, in his state of sub-consciousness, he'd suck it back up. Then the whole process would start again and so on, all the way back to Hull. Whilst I was laughing to myself, there were several tutts and shakes of the head from the other passengers. It was the most controlled and lengthy spell of dribbling I've ever seen at a day out at the football. Needless to say, Tony was not in good books with the 'then Mrs Cline' upon his return.

So during today's drive, after recalling a few old football memories, both Tony and Annerley decided to tell two new stories about themselves. Whilst neither of these are really football related, they amused me so much that I thought I'd share them with you. If nothing else, hopefully they'll help to portray these two individuals as characters in the book and part of this season's journey.

First up, Annerley's story.

Tony and Annerley had decided to take the kids to watch up and coming band 'The Vamps' in concert at Scarborough. This involved a few days away, a few drinks and a hotel stay. The stage was surrounded by water, with crowd thereby separated. None the less, the usual fluorescent jacketed stewards were in presence.

A great evening was had by all, although the kids were a little disappointed when the drummer, having thrown his drumsticks towards the crowd, saw them fall just short and into the water. Annerley, seeing the disappointment etched on their faces, waited patiently until the set list was complete and the band had departed the stage. Saying nothing to anybody, she seized her moment.

Rising from her seat, she started running towards the water. Seeing a gap between the stewards, she discarded her slip on shoes and jumped into the water in an attempt to retrieve the drumsticks. She had envisaged it to be not too deep. However, Tony and kids looked on aghast, as Annerley immediately disappeared, totally submerged under the water. This was not the edge of the Caribbean, blue and crystal clear, but a dirty North Yorkshire lake. Annerley couldn't see two yards in front of her face.

Eventually after several gulps of rat infested water, she located said drumsticks, holding them in the air in jubilation, swam to shore and climbed out. Apparently she did not look like a Pamela Anderson in an old episode of Baywatch! Her hair and clothes stank, with soggy green moss all over. The stewards and a policeman immediately wanted a word with her.

Tony and kids until this moment had been motionless in shock. He then sprang to action, accustomed to such questioning from football days out, and told her not to supply a name or address until the policeman confirmed if she was going to be arrested or not. Probably not wanting to fill in any paperwork and after some persuasion, she got lucky as the policeman said no, she wasn't being arrested.

For some reason, Annerley then nearly gave the game away, as she offered to supply these details anyway. Again, aghast faces from Tony and kids. She then offered a false name and address she knew didn't exist. Tony covered the kids mouths up just before they uttered the words, "*That's not your name*" or "*You don't live there*".

And so with drumsticks prizes in hand, the party proceeded to catch the bus, Annerley still dripping wet with stagnant water, and walk through the reception at The Grand Hotel, Scarborough. Classy chick that Annerley!

I asked Taylor if he still had the drumstick souvenir. He said, "*I think it's in my bedroom somewhere*". Kids today eh – grateful or what?

The next story involves Tony and shall be referred to as "The Broccoli Incident".

Having decided to have a family Sunday dinner, a trip to Morrisons in Brough took place to purchase the requisite necessities. Tony was despatched to get vegetables which were to include some broccoli. As is the case, these were stored in a chiller unit, the broccoli located near the top. As Tony reached for it, he suddenly felt his back go into spasm and he couldn't move. He was stuck, leaning towards the chiller, with hands resting on the top, effectively holding himself up.

A few minutes went by until Annerley found him in excruciating pain. As Tony struggled to keep still, in agony, he started knocking things off the shelves, carrots, onions, you name it, all were now on the floor.

Annerley could do nothing else but go and seek out a Morrisons staff member for some help. The aisle was soon cordoned off, preventing other shoppers assessing the scene, leaving Tony to be on his own. This obviously didn't stop numerous and curious onlookers peering at Tony in distress.

Tony was by now, getting a bit colder, so the helpful Morrisons staff provided him with some official Morrisons chiller shelf stackers gloves, and padded Morrisons jacket. He was now looking like a bona-fide Morrisons employee, 'The broccoli shelf stacker'.

With his back still not easing up, there was nothing else for it, but to call for an ambulance. This duly arrived and Tony was carefully placed onto a stretcher and blue lighted to the A&E department at Hull Royal Infirmary, family in tow.

Noticing Tony's new apparel, the ambulance staff immediately assumed an accident at work, *'where there's blame, there's a claim'*, and said that he'd soon feel better at the thought of a payout. Things got worse when under the expert care of the nursing staff, the latex disposable gloves were donned and finger promptly placed up his back passage. Much Diazepam later and Tony's back eventually eased up a little and he was allowed home, albeit requiring several visits to the loo. No-one felt hungry anymore and certainly no-one fancies broccoli anymore!

Anyway, stories now told, back to the football.

MK Dons are the 'bastard' child of the now defunct Wimbledon. And they are the exact thing that most of us football fans, who like our football history and nostalgia, despise.

Basically Wimbledon were a team who rose from non-league football to the top of the football pyramid, stayed there and even had the temerity to win the FA Cup, against Liverpool, and against all the odds. This is an achievement that, whilst we have come close, have still not achieved.

And then Wimbledon encountered financial difficulties (sound familiar?), and a certain Peter Winkelman seized an opportunity, bought the football club previously called Wimbledon, and promptly moved them sixty miles away to a soul less place called Milton Keynes. A name change later to MK Dons, and it almost seemed that Wimbledon and all that history, had vanished overnight. So little has MK Dons got to do with Wimbledon, that even the replica FA Cup in the trophy cabinet has allegedly been returned.

Can you imagine how you would react if Hull City were renamed and moved sixty miles to say somewhere like L**ds? Hardly endear you to carry on supporting them would it?!

We finally arrived at the Stadium MK to experience another new 'ground tick'. We were there extremely early at just gone midday, so the thought of a few beers was in our minds. However, if anyone has ever been to Stadium MK, you'll understand that this is not your usual football ground.

It's in a place surrounded by no houses whatsoever, and certainly has no 'old fashioned' boozers. The ground is in the middle of a modern shopping complex, so is surrounded by all your High Street stores. This was enough for Annerley, who immediately left us at this stage to seek out some retail therapy, only to be seen again at about 2:59 when in our seats inside the ground.

Being there early we parked right outside the away turnstiles, for the princely sum of £7 and looked at our choice of watering hole. This consisted of no pubs, but eateries such as Pizza Express, Frankie and Benny's, Nando's etc etc. It all felt very reminiscent of a shopping mall in America and not how we have been brought up watching City. It felt incredibly unusual.

We settled for Frankie and Benny's and delighted at having to pay about £4 for a bottled beer. I was glad we didn't have to do this every week. If this is the way forward for football, then we'll certainly be witnessing a very different type of football supporter.

As the time ticked by, we witnessed some of the Tiger Travel coaches arrive dropping off the 'Cod Army'. Many not wanting to pay the exorbitant alcohol prices, just continued drinking the red wine from their Lucozade bottles that had been part consumed in the coach.

One particular chap, along with inflatable guitar, looking a bit glazed, was receiving repeat chants of *"You're just a shit Ed Sheeran"* him bearing an uncanny resemblance to him. He then proceeded to place his guitar on a steward's head some thirty yards away (akin to the 'alien on his head' scenario at Sheffield Wednesday) to rapturous cheers from the City contingent. Taking his moment of fame, the Ed Sheeran lookalike, then turned round to rejoin us, only to instantly fall over a bollard. This brought even more cheers. We all love to laugh at someone else's misfortunes.

Three o'clock was approaching and so we entered the turnstiles. There were about two thousand six hundred away fans but it was abundantly clear that this ground will never fill. It's a nice piece of architecture and well designed, but is just in the wrong place for football and far too big for the likes of MK Dons. It just doesn't feel like a football stadium. Its capacity is in excess of thirty thousand. The crowd today, even with reduced prices, was about sixteen thousand. As such, there were ridiculous numbers of empty seats and executive boxes.

In an obvious attempt to subdue the away following, the City fans were housed predominantly in the upper tier behind one of the goals. Imagine a mini Newcastle if you will, a toy town version. Whilst beneath us were rows and rows of empty seats. A poor ball girl of about eight years of age, was struggling to return the ball into play once the game started, it requiring about three relay throws until the ball eventually reached the pitch again.

As a result the atmosphere was fairly quiet and I can't recall any singing from the MK Dons fans. We could have been anywhere and playing anybody, which is I suppose quite appropriate for MK Dons.

Naturally, and following the recent good performances, City were unchanged. The subdued atmosphere may have affected the City players as we certainly didn't play as well in this game. We didn't need to, as MK Dons really weren't very good. They were equally as intent on playing as badly in the second half as they did in the first. I'd be surprised if they don't get relegated. They are at best, a League One team, in a soul less ground, far too big for them, playing in place of a team whose identity and league place they acquired, not achieved.

It was also Halloween but no scares were encountered. They had a fairly lively left winger who troubled Odubajo a bit, resulting in Moses getting an early yellow card. They enjoyed a fair bit of possession but never really troubled McGregor.

After some early MK fouls prevented City getting to the heights of recent performances, we took the lead when good work from Hernandez won us possession high up the pitch. He slotted the ball across for Elmo to tap in easily at the far post to put us one up after twenty minutes or so.

The game was a bit easy and City became sloppy, giving possession away, but MK couldn't do anything with it, not in an attacking threat anyway. Elmo had a great chance to kill the game off just before half time when he latched onto a ball behind the MK defence, rounded the keeper, and with an empty net begging, proceeded to put his shot over the bar. A real Ronnie Rosenthal moment.

Half time came and brought me two amusing moments.

Firstly the chap sat in front of me, clearly had the munchies, as he returned from the kiosks with no less than three meat pies to himself, all smothered in ketchup. Then when nature called, desperate to relieve myself of some of the

£4 Frankie and Benny's bottles, I saw a grown man go into the toilets holding a cup of coffee in one hand, and wearing a foam finger on the other hand. Must have been a sit down affair?

Most of the second half was spent talking to a Sheffield United supporter sat next to me. He wasn't lost but had met up with some City supporting friends rather than watch The Blades at Crewe. Who can blame him? He assured me that MK wouldn't score in a month of Sundays and added that the song being sung about David Meyler, *"...He used to be shite, but now he's alright..."* was a bit harsh. I tended to agree and David Meyler himself later took to Twitter to say as much. It was decided to do something about it for the next trip to Brentford, the following Tuesday.

Lots of home possession and giving the ball away, or interceptions by both teams continued with few chances being created. Brucey closed the game up, and took off both our strikers, replacing them with Diame and Maloney. It didn't matter, as in the last minute, a delightful back heel by Maloney, played in Diame, who opened up his body and slid the ball in off the far post. Two nil City and another three points in the bag.

If we'd played better, we could probably have won by four or five, but we did enough and consolidated our position in the upper echelon of the league.

Hopefully we won't have to go back to this place again.

Roll on Tuesday and Brentford away, a proper football ground.

"...EASY, EASY, EASY..."

CHAPTER 26

BRENTFORD (A) – TUESDAY 3ᴿᴰ NOVEMBER 2015

"...THE DAVID MEYLER SONG..."

This was one of the four 'stupid' away fixtures that the FA computer had thrown up for City – a midweek away game, not in a school half term, in West London. To be fair, I was quite looking forward to this one, it's the later away midweek fixtures at Ipswich and Reading that might be slightly more challenging.

I can only recall being to Brentford once before, but had fond memories of it. Firstly City won 1-0 courtesy of a Rob Dewhurst goal back in 94/95 on Bonfire Night, almost twenty one years ago to the day. Secondly, I remember it as it has four pubs, one on each corner of the ground, The New Inn, The Griffin, The Princess Royal and The Royal Oak. So we obviously went in each one. The advert might read, *'Probably the most refreshing football ground in the country'* (albeit one of these, The Royal Oak is now closed).

So a few weeks ago, we decided that we'd be partaking in the hostelries and train travel was booked. Thomas <u>had</u> to attend this fixture as we'd booked tickets in our Family and Friends railcard, so down to London and back for less than a tenner each. So the morning brought a headache – it's a problem that I suffer from, as does my father, as did his and so on. Funny how sometimes they are convenient.

The only snag being that as Hull is such a Northern outpost, it is impossible to get all the way back to Hull from London for a midweek fixture. Therefore train tickets could only be booked to and from Donny, and minibus was organised for the missing leg of the journey.

In the end eight of us attended, Bri and James Lee, Shaun, Steve, John, Dobbo, Thomas and I. We were then referred to as 'The Brentford Eight'

An early pint in The Hop Pole set the scene, before minibus to Donny. This was followed by another pint whilst waiting for the train, then we boarded and were London bound. Many discussions took place on the train, punctuated constantly by the 'scchh' of beer ring pulls or bottle tops being undone. However, the main focus was on trying to come up with a new song for David Meyler.

He had publicly commented after the MK Dons match, that he wasn't over enamoured about his last one which involved the words, "..*he used to be shite, but now he's alright..*"

As you may have gathered, football songs amuse me. Both the words, the timing of them and the fact that when being sung, everyone knows exactly when to stop and how many verses to sing. And who starts them off in the ground? It usually only takes one or two individuals to lead the first few words, and then hundreds if not thousands join in en masse. It's like they feel it's their mission, their duty in life. Maybe they have really boring jobs and football is their release to be a leader at the heart and soul of a band of brothers, united in one cause; an alter ego if you like. It's a good job they do, as any football ground without terrace singing and chanting can be a bit soul less.

There are probably only a handful of different tunes to football chants. We are in the main, simple folk, and different sets of fans just change the words to adapt to their own team, or to point ridicule at the opposition team.

Going further back, the question that maybe needs to be asked is, who in the first place actually decides upon the words? I've never made one up myself and 'got it started'.

Today on the train we actually did take part and witnessed it first hand. And then we joined in to educate the masses to 'get it going and known'. Mind you, none of Thomas' or my suggested words actually made it into the final rather simple version. The end version was (to the tune of Lola by The Kinks):

> *"He runs all day and he won't run away*
> *He scores at home and he scores away*
> *Ohh, David Meyler*
> *Ohh, David Meyler"*

Repeat over and over again.

Now this was very simple, but proof of whether it would catch on would only be known once in the ground.

There were a few more tasks ahead of us yet. Namely catching the Tube to South Ealing, along the Piccadilly Line, walking down to the ground and revisiting those pubs, well at least the three that are still open.

Being Northern Oikes, this wasn't plain sailing. Four of the Brentford Eight, Bri, James, Thomas and I managed to accomplish this with a minimum of fuss and were soon in The New Inn, an Irish themed pub, tucking into Guinness. The remaining four found the big smoke and the London Underground a bit more complicated. Basically, yes they got on the Piccadilly Line, but on the wrong tube which rather than branching off to South Ealing, headed to North Ealing.

They eventually caught up with us, after a black cab ride and a stop off at a totally different Irish pub. By this time, Bri and I had supped numerous Guinness and were deep in conversation with some Austrian lads. They had travelled over to watch Brentford on the Tuesday and Chelski on the Wednesday in the Champion League. We tried to persuade them that City were the team to support but they had already bought their Brentford scarves!

Many more City fans came into the pub and it was good to briefly meet up with John Oxley, an old school friend.

As a result of the delay however, kick off time was fast approaching and there was no way we'd have time to take in all three pubs. We hastily walked to The Griffin, located near the away end but found the bar five or six deep with patrons spilling onto the street. With thoughts of the following morning at work (and school), we decided not to queue but instead entered the ground ready for the match.

Nasty burgers and pies were consumed to help soak up the liquid diet. Watching football on your travels is not a healthy lifestyle.

Now I have never had any intention to live in London, but if I did, Brentford is the type of team I'd probably choose to support. It's a good old fashioned ground, having a mixture of terracing and seating areas, is positioned in a housing area, is accessible by the tube and of course has a few pubs. It's on the small side, so is usually fairly full, and this kinds of adds to the overall atmosphere. Even better on a night match under the lights, which all adds to the experience.

The away end is a mixture of lower tier terracing, and upper tier seating. It probably only holds about 2,000 and tonight I estimated about 1,000 or so City fans had made the trip. Not too bad for a midweek trip to the capital.

We being 'old schoolers' and even Thomas, having enjoyed his Accrington Stanley experience, had opted for the standing area. This area has a fairly low roof which adds to the acoustics if the fans are in full song, and Brentford added to the occasion by turning off the lights in there, whilst the game was in progress.

Yes, there were times when you struggled to see all the action on the pitch, particularly if someone tall was stood in front of you. But you were free to move around the terrace to gain a better vantage point, something you can't do in all seater stadia, unless seats are empty I suppose. Although people always feel compelled to sit in their allocated seat. You see them at away games holding their ticket looking for their exact seat when there are thousands of empty seats around them.

Tonight, at Griffin Park, somehow, all the component parts just made it feel like a proper football match. Or maybe that was just because I'd had a few pints of Dublin's finest?

The game kicked off with Brentford, particularly in the first half, looking very neat and tidy. Like ourselves, they were on a good run of form and both teams were looking for a fourth successive win.

Their football was incisive, they played to feet but also weren't afraid to put it into the box early. City's defence was a good match for this though and a combination of initially Dawson and Bruce Jnr were an equal match. Bruce Jnr got his inevitable injury and was replaced by Maguire, who also performed admirably.

McGregor made a good save with his feet early on, and we only had a couple of half chances in what was a cagey close fought first half, Brentford probably shading it. So we were happy to go in at 0-0.

Midway through the first half, the first airing of the new David Meyler song was made. Obviously it took a few renditions but patience is a virtue, and with it having no complicated words, it soon caught on.

Throughout the full duration of the night, we probably sung it on and off, for about twenty minutes or so. Time will tell if it gets repeated at future fixtures, but it has already had a write up in 'When Saturday Comes'! If it does catch on and is here to stay, we'll claim a very small element of its success.

That being said, it's funny how, despite singing it over and over again, once on the way home, we couldn't remember the tune! A bit like when you watch a band in concert. You remember what song they came on to, the last song, and some songs in between, during your journey home. The day after, it's all a bit of a blur.

City came out for the second half much improved and basically showed their class overpowering Brentford. This was great as they were attacking our end – always better to see the action close up. In addition, being vertically challenged, Thomas and I managed to find a concrete pillar at the back of the away end to stand on. This gave us a better view over the heads of anyone over about 5' 8".

The back of the away end, made of corrugated steel, provided a sort of musical accompaniment when whacked with the sole of your shoes to the ever repeating chorus line of the Meyler song. Our hands were getting a bit sore with all the clapping, so always useful to alternate between limbs!

The central pairing of Meyler and Livermore again excelled and we started to get down the flanks, with both full backs overlapping. This eventually led to our first goal.

A great through ball by the underrated Clucas, and Robertson bombed on to latch onto it and tuck away for a 1-0 lead. This was Robertson's first competitive goal in City colours and he sure enjoyed it in front of the travelling support, pointing towards them as if to say, *"that's for you lot"*. He certainly seems like a confidence player so hopefully this goal will go on to inspire him to subsequent good performances. We decided at that point, that pictures of his goal celebration would form part of our book and Twitter page @46_and_counting

Brentford briefly retaliated and hit the post, and were then awarded an indirect free kick inside the box after the referee alleged a back pass. It took an eternity to take it, but predictably, the shot cannoned off the wall.

From then on City showed that they are a level above and controlled the remainder of the game.

Like the previous game, both strikers came off, Diame on for Akpom and Huddlestone replaced Hernandez. And like in the previous game, it didn't seem to matter as we eventually scored again. A corner was only half cleared and Maguire shot goalwards. The keeper failed to hold it and Clucas was on hand to poke it home, two nil and game over.

The away end went ballistic, and the chant was *"We are going up, we are going up"*.

Meyler could have added a third but shot straight at the keeper – a goal tonight from Meyler of all players, would have been the icing on the cake.

The full time whistle blew and as a result of Brighton's draw, City were top of the league. What a great feeling. What a great night.

Brentford were probably one of the better sides we have so far faced, yet we still kept a clean sheet and eventually won at a canter. Even their manager said we were the best team they had faced this season – it's always re-assuring to hear the opposition respect and praise you.

We walked back to the tube station, and ironically bumped into the Austrian posse again, promptly reminding them that we'd said City were the team to follow. We met Sue our next door neighbour, who sober as a judge, did her usual chaperone work ensuring we were all deposited together at Kings Cross. The 11:30 last train finally arrived and we boarded the train reflecting on the evening.

Brentford away. Proper old fashioned football. Open terraces, lots of beer and a 2-0 City win. Ace.

It felt good to be a City fan and confidence was high. We'd had an excellent away trip, with good company, watching City from a proper old fashioned terrace. Not an event that happens too often nowadays. If we keep playing like this and getting results, nor will it happen too often again in the future (as we'll be in the Premier League).

As the train headed back up to Donny, several of the party bobbed off. I've always found trains and planes difficult to get any decent sleep on, you never seem to get comfortable. Thomas was finding the same. After getting back on our minibus, Thomas and I were last off and we eventually walked through the front door at 3am.

It felt like we'd only just closed our eyes when the alarm went off in the morning and time to get ready for school and work. The day felt long but we both survived, probably still high on that feel good factor that being top of the league creates.

Was it all worth it?

Too bloody right it was!

"..E-I-E-I-E-I-O, UP THE FOOTBALL LEAGUE WE GO.."

CHAPTER 27

MIDDLESBROUGH (H) – SATURDAY 7TH NOVEMBER 2015

'LEST WE FORGET'

It almost feels like many of the last few chapters have all started with, 'this will be a stern test for City', or something along those lines. Today was no different.

Middlesbrough were, and still are, the bookies favourites to win the league, even though we were top of it, so we'd have to be at our best.

Discussions on the train home from Brentford (well before some of us fell asleep), were, *'would you take a point on Saturday?'* After four wins on the bounce, confidence was high, so the resounding answer was no. We clearly wanted to beat them and try and start putting some points difference between us.

I wanted to beat them even more when many of their fans were clearly disrespectful when *'Ode of Remembrance'* was read out and a minutes silence followed. Some of the Boro' contingent did not remain silent.

I'm always quite moved when these annual ceremonies are carried out at the nearest home game to Remembrance Sunday. This is in remembrance for brave men who fought in the name of our country.

So as we listened to the fourth stanza of Laurence Binyon's poem, *'Lest We Forget'*;

"They shall grow not old, as we that are left grow old,
Age shall not weary them, nor the years condemn
At the going down of the sun and in the morning
We will remember them"

And the Bugle played The Last Post, I always feel kind of humble. It's only a football match we are about to watch.

A section of the Boro' fans clearly did not feel the same way as me.

This pissed me off. Fucking take them to the cleaners City!

My latest lucky trait is a stern belief that if I'm polite to people, and do generous things, which includes putting loose change into any charity buckets, then good things will happen to City. It's been working so far this season.

Naturally, this also has to go hand in hand with the 'lucky pint' before kick off.

The football widow was at work this evening so her place and today's gassy concourse pint of lager, was to be shared with our latest guest, my twin sister, Anne.

Now in football terms, Anne until today, was a football virgin. She'd never attended a real life football match, so as part of this journey, at some point it felt natural that she be 'broken in', so to speak.

Pinning Anne down to a spare slot in her diary is not always so easy. She has three children of her own and is now in a relationship with partner Alan, who also has three kids of his own. That's eight of them altogether, like the 'little old woman who lived in a shoe', so this usually involves her diary being fairly full, with something going on.

However, she'd managed to find a spare slot for Saturday 7th November, so Boro' at home was 'her match'.

I'm surprised she hasn't been to a game before, as in reality, she can be a bit of a 'ladette'. Quite happy to swill pints rather than halves or a glass of wine, or a fruit based drink for the ladies (as Al Murray would say).

She also likes to be a bit of a wind up merchant.

Going back many years, when a crowd of us used to frequent the pubs in Cottingham, when you'd go in wearing your best shell suit or trackie, and the pub was full of people watching England play in the World Cup or Euros. Anne would often come in and ask questions like, *"What colour are England in?"*, or *"Which way are England kicking?"* just to wind up the blokes watching.

So today she was in her element, as she soon had pint in hand, and had shared some money with the concourse bookies. She felt quiet at home and enjoyed herself. I did ridicule her for putting a fiver on a Boro' 2-0 win. It wasn't quite so 'sharing her money' with the bookies, rather more, 'handing it over'. My offering of a £2, 2-1 City win with Diame being the first goalscorer, whilst a lot closer than Anne's, proved to be a case of, 'close but no cigar'.

As it turned out, Anne's partner Alan was also at the game, having had a late call up into a Corporate box. *"Ring him"*, I said, *"We can meet him if you want?"*

"No, I don't think I'll bother. I think the afternoon is all free, so he'll be in a right mess already" came the reply.

Needless to say, Alan did text Anne during the course of the second half, telling us that he was a little lost and couldn't remember what box number he was in. All he could remember was that it was about the third or fouth one from the North Stand, miles away from our seats in the South West corner.

Perhaps he was angling for a lift home. He didn't get one from us, but trust he found the correct box to resume drinking.

Alan followed up with another text asking *"Where are you?"* Anne, knowing what state he may be in, simply replied, *"Give me a wave, I'm the one wearing a Superdry jacket!"*

I'm not sure if Alan spotted her or not, but no doubt he turned up later in the evening feeling all amorous.

So, after we'd supped our lucky pint, bets had been placed, and Remembrance Sunday proceedings observed by most, the game started. I was a little apprehensive as to whether Anne may ask lots of daft questions. Her being a football virgin and all that, I was expecting to have to explain the offside rule or something. I recall once taking a South African chap to City for his first football game. Within the first thirty seconds or so, one of the keepers caught the ball. At this point the first of umpteen questions was, *"What's he doing using his hands?"* It was a long afternoon.

However, today Anne sat there quietly taking it all in, waiting for a goal to be scored.

City played really well today against a good Boro side, and once we went 1-0 up, we strolled to victory, making the game look oh so easy.

The opening stages were a tight and cagey affair, both teams quick to get men behind the ball to close the game up, and in an attempt to try and retain possession. City were just better at it.

Boro had a bloke called Fabbrini who looked lively, albeit he did sport a terrible mullet, and had a tendency to throw himself about a bit.

But in the main, City dominated and looked far more dangerous. Clucas had a free kick tipped over and Elmo shot tamely straight at the keeper, when well placed.

We passed the ball quickly and again, Meyler and Livermore were outstanding in midfield. And Livermore it was, who was very integral in our first goal. Mullet man ran into Livermore, arms flaying and appealing for a free kick. The referee was having none of it and City broke. The ball eventually found Elmo who curled a great cross to Diame to volley home unmarked from about eight yards, keeper motionless.

Anne was off her feet cheering and clapping. *"Fucking get in there"* was my shout.

Like previous games, City's opponents couldn't muster up any real response in the second half, and we continued to dominate possession. Such that it only felt a matter of time until we scored again (albeit, it is so much more relaxing to watch once you have a two goal cushion).

Chances came and went for City, Diame volleying over, Dawson heading close. Then the second goal came just moments after Boro's best chance of the match. A Stuart Downing cross to the far post was volleyed goalwards by George Friend, but McGregor made a very good save. Whilst not being called upon too often in recent games, he is having an uncanny habit of doing his duties when called upon, and hopefully the Wolves debacle is now well behind him.

From McGregor's save, Odubajo and Livermore broke forward and set up Meyler. His shot was going wide but Clucas managed to get a boot to it, and diverted the ball into the bottom corner. Again keeper left stranded and 2-0 City.

Now in the back of my mind, thoughts of my bet came to the fore. It was about 70-1 I think. Did I want Boro to score a late consolation, still get the three points and collect £140 winnings? Tricky one.

Brucey made a few changes, each player going off, Hernandez, Diame and Meyler, receiving a standing ovation, the crowd appreciating a complete team performance. Akpom, Hayden and Huddlestone came on, and eventually Huddlestone ensured the bookies won again.

Elmo nicked the ball from a sloppy defensive pass from George Friend and passed it to Huddlestone. From the corner of the box, and with some swagger, he stuck it in the far corner, once again, keeper left standing for the third time of the afternoon. Three nil and emphatic.

Anne had laughed at me putting up our flag at the back of The South Stand but overall I think she enjoyed her day out. She quickly sent a text to the football widow, to tell her that she had loved it, had been in the club shop, bought a half season ticket, and was now wearing the full kit. For a moment she believed her.

I was at pains though to remind Anne that not every game was like this. Sometimes we lose.

That being said, we haven't lost for a while now, and after all the weekend's results, we remained top on goal difference. If only the season could finish now. We are now top, and there to be shot at.

However, the week had brought two excellent wins against teams of genuine threat from in form Brentford, and now Boro. Five wins in a row, no goals conceded in any of them and some real consistency – exactly what you need to be successful in The Championship.

And then on the way home came the punch, when Anne asked if I would lend her some money so that her and Alan could buy a bigger shoe (house) to put all their kids in. We weren't talking loose change in a charity bucket here, with possible lucky connotations. Maybe I won't ask her to come again, it might turn out to be very expensive.

However, City had put me in such a great mood, so I agreed. Funny how the performance of your team can effect your whole mood swing.

Hell watching City at the moment actually seems enjoyable – much better than scrambling around for points in The Premier League.

Maybe we could even win the thing?

"...WE'RE GOING UP AS FUCKING CHAMPIONS..!"
(WELL TODAY WE ARE ANYWAY)

CHAPTER 28

BRISTOL CITY (A) – SATURDAY 21ST NOVEMBER 2015

'SHED END, SHED END, GIVE US A SONG'

Unfortunately, after such a good display against Middlesbrough, we were forced to have a weekend off as it was an international break. This was a shame as City looked like they had just clicked into shape and eventually today, we looked a little rusty. More of that later.

In the fortnight between fixtures, we managed to squeeze in two moments of footballing interest. Firstly we attended a superb Hull City Official Supporters Club 'Meet the Players Night' at the KC. The four players in attendance were Greg Luer, Sam Clucas, Tom Huddlestone and captain, Michael Dawson. Soon the floor opened up for a Q and A and I quickly whispered to the football widow not to mention this book.

So as the microphone was taken around the room, it was mainly young children who put their hands up, and asked the questions, introducing themselves as, James, age ten, David, age nine etc etc. Then my dreaded moments came.

Meet the Players. Daws asks, 'You're doing what? Going to every game …?'

Thomas put his hand up and loudly said, *"Tom, twelve"*. *"Yes son, what's your question?"* asked Steve Jordan, the compere. Thomas having watched far too much Sky TV, asked, *"Who's the longest in the shower?"* He's only twelve! The question was quickly changed slightly by the compere to *"Who is the last out of the shower?"* after much laughter around the room. For the record, the players all agreed that Michael Dawson was the vainest.

Then to compound matters, the football widow, raised her arm and said, like a little schoolgirl, *"Suzy, forty four"*. This caused a little titter around the room. She then went on to briefly outline this book and what we were doing, unfurling our flag from Thomas' rucksack. This actually got a round of applause and I suppose we suddenly became aware that we'd have to now decide how to promote this book and make people aware of its existence so that they might eventually buy a copy, rather than us being severely out of pocket, and left with a garage full of the bloody things.

The players were fully supportive of it (what else could they say?) and during the period of autographs and pictures, we took the plunge and asked Michael Dawson, our captain, if he'd write the forward to it. Although not exactly sure what this entailed, he was keen to agree, to which we were delighted. As events ultimately unfolded during the season, we changed this to the HCST.

The second football moment of interest before the Bristol fixture was when on the blank weekend, I decided to go and watch my local team, Walkington FC. They literally play about 300 steps from our front door so I thought, why

Are the Bunton's really small or are all footballers just tall?

not? The match was action packed, but I particularly remember it for one moment. The sort of moment you will probably never see at a professional football match anymore, but are highly likely to see at levels below.

All game long, the opposition number nine, had been niggling away at one of the Walkington players, the player being the smallest and probably the youngest on the pitch. He probably thought he was an easy touch and somebody he could bully. Fair play to the young lad though, he didn't back down or retaliate. After one final elbow at a corner, I noticed one of the Walkington centre halves, (who was about six foot six inches by the way) have a word with the youngster. He pointed out to him who the perpetrator was, number nine.

Within a few seconds, the ball was launched up the far end of the pitch and with that, most eyes followed the ball including the referee. For some reason I stayed watching the number nine. Shall we just say, he went down to the ground clutching his face with claret spilling out of his nose, the ball nowhere near! A melee ensued with both teams, and several spectators on the pitch. The centre half had quietly sloped off and the referee powerless, as he hadn't seen a thing. The number nine was still on the floor clutching his face, but eventually got up. To try and redeem himself and (excuse the pun) to save face with his team mates, he then tried to swing a few haymakers, which hit absolutely nothing, and he looked even dafter. He was then immediately subbed. As the saying goes, what goes around, comes around, he had deserved it.

I just thought, I'd love this to happen in say a Premier League or Championship game, which would certainly fire the crowd up.

The Bristol City away fixture had been pencilled in the diary for a while. It being near(ish) to Christmas, we had decided to all travel down and meet up with my mum (who lives in Cardiff), and eldest sister Jane, who lives in North Devon. Altogether, ten of us had agreed to meet up at The Bristol Marriott and make a weekend of it. I was however, having some pangs of guilt as this weekend was in fact Charlotte's birthday and here I was dragging her down to Bristol, sitting in a car for hours on end.

Charlotte being Charlotte was quite happy to go along with it, but to ease my mind, we had arranged to book a nice Italian restaurant on the Saturday evening with a few presents and a birthday cake (just what a 15 year old wants).

As it happened, Sky eased the situation by deciding to choose this match as a Sky Live fixture and moved the kick off time to 12.30. We'd be back in plenty of time after the game.

So we drove down on the Friday night after school. Upon arrival, my niece Hannah (aged eight) said that she would like to go to the game. I hadn't bought enough tickets. Despite several phone calls the following morning, City informed me that they couldn't sell me one (even if it was reprinted on the day and I collected it at the ground), and Bristol categorically said that no tickets could be bought on the day of the game. This all seemed ridiculous to me, as there were loads of empty seats in the City end, but hey, rules are rules. For some reason, her Dad (Steve) and Grandpa (Norman) were quickly offering her their tickets, but in the end she decided to stay with 'the girls' and go for lunch in Bristol, probably a smart move as the afternoon's events were not the best introduction to football.

I'd done a bit of research and had found out that due to ground redevelopment being carried out at Ashton Gate, it currently only had three stands and there was limited car parking. We could actually get a river boat taxi from near our hotel, get dropped off at a nice pub called The Pumphouse (for a pre match lucky pint) and take a short walk to the ground. What a way to go to a football match.

I may as well not have bothered with the research.

Our hotel was practically next door to a shopping centre, in particular a Harvey Nicholls. The football widow wanted to go in and I could hardly say no. As it turned out, we went in and after a few credit card PIN entries, I was duly informed that we had now completed all of our Christmas shopping. It was still November. Oh well, that saved me a job. I forget sometimes how efficient I can be.

Not to be outdone, Thomas informed me that he needed a new jacket, so House of Fraser was next and the new football casual, promptly selected a Lyall and Scott number, choosing to put it on instantly. He's hardly been out of it since.

So there was no time for boat trip and pub visit. A quick call to the hotel reception and taxi for six straight to the ground it was. One slight mistake was I didn't organise one for the way back.

This was another new ground tick and upon arrival at the ground, it soon became apparent that it was not located in the most salubrious part of Bristol. In fact it was a dump. Not quite on a par with my worst ever away visit, Luton, but not far off. Luton really is a shithole, the place, the ground, everything. And I say that coming from Hull, the town often voted in the top ten crap places to live.

Also joining us at the game today was Steve, my elder sister's husband. Steve is really a Rugby Union fan, often visiting Twickenham for England games. The 2015 Rugby World Cup had spoilt him recently, not necessarily by England's performance on the pitch, but certainly by the hospitality off it. And as for attending away fixtures, what could possibly compare with seeing Jonny Wilkinson's last minute drop goal to win the Rugby World Cup in 2003. Basking in the sunshine and local lagers watching England beat the Wallabies on their home turf. A Hull City away fixture at a part built Ashton Gate was going to struggle to grab Steve's attention.

Steve has spent many a long hour freezing at Twickenham for the fun of watching rugby, usually equipped with his England beanie hat to protect his head (as his number one haircut doesn't really do this). He had come prepared for today's match, as the weather forecast had predicted biting cold winds and low temperatures. Although it was extremely cold watching, for some strange reason Steve chose to keep the fluffy Tiger hat that his totally football savvy wife had suggested he borrow from their three year old, Eleanor, safely tucked in his pocket.

Today he said the one thing he was looking forward to was a meat pie!

Not a good start, Ashton Gate really must be crap, as it didn't sell any. A football ground that doesn't sell meat pies, whatever next? Steve was crestfallen, so we hoped the football might improve the situation.

The ground itself certainly does currently only have three stands, with much building work in progress. This weekend, we will have travelled over four hundred miles to see this. Last season one particular fan, Ron Swift, soon to be known as 'Eastend Shedman', only had to travel to the end of his garden, to reap the benefits of these building works.

The Eastend Shedman was able to watch Bristol City for free, with the best and cheapest seat in the house, thanks to the redevelopment work. Basically he watched from the roof of his garden shed!

The old East Stand was demolished at the end of the season prior, making that end of the ground totally clear. Houses nearby, and with the help of a step ladder and a foot up on the neighbours fence, Shedman was able to watch in clear view, from the top of his shed at the end of his garden.

He even made a sign, christening it The Shed End, and after a few games, the crowd started singing, "*Shedman, Shedman, give us a song*" and "*Shedman, Shedman, give us a wave.*" And so his cult status started. He even started giving money to charity whilst not having to pay for a ticket. This fact was not lost on the club, as when the new stand eventually blocked his view, they gave him a proper seat in the stadium for the rest of the season.

If I thought the football might cheer up 'pie-less' Steve, I was sadly mistaken, particularly in the first half. City seemed sluggish and were slow into any tackles. This in itself ended up bringing a spate of yellow cards and there was a distinct thought that we may not end up with eleven players. It was also very sunny (although this didn't stop the floodlights being on), and this seemed to cause us difficulty in picking the ball up.

We gave a number of free kicks away, some in dangerous positions. McGregor tipped the first set piece over the bar. We were also loose in possession and were guilty of miscontrolling the ball several times.

We did create a few half chances in the first half with Maguire having the best effort. Dawson was the next one in the book. It meant a suspension but worse, he pulled up with an injury that would ultimately mean three or four weeks out. We'll miss his leadership qualities.

Robertson was next for a yellow with a clumsy tackle. He too, is now suspended. Worse again though, as we conceded from the resulting free kick. The ball was crossed in and despite a couple of chances to clear, the ball eventually fell to Kieran Aguard to swivel and turn it home. It was the first goal we'd conceded in ages and it was a sloppy one which could have been avoided.

City responded reasonably well and Livermore was unlucky not to equalise just before half time with a piledriver which was somehow tipped over. However we went in one-nil down and the omens weren't looking good. Steve could sense my frustration.

The second half was better by City. We had loads of possession and several chances but sadly didn't get enough of them on target. Bristol weren't exactly adventurous in looking for a second goal.

Akpom had been selected for the rested Hernandez and had struggled to hold the ball or influence the game so he was ultimately replaced by Maloney. Within ten minutes or so of coming on, this paid dividends as he equalised right in front of us.

McGregor's kick forward was cleverly flicked on by Diame, and Maloney broke the offside trap and raced through on goal. He took time to compose himself and finished neatly into the top corner. He promptly ran right over to our corner and celebrated in front of us. This was great for Thomas and I who went mad celebrating. It also got a great caption of our flag on the TV! Charlotte meanwhile, had been complaining that it was cold. She had come to the match in November in a crop top and a pair of those stupid jeans – the one's with fashionable holes in the knees, which actually cost more to buy with holes in, than without. She did not want to be seen on TV so covered her face. Never one for the limelight, even if it was her birthday.

In the final fifteen minutes or so, City had chances to win it. An Aluko volley went just wide and Clucas headed wide right at the death. But it was not to be, and we had to settle for a point. A little disappointing against a team who appeared to be quite happy with that, and one that we should be beating if we harbour promotion dreams. However, we did not play at the levels we have being doing so recently. Dare I say it, but we are missing Meyler, 'the accidental footballer' (who was injured with Ireland during the international break) and his energy in midfield.

Still unbeaten though, and the point kept us top of the league, just.

We then proceeded to have to wait ages for a taxi back to the hotel (mainly due to my lack of planning). However when we finally got back, the early kick off did mean there was ample spare time to go to the bar. The football widow soon found a drinking buddy at the bar to share the 'Two for One' cocktail offers, whilst I supped a few pints of Guinness. The kids ate chips and eventually left us to go up to our room.

Soon after, my mum joined us and it was with great delight when she told us that she'd been given a pass for the executive lounge, where, from four o'clock onwards, you could get free drinks. Basically this turned out to be an unmanned room, already laid out with bottles of beer, wine, canapes and nibbles. All you had to do was put mum's room key in the door to get access. Now my mum is not much of a drinker but she was today, as between us, we all took turns to frequent the executive lounge and smuggle drinks out. Mum was getting a little concerned. I wasn't!

The hour soon came round to the teatime kick off on Sky. I asked Grandpa if he could go and ask the bar staff to put on Man City v Liverpool. We were soon outnumbered as a dozen or so Real Madrid fans came in and the general consensus was to put on El Clasico, Real Madrid v Barcelona from The Bernabeu.

We were in an English hotel, and the choice was to watch Spanish football. The Real Madrid watchers weren't even drinking. So to be obnoxious, I decided I'd support Barcelona, just to wind them up. Barcelona then proceeded to give them a football lesson and easily ran out 4-0 winners. The Real Madrid viewers were not happy, particularly as I cheered every Barcelona goal.

It was only after the third goal, that I noticed one of the Madrid supporters was only a young boy. Seeing the angst on his face, I decided to apologise and went up to speak with his father. Always on the lookout for a potential story, I explained that I was writing a book about football, predominantly Hull City.

I then asked his son, Ingo Fernandez-Aceytano (aged eleven), how he was feeling about the Madrid game. I asked him if he could put his feelings into words, and went to the bar to get him a pen and paper. It turned out that Ingo was actually at a boarding school learning English and he promptly wrote his feelings, both in English and Spanish.

I suddenly felt a bit of a neanderthal.

I have no idea if his Spanish is the same interpretation as the English. For all I know, he might have called me all the names under the sun. However his closing sentiment, kind of also summed up City's result today.

Spanish version

Para mi es al partido mas importante del ano, dificil y me gustaria ganar porque no me gusta perder contra el Barcelona.

Pero la liga es muy larga y lo importante es como terminan las cosas no como empiezar.

English version

For me, this is the hardest match of the year. It's hard and would like to win it because I don't like losing against Barcelona.

But the league is very long and the important part is how the things finish, not how they begin.

With that, we were informed that we had about two minutes left before we had to go to our restaurant. A hasty dash to our room and off we went.

I hope Charlotte enjoyed the weekend. She certainly enjoyed listening to her new One Direction CD for three and a half hours during the drive home on the Sunday. I wasn't quite so sure.

"...THERE'S ONLY ONE SHAUN MALONEY..."

CHAPTER 29

DERBY COUNTY (H) – FRIDAY 27TH NOVEMBER 2015

"CRAP ON THE TELLY"

I wish Sky would stop selecting City to be the live game. The old adage of *'City are always crap on the telly'* came home to roost again, as we were outplayed and out thought by Derby, and ceremonially dumped off the top of the league. It had lasted just three games, perched at the top.

There is no great shame in losing to Derby, as they have assembled a very good squad, with great strength in depth. And in Chris Martin, they have a good frontman who can hold the ball up and retain possession for the team. If it hadn't been for a dismal run at the back end of last season, they should have really got promoted last year. Perhaps they have learnt their lesson, and I have no doubt that they will be very close this season. If we finish above or one place below them, we should all be happy City supporters.

Tonight was disappointing though on a number of fronts.

Not only did we lose top spot, we also lost our unbeaten home record. It will have also greatly dented confidence.

The manner of defeat was also a little disappointing. I've certainly seen us play worse, but our game plan currently seems to be not to concede early goals, to stay in the game if you like. This must be evidenced by the lack of early goals we score, most seem to come either late in the first half or in the second period. As a result, we are not that adventurous in the opening stages of matches. So when, on the few occasions to date, we do concede early, it seems to really knock us back and struggle to think of a plan B.

We really aren't that comfortable in chasing games. I recently found out that under Steve Bruce, we have conceded first in sixty seven league games. We've lost fifty five of those and only won five of them. Admittedly, many of those games will have been against Premier League opposition, but it's still a fairly damning statistic. Concede first, and we appear knackered!

In very wet and blustery conditions, Derby passed the ball much crisper along the floor than we did. Where we made twenty or so passes, sideways and from flank to flank in an attempt to get forward, Derby played three or four incisive ones and so generally, looked much more threatening.

So when Derby went two nil up just after the half hour mark, you could almost see the City players looking at each other saying *"What now?"* We just looked bereft of ideas.

We'd had signs of an early goal when Cyrus Christie had been allowed to run all the way from the halfway line unchallenged to our six yard box, before Maguire eventually stopped him. I say unchallenged. A couple of 'dangling legs' may have been proffered, but that does not constitute a tackle. The warning signs were there.

Then Andreas Weimann, so often the tormentor of City in his Aston Villa days, cut through the middle of the City defence. He was half tackled by Davies, the ball fell loose, three or four City players looked at it leaving it for each other, and Jacob Butterfield said thank you very much, and swept the ball into the bottom corner from just inside the box.

Cue glum faces and groans in the crowd.

With suspensions and injuries to Dawson and Robertson, we started shuffling the pack. We had started with Odubajo at left back which hadn't worked. He was moved to his preferred position of right back and Clucas dropped into left back. I'm not sure that worked either. There was a gaping hole tonight at the left back slot (oh for a versatile Liam Rosenor?) and we missed the leadership skills of Dawson who is certainly not afraid to put a tackle in.

This seemed a constant theme of the night, with players constantly changing positions. Late in the game we actually subbed Davies and moved Livermore to centre back.

This constant changing certainly did not help City, and Derby soon took an unassailable two nil lead when Butterfield again sent a low volley past

McGregor from about twenty yards. At two nil up, Derby were not going to lose. They worked well without the ball, and broke incisively.

We did have a couple of chances before half time, with Scott Carson saving well from both Huddlestone, and then even better from Hernandez.

In the second period, City had plenty of possession, Derby relatively happy to let us have this whilst getting men behind the ball. In the main, our play was laboured and predictable, although we did create a few good chances with Maloney twice coming close. First he curled a shot just wide when he should have scored, and secondly, had a rasping shot tipped over. Had one of those gone in, then we may have had a grandstand finish. But in truth, Derby were worthy winners.

It was a frustrating night after the euphoria of Brentford and Boro', it felt like we'd been knocked down a peg or two. Maybe this promotion thing won't be quite so easy after all (albeit I certainly never thought it would be).

To make matters worse on the night, I also have to make a confession.

Tonight we let our ranks be infiltrated, we were joined by forces from the dark side. We had invited a couple of guests along, Jon Booth and son, Oliver, in the hope that they would be royally enthralled by a swashbuckling Hull City performance. They could then see for their own eyes just how football should be played in The Championship.

The reason? They support TWS. For those readers not already in the know, TWS refers to The White Shite, also known as Leeds United, or correctly spelt, L**ds United (as it is a swear word).

My plan had backfired. Derby, not City, had shown them how to play. This did not bode well, as our next league game was L**ds away.

We have known Jon for a number of years, and despite his terrible taste in football team, he is always a pleasure to be in the company of. And whilst I question his parenting skills for allowing his son Oliver, or Ords as he is referred to, to be inflicted with the same disease as himself, Jon has in fact, only done what I have subjected to Thomas. We have subjected them to a life of torment, with too many ups and downs following the fortunes of our respective teams. If we had to go through it, so can they!

That being said, I reckon Ords, currently only seven years old, is *'there for the turning'*. He has a grandparent who is actually a City supporter, and secretly I believe Ords has a foot in both camps. Tonight, he provided us with a running commentary of the game, constantly giving the City players, for whom he knew all the names, instructions and guidance. *"Through the middle, out wide, have a shot"* he said. If only they could have heard him from our position towards the back of The South Stand, and executed his instructions, maybe the result may have been better.

Jon may not like me for saying this, but I reckon there is still a young Tiger in young Ords yet. It's not been totally drummed out of him, even if dad does like dressing him in L**ds United fancy dress.

Jon was particularly helpful tonight in making life easier for me. Instead of me having to extract stories out of him for the purposes of this book, he went one better. He typed up and e-mailed me a couple.

I have read these now and hope Jon won't mind but I've tweaked them slightly. I simply can't write anything that glorifies L**ds United! After all, this is a book mainly about Hull City, not TWS.

First up, Jon's story about the introduction of Ords into the 3pm Saturday world of football. Spending quality time with your father, listening to him and others use foul language, an inauguration into that thing we all love and hate, professional football. Note these are predominantly Jon's words, but even though it's about L**ds, I'm sure we can picture ourselves in a similar situation.

*The day had arrived. It was time to initiate Ords into the 'fold' – it was to be his first L**ds United game at Elland Road. Jon felt that at four years old, his sight and senses were of sufficient maturity to warrant this. In any event, residing in Hull with a large proportion of family and friends supporting the Tigers, who were currently riding the crest of a wave (L**ds were not!), Jon needed an ally.*

Ords approached his initiation in a relaxed non plussed way taking no part in the pre match deliberations in the car on the outward journey, choosing to sleep instead. Not a good start but understandable as he could hardly speak anyway.

As they took their seats in the rickety old West Stand, Ords still appeared to be taking everything in his stride. How rude and irresponsible thought Jon, he should be excited, it's his legacy. It was customary to stand on the seats greeting the team onto the field with a chorus of 'that' L**ds United song, 'Marching On Together'. Jon strategically placed Ords onto his seat and proceeded to engage himself in ritual chanting, engulfing himself into his own 'Elland World'.

As the song was approaching its end and the players were lining up for kick off, Jon nocturnally looked down to assess his son's progress. To his dismay his seat was empty – the game had not even started. Where had his son gone, how could he treat this occasion with a disappearance, with such disdain. Was he making his way home already to the KC?

Jon's fatherly instincts returned to the fore and panic started to grip him. His only son and heir to the Elland Road seats had 'done one'. It was only then that he assessed the empty void in detail and as the singing subsided, he could hear a tiny voice squeal, "Please help me Daddy"

The West Stand seats were old wooden fold down ones and Ords had disappeared down the back of the seat as it had upturned. Jon had found his son and he could at last try to enjoy his first taste of football, only this time choosing to spurn the unreliable, temperamental old seat in preference to Jon's knee for the duration of the game. What a surprise, Jon just had to keep him awake now!

The journey for Ords had begun in somewhat of an unconventional and painful manner. Only problem for him was that now being a L**ds fan, there would be much more pain to come on all fronts.

The second story involves Jon and friend, from many a year ago. Remember those years when L**ds were really chasing the dream. Monetary matters had gone out of the window under Peter Ridsdale's command. Expensive players were bought in, even expensive goldfish were bought in for the Boardroom. They enjoyed European nights almost, I say almost, getting to a European final, with no thoughts of the monetary and eventual consequences.

Jon was already on board with all this, and was obviously taking the same approach, taking out an increase on his mortgage at the time to fund his many European trips. There's dedication for you, or maybe stupidity? Having had the briefest taste of this ourselves at Lokeren, I can see how you could become hooked.

Again, the following story, which Jon likes to call 'The Pope is a L**ds fan' are his words not mine, so don't shoot the messenger.

It seems a lifetime ago now, when L**ds United were riding high and featuring prominently in the Champions League. Instinctively knowing full well that this might be short lived, Jon and fellow L**ds fan Patrick, decided to enjoy as many of the away fixtures as they possibly could. This took them to Madeira, Milan, Rome, Madrid, Moscow, Prague to name a few. What was enlightening about those away trips was the many thousands of like minded supporters following the same sentiment.

Whilst they had many stimulating experiences in these fabulous Cities, it was their trip to Rome playing against Roma, that stays with them, and not because of the football. As usual with these Champion League excursions, they were not only there for the football, but to experience the culture, the history and magnitude of such famous Cities, usually travelling for three to four days to savour the whole 'pie'.

On this particular trip, once in Italy, they travelled by train to the Vatican City of Rome where they were greeted by the usual army of taxis, there to take advantage of the unsuspecting foreigner. As they had time to kill before checking into the seedy 'bed and breakfast' establishment that they had sought (true Yorkshire thrift), they decided to take the perky Italian taxi drivers offer of a sightseeing tour, and as he spoke fine English, this became even more palatable to Jon and Patrick. Us arrogant English do tend to expect wherever we go, that our compatriots articulate the English language.

They proceeded to circle such icons as The Colosseum, The Pantheon, The Roman Forum, Trevi Fountain, Piazza Novana, The Spanish Steps, Palatine Hill, Circus Maximus etc etc. The highlight of this elongated journey was of course the great Vatican City, the home of The Pope himself. The pair could have sworn they saw him looking down on them.

They were eventually dropped off at their seedy B&B, miles out of the City centre, in the bowels of Rome, far removed from the sights they had just experienced. Two Yorkshire men brought back down to Earth.

That evening they had arranged to meet some of the L**ds United administrative and marketing staff who had travelled to the game, at a fish restaurant, which turned out to be many leagues away from their B&B, in a much more respectable part of this great City. It seemed to take an eternity to get there, bad planning they thought, but they would enjoy the subjective conversation, getting the inside track on the match the following night, whilst munching on fine Italian seabass and guzzling many glasses of Peroni and Italian vino. Many hours later, and 'three sheets to the wind' many of the party were taking their leave returning to their temporary residences.

Jon and Patrick decided to walk off their excesses, to clear their heads before tracking down a taxi. After half an hour or so tramping through the streets of Rome, Jon asked his friend what the name of their B&B was so that they could return and get some shut eye, preparing for the big game the following day. Patrick proceeded to tell Jon that he had forgotten the visiting card with the name and address on, deciding to concentrate more upon his vanity and generally tarting himself up for the night out, totally forgetting the logistical practicalities.

They were stuffed. Not only did they not know where they were staying, but the vast array of Roman taxis had all gone into hibernation as there was not one in sight. After a few moments of reflection, they began a series of colourful arguments, blaming each other for their predicament. It was clearly getting them nowhere. All of their friends had gone in different directions, clearly knowing where they were going. These two dumb Yorkshiremen though were miles from home, miles from their temporary home, wherever that may be. To add insult to injury, there was not a soul in sight.

By now, the over indulgence and intoxication was wearing off and temperatures began to drop. A strange but eery mist began to fall, permeating their paths as they strode on with no sense of direction.

As the mist thickened, they suddenly saw a shaft of light coming towards them. It was not only a car, but a taxi. At last, something positive. They waved their arms frantically bidding the taxi to stop. The problem was that when it did, and they both clumsily piled their tired but relieved torsos into the back seat, what were they going to say? They did not know where they were staying.

What happened next, Jon believes was the Pope looking down on them.

The weary Italian taxi driver articulated, "where would you like to go?" At this point, an embarrassed silence followed. Both Jon and Patrick looked at each other, each shirking responsibility for the predicament they were in. The taxi driver turned round and to their amazement, it was the same taxi driver that had some hours ago, shown them the sights and sounds of Rome. In a City of a thousand taxis and population of three million, what were the chances of that?

The taxi driver clearly remembered their destination having dropped them off earlier. It was about fifteen miles away.

Their prayers had been answered. The Pope was watching and had blessed them with the gift of homeward transportation. He had saved them from the jaws of uncertainty and an uncomfortable evenings slumber in the ghettos of Rome. He had delivered them from evil, for thine is the Kingdom, the Power and the Glory, forever and ever. The Pope is a L**ds fan!

Great story from Jon and it certainly lifted my mood after City's loss.

However, if the Pope really is a L**ds fan, then I feel sorry for him. Unfortunately for Jon (and maybe The Pope), but not the rest of the non L**ds world, the dream came crashing down. The goldfish were sold and the money had all gone. L**ds plummeted down the leagues and changes of ownerships followed, initially madman Ken Bates, and now Cellino. The rest of the football world laughed, 'no one likes L**ds', but Jon still has his memories.

Hold on to them Jon, I can't see them coming back in your lifetime. Maybe in Ords' lifetime, that is if he hasn't become a Tiger by then!

"...WE'RE NOT VERY GOOD, WE'RE NOT VERY GOOD, WE'RE NOT VERY..."

CHAPTER 30

MANCHESTER CITY (A) – TUESDAY 1ST DECEMBER 2015

"THE CUP RUN IS OVER"

The saying in football goes that after a disappointing result, the first thing that a player and manager wants to do is to get back on the pitch and put things right again. This season with a good Capital One Cup run, and more games in The Championship, lots of opportunities present themselves.

So all we had to do was dust ourselves off from the Derby defeat, forget feeling sorry for ourselves, and put in a performance in our next game. The only problem? Next up was Manchester City away in the Quarter Final of The Capital One Cup.

Not long ago, Manchester City were in the football wilderness (a bit like us). Back in 1999, they just edged past Gillingham in the old Third Division play off final. Two nil down with only three minutes to go and The Gills looked victorious. However, late goals from Kevin Horlock and Paul Dickov forced a draw, extra time and eventually a penalty win.

Since then, and very much akin to Chelski, they've been taken over by a multi millionaire, Sheik Mansour, who throws money around like confetti. In a recent survey, he was valued as being worth £20billion. In the build up to this game, the owners sold a thirteen per cent stake to a consortium of Chinese investors for £265million. That valued the club at about £2billion. That's billion not million! At the moment, I suspect if you guaranteed City's existing debts, you could probably buy it for £2.

There seems no end at the moment to the amount of money being thrown at football, be that by owners who simply have too many noughts in their bank balances, or by Sky. None of it appears to be filtering down to us, the fans, despite recent public clamouring to do so.

Tonight's game just emphasized the gulf that is being created by those that have and those that have not. And most of it I do not like. That being said, I'd probably be a total hypocrite as if somebody owning £200billion suddenly came and bought City, I wouldn't be complaining.

However, I haven't and never will forget all those days of basement football. The dream has to be kept alive for all those at the bottom, the wannabies to really believe that they can get into The Premier League and stay there. Stoke, who went up with us in 2008 have achieved it. However the same rich list showed their owners, The Coates family, as being worth £925million. Even Leicester, currently top of the Premier League, have a Thai owner worth a reported £1.4billion.

The gap is becoming bigger and bigger and I doubt if Hull City can ever expect to amass such wealth.

That being said, shocks can still happen in football. So as the five thousand travelling City following, armed with a reduced £10 match ticket and subsidised coach travel made their way to the game, and an air of belief existed.

We were located at the far right hand side of the City end, housed in the upper section of the recently enlarged South Stand. As I gazed to my left, it really did look a great site with almost every seat occupied. Not bad for a cold Tuesday night in November.

Another example of the great divide. Whilst the City end looked full, the rest of the ground did not. Yet still, just over thirty eight thousand souls attended the fixture in a ground which now holds around fifty five thousand. The ground was two thirds full for a Cup Quarter Final, and there was a distinct lack of atmosphere. I suspect the home contingent whilst clearly wanting to win to reach the semi-final of the Cup, just expected to roll us over, after all we are only little old Hull.

Old visits to Maine Road were met with memories of a tired looking old ground in a shady area of Manchester. Not any more. Shiny new ground courtesy of a Commonwealth Games legacy and shedloads of subsequent money, have resulted in a very impressive stadium. The exterior is particularly good with plenty of kiosks serving food and drinks, and tonight even a stage with rock band playing, and mock 'mosh pit'. You won't see that on Walton Street.

However being away fans, as evidenced by the requested showing of our match tickets in the queue, we obviously weren't allowed to drink in these facilities. We were promptly told that the only place we could have a beer was on the concourse inside the ground. Great customer service, it was only a forty six year old bloke with a twelve and fifteen year old, asking for a drink, not a coachload of hooligans.

So we were directed towards the away section. This game was taking place after recent ISIS attacks in Paris, which involved both a rock concert and a football stadium. So security at such venues has risen ever since. Tonight this meant that The Greater Manchester Police insisted on all spectators being searched, both in person and any bags. Obviously this meant that queues developed.

Now I'm not one to worry about terrorists and all that. In my mind, if you do worry and stop living your life as normal, then they have half won already. They needn't have worried too much about the security measures at our sporting fixtures. It's all well and good, The Greater Manchester Police insisting on searches, but if they do, don't give the job to stewards being paid about £7 an hour. They really don't care. As we approached the front of the queue, no search at all was carried out on any of the three of us attending the game. Our bag search consisted of unzipping the rucksack and peering in. We were simply asked what was in it, to which we obviously replied *"Just a flag and some scarves"*. They just took our word for it and didn't even bother looking.

We took our seats and watched on the large screens our starting line up announced. For me, that told me we had almost given up already. We weren't the only Championship team to do this tonight, all three fielded allegedly weakened teams. Now I find this somewhat hard to follow. This is a quarter final of a cup competition – a stage we've never reached before. Yes, we may well have lost had we fielded our strongest available starting line up. We may have got injuries ahead of what may be seen as more important league games, but at least we'd have gone out fighting. I'd have certainly felt a lot better. Tonight I just kind of felt we'd surrendered any possible chance of an upset before a ball had been kicked.

I do understand the sentiment of sticking with players who had got us to this stage of the competition, but something just didn't sit right with me. I'll quite happily eat humble pie if we go in to win on the following Saturday in the league, but at this moment, I couldn't help but feel underwhelmed.

Man City fielded a pretty strong line up. Mind you, they can as they probably have two full teams, most of whom would get in the first team at any other club. Their answer to not winning the Premier League last year? We'll go and spend £54million on one player, Kevin De Bruyne. Tonight we simply couldn't match him.

The match started and it was evident to me that City's game plan was to try and stay in the tie as long as they could, then have a go in the last twenty minutes or so. To an extent, this worked even after Wilfried Bony had but the Blues ahead after only twelve minutes, knocking in a De Bruyne shot that ricocheted off the post. However, it felt like Man City could simply step up a gear when they felt like it, and towards the end, they did.

In truth, we never looked like troubling Man City. Against a big team, clearly you expect them to have the lion's share of the possession. You therefore have to work that much harder to win the ball back, and when you do, to keep it. We simply didn't do either tonight and it was all too easy. Too many players were shrinking violets choosing to pay too much respect to the opposition. Yes I expected to lose, but not quite so tamely.

Akpom with his pink boots, short sleeves and gloves (never quite get that one) failed to trouble the back line of Man City, and it was only when Hernandez, Diame and Snodgrass (to a great reception) were introduced did we have any real forward momentum.

But unfortunately Man City just moved up the gears and three goals in the last ten minutes eventually gave them a rather flattering 4-0 lead. The last was fairly comical to me, when a free kick just outside our box went in. Elmo, trying to help out dropped back onto the post only for De Bruyne to smash it between him and Jakupovic.

We had something to cheer about when Robertson scored a fine consolation goal in injury time but it was scant reward. Our first visit to the quarter finals ended in somewhat of a damp squib and just confirmed to me the gulf that exists in football today. In all, I was a little bored and Leicester at home seemed ages ago. During the drive home (both Thomas and Charlotte fast asleep) I did question whether I am actually missing The Premier League. Do we really want to get promoted, assuming we can actually achieve it, and subject ourselves to that most weekends?

Great stadium, great wealth, but give me Brentford away for a trip any day.

"..WE'RE GONNA WIN 5-4, WE'RE GONNA WIN 5-4.."
(JUST NOT TONIGHT)

CHAPTER 31

L**DS UNITED (A) –
SATURDAY 5ᵀᴴ DECEMBER 2015

"PIE IN THE SKY"

For some City supporters, they might see this as the biggest, most important game of the season, an away match against TWS. A chance to gain victory and bragging rights over a team they see as their biggest rivals.

I don't quite concur with this. To me, L**ds are just another team. I don't particularly look out for their scores, nor do I wish them any ill feelings.

Don't get me wrong, I'm not saying I like them. After all isn't it an unwritten rule that you have to hate them? They don't want anyone to like them anyway, I think they kind of revel in being unliked, an unwanted child.

But I don't particularly see them as rivals. Yes, they *were* the nearest team geographically to City, who were once successful. However, our paths, and the success of each team always seem to have been going in opposite directions, certainly in the majority of my lifetime to date watching City.

When L**ds were at their pomp spending money like no tomorrow, City were languishing in the lower reaches of the Football League. L**ds were on their way up, we were on the way down. Then when all the money had run out at Elland Road and administration inevitable, TWS sank down the leagues from their perch. City meanwhile rose from the mire and roared to The Premier League. We were on the up, they were on a downward spiral.

Yes our paths crossed, but rarely have we both been challenging for the same honours in whatever league that may have been, during the same season.

So as a consequence, I do not really make direct comparisons to them.

A warm welcome as usual at L***s.

My first taste of football at Elland Road with City was in the 1989/90 season, when a case of '*next goals the winner*' (as longs as its L**ds) saw TWS edge City out in a 4-3 thriller. If you can't recall the game, I would advise you to go on You Tube and watch the highlights.

L**ds were challenging for promotion from the old Second Division (now The Championship) and had a team of household names, most noteably being Vinnie Jones and Gordon Strachan. We included the likes of Dave Bamber, Ken De Mange, Heremaia (Harry) Ngata (an unused substitute on the day) and the late Iain Hesford in goal. We did have some excellence as well mind, with the likes of Wayne Jacobs, Richard Jobson and Andy Payton.

On the day we gave them a run for their money.

TWS went in front through a Lee Hendrie header (from outside the box) which looped over the tracksuit bottomed Hesford, who later became a publican I believe and was the only player I've seen smash the frame of the goal, and stop play in an away fixture at Sunderland. City equalised through a Payton penalty, only for Vinnie Jones to hit a thirty yard worldy. More famous for grabbing Gazza's testicles, I do believe he was actually an under rated player.

Another Payton penalty saw us equalise and then we went 3-2 in front through a Bobby Doyle screamer, which was a match for Vinnies effort, with only ten minutes or so to go. Imre Varadi equalised and then the diminutive Strachan broke City hearts when he struck the winner in the 92nd minute.

Leeds went on to win the league that year. City finished fourteenth in our usual no-mans land.

From then on our paths never crossed again until 2005. We were free to play the likes of Chester and Scarborough while they entertained the so called big boys.

Even when we did eventually meet up again, we failed to beat them at Elland Road, and we had to go all the way back to 1987 since we'd last beat them on their patch.

That was until September 2012, our second promotion year from the Championship. This fixture was a weird experience for me as I didn't watch the game from the usual designated away seats. By this time, I'd become friends with Jon Booth, who I have already introduced by way of being our guest at the recent Derby home fixture.

For this particular L**ds away fixture, Jon had asked if I wanted to join him for the evening. A couple of pints in the Billy Bremner suite and then watch the game from his usual seats in the West Stand. It felt rude to say no!

Clearly I wasn't thinking properly. Maybe I just expected City to get rolled over again and it would be relatively easy to get through the full ninety minutes sitting with the opposition.

Now I'm not sure if you've ever watched a City game from the opposition seats but it's not that easy. Particularly when the team you're supporting secure a first away win at a ground for twenty five years. You simply can't just sit on your hands and not show any emotion.

On this night, we were sat just about on the half way line, clearly no colours on show. We could see the City faithful just to our right hand side (no longer being housed in what I like to call the cheese slice of yellow seats which used to accommodate away fans).

The game started in a usual manner for a City game at L**ds. L**ds were awarded an early penalty when that lovely gentleman El Hadj Diouf theatrically fell to the ground. It wasn't even in the box. Spot kick was duly despatched and City trailed 1-0. However, City came roaring back and late in the first half, we led 2-1 thanks to goals from Elmo and Faye.

I greeted the first goal with an inner smile, the second with a mini fist pump low down, that only I could see. The groans around me as the second went in made me chuckle, very quietly.

City were the better team and with about fifteen minutes to go, a swift counter attack saw Koren sweep the ball home. 3-1 up and game over surely. I momentarily forgot where I was, stood up and celebrated, pumping my fist in the air and shouting *"Fucking get in there"*. Whoops!

I promptly sat down kind of hoping that nobody had noticed. The fact that obviously nobody else had stood up made it a bit clear to see. Some of those that noticed were not shy of telling me what they thought. Fortunately Jon calmed them down and other than a few sly knees in the back near full time, no lasting damage was done. Good job I wasn't sat in their South Stand.

The remainder of the match was spent with eyes focused on the pitch, ensuring no eye contact was made with those sat near. L**ds scored a very late consolation goal which led to some ironic comments coming my way, but it wasn't enough and City held on for a 3-2 victory.

City eventually got promoted in the runners up spot, TWS finished thirteenth. Almost the polar opposite of that first Elland Road experience back in 1989. That's football for you I suppose, it can go in cycles.

So in all, todays match was nothing overly special to me. Just hopefully another chance to get three points. L**ds had only won one home game all season.

We'd nearly decided not to go. This weekend was the first event of Tribfest at Sea, an event where a lot of tribute bands play on the ferry out of Hull to Rotterdam, ultimately onto Amsterdam and back. What a way to spend the weekend, drinking copious amounts of alcohol, watching live music and then visiting Amsterdam, with all that it has to offer.

Next year, once this book is out of the way, we'll definitely go!

Today though, seven of us travelled together. Tony and Taylor Cline, Taffy, Big Al, James Lee, Thomas and myself. We parked up at The Drysalters pub as it provides the best and quickest means to get away post match, and is also open to visiting supporters.

In here we experienced the fact that the youth of today cannot help themselves when surrounded by electronic equipment. Taylor and Thomas found themselves sat right in front of what I think was the PA system, probably used on karaoke nights in the pub. Little fingers were soon pressing buttons resulting in loud noises being emitted. This soon stopped when the rather rotund, heavily tattooed, and menancing looking glass collector told them, in no uncertain terms, to stop it. The boys looked a bit sheepish and asked when were we leaving.

A short walk to the ground and the game soon started. Well L**ds did and City didn't. During the first half, L**ds were 'up for it' much more and won most tackles, were first to the ball and generally more incisive. We looked laboured and sluggish.

This seasons particular fixture against TWS had been surrounded by a certain amount of furore over the current L**ds owner, Massimo Cellino, with regards to his now entitled 'Pie Tax'.

Basically, in another way to try and extort more hard earned money out of football spectators, the club had forced spectators in the South Stand to pay for food and drink, whether they wanted it or not. This was achieved by making them all pay a £5 increase on their usual matchday ticket, which can be redeemed at the catering kiosks. It's not as if the tickets at L**ds are not high enough already.

Certain sections of the L**ds fans had called for a walkout on the seventeenth minute (Cellino having a superstitious dislike of the number seventeen) in protest at the price hike, dubbed the 'pie tax' by fans.

As it turned out, it was all a bit of a damp squib as only a smattering of L**ds fans actually did walk out. A small minority actually threw some pies onto the pitch. Had Hesford of that 1989 match still been playing, I dare to suggest that he might have actually picked one up and eaten it.

The terrace banter was evident as usual with chants of;

"Sit down and eat your pie, sit down and eat your pie" and

"That is embarrassing, that is embarrassing" when hardly anyone walked out.

An early injury to Alex Bruce and Davies came on to replace him. We'd later finish the game with Huddlestone at centre back when Maguire also went off injured, albeit by then the damage was done.

It came as no surprise when TWS took the lead on the half hour mark, although it all seemed a bit easy. A ball down the L**ds right dissected Robertson, and Stuart Dallas crossed easily and Chris Wood glanced a neat finish past McGregor. Overall I thought Wood had a good game for L**ds today. A target man who can hold the ball up, something I seem to have been craving for.

Wood promptly celebrated in front of the South Stand, standing on the advertising boards, arms aloft. The L**ds fans surged forward, one over the barrier to celebrate with Wood directly, embracing him. It was all fairly harmless but some over zealous stewarding soon ensured that the fan would see no further part of the action, as he was unceremoniously dragged out of the ground. He was later followed by a colleague who decided it would be a good idea to throw a punch or two at a steward. Not the wisest of moves. Cue the heavy handed old bill this time to escort him off the premises, about six of them.

L**ds continued to press and harry City, putting them off their stride, not that we'd got into one, and they generally had much more intensity to their game.

Things got worse when on the stroke of half time, some lacklustre defending and ball watching, allowed time for Adeyemi to slam a shot home from close range. City coming from behind to win in recent times is a rare thing, but from two-nil down, practically unheard of.

Half time came, we sat down having stood as is usual at an away game, and I contemplated what Tribfest at Sea was like. The first half City showing had been beyond awful.

A bit of banter took place on the terraces. TWS mocked us by singing *"You should have gone Christmas shopping, gone Christmas shopping"*.

Rather below the belt, City replied with, *"He's one of your own, he's one of your own, Jimmy Saville, he's one of your own."*

The second half was a completely different affair. City came out and bossed it. We quickly pulled a goal back when Elmo headed in from close range. Game on. It was like the Alamo, just without loads of clear cut chances, if you can have such a thing. The ball spent almost all of its time in the L**ds half, but not in their net. Had we scored again soon after Elmo's goal then we very well might have gone on to win it. However we didn't. Akpom had a great chance near the end but somehow headed wide. The minutes ticked by and L**ds hung on.

Overall for 'their' first half display, they probably deserved the win. Overall for 'our' first half display, we didn't.

Steve Bruce summed it up pretty well with his post match comments and I paraphrase,

"We've had an awful week. That first forty five minutes was as bad as I have seen from us since I came here. I don't give a monkeys what names are on the shirts, but the next time we play, I will have a team that shows the right attitude. You have to win your headers, and tackles and earn the right to play. We did that in the second half when we were relentless, but the first half was unacceptable. If we are going to challenge (for promotion), we have to make sure we do better than that"

Couldn't have said it better myself Steve. Can you sort it out for the next game please.

"...SHOULD HAVE GONE CHRISTMAS SHOPPING.."

CHAPTER 32

BOLTON WANDERERS (H) – SATURDAY 12TH DECEMBER 2015

"STOP THE MUSIC"

Today we had the chance to make a statement to the rest of the league. If we really do have aspirations of promotion, then today was a fixture that should have been a convincing win and three points.

City were still in the upper echelons of the league, Bolton were bottom. It is fair to say that Bolton are in a right mess.

They had won only one game in the nineteen they'd played so far this season, and they stood rooted at the bottom of the league.

The manager Neil Lennon was also under the spotlight. Allegedly Mr Lennon had been engaging in extra curricular activities with not one, but two women, in addition to his partner. When one of the women threatened to go public with details of their affair, it was claimed that Lennon told her, '*he could put a knife to her throat*'. Hardly the backdrop to encourage a struggling team.

Bolton are also in financial meltdown. Their current owner, Eddie Davies, had gone on for a number of years basically lending the club millions after millions of pounds. First it was £30 million, and at the last count as shown by the most recent accounts, it was £172 million. That is a staggering amount of money and obvious questions of '*where's all the money gone*' are posed. It beggars belief how both the owner and club allowed it to get so high, they clearly got the most basic business rule wrong, spending more than you earn.

The recent years of doing well in The Premier League are all very well and good from a football point of view, but clearly throughout that time, Bolton were living well beyond their means. Maybe they thought it was okay as it was the owners money and not borrowed from a financial institution, but it wasn't okay.

Debt is bad in football, just ask L**ds and Portsmouth, to name a few.

Bolton's owner has now said enough is enough. His lending is no more and who can blame him. However the underlying problems still remain, living beyond your means, especially as they are now plying their trade in The Championship, and not The Premier League. The owner is prepared to write off the vast majority of his £172 million loan and is looking for someone to sell to. But what is it though that is actually up for sale?

Whilst this is all taking place, insolvency experts have been brought in, training grounds are up for sale, car parks up for sale, players and staff have not been paid their wages and the taxman has issued winding up proceedings.

All sound very familiar even if some of the numbers are different?

Take note Chelski or Man City, and others, What if your owner(s) were to suddenly stop the money pipeline. Could you survive?

So as Bolton now struggle at the bottom of the second tier with no money to improve the team and praying for a fairy godmother to magic them out of the mess they are in, I wonder if those fans think the good times recently had were worth it.

Today we had the opportunity to ask as we were joined by a good pal, Ged Lees and son Matthew who are both Bolton supporters. The Lees family now live in York and we had selected both this seasons fixtures for a get together, an excuse for a few pints and a bit of football.

As it turned out, about another twenty people or so attended the get together, as the football widow had decided to invite a load of people round for the evening. She was therefore up to her neck in it, cooking, baking and whatever else. We therefore chose to get out of her way and departed towards the KC soon after the Lees had arrived.

I asked Ged about Bolton's current predicament and he did admit to having fallen out of love with football a little at the moment. Understandable I suppose. He struggled to see what possible outcome there could be other than almost inevitable administration, if a buyer could not be found soon. This in itself would lead to a hefty points deduction, not something a team at the bottom of the league requires in their fight for survival.

However Ged fondly reminisced of attending various Bolton games, in particular the 2007/08 season, which whilst not their best finish in The Premier League, did culminate in reaching the last sixteen of the UEFA Cup. This included a 2-2 draw away at Bayern Munich, during an unbeaten group stage. They then went on to knock out Athletico Madrid before eventually going out to Sporting Lisbon. Not a bad sounding campaign.

Their squad list was also fairly impressive, including the likes of Nicolas Anelka, Gary Cahill, Jussi Jaaskelainen, Ivan Campo, Gary Speed, Kevin Nolan and Kevin Davies.

I told Ged that 2007/08 was also a pretty good season for Hull City with a first ever promotion to The Premier League courtesy of the play offs.

We also recalled previous games between the two teams.

Ged distinctly remembered a game back at Boothferry Park in April 1993, when a certain Phil Brown was playing right back for Bolton, as they were on course for promotion. City were not and eventually finished in twentieth place.

Bolton were down to ten men after Alan Stubbs had been sent off, and as the game entered its last ten minutes, the score was level at 1-1. Then John McGinley diverted a shot into the net and many of the travelling Bolton fans got on the pitch. Ged didn't confess if he was one of them fearing a very delayed banning order. The game was delayed for several minutes as fans spilled out in front of the supermarket North Stand and North East corner (which was still open in those days), and when eventually restarted, Bolton went on to win 2-1 and ultimately gain promotion.

There would be no pitch invasion today as firstly, there was a very poor Bolton following, and secondly, they had very little to celebrate.

I recalled City playing away at Bolton back in a League Cup tie during David Lloyds regime. Unhappy with Lloyds antics, the City fans decided to grab some media attention and make a statement. The Bolton match was selected and rather than a pitch invasion, it was decided that several hundred tennis balls be thrown on the pitch to disrupt the game. This was amusingly ironic as Lloyd, a former tennis pro, was at the time, the Davis Cup captain. It was noted by Lloyd who soon after departed City. As a post script note, in February 2016 very similar actions were taken by Borussia Dortmund fans as a protest against high ticket prices. Bloody copy cats!

I also recall our last trip to Bolton in February 2013 when, again attending with Ged and Matthew, City were on the wrong end of a result. In the car on the way there we all gave our score predictions. Matthew suggested a 4-1 victory to Bolton. Ged and I immediately laughed and told him to stop talking silly. What does over sixty combined years of football following mean. City were 3-0 down after about only seven minutes, eventually going on to lose 4-1. Thomas was extremely distraught, but neither Ged or Matthew gloated. They had no reason to as Matthew had gone through with his convictions and put a bet on his 4-1 scoreline so was 'rolling in it'. City eventually got promoted.

As we arrived at the KC, it was pouring down and with all that build up, it felt like it had all the hallmarks of 0-1 home defeat. Ever the pessimist.

The Lees headed towards the away section and we took up our usual position in the South Stand. Due to the unconvincing nature of the game about to unfold, we kept in regular contact during the ninety minutes via text. Never happy, I bemoaned the quality of City's play, Ged just replied, "*Try being a Bolton fan*".

Dawson, Davies, Meyler and Akpom were recalled to the starting eleven following back to back defeats to Derby and L**ds, but Hernandez was missing.

The current plight of Bolton was aptly summed up after only three minutes when one of their free kicks was smashed into the head of one of their own players, who was completely poleaxed.

City soon began to impose themselves and opened the scoring within twenty minutes. Akpom fed the overlapping Clucas, whose cross was met with a volley by Elmo. His shot was blocked by David Wheater on the line, but the ball fell to Akpom to fire home past Ben Amos in the Bolton goal. Just the luck when you are at the bottom, but all good stuff for us.

What immediately followed was not good stuff.

For the first time ever at the KC, someone had the idea to play that awful thing that is music immediately after a goal. And so 'Tiger Feet' boomed across the PA. Almost immediately and midway through a goal celebration, (something that should be the highlight of any football experience) the cheers turned into boo's. And just after we'd scored!

Charlotte even turned to me and said, *"Get that off, that is embarrassing"*. I couldn't argue. Fortunately it was the first and last time it happened as social media went in meltdown with its disapproval.

And almost from that moment on, any atmosphere was lost. This was replicated on the pitch and the game was extremely 'patchy'. Bolton were poor, a team devoid of confidence, merely happy to stop City scoring, being negative and time wasting even when they were losing. What's that all about?

The referee wasn't helping either, being over officious, blowing for lots of free kicks and then insisting they be retaken from 'exactly' the spot he chose.

Bolton posed a little more threat just after the break and Neil Danns struck the base of a post, but chances for either side were at a premium. City needed to score a second but didn't and so we had to leave thinking City could have done more. Whilst the 1-0 win wasn't overly impressive, it was very welcome. Co-inciding with draws for both Brighton and Middlesbrough, we made up some ground and moved up to third.

The win did come at a price though as just before the end, captain Michael Dawson limped off. This was his first game back from injury and it was later revealed that he'd go on to miss another six weeks or so.

As we descended into the depths of the Hull night, I refrained from ribbing Ged and Matthew. Instead we returned to feast on the football widows culinary delights and get pissed in football harmony.

"... WHERE'S YOUR MONEY GONE, WHERE'S YOUR MONEY GONE ?...."

CHAPTER 33

"NEVER LEAVE EARLY"

Following the rather drab and tame affair at home to Bolton (albeit we still chalked up three points), we had the chance to accumulate some more points with another eminently winnable home game against Reading.

As the season is progressing, I'm trying to recall if we swaggered our way through many matches in our last Championship promotion season. To be honest, I don't think we did. Lots of close affairs won by the odd goal but constantly picking up and accumulating points. I think that pretty much sums up how to get out of this league.

After tonight, we'll have played all but two of the sides in the league and possibly with the exception of Derby, I've not seen any team that has really impressed me. So there is nothing to stop us ensuring a top two place. All we need to do is stay somewhere near averaging two points a game and that should guarantee a top two slot.

So despite having tailed off a bit since the Middlesbrough and Brentford games, I was still fairly optimistic going into this particular fixture.

That being said, we had the curse of the Sky TV cameras on us again. In December, Sky were running a thing whereby they screened ten live football league games in ten days, with Ian Holloway attending all ten, providing the alleged expert comments. This was game number six in the ten game saga, and as a result our normal Tuesday night midweek slot had been moved back to Wednesday. How dare they once again mess up our rituals.

It also brought back the return of Super Paul McShane, and Stephen Quinn or Quiniesta, as we fondly referred to him. In my mind both had been good servants to City during their time and I'm sure they could have added something to this season's squad. But this was not to be the case and both had moved on to Reading. Our loss, their gain.

McShane in particular always gave 100% on the field, always typifying the phrase 'he bleeds black and amber' This was demonstrated in the final league game last season against Manchester United when carrying on after being savaged by the terrible Marouane Fellaini. Whilst Quinesta didn't actually make it off the bench tonight, both players received a great reception from the City faithful.

There was a new City fan sat next to us tonight which caused me a little snigger. He must have been about six foot nine or so and looked extremely uncomfortable, his legs crammed behind the seat in front, knees almost in the back of the spectator in front.

Injury to Michael Dawson at the end of the Bolton game meant a start for Harry Maguire, and fit again Hernandez replaced Diame up front. Livermore was handed the captains armband in Dawson's absence and he eventually won us the match with a captain's inspired fightback.

Yes for the first time in a long long time, City actually came from behind to win a game. I think we last achieved this against Sunderland on Boxing Day, almost a year ago. Admittedly we don't lose many games from winning positions which is why it seems to be so important to score the first goal.

So why oh why do we recently seem to be so slow out of the blocks in games, serving up mediocre first half performances? Tonight's first half showing was one to forget, it almost gave the showing at TWS a run for its money, almost but not quite.

It can be extremely frustrating to see this City side repeatedly decline the chance to seize the initiative in games, granting it instead to so called lesser sides. This gives them more confidence from unexpectedly matching us. Tonight Reading were in the ascendancy for the majority of the first forty five minutes.

City went sideways and backwards and seemed to be playing several long balls which came to nothing, and effectively gave Reading the ball for the main. Reading in contrast made intelligent runs and caused us all sorts of problems. We'd had a couple of early warning signs with McGregor twice saving well early on, and Odubajo made a good last ditch tackle on Vydra.

So it was no surprise when Reading finally took the lead, and it was a very good goal, even if it pains me to say so. Robertson was attacked down the left and the ball was passed across the edge of our box. Two slick lay offs led to Blackman free in the box and he produced an unerring finish to smash the ball into the far corner.

Whilst falling short of actually applauding the goal, I nodded in appreciation. I'd have been proud had City scored such a goal. Charlotte looked at me and asked what I was doing. I just tried to explain that I thought it was a very good goal. "*How can it be*" she asked, "*We didn't score it.*"

City continued to struggle and there were mutterings of frustration eventually leading to chants of "*This is embarrassing, this is embarrassing.*"

Blackman came close again just before half time clipping the top of the bar with a free kick and to be honest, it was a relief when the half time whistle came. Nearly all of City's players had been ineffective, barring Livermore.

Big Billy Whitehurst, the guest on the pitch at half time summed it up when asked by Steve Jordan what he thought of the first half. Billy, never one to waste words, just replied "*Crap*".

Surprisingly no substitutions were made at half time but as later revealed during a post match interview, Moses Odubajo did say that they'd all been given a 'rocket up the arse' during half time. Too bloody right they were.

It at least meant that the City players did come out with more urgency. In contrast, and for some reason, Reading, rather than going for a second goal and maybe killing the game off, decided to stick with what they'd got and turn to time wasting.

This all contrived to help City start to create some half chances. Odubajo should have scored and sensing the tide was turning, the North Stand really started getting behind the team. Chorus' of "*We're Hull City, we're Hull City, everywhere we go, everyone will know, we're Hull City*" echoed around the KC, and near the hour mark we equalised.

Hernandez played in Clucas, who in turn found Elmo. His shot was well saved by Bond in the Reading goal, but 'Johny on the spot' Hernandez was there to pick up the rebound and poke home from his customary range of about three yards. One all and now game on.

It's worth pointing out that after the hype following the 'goal music' at the Bolton game, thank god we were not repeated to another rendition of Tiger Feet. The PA was noticeably quiet. Instead the razzamatazz on display was large City flags being unfurled by the ball boys, very akin to Arsenal.

City looked reborn after equalising and looked a different side to that of the first half. Reading a shadow of themselves, and purely intent on slowing the game up to waste time.

The next chance fell to Akpom, who after a one two with Hernandez, only had the keeper to beat. He didn't and the keeper pushed the ball over the bar. Moments later, Akpom was promptly substituted. Had he scored he may not have been.

Wearing the ridiculous combo of short sleeves and gloves, Akpom decided to spit his dummy out. Approaching the dugout, he angrily threw his gloves into the floor, clearly not agreeing with the managers decision. Bruce gave him a stare that almost said, *'get used to the bench for a bit son'*. In fairness, Akpom apologised for his reaction afterwards on social media, but I suspect he'll have to work hard for a starting berth now.

We entered the final few minutes of normal time and as is common place at the KC, I observed many home fans leaving early. Why?

City continued to press and with the clock ticking down, Reading ended up with only ten men. Their left back got injured right near the East Stand touchline, and whilst remaining on the pitch about a yard in, clearly in an attempt to waste more time, he was finally ordered to leave. They'd already made all their substitutions in previous attempts to waste time.

And then City snatched victory. Never a better time to score a winner.

Odubajo burst past a Reading defender and pulled the ball back to substitute Snodgrass. He laid it off to the other subs, Maloney and in turn to Diomande. All three appeared to pass up the opportunity to score but eventually the ball rebounded off the Reading keeper and Jake Livermore arrived to thunder the ball home. 2-1 City. Those early leavers would be regretting it now!

With all the previous time wasting, the fourth official displayed seven minutes of injury time to groans from the home crowd. We needn't have worried as the king of all time wasters, Alan McGregor came to the fore. He expertly wound the clock down, comically 'accidently' kicking the ball away when bending down to pick it up. Take note Reading for future.

No scares were encountered by City. In fact Meyler had a chance to add a third but much to my dismay (as I had a few quid on a 3-1 home win) he failed, pulling a tired shot wide after running half the pitch.

The final whistle blew shortly after and we all filed out relieved, but ecstatic after a fairly dramatic finale.

Can we please just do it the easy way next time though, and start matches like we finished this one? Who knows how important that last minute winner might be come the end of the season.

"...LIVERMORE, LIVERMORE. LIVERMORE, LIVERMORE..."

CHAPTER 34

ROTHERHAM UNITED (A) – SATURDAY 19TH DECEMBER 2015

"HOW SHIT MUST WE BE, YOU'RE WINNING AT HOME"

Let's get this out of the way, this is probably going to be a fairly depressing chapter.

After a poor performance in our previous away game at L**ds, followed by a fairly abject display at home against Bolton (albeit ending in victory), this showing capped both. It's safe to say that this was the most disappointed I had felt so far this season.

During the weeks build up to the game, Rotherham's manager, Neil Redfearn, was quoted as saying that his team were nowhere near good enough for The Championship. Their lowly league position also suggested as such, and they had only won two games at home thus far. Surely a formality then, may as well just give the three points to Hull City.

Unfortunately things do not work out that way and are never that easy.

The day started off reasonably well, but eventually went very down hill.

A fair number of us had met up for a few pre match ales. The initial proposed meeting point, an ex Railway Servicemans pub, proved to be fruitless, as the curtains were shut and no-one was at home! So a quick walk down the road saw us end up in The Prince of Wales for a few pints.

Already Thomas wasn't happy as there was no grub on sale.

This was City's first visit to the New York Stadium. It's okay, but smacks of never wanting to really hit the big time. The old Millmoor ground is in very close proximity and this brought back memories of a couple of visits there.

The first involved me travelling to a cup tie on my first 'Special', the days when British Rail, as it still was, would put on a train just for visiting supporters. They were usually carnage with empty beer cans rolling around the carriages. They were fun but have long since stopped.

The last was all the way back on 28th December 1997 in the old Division Three when City came out on the wrong end of a 5-4 defeat. If memory serves me right, I think it was a lunchtime kick off as I ended up going with a few inhabitants of the Cross Keys pub, including the then landlord.

Rotherham raced into a 5-1 lead, Lee Glover helping himself to four goals in the process. City roared back with Duane Darby and Glyn Hodges both getting braces to pull it back to 5-4. City then piled on the pressure and we were thinking of an improbable 6-5 'Orient-esque' comeback (where we came back from 4-1 down to win 5-4, although I can't claim to have been there). The late surge, very much like most of City's history in the 90's, didn't end in victory though.

However, we had fully enjoyed the afternoon, and as the pub landlord had accompanied us, it qualified us for an extremely late night session back in Cottingham.

Our seats today were on the very front row and we planned a goal celebration should City score at our end and celebrate just in front of us. This would have involved us throwing on a City scarf and hat to see if the scorer would don it. We may as well have left them in our bag, we weren't to trouble the scoreboard today.

A quick blast of 'She Sells Sanctuary' by The Cult (great tune) before kick off had me humming and tapping my feet. Thomas, by now tucking into a pie, looked at me, shook his head, and told me I was embarrassing. He may have a point.

And then it started raining, we got wet and the match started. This didn't cheer us up either.

Almost from the off, our display was nowhere near good enough for the calibre of our squad. A squad that just a few weeks ago blew away Middlesbrough, and looked so impressive.

Rotherham fielded five in midfield and just seemed to outfight us and want it more. That being said, without our assistance, I'm still not sure whether they would have scored or not. Both their goals arose from a great deal of help from us.

Midway through the first half, Odubajo conceded a penalty after he dallied in trying to clear a corner and then clumsily tripped a Rotherham player. It was a penalty and Lee Frecklington smashed the ball home.

Akpom had a good chance to equalise just before half time when Hernandez fizzed a ball to him across the box, but despite being only a few yards out, he appeared to try and chest the ball in, and completely fluffed it.

City started better in the early parts of the second half and when Robertson burst away to play in Akpom, we were ready with our hat and scarf for the ensuing celebrations. No, Akpoms shot beat Lee Camp, but bounced back out off the upright. Bollocks.

And then on the hour, the other full back, Robertson, lost possession just outside our box to Joe Newall, who promptly, smashed the ball past McGregor. 2-0 down and a mountain to climb.

However, despite enjoying over 60% possession and having eighteen shots (only three on target), you just knew we'd end up with nil. Not for the lack of chances though. Livermore played a lovely ball through, again for Akpom, who thinking he was offside (he wasn't), simply didn't bother going for it, and stood motionless.

It wasn't Akpoms day as shortly after, he broke clear, beat Camp, but once again, saw his effort cannon off the same post he'd hit earlier. He then failed to play in Hernandez, unmarked only six yards out, choosing instead to shoot himself, a shot that was saved at the near post. Hernandez flayed his arms, as did many of the City following.

Maguire could have scored a consolation goal late on when I believe he headed wide at the back post, unchallenged from a corner. I missed it as I was untying our flag. I'd had enough and wanted to get out of there.

The PA blasted out Frank Sinatra's 'New York, New York' to rejoice their victory. *"Fuck off"*, I mumbled. We then sneaked away, almost unnoticed.

We left feeling very dejected and the car journey home was quieter than normal, all of us trying to fathom out what was going wrong with City's performances. Over to you Steve Bruce.

What is more worrying, is not necessarily the results, it's the insipid performances. I understand a player, or players, having an off day, but being outfought by teams, which are clearly nowhere near as good as us, is unacceptable. However, Steve Bruce has experience of all this, his CV says so. We have to remain confident that he will turn it around.

We are still in a decent position and well placed to challenge for promotion. We just need to halt this slide sooner rather than later, and as the banner says, 'In Bruce We Trust'.

As I sat at home later in the evening, trying not to look at the league table, and work out what it would have looked like had we won and not lost, my mind turned to recall games where I'd come away feeling as dejected.

My history of watching City could produce a long list, but one sprang to mind and hopefully this story will lift the rather downbeat mood somewhat. It certainly brought a smile to my face.

I'm taking you back to the days of Mark Hateley!

When Mark arrived at Boothferry Park, there had been little to cheer about. Things were bad. So the arrival of an ex England player, prolific in front of goal at a number of big name clubs, as our new player manager really led us to believe that things were going to improve. He had an enormous ego and we went along with it (initially at least).

His opening game of the 1997/98 season saw us trek over to Field Mill to take on Mansfield with renewed optimism. We lost 2-0, convincingly!

The season was a disaster and we eventually finished third bottom of the old Third Division. Due to an injury, Hateley didn't play between October and April. In all, he made fourteen appearances that season and didn't manage to find the back of the net. The renewed optimism had all but evaporated.

However, we'd survived the season and as all of us football fans do, we looked forward to the next season with blind faith. Surely in the 1998/99 season, Hateley would show us the skills he used to produce?

So after he finally got on the score sheet (at a game I did not attend) in a 2-2 draw at the mighty Chester City, I thought that was it. Next up was a home game against Peterborough United, the second home game of the 1998/99 season. I was convinced that I'd see him score for City, for the first time with my own eyes.

This was pre-marital days for me, so the Friday night involved the usual ritual of going down to the pub. Whilst there, I engaged in conversation with one of the young barmaids, who expressed an interest in watching Hull City. As the conversation developed, it was agreed that I'd pick her up the following day and we'd go to 'Fer Ark', watch the game, and then go out for a few drinks thereafter. Result.

So, after a splash of after shave, I duly turned up expecting both a Hateley goal, victory for City, a few drinks, and then who knows what?! Happy Days.

We took our position towards the back of the terracing on Bunkers Hill in a relatively sparse crowd of just over four and a half thousand (things were really that bad).

We watched Hateley run his hands through his long, slightly receding locks with almost visible bald patch, and waited in anticipation. This was going to be the day.

Peterborough started in the ascendancy, Steve Wilson pulling off a number of good saves to keep the score at nil nil.

My partner for the day then proceeded to light up (you could at football grounds in those days). As I looked closer, this was not a Benson and Hedges, it was a pre rolled joint. The smell of weed permeated through the air and all eyes turned focus from the pitch to see which spectator had the audacity to light up in such a public place. I made no eye contact with anyone but could feel myself edging away, distancing myself as if to say, *'she's not with me'.*

And then, ten minutes or so later, her legs gave way! Her feet slipped on the decaying crumbling steps and she bounced off any spectators within her proximity. It was like the parting of The Red Sea until eventually she came to her resting place, face down, legs akimbo.

For a split second, I contemplated doing a runner. But my good nature got the better of me and I went to her assistance. After all, I may have needed to get served in the pub by her at some point in the near future.

A fellow spectator helped me drag her to the concourse and then a steward also helped her into a wheelchair. Her legs were like jelly, they'd gone. I shook my head, but just thought the sooner I get rid of her the better. I agreed with the steward that I'd leave her there while I quickly collected my car to come and take her home. I legged it out of the ground, collected my car and drove right up to the South Stand turnstiles.

For those that can recall, to get out the back of the South Stand, you had to go down a number of steps. This was slightly problematical for someone who had temporarily lost use of their legs, but eventually the steward and I managed it, both of her legs clattering against each step. Finally, I shovelled her into the passenger seat of my Ford Fiesta.

This had all taken place in the first half and just as I was about to climb in the car myself, the home crowd cheered. Not that I knew at the time, but Hateley had taken advantage of a shove in the box, fallen over and won a penalty. Needless to say, he promptly demanded the ball and beat the Peterborough keeper to score his first home City goal. I'd missed it!

I looked to the heavens, put the keys in the ignition and sped off. Miss Jamaican Weed just gazed straight ahead, totally oblivious of what had just happened. As I dropped her off at her house, her brother answered the door, clearly in an equivalent state. Bad choice I'd made eh?!

I descended back to the pub and eventually went home alone.

Hateley never did score another home goal. He did score away at Scarborough but I missed that as well, and eventually in November, he was sacked. It was down to Warren Joyce to rescue the season, later to be dubbed as 'The Great Escape', finishing fourth from bottom, with Scarborough being relegated from the Football League.

Moral of the story?

In these recent times, when you think things are bad at City, believe me, they aren't!

"...STEVE BRUCE...IN BRUCE WE TRUST..."
(NOT MARK HATELEY!)

CHAPTER 35

"WE'VE ONLY GONE AND BEATEN THEM"

Normally I'd say that I always look forward to a Boxing Day fixture. The attendances are usually up and there seems to be more atmosphere. It also gets you out the house and stop you eating more turkey and chocolates, and if nothing else, it always seems like a good excuse to have a couple more beers. That is unless you end up playing an away game umpteen miles away.

Or even worse, against bloody Burnley!

That was our prospect today. Up at home against our nemesis. I think the statistics showed that in the last ten meetings against Burnley, we'd won one and lost the rest. Hardly awe inspiring.

And then, the last time we played them, I came up with this stupid notion of then trying to attend every game and writing a book.

Anyway no point moaning about it. We've got to play everybody twice at some point, and poor runs are there to be broken eh?

It being Boxing Day, the whole family had decided to go. The football widow did the honourable thing in driving and it was agreed that we'd venture into The Malt Shovel for a couple of jars pre match.

This was much to Charlotte's dismay. A pub full of sweaty middle aged men, drinking beer and predominantly talking nothing but football. She buggered off with Thomas for half an hour or so to get something to eat, returning to see the entertainment.

This was like going back in time, as on show this afternoon was Play Your Cards Right. Bri Lee was doing his best to be Bruce Forsyth, but he'd unfortunately not brought along any 'Dolly Dealers'.

A quid bought you the chance to shout out the usual 'higher' or 'lower' predictions, first to finish taking the pot. We don't go for anything too complicated in Hull. Today between us, we either couldn't count or as Mr Forsyth would say, *"nothing for a pair in this game"*, or *"what an awful deck of cards this week"*.

Nobody seemed capable of winning it as time after time, the participants failed to predict correctly. Some people sat there with a fivers worth of tickets hoping to get their number called out for the chance to win. There were already suspicions of a fix when practically the whole Lee family had been called up, and then Bri's dads number was drawn out.

A chorus of *"He only bought one ticket, he only bought one ticket"* rung around the pub. Nonechalantly, Bri Lee Senior called them all right, collected a pot full of £1 coins and returned to his seat, half pint of bitter in hand and grinning like a Cheshire cat!

Fun and games over, we vacated the pub and headed up Anlaby Road. Now if there is one good thing I can comment about Burnley, it has come as a direct result of trying to write this book.

After finally meeting my preferred printer, Duncan at YPS in York, one of the books he'd help to print and publish was one entitled "Got to Be There". It's written by, in his own words, an extreme supporter.

The author is a chap who, due to his own devotion and love of his team, changed his name by deed poll to Dave Burnley (he said he is an extreme supporter).

The book tracks through the years and adventures of his travels following Burnley Football Club, regardless of what far flung places they are playing. What makes this all so much more complicated is the fact that Dave lives in an isolated village in the Potteries, some seventy five miles from Turf Moor, and he has never been able to drive. This therefore involves the start and end of each trip requiring a ten mile bike ride to the nearest train station and / or lots of hitching a lift. He perpetually takes a sleeping bag just in case he can't get home, requiring bedding down for the night anywhere, and countless days off work in the numerous jobs he has held. And all of this is always carried out on a shoestring budget.

The book spans an initial twenty three year period up to 1987, seeing Burnley move around all four divisions of The Football League, but no game is too small to consider not attending. During these years, I think he missed one fixture, and this includes all pre season friendlies, either in the UK or abroad, in addition to the then midweek Anglo Scottish Cup fixtures.

He really does take supporting a football team to a new level. Either that or he is barking mad. I'm not trying to plug the book or anything but for football fans, it is genuinely a good and amusing read.

As I entered the turnstiles today, I wondered what Dave Burnley was thinking now. Was he relishing yet another Burnley victory over Hull?

As expected, there was a good away following from Burnley, with the usual array of away supporters for a festive fixture in fancy dress Santa outfits. City meanwhile had placed one of those paper clacker things under everyone's seat with a Christmas message from Steve Bruce. They either get left behind for some poor sods to clear up, or your kids take them home and not content with annoying you with it for ninety minutes at the game, carry on doing it at home. Then, they just leave it to clutter their bedroom up. Fortunately, Thomas, football casual in the making, considers this not to be cool anymore so I'm saved from this fate.

The atmosphere was good today, albeit this wasn't down to the opening exchanges on the pitch. The early stages demonstrated that Burnley were fairly one dimensional, playing either long balls for Andre Gray to chase down the channels, or alternatively and more frequently, to try and find the head of Sam Vokes, hoping to feed off knock downs. Today, this didn't work very well and City coped with it admirably. As Bruce Forsyth might have said, "*We were so much better than last week*" (a reference to the disappointment of Rotherham away).

Maguire was looking comfortable and during a passage of the game, as Maguire shielded the ball out, physically holding off the advances of a Burnley player, I found myself replicating his actions in my seat, actually nudging the bloke sat next to me. I've also been known to head corners home!

Diame had a rasping shot pushed wide, Maguire had a header saved, but generally there were few clear cut chances in the first half. We were generally controlling the game, with Livermore totally out muscling Joey Barton, but for a change, the inevitable Barton red card didn't happen. Last time at the KC, he got red for attempting to punch Huddlestone in the nether regions.

Just prior to Christmas, we had sadly heard the news of another death of a friend of ours, this time Chas Jackson, a fervent City supporter. Chas was a lively character, who always seemed to be in the pubs around Cottingham, hovering around the bandit, ready to move in like a vulture when he thought it was ready to drop.

You'd always know when he was in the pub, as his stand out yellow Mr Bean mini would be parked nearby. On one occasion with Chas not looking, a few of us sneaked outside and literally picked it up, moving it in its parking spot so it was physically impossible for him to get out. It was highly amusing for us watching Chas' face when he went out to it. However, this usually meant he'd just go back in the pub and stay for a few more.

It was a fitting tribute in early January when his funeral was held at a packed out Haltemprice Crematorium, standing room only. Today he was remembered just before half time on the screens.

And with that, as if in tribute to Chas, City came out much better in the second half and put on a display that was far too good for The Clarets. The increase in tempo also saw the atmosphere levels rise, with lots of singing and chanting from both sets of supporters.

It was not long after that City took the lead. Livermore retaining the captains armband in Dawson's absence, again led by example. Just before the hour mark he latched onto a Clucas cross and volleyed past Heaton into the bottom far corner.

From that moment on, there was only one winner. City turned on the pressure. Maguire headed over, Diame shot wide when he could have played Hernandez in. Burnley did have a rare chance when a Dean Marney cross eventually found Gray, but he smashed it wide from about eight yards. Having tried to sign him earlier in the season, this led to the usual derisory chants of "What a waste of money" and "You should have signed for a big club".

He was made to pay for his miss, when soon after Diame found Hernandez, who cut inside and curled a shot past the helpless keeper. 2-0 and definitely game over. I could relax into the back of my seat, rather than perch on the edge.

This time the goal led to chants of "Santa, Santa, what's the score?"

Burnley made a host of substitutions in an attempt to change the game. One of them saw George Boyd taken off to warm applause from the City crowd.

City also made some changes which continued the recent trend of ending the game with no recognised strikers. Today, Clucas finishing off as the loan attacker. No worries though, as the new loan attacker added a third in injury time to complete a comprehensive 3-0 City win.

The win lifted us up to third, just outside the automatic places and this was so much better than at Rotherham and against our 'bogey' team. How can practically the same players produce such differing peformances? Is it a co-incidence that most of our poor performances have been away fixtures, are we not up for the fight?

Soon time to find out. The next fixture is in only a few days time, away at Preston.

"...SANTA, SANTA, WHAT'S THE SCORE?..."

CHAPTER 36

PRESTON (A) – MONDAY 28ᵀᴴ DECEMBER 2015

"DEAD LOSS"

By the time you are reading this, you'll probably know all about this match and result. City were simply shocking.

The previous two away fixtures at TWS and Rotherham had hardly been vintage City away performances; this one surpassed them both.

In between, the home fixtures had somehow all resulted in wins against Bolton, Reading and Burnley with some decent patches of football. In particular the last result against our bogey team had convinced us that maybe our sticky patch was over. Surely we'd go back to performing at the levels we should be capable of? Certainly not on today's showing. How Preston only scored one, I'm not too sure. The trip certainly vanquished any Christmas spirit that was left in us.

There was a decent following from The Cod Army, with around 1,500 fans making the trip to Lancashire. There had been some mild speculation that the fixture may be called off, as during the preceeding few days, both Lancashire and Yorkshire were engulfed in heavy rain, resulting in severe flooding.

In hindsight, we wish this fixture had fallen foul of the weather. But alas, this was not the case, and numerous cars and minibuses were seen on the M62, including one from The Malt Shovel, with the customary beer swilling commencing at nine am. Many a glazed eye were noted at Hartshead Moor Services on the way home, as Ginsters pies were being purchased to soak up the intake. The events in the preceeding few hours will have sobered them up somewhat mind.

Today though for us, it was just Thomas and I making the trip. A busy social calendar (very unlike me!) had meant that the previous day had involved far too much alcohol being drunk in The Dog and Duck, then the Barrel in Walkington, and then back at home. As a result, I was extremely slow to emerge from my pit, Thomas no quicker. A quick slug of Lucozade and intake of painkillers would hopefully address the issue, although I then realised that I had to walk to collect my car, which had been abandoned at the pub the day before.

The fresh air had a slight effect, and I returned to collect Thomas. This did all mean that we were slightly later setting off than was originally planned. Well it would if I ever actually planned anything.

We eventually rolled into the Deepdale area of Preston at just gone two with the traffic at something of a standstill. The sat nav suggested the ground was only just over a mile away and I noticed several cars turning off to park in a nearby cemetery. There were many attendants donning their usual fluorescent jackets, so naturally I assumed that this was a match day parking service. I should have suspected something was not quite right when no attendant actually asked me to line their palm with silver. We just made a hasty retreat, thinking we'd got away without paying, and briskly headed towards the ground, Thomas by now with food on his mind.

We would later discover the error of our ways.

This was a new ground for both of us (not quite sure how it had so far eluded me) so were quite looking forward to the visit. Particularly as the second half display against Burnley had convinced us that we were 'back on track'. Preston had done little in the early season encounter at the KC to suggest anything other than a City win.

What have I already said about expectation rather than hope? I should know better. Why do us football fans so easily try to erase the poor performances, excusing them as a blip? For some reason we'd conveniently forgotten about the Rotherham and L**ds debacles, and the first half displays against Reading, Burnley and most of the Bolton fixture.

So after Thomas had refuelled himself, (my stomach was not yet ready for such a food challenge) we arrived at the ground. A relatively neat little ground, albeit not a patch on the KC. Personally I always think that grounds look complete when the corners are also filled in. This is not the case at Deepdale. Our flag was attached to the seats, albeit nowhere in line with any camera's, so highly unlikely to be seen by anyone, but at least we tried.

A quick Guinness (can at the ridiculous price of £4.50) supped just to check my condition and seats were taken.

For some reason, three major changes were made to the City starting eleven. Diame and Odubajo (who was injured) were dropped, but probably more disappointingly, Hernandez was only on the bench. Instead we opted to play Clucas up front with Akpom and a first start in over fifteen months was given to Snodgrass. Why we couldn't play our top scorer, I'm not sure. I've mentioned it before, but a professional footballer should be capable of playing two or even three games in a week. Hell, comedian Eddie Izzard once ran forty three marathons in fifty one days, he's not even at athlete.

The City following clearly were in agreement, as within minutes of the kick off, Hernandez's name was being sung. Generally the City fans started off in good voice.

Clearly part of 'the job' of football supporters should be to get behind the team, particularly when they are not playing well. However, this can prove to be a challenge when, time after time, the players simply do not perform well. They have to give some sort of excitement to get the fans off their seats. The L**ds and Rotherham performances had tested our patience and this display was even worse. As a result, the support did understandably wain. It was difficult watching and the inevitable just seemed to be about to happen.

Preston could and should have been out of sight by half time. They had numerous gilt edged chances, each of which were squandered. A combination of poor finishing and last gasp deflections somehow kept us at nil nil. We didn't have a shot on target in the first half. Come on City, give me something to write about!

Preston simply wanted it more. They won tackles, pressed us well and some wayward passing by City simply gave the ball back time after time, and seemed incapable of holding it up in any advanced areas. There were many culprits in black and amber.

As I sat at half time, trying to take some positives, I convinced myself that we'd ridden our luck. Maybe we'd keep a clean sheet somehow and nick a 1-0. Stranger things have happened. I must have still been pissed from the night before, deluding myself into that.

Meyler was one of the players made to pay for the first half display and was replaced at the break by Huddlestone. You could have almost taken your pick.

We started slightly better (it couldn't have been much worse) and Tom had our first shot which was pushed just round the post. Akpom was then played through and did actually score, but the linesman had already flagged for offside, not for the first time. The linesman clearly wasn't on our side, as he would re-inforce later on.

Akpom's gloves had returned for the second half. He must have retrieved them from the dugout after the Reading game. It wasn't even cold, but this time he did manage to keep them on after being substituted for Hernandez just after the hour mark. Our brief upturn in performance had just about run out and Preston once again, took control of the game.

A needless and rash challenge by Huddlestone on the right hand edge of our own box, brought him a yellow card and eventually led to Preston taking the lead. The ball was simply crossed in across the floor and Paul Gallagher slid home through a crowded box for a 1-0 lead. It all looked far too easy.

City didn't have an answer. This was Preston for fuck sake, not a promotion rival, but they fully deserved their win. There was some 'harem scarem' football in the last few minutes with City lofting some balls into the box.

Hernandez had an air shot and in the last minute of injury time, a moment of controversy. From a City corner, the ball reached Snodgrass who half hit a shot. The ball found Hernandez who back heeled it goalwards from his customary position inside the six yard box. We were sat on the second row, and from our vantage point, it looked like it had crossed the line, before a Preston player hoofed it clear. Unfortunately the linesman and referee did not share this point of view and almost immediately blew for full time. The City players were convinced it was a goal and a melee then ensued on the pitch. Many City fans also ran down to the perimeter fencing to vent their anger at the decision, and for a split second, I did think a mini pitch invasion was on the cards.

To be fair, it would have been very harsh on Preston if we had snatched a draw. We didn't deserve it (although we would clearly have been delighted by it). Thomas kicked many a plastic seat in frustration, I just chuntered many a swear word. We weren't on our own.

In contrast, the players no doubt had a nice warm bath, and a nap on their luxury coach ahead of a night out clubbing.

We retrieved our flag and trudged back to our car. Why do we bother?

We discussed what was going wrong with City, but simply couldn't come up with any real answers. It's not just as if a selection of players were under performing, it was many, no most of the squad. How can we go from despatching top teams like Middlesbrough and Burnley, to such abject performances against lower placed teams? Is it because we just turn up expecting to win? You could forgive this once, maybe twice at a push, but not on so many occasions.

It is beginning to take the enjoyment out of these away trips. That excitement when you set off for your next adventure, your next chapter of your City experience, a football day out, is being replaced by the anticipation of a dismal performance. I did not want watching City to become a habit or a chore.

Our dismal mood was about to get worse.

Upon finally reaching Preston cemetery, it was very evident that it was closed! Entrance gates, ten foot high, padlocked up, with just one solitary car parked in it…ours! Perhaps it wasn't match day parking after all.

Bollocks, what now..?

We scaled the gates to at least sit in our car and contemplate our next move. I suggested to Thomas that we may need to sleep in the car overnight if we couldn't get out. Clearly he was not too keen on sleeping in a cemetery for the night. A quick drive around clearly showed all gates firmly padlocked, and cemetery office closed.

However, the miracles of modern technology and mobile phones came to our rescue. A quick search on the internet under Preston Council, suggested an out of hours emergency telephone number to call. Two calls later and a friendly old man called Joe said he would be with us in ten minutes to unlock the gate so we could get out. Thomas was relieved to say the least. We'd had enough of Deepdale for one day, in fact for a few seasons.

Thomas just wanted to go home. I was in need of another drink again.

"..WE'RE SHIT AND WE KNOW WE ARE.."

CHAPTER 37

QPR (A) – FRIDAY 1ST JANUARY 2016

"HAPPY BIRTHDAY THOMAS, FROM ROB GREEN"

Now I'm not sure if I was in trouble for this game or not.

Originally the fixture had been scheduled for Saturday 2nd January, which is also Thomas' birthday. As such it was always his choice as to what to do with regards to going to the football. It had been decided that we'd all go away for New Year to Filey, and then on the Saturday, just Thomas and I would get up early and travel to London.

And then Sky decided to move the fixture and bring it forward to New Years Day.

As a result, family discussions then ensued, and Filey was cancelled. We were off to London for a few nights instead, setting off on New Years Day. No influence exerted by myself, honest. It was clearly going to cost us (these southerners know how to charge) and the visa card needed to be ready. The football widow duly arranged train tickets and hotel.

Just prior to the game, the night before made the football widow and I realise that we were getting old and that our kids, well, weren't kids anymore. Charlotte informed us that she'd been invited out to a party, as had Thomas. We hadn't! Whilst Thomas' was just around the corner from our house, Charlotte's required a lift there and back, just after midnight. The football widow kindly volunteered, and being 'Billy No Mates', we decided to gate crash Thomas' party and stay in the kitchen with the adults. Hey, this was no different to the 'night before' preparation for a City match that used to take place years ago. Have a skin full and hope you feel okay the following day. Only slight problem was that the train was due to leave at just gone eight am in the morning.

New Years Day.
The Bunton's on tour in the capital. Christine's favourite watering hole.

Good job then that the football widow acted as the alarm clock and ensured we all got out of our beds and to Brough station on time. We were then promptly informed that our train was no longer going all the way to London, but would be stopping at Doncaster.

Now, train tickets are extremely confusing to me nowadays. Different train companies, supersavers, railcards, etc etc. We were told that for the tickets we had purchased, we needed to then travel from Doncaster to Sheffield, and then on to Kings Cross. This seemed ridiculous, as it effectively added an extra hour and a half to our journey. A quick check of the train listings on the board showed that within the next twenty minutes, there was another direct one to Kings Cross. Stuff it, we decided to jump on this anyway and just smile nicely.

This seemed to work, albeit annoying the jobsworth ticket conductor slightly. She wasn't displaying a lot of New Year cheer.

Whilst we waited for this train, I was amazed by how many other City fans were also there. I'd thought that with the game being on Sky now, and on a New Years Day, that the City turnout would be fairly low. I think just short of one thousand actually made the effort.

We spoke with a group of older City supporters who had been watching City since 1963, one of the party stating that he'd recently attended his 1,000 City away game. Some feat that.

Once arrived in the capital and bags deposited at the hotel, it was off into the bright lights. Well, more like the damp and cold of London, it was freezing.

First up was a few beers in an old haunt of the football widows, The Glassblower pub near Piccadilly Circus. This is a particular pub that the football widow used to frequent with her mum Christine, on numerous visits they used to make to London. Without fail they would ensure at least one drink in the pub. As a family, we have kept up this homage ever since and it helps to bring back fond memories of her. Unfortunately Christine now suffers from dementia and is a shadow of the lovely energetic, full of life person that she used to be. It's a very cruel disease, and in a weird sort of way, is harder for the loved ones of those actually suffering from the ailment. They can see the person slowly slipping away, whilst the individual themselves is actually, fairly oblivious to it all. I'd always intended to donate some of the proceeds or profits (if it ever makes any!) of this book to some charity or other. So as I worked my way down another pint of Guiness sat in The Glassblower talking about the football widows mum and best friend in life, it seemed obvious that the charity should be Alzheimers Research. So thanks for buying this book. Not only do I hope you find it mildly interesting, but you have also contributed to a very worthy cause.

Anyway, this trip was not all about me, so as the bottom of my pint glass was in view, requests from the rest of the family were to do a bit of retail therapy. So Oxford Street it was.

It seemed like the rest of the world was doing the same thing. Far too many people on not wide enough pavements, either dawdling in front of you, or all walking in the opposite direction. However, mission accomplished to some extent, as between them, they ended up with various shopping bags in hand. I was constantly looking at my watch, and Underground map, deciding what time we should be heading for White City on the tube.

Eventually I won and we set off for the match. This was the very first time I was to attend a football match carrying shopping bags! How very football touristy! There was also an insistence as we later entered the turnstiles, that the stewards search each bag. Unfortunately for Charlotte, this meant searching her new Calvin Klein bag, looking through her newly purchased underwear!

Shepherds Bush is a strange part of London, and Loftus Road is not one of my favourite football grounds. The surrounding area all seems a bit run down and the street names all seem a bit odd. Many have South African connections and I was also later to find out that there is even one called Batman Close. No word of a lie, stick it in Google Maps. Some local councillors must have deliberated and actually discussed it at taxpayers expense. Batman Close I give you, you can just see Delboy and Rodney running down there now.

We bumped into my boss William Clark and daughter in law, Zara Holland outside. Zara is the current Miss Great Britain but hey, "*Nah, nah, nah, nah, she's from 'Ull and she's from 'Ull*", they'd both decided to come and watch the next chapter of City's season.

The ground itself doesn't seem to have had much work carried out on it recently and it has about the least leg room ever. The concourse behind the seats for the away fan is miniscule and as for the toilets at half time, you may as well just piss in your empty beer bottle.

We also bumped into an old friend, Jo Irvine, just before kick off and shared a pre match beer. Jo and family were all doing the same as us. All using football and City as an excuse for a weekend away. Or maybe it is actually the football that is bringing us all together? Jo is now a counsellor. I thought I'd make a note of her number just in case City lead me to requiring her services!

Jo promised to send me a little football related story for inclusion somewhere. This duly followed at the Fulham away game. On this day her son Benji had travelled down to London again to follow the fortunes of City. Little did he know that he'd actually gone with both his own and his mum's car keys, and as a result, Jo was housebound for the day. Nothing else to do, she was forced to tune into Burnsey and listen to City.

As the 5.15 kick off time approached, we took our seats, cramming our bags and legs into the small space between the seats in front of us. For some reason today, City performed a pre kick off team huddle and they kicked towards the away end first half.

Our overall performance was certainly not of the heights of the second half display on Boxing Day, but in the end, it was sufficient to overcome a very poor QPR team. This was a limited QPR team devoid of the spearhead in Charlie Austin. To the viewers on Sky, it probably was a pretty boring game. And much of it was, but after appearing to be cruising to victory, we nearly threw two points away, eventually coming out 2-1 winners with a last gasp goal and so our feeling was good. Just the sort of resilient display that promotion seasons are made of? It also moved us back up to second place in the table behind Derby.

The match was restricted to only a few clear cut chances and it took until the hour mark to see the first real passage of skilful play. A fine run by Diame, and exquisite pass with the outside of his foot, set up Hernandez, who smartly volleyed home from about twelve yards to put City one up.

QPR huffed and puffed a bit but it never felt like City were in too much trouble. In fact had we demonstrated a bit more cutting edge in the final third, we could easily have despatched them three or four nil. Maguire put in a good display again and midway through the second half put in a fantastic tackle that left not one, but two QPR players on the floor. Not something you see very often nowadays, where tackling is a bit of a dying art.

However as the cliché goes, a 1-0 win is always a slender one, and with only about three or four minutes remaining, a lovely cross from Matt Phillips saw Polter power home a fine headed equaliser. It seemed like we had thrown two points away.

QPR though were in generous mood and decided to gift City a late Christmas present.

In the final minute, former England goalkeeper Rob Green, came out to meet an inswinging left wing cross from Clucas. As he did, he collided with Grant Hall, and the ball richocheted in, off the unwitting Diomande, who had only come on as a substitute a few minutes earlier. Diomande didn't know an awful lot about it, but at least he was in the right place at the right time, and hell were we grateful.

This was our first away win for two months and hopefully confined those displays at L***ds, Rotherham and Preston to some dark place not to be repeated. The full time whistle soon went and the rest of the family could now enjoy a couple of days in London with me being happy, rather than a miserable old sod.

The next thing to start thinking about was that stupid bloody transfer window. The New Year meant it had opened again and all sorts of rumours would start about whether City players would leave or not. With the expectation of any new arrivals unlikely, it almost goes without saying that we need to keep hold of the vast majority of this squad to give us our best possible chance of promotion.

On the train journey home, I read an interesting article about Jean-Marc Bosman. This was the chap who twenty years ago instigated what is now referred to as the Bosman ruling. Many footballers have been noted for historic events, the Cruyff turn, Fergie time, the Matthews final. But few can have actually changed the game as much as an unknown (at the time) Belgian Standard Liege footballer.

At the time, Bosman wanted to move clubs from Liege to Dunkerque, at the end of his contract. Liege, being in financial trouble, had already cut his wages by 75%, and then demanded a very high transfer fee. Bosman and his lawyers sued Liege, the Belgian FA and UEFA, for restraint of trade. The legal proceedings took five years and no club wanted to touch him. His career was practically over.

Ultimately, twenty years ago, the player emerged from a European Court of Justice with a win that changed football forever, enter the Bosman ruling. From that moment on, players at the end of their contracts could move clubs without a transfer fee being involved. No longer would there be limits on the number of foreigners that a club could play. The power almost instantly switched from the clubs to the players. They now hold all the aces and demand ridiculous amounts of money, as do their agents, and ultimately the money leaves the sport altogether. Little thought for paying supporters, grass roots football and alike.

Bosman finally agreed to a damages settlement for his legal victory and was forced to begin a life outside football. None of this was successful, he had various failed business investments, a bankruptcy, and ultimately becoming an alcoholic, eventually leading to a jail sentence for assault.

Nearly every player since has ended up benefitting from the Bosman ruling, apart from Bosman himself. He'd changed football forever.

Let's hope City manage to get to the end of January without any of the hype that Sky Sports thrust upon us. Jim White, don't bother coming to the KC please!

A New Year, a City win. Keep them coming until May.

"...DIOMANDE, CITY'S TWENTY FIVE..."

CHAPTER 38

BRIGHTON (H) FA CUP ROUND 3 – SATURDAY 9TH JANUARY 2016

"# NO BROWNIE POINTS"

This was the first fixture of the season whereby I got a bit of a telling off by the football widow, albeit not in so many words.

A couple of years ago we had treated Charlotte and a friend to a weekend at Centreparcs in Sherwood Forest for her thirteenth birthday. She had really enjoyed it, the independence of going out on her own with loads of activities to do. Thomas had not forgotten and had reminded us, well well in advance of his thirteenth birthday, that presumably we would be doing the same for him. We could hardly say no.

So before the fixtures for this season had been released, the lodge had been booked and we were to share the weekend with Honest Dave the bookie, Jo and Bertie Talbot. At the time of making the booking, I just crossed my fingers and hoped that fate would be kind to us, maybe we would be playing Derby or Forest away.

As it turned out, the weekend happened to be FA Cup third round weekend, so in early December, as the draw was being made, I crossed my fingers again. Please be kind and give us a fixture not too far from Centreparcs. It turned out to be Brighton at home.

Now this could have been a lot worse, albeit there was the real threat of City getting a draw, resulting in a midweek away replay at Brighton. Hardly an easy away fixture. Would I have gone to keep up the 100% record for the season, or would I have made an excuse? Fortunately we'll never need to know.

Plans were made in the weeks building up and both Thomas and Charlotte were allowed to take a friend to Centreparcs. This clearly meant that they would entertain themselves and other than being fed, very few parenting skills would be required. This left much free time for drinking and gambling with Honest Dave. My FA Cup predictions were looking good for a several hundred pound pay out until about the seventy minute mark, but then it all went a bit Pete Tong. Honest Dave though softened the blow by winning 'a monkey' on Brandon Stones in the PGA golf. Maybe that's why he's a bookie and I'm not.

In the days leading up to the weekend, Thomas had shown his hand and his 100% attendance record was to be sacrificed. He didn't feel it was fair to drag his friend (dare I say it, a L**ds fan), back to Hull for a cup game against Brighton with both teams likely to field weakened teams. Not only that but the lure of the rapids and swimming pool were too much of a temptation for them both. No, Thomas said that his 100% attendance only counted for the league games, after all it is called '46 and Counting'.

I couldn't argue really. Maybe I should have been doing the same.

The football widow also agreed and I assumed believed I would come to the same conclusion, thus ensuring a hassle free, uncomplicated family weekend away. I put my case to the defence that:

–   As the kids both had friends in tow, they'd barely notice I wasn't there

–   Not being able to swim, the rapids were no draw for me

–   I'd kick myself if this was the only game I missed.

I think it was a hung jury, and reverse psychology came into play. "*Oh, you just decide*" the football widow said. In real terms this probably meant, "*Surely you are not going?*"

Needless to say, I decided to travel back to Hull on my own.

So around lunchtime, as the drinking had just commenced, I got my car keys and drove back the seventy miles or so from where I'd driven just the night before.

In recent years the FA Cup has come in for a bit of negative comment and has at times not been taken seriously by some teams. The riches on offer in The

Premier League seem to have dictated that, it is far more important and the FA Cup can play second fiddle. In fact some teams, albeit they won't admit it, are probably not that bothered if they get knocked out in the early rounds. It's one less thing to worry about, and as such they field effective reserve teams.

I can't share that view at all. The squads are big enough to accommodate this. You can't tell me that every single City fan or player, involved in either the Sheffield United semi-final or Arsenal final didn't enjoy it. I'll certainly remember them for the rest of my life and would love to repeat the experience. Hull City at Wembley – what's not to enjoy?

However, driving back to Hull today. I knew it would feel miles away from a Wembley experience. They would be 'weakened' teams played and the stadium would be half empty.

I, along with Bri Lee and Shaun Weaver, decided to change our normal matchday routines slightly. We all agreed to watch this match from The North Stand instead of our usual seats, in the South and East Stands respectively.

So after having entered my usual turnstile in The South Stand, I simply walked all the way along the concourse on the West Stand, back along the seats and onto the North Stand kiosks. A quick pre match pint and Bri and Shaun soon turned up, fresh from The Malt Shovel. We ambled up to some empty seats at the top just to the left of the goal, within very close proximity of the Brighton fans, about 400 or so of them. We then stood for the whole game and the experience was very enjoyable, much more like watching an away game.

The overall attendance edged just past ten thousand, albeit social media was later in a bit of a frenzy about the inability to pay cash on the turnstiles, driving more 'last minute decision makers' away. So far this season, the attendance figures have been a bit disappointing. We are in the upper reaches of The Championship, the KC has been something of a fortress, yet we struggle to ever get past the seventeen thousand mark unless the away support swells the numbers.

Anyway, today as ever, the North Stand attempted to create an atmosphere with constant chants and singing which was good to join in with. The South Stand simply doesn't. The banter with the adjacent Brighton fans was mildly amusing as well, with one particular Brighton fan, who must have been in his mid forties if not early fifties, constantly gesticulating to the City fans. Until he was quietly spoken to by 'The Old Bill' that is.

Both teams made many changes to their starting line ups, compared to those in their previous league fixtures, utilising their squad depth. All I can say is, that whilst we didn't stuff Brighton in scoreline, we won at a canter. Considering they are currently a genuine promotion rival in The Championship, this convinced me that we should quite easily finish above them. Our squad depth and quality is much better than theirs. Whilst I always suspected it, the events on the pitch today simply proved it.

Due to injuries, Cty's back four remained the same, but elsewhere, second string players were given an outing. All of Isaac Hayden, Ryan Taylor, and Sone Aluko impressed me today, and staked viable claims for future inclusion in the squad. Adama Diomande also started his first game, and looked lively before going off injured.

Basically City dictated the game from the outset and had numerous half chances and lots of possession. Brighton hardly threatened to score at all.

It was pleasurable on the eye and all that was really missing was the killer instinct which would have put the tie beyond doubt well before the final whistle. Robertson constantly had the beating of the 'tramp looking' Brighton right back, Calderon, and for me, he was our man of the match. That accolade actually went to Robert Snodgrass, who is improving with each minute of playing time on the pitch after such a long lay off. Today he ended up being the match winner.

Just before half time, a City corner was only half cleared to Huddlestone on the edge of the box. He tied to create space for a shot and the ball eventually fell to Maguire. 'Twinkle Toes' skipped past Dunk, who clumsily lunged at him. The referee immediately gave a penalty, and it was.

Up stepped Snodgrass who smashed it down the middle, beyond the keeper. Rob promptly ran towards the City medical staff, with whom he'd spent most of the preceeding fifteen or sixteen months, to celebrate. Nice touch.

I asked Shaun, 'famous in his own lunchtime' and once a keeper for Fish Trades FC what he tended to do at penalties. So many nowadays seem to go down the middle and I'd be tempted to stay there. He reckoned he did so for about one in every three penalties. He didn't though admit to his actual penalty saving record!

The second half was much of a repeat of the first, but City couldn't quite get a second goal, which would have killed the tie off. Aluko had the best chance when clean through, but couldn't beat the advancing keeper.

As the clock ticked down, my 'glass half empty' mindset kicked in and I just knew that Brighton would at least get one chance. When you've watched so many football games you just get a sense of how these things work out. Surely they wouldn't snatch a draw and a bloody replay?

They didn't but they came close in practically the last minute. A half shot by Crofts from inside the area bounced off the top of the bar and away to safety. My heart was in my mouth for a split second, but fortunately the referee soon blew for full time and I was saved from a possible midweek trip to the South coast. We were into the Fourth Round and the eventual draw pitted us away at either Braford or Bury – a real chance to progress even further.

As the rain descended, I travelled back down the same road for the third time in twenty four hours to rejoin the family at Centreparcs. They'd barely noticed I'd gone!

One more game chalked up, but now at least one more to attend.

"...SUPER, SUPER ROB..SUPER, SUPER ROB..SUPER, SUPER ROB..SUPER ROBERT SNODGRASS..."

CHAPTER 39

"A DOUBLE OVER THE WELSH"

After a break for the FA Cup match, another home game to follow against Cardiff back in The Championship.

On paper, this could have been a testing game, Cardiff were sitting just outside the play off positions, so this could have been a potential banana skin. Surely our tremendous run of home results will end soon?

The progress of the two teams have recently followed similar paths. Who can forget that momentous day back in May 2013 at the KC. All City had to do was at least match the result of Watford, who were playing L**ds at home, and we would guarantee promotion back to The Premier League. Cardiff, our opponents that day, were already promoted. In usual City style, we didn't make it easy.

After going a goal down to a Frazier Campbell opener (no need to celebrate like that Mr Campbell!) we fought back to lead 2-1 through goals first from Nick Proschwitz (yes he did score the odd important goal) and then Paul McShane. Then a City penalty in almost the last minute to seal it. Only for Proschwitz to blot his copy book again, and become just about the only German to ever miss a penalty. Cardiff then charge up the other end, win a penalty of their own and calmly slot it home to level it at 2-2.

Tenterhooks we were on but fortunately TWS did us a favour.

Cardiff were immediately relegated, we followed the season after.

However, of recent months, Cardiff look to be struggling. The previous Sunday, they were ceremoniously dumped out of the FA Cup at home to Shrewsbury. The match was watched in a stadium that holds 33,280, by a crowd of only 4,782. Hell, we thought our crowds at the KC were down.

On tonight's showing, the crowds will continue to dwindle as their performance was absolutely shocking. About 150 of their fans had made the long trip tonight and I felt for them. It's sometimes not easy being a football fan.

The previous night's results saw Derby only draw, so a City win meant we could leapfrog them and go back into second place, an automatic promotion spot.

It was bitterly cold at the KC and numerous layers were donned in an attempt to stay warm. Thomas just tried to do this by the intake of meat pies and hot chocolate.

City eventually won this game at an absolute canter, ending up 2-0 winners. It was an odd game, as other than a chance for Cardiff at nil nil, which was just lifted over McGregor's crossbar, I can barely recall him having to make a save. It was all so easy that once the first goal scored by City, it was almost a bit boring. City bossed the midfield, Livermore once again excelling, and dictated the play so much that the result was never in doubt.

I came away from the game a little unsure as to whether we were good or Cardiff totally inept. Is the standard of The Championship really quite poor? After all Cardiff were sitting handily in ninth position. I concluded that tonights game was really poor, and City won comfortably without having to actually get out of second gear. In fact, had City really gone for it a bit more, I'm sure we could have scored a hatful of goals.

Rich Hewson joined us this evening and having shared many a season watching City struggling in the bottom leagues, we asked ourselves if we should really be disappointed with only a 2-0 home win! We both believed we could have scored at least four or five against tonights opposition. Should we feel guilty for expecting too much and saying we were bored despite winning?

Cardiff constantly gave the ball away, apparently intent on trying to create openings for City. We were guilty of being wasteful of several of these. Diame in particular with some fairly woeful finishing. Sometimes he can be excellent and unplayable at this level, sometimes a luxury. Hernandez wasted a great chance when one on one with the keeper, taking too long and the chance was gone.

Almost identical to the Brighton game, City finally opened the scoring just before half time when Maguire was fouled in the box following a Clucas corner, and the referee pointed to the spot. This time, Hernandez stepped up. I immediately recalled his miss at Forest away, but no mistake this time as he expertly drove it into the side netting beyond the reach of the Cardiff keeper David Marshall. 1-0 City and from there, there was no chance of a City slip up. Hernandez celebrated by jumping into The West Stand, where somebody appeared to have a Uruguay flag. The referee promptly brandished his yellow card.

I always find this ridiculous. The aim of football is to score a goal. Yet you can't 'over celebrate'! What should players do, simply trot back to the halfway line and start the game. Us fans *want* to see over the top celebrations, we want to see some practice having gone into it, well choreographed etc etc! Later in the season, a Dumbarton player actually got booked for hugging his mum, who was stood in the front row behind the goal!

Thomas certainly started to take more of an interest in the game from that point on, as he had put £2 on a 2-0 City win, Hernandez as first goalscorer at 22-1. Well, I'd put the bet on for him.

Half time approached and Rich descended to the West Stand concourses. Not usually sitting in these seats, Rich obviously lost his bearings when returning with dirty hot dog and coffee, as he looked somewhat dumbfounded trying to locate where we were sat. It was almost as if he'd never been to the KC before but typified how we all have our own match routines and familiarity with different areas of the ground. I waved at Rich and he noticed us, shaking his head at his own stupidity.

The players re-emerged, many not bothering to run over the cones especially laid out for them. Ever notice how some are told to go back, but then do it so half heartedly?

The second half resumed and City had a few more chances. Maguire (we'd all love him to score!) poked a far post volley at the keeper, and soon after Clucas put City 2-0 up.

Odubajo played in Diame down the right. His pass found Hernandez, the ball looped up in the air, and just as it looked like the chance had gone, Clucas smartly swivelled and volleyed it into the bottom corner, the keeper motionless. Game over really.

City then seemed to take their foot off the gas a bit and whilst Cardiff enjoyed a bit more possession, they never really threatened the City goal. One good bit of play saw a nice one two between Diame and Hernandez but the latter just poked the ball over the bar. But all in all, it was a little disappointing that we seemed to show a lack of ambition to really go for it and score a few more.

Charlotte and Thomas seemed to stray their attentions from the action on the pitch as they decided to play guess the M and M colours. Basically you had to close your eyes whilst the other picked an M and M for them and put it in your mouth. You had to then guess what colour it was. I was useless. Thomas was ace. Too much practice I reckoned.

City made some substitutions which suggested that the manager was content to see the game out. Hernandez came off for Huddlestone, Aluko and Hayden also came on, reward for all three re their impressive displays against Brighton, but it somehow felt like we were going through the motions.

Thomas certainly wasn't bothered, as his bet was coming in. A late flurry of chances had him sweating, and believe it or not, he was actually asking us not to score! I can't believe I've ever done that.

Clucas had a number of late chances, first from a long through ball by Huddlestone but he failed to go direct for goal and the chance was gone. Then he was denied by Marshall when he should have scored, and then Meyler also had a shot saved. The final piece of action summed up the night. A half chance for Cardiff resulted in a terrible shot being skewed wide. Ironic cheers from the small Cardiff following. Chants followed from the City fans of *"..You're not very good, you're not very good, you're not very, you're not very, you're not very good. Shit. Ahhhhh.."*

The referee soon put Cardiff out of their misery and blew for full time. Thomas gave a quick fist pump. Not for a City win, but for the fact that he'd 'beat the bookies'. God help him when he has to start putting his own stake on.

"...BETTING – WHO SAYS IT'S A MUGS GAME?..."

CHAPTER 40

CHARLTON ATHLETIC (H) – SATURDAY 16TH JANUARY 2016

"AS SICK AS A CHARLTON FAN (AND THOMAS!)"

Today brought up a third home game in a week, and it was not an enjoyable one for the travelling Charlton fans, or Thomas come to that.

After our early poor show at The Valley where Charlton scored a 98th minute winner, and we paid twice to get in for the privilege, I really wanted us to give them a whalloping. The omens were all good for this to happen.

Charlton had been on a slump almost ever since they beat us and now sat towards the bottom of the table. Midweek had involved their fans travelling up to Huddersfield. This resulted in a 5-0 gubbing and their manager got sacked. The club were that embarrassed by the defeat that they refunded the travel costs for all those attending.

The following Saturday saw them have to travel all the way back up to Yorkshire again. That's almost as bad as City having to play, say Brighton away followed by Cardiff away within the space of four days....oh, done that one. Stupid fixtures though, absolutely no thought for fans.

This time, three hundred and sixty nine Charlton fans made the trip and come the final whistle, I felt for them. If 5-0 wasn't bad enough, today they went for one more, ending up on the wrong side of a 6-0 drubbing. They were completely outclassed by City in every department, and each and every one of the Charlton fans must have felt sick at their teams showing.

They weren't the only ones to feel sick on this day. One of our 100% attendances came to an end today, and nearly mine as well.

As a family Christmas present, the football widow had bought the Bunton household a lazy Spar. So on the previous evening to this match, Thomas had spent far too long in it with his mates, no doubt ingesting far too many E numbers. This was then followed by an impromptu sleepover at his mate's house, which will no doubt have involved a late stop up. I just said, *"that's fine, just make sure you are back home no later than 1.30ish Saturday lunchtime, ready to go to football."*

Thomas duly turned up the following day, late as ever, me itching to get going. My timekeeping is usually pretty rubbish but I hate being late for kick off, so always set off earlier just in case. So by the time Thomas rolled in, I'd already started pacing around, constantly looking at my watch.

We eventually parked up in our usual spot and set off to walk to the KC, cutting up some side streets and onto Anlaby Road. Charlotte had come with her pal Izzy again and the girls were off at a gallop, clearly excited. Thomas meanwhile was being his dawdling self, carefree and seemingly in his own little world.

"Come on Mr B", I called, as he lagged a few yards behind me.

"I don't feel very well" he uttered, *"I need a drink."*

"Thomas, I can't magic one up. There's a shop just around the corner, we'll get one there" I snapped.

However, Thomas didn't make the corner in time.

As we approached the old, now derelict cinema on Anlaby Road, Thomas promptly threw up. I ushered him to the side of the road, but at least three more 'heaves' soon followed. He really didn't look that well.

I glanced at my watch. It was by now 2.45pm. What to do now?

"C'mon Thomas" I said. *"We'll have to take you home, you can't go in feeling like that"*

"But I can't miss a game, nor can you" he replied

"Don't worry, it doesn't matter" I said. The glum feeling of breaking our 100% attendance though was, I admit, in my mind.

If we'd taken him in, for all I know, he might have been sick in someone's hood sat in front of us! So that seemed it. '46 and Counting' would be no more, it would be 45 at best.

Not to be defeated, Charlotte and the football widow sprang into action. A quick couple of phone calls and they'd organised for us to meet up at Willerby where Thomas would jump out of our car and go back home with the football widow to recuperate. It felt strange going in the wrong direction at nearly 3 o'clock on the day of a home game. At least we should be able to make it to our seats not too long after kick off.

A quick drop off for Thomas, and we did an 'about turn' back to the KC. With time of the essence we parked in Walton Street and walked spritely towards the ground. The game had started and I was already checking my phone for score updates. As we approached the stadium, with about ten minutes on the clock, there was an eery silence and not much chanting could be heard.

And I promise that this next line is no word of a lie.

I turned to Charlotte, in a slightly agitated state, and said *"I hate being late and missing the kick off"*

"Don't worry" she said trying to comfort me, *"we never score early goals."*

I smiled (she's actually taking it all in!)

And with that, almost at the precise moment, the KC erupted into noise!

As I found out later, Hernandez had charged down a Charlton clearance on the half way line, ran through and slid the ball under the keeper. 1-0 City, and we were on the wrong side of the stands!

We were soon in though and the avalanche was about to begin.

Charlton were extremely poor, but as the saying goes, you can only beat what is in front of you. From the eighty minutes or so that I witnessed, City totally dominated, and scored some excellent goals, both individual and team goals.

Not long after we'd taken our seats, Hernandez scored again. He picked the ball up just inside the Charlton half and was allowed to head towards goal unchallenged. Once at the edge of the box, he curled a crisp shot past the Charlton keeper. 2-0 and already game over.

Texts were exchanged with Thomas who was clearly annoyed at missing the game. I just sensed we were going to get a hatful and he'd miss it.

I tried to recall matches that I'd attended not feeling well and the one that most sprang to mind was an away game at Stoke on a New Year's Day. God knows why I bothered going. We'd stayed up until about five am in the morning drinking, and I was extremely worse for wear. Fortunately I wasn't driving but can recall sitting in that rubbish Harvester's pub near the ground, unable to even look at a pint never mind consume one. A pub is not the place to be when you feel like that. It took me all my powers of concentration all afternoon to not be ill. I barely noticed any of the 1-1 draw, and to make matters worse, I think we also got a parking ticket.

So I knew we'd made the right decision to take Thomas home. His 100% record over, but he still enjoyed listening to it on the radio at home with the football widow, even if he was a bit envious.

The day's events also involved a well respected twenty first minute round of applause for Rob Brown, a City fan who had recently lost his battle with Leukemia, aged only twenty one. The whole ground stood in unison, including the Charlton fans, and joined in. A fitting tribute.

Soon after, we scored a third goal, a nice team goal this one. A lovely flick from Hernandez to Clucas, who played in Snodgrass, who stepped inside and curled a lovely left foot shot from just outside the box.

Charlton had a header just wide with one of their rare attempts at goal. And then just before half time, it was 4-0. A lovely piece of play and a one-two between Clucas and Robertson down the left, ended up with Robertson cutting the ball back from the bye line for Hernandez to tap in. A hat trick in the first half. There was still time for Clucas to come close with a rasping drive but the team soon left the field thereafter to a standing ovation.

This felt like payback for that early season woeful display at Charlton. Even Michael Dawson had referred to it when we met him at the OSC Meet the Players Event.

By now, texts from Thomas were pouring in. He was gutted although I'm sure the scoreline was making him feel better. It can't have been doing the Charlton fans any good and I did wonder what the new Charlton manager could possibly have said during his half time team talk. One of those Sunday morning clichés maybe, *"Come on lads, it's still 0-0."* As if!

Whatever he did say, there was a moment where it appeared as if the Charlton goalkeeper had seen enough. He finally emerged about a full minute or two after the rest of the team. Maybe he needed a dump at half time?

Unlike some other games this season, City were not content to sit on their lead, and were going for the jugular. Livermore was impressive in midfield, showing strength in winning balls, holding off Charlton players and generally dictating play.

Clucas came close, in fact should have scored after some neat work from first Snoddy, and then Diame, but Sam ended up shinning the ball over the bar. The crowd were certainly enjoying it and there were chorus' of:

"We're the North Stand, we're the North Stand.." followed by;

"We're the East Stand, we're the East Stand.."

And today, are you ready for this, there were even chants of

"We're the West Stand, we're the West Stand.."

Wonders will never cease! Only us miserable buggers in the South Stand to join in now.

And soon after the crowd were off their seats again with arguably the best goal of the afternoon. A nice passage of play and some one touch possession saw Robertson knock the ball inside to Snoddy, who tee'd up Diame to volley into the net, again from outside the box. 5-0 to a rampant City.

The crowd were clearly enjoying this and the only thing missing was a goal from Harry Maguire. Whenever he got the ball in their half the crowd were urging him to *"shoot, shoot"*. He's becoming a bit of a crowd favourite after some sterling performances, deputising for the injured Dawson.

Snodgrass, Clucas and Diame all had half chances before Isaac Hayden rounded off an excellent display with a deflected shot that left the keeper wrong footed and eventually on his backside. 6-0 – a demolition job.

Just one thing City. And I know this may sound greedy.

Can you repeat this sometime soon, so Thomas can witness it first hand.

"...HERNANDEZ WHOAH, HERNANDEZ WHOAH, HE CAME FROM URUGUAY, TO EAT HULL PIE..."

CHAPTER 41

FULHAM (A) – SATURDAY 23RD JANUARY 2016

"BACK ON TOP"

City had won the last four games on the trot, only conceding one goal, culminating in the emphatic 6-0 drubbing of Charlton. When you are winning, the prospect of another away game involving a decent amount of travelling hardly comes into the equation. You are going.

Not that we've got a choice this season anyway, but even if we weren't trying to write this book, a trip to Fulham *would* have been on the agenda anyway.

Craven Cottage is a cracking ground, in pleasant surroundings, many local pubs within easy walking distance, and when City have been in town, we've usually enjoyed an excellent atmosphere in the away end, along with some half decent results.

Who can forget Manucho's last minute winner back in March 2009, during our first season in The Premier League. After good set up play by Richard Garcia, Manucho tapped home to steal three points.

I also vividly recall that game as we sat in an area of the ground referred to as the 'neutrals area' or 'mixed zone'. Never come across this at any other ground or heard anything so ridiculous in my life, but we did it anyway as the tickets were much cheaper (tight northerners). It was a surreal experience not knowing whether to keep quiet or be animated. It just seemed to be full of 'football tourists', taking selfies, wearing the dreaded half and half scarves, not really knowing what was going on. We soon upped sticks and relocated to the City section via the back of the stand and promptly went ballistic when Manucho scored.

That season we failed to win any of our remaining ten league games, and that win at Fulham was our only win in our last twenty two games. However, the win effectively helped to keep us up that season (helped by the fact that Newcastle were rubbish) and we were eventually treated to Phil Brown's karaoke version of 'This Is The Best Trip I've Ever Been On' at the KC on the final day of survival. In typical City style, this was a defeat!

We also enjoyed a spirited 2-2 draw in April 2014 when late goals by Jelavic and Shane Long rescued a point and all but relegated Fulham and secured our safety.

So this four hundred odd mile round trip was always a definite. Bri Lee joined us again today and after an early start, we were soon parking up at our usual West London stop off at Ruislip Tube Station, just gone 11.30ish. One tube change and we were departing at Putney Bridge ready to meet up with The Clines in The Rocket Pub, just over the River Thames.

The pub was well populated with City fans, familiar faces everywhere, all come down for a day out 'on the pop', a bit of football thrown in. We enjoyed a few decent pints in proper glasses, albeit the number of mine were restricted being the designated driver for the day, and the banter was flying. As the clock ticked past 1.30, the 'house rules' on match days dictated that proper glasses and bottles had to be dispensed with, and in place, all drinks served in plastic glasses. How ridiculous. The fact we'd been drinking already from pint glasses and bottles for an hour and a half and that the tables were strewn with empties seemed to be lost on the bar staff. But hey, rules are rules.

The first signs of City's widespread following soon came to the fore as Bri's nephews Daniel and Kieran joined us. They'd just flown in from Jersey especially to see City and enjoy a night in the Capital. From now on we obviously referred to them as The Jersey Boys, although they were not donning red jackets.

I had a brief chat with some Fulham old timers who were sat at the table next to us. I enjoy pre match pubs where fans can mix and chat, rather than this 'No Away Supporters' rubbish. Have a bit of banter, enjoy and exchange conversations and then pass ridicule and hurl abuse at them once inside the ground!

Today, Jeff, Bernie and Phil, who between them had clocked up too many years watching Fulham that they cared to mention, had a general air of despondency about them, fully expecting City to be victorious. They reminisced about previous Fulham players and generally concurred that a player from the 60's called Tosh Chamberlain to be their favourite. A character who would play with sleeves rolled up and apparently possessed one of the hardest shots in football. Sometimes he'd score a spectacular goal but often they weren't in the general direction of the goal and allegedly he once struck the floodlights. Other noteable claims to fame included being seen puffing the remainder of his half time cigarette after the second half had started. He was also once seen taking a corner kick, missed the ball altogether, instead booting the corner flag sending it in the general direction of the goal. Real Sunday morning stuff.

A quick sup up and we relocated to The Temperance where more City fans were in presence including Jonny Mail who was certain to leave his mark on the day later.

An attempt to have a final pint in The Eight Bells was thwarted due to the fact it was rammed and operating a 'one in, one out' basis.

So we sacked off the idea of waiting and instead headed to the ground, munching on obligatory dirty burger en route. It's a pleasant stroll through park area and Thomas was highly amused by the London accents of the Fulham supporters walking in front of us. All at a few decibels too high and frequently punctuated with lots of *"facking hells"*.

Soon we were in the ground and were promptly told by the stewards that due to 'health and safety reasons' (whatever they were, they couldn't elaborate further), no flags could be hung up, so we just took up our seats near the front, me chuntering. Initially Bri had descended to the back of the stand. We knew that as we could hear his dulcet tones singing.

As the game commenced, there was a lack of atmosphere surrounding us, with many fans choosing to sit down as opposed to the obligatory standing up at away fixtures. In fact there was a bit of animosity between certain sections of the City fans, resulting in a mini tussle, one chap ending up on the receiving end of a few jabs in the face. We decided we'd relocate to Bri's vicinity in the second half.

On the pitch Fulham started well, enjoying a lot of possession without really penetrating our goal too much. City weren't playing particularly well, but soon fashioned out the best chance of the game. Diame played Hernandez clean through but his shot was well saved low down by Lonergan in the Fulham goal. Hernandez should have scored really to get that all important first goal, but considering the run he has been on lately, we'll excuse him.

After that Fulham continued to control possession, whilst City struggled to get any real momentum. However, for all their possession, Fulham didn't really create any chances and probably overplayed a bit. It was almost as if we were just keeping them at arms length.

Their best chance fell just before half time. Dembele passed to ex Tiger Cairney, whose shot was only half saved by McGregor. As the ball trickled goalwards it seemed that Kacaniklic would simply tap it into an empty net, but somehow Odubajo got across and just got to the ball first, flicking it onto the Fulham player and over the bar. As good as a goal that challenge. This wasn't to be the last telling moment that Moses had in the game.

As half time approached, I received a text message telling me that an old mate, Dave Waters (who I've already mentioned bumping into in Lokeren) was at the game. We exchanged texts and agreed to meet up at the back of the stand at half time and relocate towards the back of the City contingent, to watch the second half. This was easier said than done as the entire crowd seemed to be there trying to sneak a half time pint in. Eventually we found them.

Dave had flown over the night before with his Dutch pal, Pete De Boer. We also met up again with Jonny Mail, who was at school with Dave (many years ago I hasten to add) and the Clines again.

Jonny Mail, practising as a solicitor and now residing in Cheshire, can often be seen at away games and is an infectious chap. Claiming to be one of a dying breed of football casuals, he's always out to enjoy himself at City. As we all decamped to the rear of the Putney End, River Thames in view, little would we know what he had started that day.

That ability to create, start and get others to sing a new song (as previously discussed in the Brentford chapter) was about to come to the fore again. And Mr Mail can lay claim to today's new ditty. He claims it is not an original and was originally sung at Everton last season, so he can't take all the credit. The original version was made up by Chris 'Ghetto of Excellence' Cooper and the original words were *"...Signed Ben Arfa on loan, Dawson at the back, Gaston in attack..."*

The words were amended towards the back end of last season for obvious reasons.

Today Jon was the instigator, and whilst he had many foot soldiers, resulting in the swelling of numbers joining in, I am reliably informed that he was the driving force. His aim for it to be this season's version of *"No silverware"* which swept us to promotion in 2008.

As the second half started, the first few renditions were voiced. Jon and backing singers energetically repeated it over and over again, firstly at fairly low volumes. However, as each repetition was aired, and those supporters unaware of it, had the time to learn it (like most football chants, it's not too complicated), more voices joined in, such that the volume increased.

It's a catchy little number and is a shoe in to be repeated at many a future fixture. In fact, I couldn't get it out of my head all the following day. By the time you read this, you'll have heard it, but it goes as follows:

"..Steve Bruce had a dream
To build a football team
He signed Diame
And sent Ben Arfa back home
Daws at the back   (this line confuses some as they all go quiet)
Abel in attack
We are Hull City
In Amber and Black.."

Momentary lapses took place but then it would pick up again a few minutes later.

On the pitch, the early stages of the second half were the same as the first. Scot Parker, now thirty five years old, was rolling back the years and generally dictating play, albeit chances were still at a premium. Huddlestone came on to replace Hayden, Parker departed, and City slowly started imposing themselves on the match.

Maguire headed just wide and then in the crowd, news came through that Middlesbrough, currently just above us and top of the league, had just gone behind at home to Forest. The volume in the away end increased and there was a sense that this was our chance. Maybe the players sensed it too? City were coming more into the game and soon after we took the lead.

Odubajo picked up a Robertson cross that was hit too long. He attacked the full back and drove to the bye line, where a Fulham defender clumsily took his legs away. The ref immediately pointed to the spot. Cue lots of jumping up and down in anticipation.

Hernandez picked the ball up, eyed his spot, and whilst the keeper guessed right and got a hand to it, the ball went in off the post. 1-0 City and only about ten minutes to go.

Hernandez whoahh'. Johnny on the spot puts us top again at Fulham away.

The volume hit new levels with chants alternating between *"We are top of the league"* and *"Steve Bruce had a dream"*, without any moment of respite. The final minutes were a joy to be a City supporter, in full vocal support for the team we follow, encouraging them to 'get over the line', and end the day top of The Championship.

City could have scored a second with Diame having a shot saved and Elmo almost getting on the end of a Clucas pass.

We did though have a couple of scary moments in the remaining few minutes with Fulham coming close, and it took a great save by McGregor from a Jamie O'Hara free kick to secure the points.

Overall, a real team effort. Not always pretty on the eye, but workmanlike and efficient. Three points that took Hull City back to the summit. I'd almost forgotten about L**ds, Rotherham and Preston. Almost.

As we congratulated ourselves and gave bear hugs, I asked Dutch Pete if he'd send me a few words to describe his first experience of attending an English football match, and more importantly, attending a Hull City match.

So for this match, I'll sign off and leave you with his thoughts.

In April 2015, I took Dave to a Dutch football match, involving my team SC-Heerenveen, against AZ Alkmaar. I showed him our city, stadium, pubs and that day he got flooded with goals and beautiful football with SC-Heerenveen winning 5-2. Dave insisted on taking me to England to show me 'real' football. It took us some time to plan the trip, but on the 23rd January 2016, it was on. It was to involve Dave's team Hull City, playing away at Fulham.

We flew into London one day earlier and were staying in a hotel (shithole) in Chiswick, close to Fulham. On the internet they forgot to mention that the beds were for dwarfs, the shower was full of mould and that you were woken in the morning with their fire alarm. But who cares, there were pubs and 'cod everywhere' (aka Hull City fans). On Friday we went for some drinks, but didn't make it too late, Dave expected a long Saturday.

After a full English breakfast (what else), we took the tube to Putney Bridge. At noon we arrived in The Eight Bells, where the first Hull fans were already drinking. Unfortunately this is not allowed in The Netherlands, drinking beers with a group of away fans in the city you are playing. So it was extremely good to see that by one pm, The Eight Bells was already full of Hull City fans, drinking shitloads of beer and supporting their team in an away match. At two pm, we went to another pub, also full with City fans, where we met an old friend of Dave's (City fan of course), who went to the match with his son.

From there we went to the ground walking through Bishops Park, City and Fulham fans next to each other, singing songs and talking about the match. We had tickets for the mixed zone, so we tried to walk over to the section housing the away supporters. This didn't work as some over zealous steward sent us back. As we really wanted to be in the away section, I tried again, playing the stupid tourist. This worked and we were finally there. The support in the away stand was really good and I don't think I heard the Fulham fans all game. Some City fans were already singing, "Is this the Emirates, is this the Emirates..?"

Apparently word spreads fast, as Dave was getting a text message just before half time from someone who had heard Dave was in the stadium too. This was when we met Ian, his son and some others. Second half we stood next to them and they were introducing some song about a dream Steve Bruce had. It took a bit of effort, but more and more were picking it up and joining in, including myself!

To be honest, it wasn't the best football match I've been to, but the fact that around two and a half thousand City fans had travelled over four hundred miles to support their team, was enough for me to have a great ninety minutes. When I almost thought the match would end up 0-0, Hull got a penalty. Easy job for the player "who came from Italy, to play for Hull City" and City went on to win.

All in all, I had a great match day. The away support in England is so much bigger and better than in The Netherlands. You're allowed to drink beer wherever you want and you can walk to the ground next to the home fans.

A week after the game, I'm still catching myself singing (in my head) about Steve Bruce having a dream!

"...WE ARE HULL CITY, IN AMBER AND BLACK..D-D..D-D..D-D........STEVE BRUCE HAD A DREAM..."

Lyrics courtesy of Jon Mail (and Chris Cooper)

CHAPTER 42

BURY (A) FA CUP 4TH ROUND – SATURDAY 30TH JANUARY 2016

"HAPPY BIRTHDAY KAY, SORRY I WAS LATE"

Now you might think that this would not stand out as the most attractive fixture of the season. Reward for beating Brighton at home in the third round of the FA Cup was an away tie, at either Bradford or Bury, who drew their first game.

This initially posed me a potential problem, as on the Saturday night I was due to attend a 50th birthday party in Beverley. The start time was 6.30, a black tie affair that the football widow was greatly looking forward to. I know that because there was a Michael Buble act on, and girls always like an excuse to get dressed up don't they?

"Does Kay's party clash with a Hull City game?" the football widow asked. *"Yes"*, I replied. *"It will either be Bradford or Bury away"* I informed her. *"Then you may have to miss it, it's only Bradford or Bury"* was the suggestion. I contemplated exactly how the football widow had the temerity to know the importance level of Bradford or Bury away. *"It's important though"* I stated. *"There'll be another important one next week"* was her repost. She was right. They're all important.

Bradford winning the replay for me would have been ideal as the fixture would have been played on the Sunday. Everyone would have been a winner. Sod's law then, Bradford lost and Bury it was on the Saturday, the same day as the party. I then found out that there was a minibus going involving a 'boys day out'. Clearly I couldn't go on it, if indeed I was going at all.

However, I accomplished the best possible solution. I made my excuses, proffering apologies to the birthday girl, Kay, and suggested I'd be fashionably late if that was okay. Kay was totally understanding and said that was fine. The football widow was also eventually cool with it all, even going on her own to the party. She's good like that. It did cost me an expensive dress to go in mind! City had better make it worthwhile.

So with all the clearances obtained, Bury it was to be.

During the midweek immediately prior to the fixture, an omen of what was to come caught my attention. Manchester City were playing a League Cup semi-final against Everton. As part of their attempt to create an interest, they had placed inflatable yellow bananas under the home fans seats.

As soon as TV pictures were aired showing fans frantically blowing them up, this took me back to football in the eighties, the 'taking an inflatable to football craze'. All very light hearted fun.

Manchester City were the forerunners of this, their trademark being the yellow banana. After some research, I found out that initially a chap called Frank Norton, first took a five foot inflatable banana to a Manchester City game against Plymouth in 1987. It was all part of a drunken bet, at which Frank had to obtain some sort of proof that he'd actually taken the banana to the game. Photographs were taken, bet won. It was a barmy August day, and before long, said banana was also 'wearing' a Man City top and had a face drawn, and also donned a bobble hat. The banana had almost come to life, and now became a regular Man City follower.

And then the number of bananas on show increased. Other fans also acquired their own, and every time a goal was scored, hundreds of bananas were enthusiastically waved in the air, a sight to behold. And then, other inflatables also started to emerge.

At the start of the 1988/89 season, Man City visited 'Fer Ark' (Hull City won 1-0!). I wasn't at this particular pub, but on that day, Frank who had now changed his banana for a six foot crocodile, was joined by a toucan, a seven foot golf club, a Spitfire, a Red Baron, a parrot, a gorilla, and enough bananas to feed a small African nation.

At one game, even the Man City team all ran out carrying a banana each, eventually throwing them into the crowd. Other fans got in on the act.

Stoke had inflatable pink panthers, Oldham had hot dogs, Grimsby had 'Harry the Haddock', West Ham obviously had inflatable hammers, and I'm led to believe that our opponents today, Bury, had inflatable black puddings!

The craze eventually died out, probably due to the involvement of PC Plod and some clubs started banning them as an offensive weapon, or because they blocked people's views. Ridiculous really, as it was all harmless fun. They were later replaced by golf umbrellas for a short while, and nowadays you can take nothing at all! The list of forbidden objects on display at each turnstile is extremely long.

The trip today was very much like a step back in time. The last time I visited Gigg Lane was way back in October 2003, when a crowd of just under 4,000 watched a drab 0-0. A certain Mr Ian Ashbee was sent off late in the piece, not for an '*Ashbee's gonna get you*' tackle, but a theatrical dive in the box in an attempt to win a penalty. Second yellow for diving, tut tut Ash.

So why did there seem to be such an interest for City fans to travel to Bury today?

A wet and muddy Gigg Lane. A Chuba hat trick and a bit of aggro thrown in for good measure.

Maybe it was the thought of being the 'big boys in town'. But more likely it was the fact that this was going to be proper old school football. A reminder of how football used to be, and still can be. When you strip away all the sanitised stadiums, match atmospheres, Sky fuelled razamatazz and hype, and immaculate playing surfaces, it is just ordinary players in ordinary settings, living ordinary lives. A world away from the alleged glamour of Old Trafford or Stamford Bridge. Football as we used to know, and the game as it was when I fell in love with it.

Thomas had brought his friend Jaden again today (think he's getting tired of following the fortunes of Newcastle) and upon arrival at the Bury Social Club outside the ground, they promptly demanded money from me for food, while I drained a couple of pints on my own like a 'Billy No Mates'.

Bury were clearly expecting a decent following. Their ground, Gigg Lane, only holds about 11,600, so to ease segregation issues, they had decided to dedicate both their South stand (running alongside the pitch) and West Stand (behind one of the goals) to the City fans for the day.

During the actual match, the irony of this was not lost on the City following. The usual home chants of *"We're the North Stand, we're the North Stand"* being echoed by *"We're the East Stand, we're the East Stand"* (with no noise whatsoever emanating from South or West stands) were amusingly flipped around today. I'm sure that will never be repeated in a long while.

The turnout in the end was a fraction under three thousand I think, with just a smattering of fans in the West Stand behind the goal. Those in the South Stand were in fine voice though, and there was some real tension in the stands.

The eighties feel continued during our approach to the stadium as Transvision Vamp's 'Baby I Don't Care' was blaring out over the tannoy. It was probably being played on a record player as well.

None of this looking for your allocated seat rubbish today, all fans free to roam wherever. We took our vantage point near to the half way line and it was clear to see that there were a few chavs on show today, all donning Burberry caps. Their position was in the far corner near an old fashioned one line electronic scoreboard, in close proximity to some like minded Bury fans, with just an old fashioned high wire fence in between. Oh, and lots of fluorescent jackets and police on triple time.

It was clear from the off that there was some amount of bating going on between the young Bury wannabe casuals, and the City contingent. Several exchanges of loud chanting warmed up the atmosphere and animosity, until eventually the Bury boys lit a smoke bomb and threw it over the fence into the City fans. This was not welcomed and several more were thrown back and forth.

As if by magic, even more police appeared from nowhere (not sure what they were doing before) to ensure the fans were separated. This didn't stop either party 'giving it large' to one another, slit throat signs, and generally lots of bravado being shown. I was a bit far away to really make any faces out, but in reality, I suggest that most of the participants were due at school on the Monday.

If nothing else, this all whipped up a ferocious atmosphere, just what an FA Cup tie should be about. So long as no-one gets hurt, no harm done eh?

City made a host of changes, in fact the full starting eleven! However, when you looked at the teamsheet, every one bar one had started numerous first team appearances. It once again, just went to emphasize the strength in depth in this City squad. When looking at it, even me the usual pessimist, was not in doubt as to who would be victorious on the day.

The one player not to have had any first team experience was Josh Tymon. This is a sixteen year old lad who was making his City debut at left back. Josh was just nine when Deano scored at Wembley, and as John Harrison amusingly tweeted later in the day, *'I've got a tin of peaches in my cupboard older than Josh Tymon'*.

It was extremely refreshing to see a youngster come through the ranks and break into the first team. This is not a feat that happens much anymore. Such is the constant craving for immediate success at most clubs, they simply choose to 'splash the cash' and go and buy players, rather than 'play the long game', nurturing young talent and giving them opportunities.

This was not lost in the City following with constant renditions of *"He's one of our own, he's one of our owwwwn, Josh Tymon, he's one of our own"*. This must have given him constant encouragement and confidence. I noticed too, particularly at the start, how the other City players looked after him. Everyone went up to him just prior to kick off, Huddlestone in particular, and we ensured the ball was passed to him immediately to get a confidence building first touch.

Overall he put in a sterling display and when eventually substituted, received a rapturous standing ovation from the City fans. One for the future hopefully. How we all appreciate this so much more than some money orientated football mercenary on a last pay day.

Bury started lively and were keen to leave a foot in, hoping to put City off their stride. The weather too was atrocious. You name it, wet, windy, rain, sleet, snow and sub zero temperatures. The pitch was not like the snooker tables we've been used to recently. Lots of brown muddy patches and water! At one point during the second half, Elmo, whilst waiting to take a throw in, tried to bounce the ball up and down. It went down, but then just stuck in the mud!

So whilst all the component parts were there for a possible upset, it never materialised and City coped with everything fairly comfortably.

Akpom fired in an early opener, slotting home into an empty net after the Bury keeper had only half saved a Meyler shot, the rebound falling nicely to Akpom. This also subdued the home posse and the tension in the crowd seemed to die down a little.

Several reprises of "*Steve Bruce had a dream...*" followed and it was all looking fairly comfortable for City as we went in for the break at 1-0.

During half time, rain turned to sleet and then driving snow. With it, the temperature dropped and it was bloody freezing (once again taking me back to that night at Witton Albion watching City in the FA Cup against Runcorn). Had the weather continued, there could have been a risk of an abandonment, something I've never experienced watching City.

The players re-emerged, and fortunately the snowstorm died off a little so we could at least see the action. Many players were wearing the customary gloves, and it reminded me of the days of Cameron Stewart also wearing a snood (think that's what they were called). Whatever happened to him?

Sone Aluko put on a good display in the second half, constantly troubling the Bury defence. For a moment, Bury thought they'd equalised, but the linesman had flagged for offside already. This didn't deter the Bury lot, who joyously celebrated. One lad even ran on the pitch, looking remarkably stupid when he realised it had been disallowed.

Seconds later, Aluko once again ran at the Bury defence and this time was tripped inside the box. Penalty. Akpom stepped up and slotted home and immediately ran to the City fans in the corner to celebrate. This only proved to antagonise the Bury lot, especially as this was followed by jibes of, "*You're fucking shit, you're fucking shit, you're fucking shit*".

The second goal turned up the volume levels in the City section though and soon Akpom got his hat trick to make it 3-0, after good build up play again by Aluko.

That was game over and saw most of the Bury massive leaving. I'm not sure whether this was an attempt to convey a 'see you outside' mentality, or just that they had to get home for tea.

There was time for Bury to score a late consolation goal but City had by then wrapped the game up and taken their foot off the gas. Job done and into the fifth round. The one season I decide to try and get to every game, and City have decent cup runs in both competitions.

We all now headed for the exits, now very cold and damp. This didn't deter Thomas asking us to wait to get a photo and signatures on our flag from the three players, Livermore, Maguire and Snodgrass, who were 'warming down' on the pitch. The players duly obliged and eventually we were the last to leave the ground, heading for the car to try and 'warm up'.

Overall, a thoroughly entertaining day and for me, certainly beats some of the Premier League offerings we have had in the past. And that is not just because we won (although that clearly helps). It was because it just kind of reminded me of why I love this game, and despite all the recent changes, will hopefully continue to do so.

And speaking of love. A quick thrash down the motorway, off with the Adidas trainers and Tacchini, on with a bloody penguin suit, and late arrival at Kay's birthday bash. I arrived just as Kay was doing her speech and was soon informed that the football widow had been mesmerised by the Buble act. Upon noting my arrival, she promptly returned back into football widow mode and brought over one of the guests to introduce me too.

I knew exactly who it was. It was only Ian Ashbee!

My mind told me to burst into song, *"He's neither here nor there, he's fucking everywhere…."* but I managed to refrain from doing so. So almost immediately, it was straight back into football talk.

"..CHUBA, CHUBA CHUBA, CHUBA CHUBA, CHUBA CHUBA AKPOM…"

CHAPTER 43

BURNLEY (A) – SATURDAY 6ᵀᴴ FEBRUARY 2016

"BLOODY BURNLEY – PART 3"

Oh god, it's Bloody Burnley again. They keep turning up in this book, like a bad smell. I really hope that after today that is it, and I won't have to mention their name again. That prospect is however, highly unlikely as since we turned them over on Boxing Day, they are in a rich vein of form.

I don't see them as a spectacular team, but they know how to grind out results and with Andre Gray up front, they've always got goals in them. Really hope we don't end up against them in the play offs, otherwise there is the distinct possibility that the first chapter of this book could be identical to the last chapter.

It felt like there were two curses on City today. Firstly, and obviously, it's bloody Burnley. And secondly, after a great month in January, in which City won all six games, scoring fifteen goals and only conceding two, Steve Bruce had been presented with the Manager of the Month Award. That usually spells a bad result coming. Today it struck again as in the East Lancashire rain, City went down to a late 0-1 defeat.

This chapter may be slightly unusual to certain others, in that the main story involves a guest, that, well chose not to attend, such is the lure of Turf Moor for a Hull City fan.

Just prior to Christmas, at a mutual friend's party, I bumped into an old friend Geoff Bradley, a lifelong City fan. For a short period of time, Geoff and I used to live down the same street some thirty plus years ago. I can recall numerous games of 'kerbie', football matches, and cricket down the street. You know, the ones that don't take place anymore as kids are too wrapped up in their rooms playing on an Xbox or Playstation. The days of 'jumpers for goalposts' and shouts of 'Car' and scrambling around to move said jumpers, or makeshift wickets, seem to have long since gone.

Now Geoff has a fantastic memory and eye for detail. Talk to him about City and he can recall all of his trips and statistics from games. I thought mine was quite good but compared to Geoff's, it's nothing.

So whilst sharing a couple of beers that day, we discussed this book thing and I suggested that maybe he come along to a game and share a couple of stories with us. E-Mail addresses were exchanged (even in this modern day, Geoff still doesn't have a mobile) and it was agreed that I'd send him a draft chapter to see what he thought and we'd maybe select an appropriate fixture. This duly took place and I proposed that Geoff maybe join us for either the Fulham or Burnley away fixtures.

Geoff soon replied and I got the gist that whilst still attending home fixtures, his days on the road and 'on the lash' attending away games had dwindled somewhat. I'm not sure whether this was down to Geoff being a much more responsible family man than me, or whether the years following City in the doldrum years had taken its toll on him. Or perhaps both. So Geoff took up neither offer, but did supply me with a great story about one of his previous expeditions to Burnley.

On this particular day, Geoff was sat with Raich Carter (the grandson of the famous Raich Carter) on an original Simon Gray special. Those readers that have heard of Simon Gray may already sense where this story is heading. Whilst on the coach, the two chaps were doing their best to complete The Daily Mirror quizword. The answer to *three down* was easy, the clue being 'Team which plays its home games at Boothferry Park'. They were both convinced that '*three down*' was an omen that City would lose 3-0 at Turf Moor. In the end, they actually lost 2-0, but this wasn't the main story of the day.

The coach to Burnley had taken the A646 route up through the Pennine Hills. As it slowly approached a stationery queue of traffic waiting at a pedestrian crossing in the village of Mytholmroyd, its brakes failed. The coach came to a stop after it sent a car in front careering into a lamp post on the opposite side of the road. The lady car driver required ambulance treatment, but by this time, Geoff, Raich and others had legged it to The White Lion back up the road.

A few beers later, there had been no word of a replacement coach when a guy wearing a City scarf pulled up in his van to ask what the story was. He said he'd take four of them to Burnley in his van. In the end, five of them piled in but the van driver didn't protest, and they all made kick off just about bang on time. About twenty five minutes into the first half, chanting was heard behind the old Longside Stand at Turf Moor, and it was a sign that the rest of the Simon Gray congregation had finally made it. At least they would have a coach to get home.

Coach number two was boarded after the game and the new bus proudly sat at the front of the convoy of City coaches waiting for the obligatory police escort out of Burnley. The local constabulary deposited them at the top of the M65 slip road, from where it was only about three hundred yards to the motorway itself.

However, by the time the coach had made it down into the slow lane, the rest of the coaches had left them for dead. A mile or two later, Geoff turned to Raich and uttered something along the lines that this coach would never make it over the M62. Sure enough, about one hundred yards short of the Yorkshire – Lancashire border, the old boneshaker came grinding to a halt.

This is the highest and bleakest stretch of the motorway in England and just about inescapable on foot. The only entertainment was to nip up to the White Rose boundary stone, stand in Yorkshire, and piss back into Lancashire.

Just over an hour later, a third coach came to the rescue. The problem being that it was a replica of the one they had just abandoned, both in looks and performance. This one didn't require a massive hill on which to break down. Somewhere near junction 31, coach number three gave up and once again, they were stranded in the middle of nowhere and running short of patience. Simon demanded everybody stay on the coach, but spotting some steps up the grass bank from the hard shoulder, a small group decided to go on an exploration. Several fields, a farm track and a country lane later, they found themselves in a hostelry on some council estate on the edge of they-know-not-where.

After a quick pint, they loaded themselves up with bottles and returned to the M62 where the rest of the party were still waiting for yet another replacement coach. Another one did turn up and they finally made it back to Ferensway at about 11.15pm, just after closing time in those days. They remembered the quizword, the 'three down' was obviously referring to coaches!

Six hours to get back from Burnley was quite amazing even by Simon Gray standards. So after a trip that in total involved one van and four coaches, a few subsequent trips that never saw City win a point, Geoff politely told me that *"Turf Moor is the place of nightmares, I think I'll pass if you don't mind."*

I couldn't argue after that story.

I myself said to Thomas after our last visit there in the Premier League that he had full permission to tell me to shut up if I ever suggested going back to the godforsaken place again. He did try and remind me of this but I suppose this book has kind of got in the way. We certainly won't be rushing back there in the future (unless we end up playing them in the play offs this season).

So after a definite 'no' from Geoff, we ended up going with Bri Lee again, and his dad Bri Lee Senior.

Bri Lee Senior used to be a horse jockey back in the day, including once riding a 25/1 winner of the Lincoln in 1961, on a horse called Johns Court. For those of you that can recall, he also led that white horse around the Boothferry Park pitch with Don Robinson perched on top wearing a cowboy hat.

Stories were told of horse races in days gone by, in particular one meeting at Pontefract involving Lester Pigott. I've tried to research this on the internet but had little joy as the race was back in the 1960's.

At this meeting, Lester already had four rides selected, all of which were favourites. The course executive asked if, for a small fee, he'd also pick two more rides so that he had one in every race. This would hopefully bump up the attendance figures. Lester agreed and one of these was a horse called Sarajass. Now this horse was extremely unfancied and had finished last on all of its previous outings, a real donkey. It also happened to be in a race with four very fancied horses and, one of which was being ridden by Bri Lee Senior, and one other, being ridden by a young apprentice on only his second or third ride. The young lad was extremely nervous, particularly being in the company of such a legend like Lester Pigott. To make the race more interesting, Lester had a side bet of £10 with another jockey called Kipper Lynch, that he wouldn't come last, which based on Sarajass' previous showings was an almost certainty.

As the race started, Lester took up position next to the young apprentice and told him that he'd look after him, *'just go round with me and you'll be fine'*. As was expected, the four fancied horses duly went about twenty lengths clear almost out of sight. Lester and the young apprentice carried on going round together, chatting along the way, until the last furlong when, with a crack of the whip, Lester and Sarajass just pipped the young apprentice at the post.

Back in the weighing room, Lester gave that grin from ear to ear, and took his £10 bet winnings, immediately passing £5 of it to the young apprentice, in full view of everyone. Bri Lee Senior swears that Lester took as much pleasure from that particular race, as he did from many of his big race wins. Oh for City to pip Burnley at the post today.

Bri Lee Junior just rolled his eyes whilst the story was being told, having flashbacks of days as a five or six year old, being dragged around racecourses up and down the country, to the delights of such places as Ayr and alike.

As we rolled into Burnley, surprise surprise, it was pissing it down. The car park at the cricket ground (our usual watering hole) was full so we parked further up at the tennis club, and decided to just go straight into the ground. No lucky pint, but the sooner we were in and out of here the better, being the thought process.

The game was played in horrible conditions and overall it was a tight affair, with one goal either way always likely to be decisive.

Burnley started the better in the first half, although their most likely route to goal was always from set pieces, corners and free kicks. Ben Mee saw a header saved by McGregor before he made an even better save, tipping over a Joey Barton header, following a short corner. The Burnley keepers main effort in the first half came from a Robert Snodgrass volley.

He was certainly busier in the second half mind, as City came out stronger. First Heaton saved well from a Moses Odubajo drive, and then he was quickly off his line to thwart Hernandez, who was clean through on goal. City's best chance soon fell to Hernandez again, who unfortunately saw a diving header from six yards go over the bar. Fine margins in the game, and had one of those chances gone in, City may well have been going home with a 1-0 win.

As it turned out, a goalkeeping error led to Burnley's winner with just thirteen minutes of normal time remaining. An Arfield cross was only half cleared to Barton on the edge of the area. McGregor couldn't hold onto his half volley, and the ball spilled to Sam Vokes, who swivelled and turned it home from close range. Mcgregor will be annoyed with himself, but as is often the case when a goalkeeper makes an error, it invariably ends up in a goal. The weather conditions were certainly not in Allan's favour today, and his error (Wolves aside), was not in keeping with his recent displays.

City couldn't muster up any response in the remainder of the game, and once again, we departed Turf Moor pointless. It was a frustrating afternoon, as a point was the least a hard fought display merited. It would also have kept some daylight between us and Burnley. After Boxing Day, Burnley were eight points behind the automatic promotion slots. They were now only just behind us and look like they have real momentum.

But hey this is Hull City, never know how to make things easy! Just hope we don't have to come here again.

"...BURNLEY'S A SHITHOLE, I WANNA GO HOME..."

CHAPTER 44

BLACKBURN (A) –
SATURDAY 13TH FEBRUARY 2016

"HERNANDEZ AND DIAME AT THE DOUBLE"

I think we must be stuck in a loop here, we've got a serious sense of déjà vu. For the third Saturday on the trot, we were making the trip to East Lancashire, this time to Ewood Park and Blackburn. The two previous Saturdays having seen us visit Bury and Burnley, all within about a twenty mile radius of one another.

Ewood Park has not historically been a happy place for City to visit with only three wins in the last thirty visits. It was one of the first away grounds that I took Thomas to, then aged just five. The occasion was our first away game in The Premier League when a looping header by Richard Garcia saw us come away with a point in a 1-1 draw.

The earliest visit I can remember making was for a League Cup match back in 1991, when an Andy Payton goal secured a 1-1 draw. City eventually knocked them out, winning the second leg at home. At the time this was something of a shock, Blackburn eventually getting promotion from the old Second Division that year through the play offs, with a certain Kenny Dalglish as manager. We finished fourteenth in the old Third Division.

The following three seasons saw Blackburn finish fourth, second and first in The Premier League. This was all assisted by the millions of Jack Walker and the goals of Shearer and Sutton. They were like the forerunners of today's Manchester City and Chelsea. The first signs of things to come and how the game would be dictated by money, it has now just risen to a totally different level. Millions have become billions.

Blackburn couldn't sustain this, and eventually after sacking Roy Hodgson, now the 'mastermind' behind the England national team, they were relegated. A string of top name managers followed, including the likes of Graeme Souness, Sam Allardyce and Mark Hughes, and they returned to enjoy a few more years in The Premier League. Ultimately a change of ownership followed, seeing a downturn in fortunes and a second relegation back to The Championship. The new owners were Venky's, an Indian company specialising in chicken meat processing, and, are you ready for this, pharmaceutical products for both poultry and human useage. According to their financial statements, they bought the club in 2010 when the accounts showed a worth of plus £26million. By 2015, they showed a deficit of £57million, a turnaround of some £83million! They also show that annual operating losses were running at £24million per year. This is not the same Blackburn Rovers anymore.

They look like, at best, they'll be staying in The Championship, and had it not been in recent seasons for the goals of Jordan Rhodes, they could well have dropped even further. I felt like we owed them one today as Mr Rhodes had denied us three points earlier in the season, when we allowed him to score an injury time equaliser at the KC. He wouldn't be facing us today though, as just prior to the end of the January transfer window, finances I suspect, had seen him sold to one of our promotion rivals Middlesbrough, in a protracted affair.

Blackburn's replacement for Jordan Rhodes hardly had us quaking in our boots. A familiar face in Danny Graham, once again sent out by his parent club on loan. Having endured a barren spell at City on a supposed season long loan in the 2013/14 season, he mustered up only one goal in eighteen games. We sent him back early. As it was today, he didn't play due to an injury.

One of the great things about doing this book is that it has made me get in contact with various people that otherwise I may not have done. One of those was our guest today, Ian Warvill.

Ian was an ex work colleague of mine over ten years ago. I'd always got on well with Ian, he's a very down to earth guy and fairly laid back. It helped that he loves to talk football, especially Hull City. I moved on from that particular employment, but Ian has since been a formidable part of a management buy out of his employer, CPD Limited, and is now a part owner of a multi million pound turnover company. Not bad for a Hull lad, but just rewards for all the hard work Ian has put in.

This period of time did not go without its fair share of troubled times for Ian. As mentioned, Ian has a deep rooted love of football and was still playing as a forward well into his forties, predominantly in the Humber Premier League, for the likes of Malet YC and Reckitts.

At the age of forty four, during one season, Ian had noticed a small growth developing on his right ankle. This wasn't causing him any great pain, so as most blokes would do, he pretty much ignored it and carried on regardless. The growth started to enlarge until eventually it was coming over the side of his boot, thus causing somewhat more inconvenience. This, added to a bit more ribbing from his teammates, persuaded Ian to finally get it checked out, fully expecting it to be nothing serious.

No alarm bells were indicated by the initial scans and checks, but better to be safe than sorry, further tests were undertaken. At no point during this process did Ian seem too concerned, although I'm not sure the same could be said about his wife, Jenny.

Eventually all the tests were complete and the final diagnosis was in. After thinking it was nothing, Ian was diagnosed as having Synovial Sarcoma. This is a rare form of cancer which usually occurs near the joints, and worse still, it is malignant. Fortunately the tests had shown that there had been no spread as yet, but just to make sure and prevent any possible future spreading, there was only one option. Off with his leg. Just below the knee.

Ian, being Ian, took all this in his stride. In a way, he said that once he was told it was cancerous, he was just relieved that it had not spread. The loss of part of his leg, whilst inconvenient, could be coped with. I'm not sure I would have had the same mental approach.

Obviously difficult discussions were had informing his children, but as a family they all rallied round. In fact, Ian even cut short his convalescence period, as he couldn't cope with the 'fussing' that his wife was making. Within two weeks, he was back at work with the aid of crutches and wheelchair looking like Pirate Warvill.

Soon after, replacement leg was measured and fitted and 'he was as good as new'. Gutted that his football playing days were over, he started helping out with coaching and even joked about being in the Paralympics.

Although, this wasn't quite the throw away line it sounded like. Since that day, Ian claims to have three legs (don't we all), all used for slightly different things. One of these is a blade, like the one that paralympians now use, and Ian is actively competing on 10k runs. This certainly makes me feel very humble, sometimes I can't be arsed to go downstairs and apparently both my legs are able.

He also quipped about being Hull's very own Oscar Pistorius, suggesting that after the latter had received a custodial sentence, he'd written to him asking if he could borrow his blades, as he wouldn't be getting much use out of them for a while! He also added though, that Jenny is now frightened to go to the toilet during the night.

A whole new meaning to the phrase, 'he's got a third leg.'

Ian even has his own 'Hull City' leg which is painted black and amber and sporting a club badge. This generally gets used on holiday to 'spread the word' of our team.

Ian was always a laid back chap but perhaps understandably, his outlook on life has changed somewhat. Basically he said don't 'dilly dally' on making decisions about whether to do something or not. Just face things head on and live life to the full. It was great to listen to and Ian was very open about it all. It certainly gave me food for thought, and when you hear stories like that, really helps you put things into perspective.

So whilst the main topic of conversation could have been a bit depressing, Ian ensured it wasn't and we arrived at Ewood Park in high spirits, and fully expecting a City win. We weren't disappointed.

Blackburn were a poor team and probably a good one for us to come up against following last week's loss at Burnley. One change saw Huddlestone come in for Hayden.

The first half was fairly scrappy, once again played in damp and miserable conditions. Few chances were created by either team really. McGregor comfortably saved a couple of shots from outside the box from Ben Marshall and Craig Conway. Diame had City's best effort, when after beating two defenders, one with a nutmeg, drove a decent effort just over the bar. It would have been a screamer had it gone in, but we went into the break at 0-0. It was a familiar tale of many first half displays this season so far.

And the second half also followed previous scripts as City exerted total dominance, almost straight from the kick off. Robertson was effective bombing forward and half chances started to be created in quick succession.

Within ten minutes of the restart, we'd taken the lead. Snodgrass won the ball just in our half, found Diame and his through ball, aided by a deflection, found Hernandez, who rounded the keeper and slid the ball into an empty net. He celebrated as the 1,311 City fans in The Darwen End rejoiced. I asked Ian if he was going to take his leg off and wave it in the air, but he declined.

Blackburn briefly retaliated and Robertson cleared a corner off the line but soon after City went 2-0 up and effectively killed the game off as any sort of contest. Huddlestone dinked a ball over the top for Hernandez to run onto. Rather than go for goal, he unselfishly squared to Diame, he this time passing it into an empty net. It all looked so easy, and was.

From there on in, City cruised to victory and many of the home fans were heading for the exits long before the final whistle. McGregor was still required to make a couple of saves, although a third goal also went begging, when Akpom couldn't beat the keeper from six yards.

Overall, we were just too strong for a poor Blackburn team. A comfortable win. If City could maintain the intensity that the twenty minutes or so after half time showed for greater periods of the game, then we would be 'blowing teams away'. But never the less, the win returned City to the summit of The Championship.

With traffic at a standstill after the match, we chose to celebrate with a cheeky pint. Jackets were zipped up so that no colours were showing and we went in the 'No Away Fans' pub The Fox and Hounds. Whilst we were glowing on the inside, the Blackburn fans were certainly sounding disgruntled.

A good day to be a City fan, great company, and cause for optimism again.

"...HE'S ONLY GOT ONE LEG, (ACTUALLY HE'S GOT FOUR ALTOGETHER)..."

CHAPTER 45

BRIGHTON (H) – TUESDAY 16TH FEBRUARY 2016

"THE PRICE OF FOOTBALL FOR NO GOALS"

Unlike many of the previous chapters, for this one, I am first going to talk about the match and guests, and then onto something more important currently happening in the game. This is predominantly because tonight's match itself was something of a damp squib, so there isn't too much to say about it.

The match promised something mouth watering, a top of the table clash in the race to reach The Premier League. City were top, Brighton third. In the end, neither team really pushed on to try and win it, more intent on ensuring they didn't lose. It didn't really have a 'must win' feel about, more a 'must not lose' feel. We all therefore left with an air of frustration as both teams nullified each other. City remained top, but the chance for us to open up a gap was missed, and a 0-0 draw was played out.

This was only the second time City had failed to score at home this season. This was mainly down to Brighton packing five men in midfield, with clear intent on show that they would be happy to be going home to the south coast with a point. City simply struggled to break them down, and looked laboured with a lack of any decent final ball to cause real trouble.

Brighton had the only real chance of note in the first half, McGregor saving from a well struck shot by James Murphy. Huddlestone fired a low drive just wide, but it was all fairly lacklustre.

The signs were there early on tonight when our guests, Jo and son Jay-j Sams turned up, only to realise that they had accidently thrown one of their tickets in the bin. What they actually had was one ticket and one receipt. Jo smiled nicely at a steward, acted a bit dumb and pity was taken, and allowed to sneak in. In fact, the cheeky cow even had the temerity to escape the queues as well.

Danny Ings wheels away to the North East Corner. City slump to a 0-1 home defeat to 'Bloody Burnley'. A Book is born.

(Getty Images)

Relegation in 14/15 is confirmed. The book is happening.

(Getty Images)

Sam Clucas gets the sesaon up and running at home to 'Uddersfield.

(Getty Images)

Modern day football, but honestly, pink boots …? Chuba Akpom celebrates a penalty shoot out win away at Accrington (who are they …?) Stanley

(Getty Images)

Allan takes a few hand gestures after a howler in our first away league game at Wolves.

(PA Images)

Abel makes the long midweek trip to Cardiff worthwhile. 2-0 to the En-ger-land (with the help of Senegal and Uruguay)

(PA Images)

The enigmatic Myler celebrates the winner against Swansea in the League Cup.

(Getty Images)

Jamie Vardy in the middle of a record goal scoring run. Big 'Arry says 'Have that, you ain't scoring against us.' Greavesy would have been proud.

(Getty Images)

Home performance of the season? The Thud seals a 3-0 win against Boro'.

(PA Images)

A player that cost more than the entire City squad puts us to the sword, and out of the League Cup at the QF stage. Money talks in todays game.

(PA Images)

A brief highlight in a 2-1 away defeat at L***s. Elmo heads in. We were shit.

(Getty Images)

Take that Joey. Influential Livermore strikes in a 3-0 home win on Boxing Day against 'Bloody Burnley.'

(PA Images)

'We're gonna win the league.' Diame dinks in to send us back to the summit at Ipswich.

(PA Images)

'Cheat Fell Over.' No luck in February, absent in May.

(PA Images)

Steve Bruce feels the pressure after defeat away to Birmingham.

(PA Images)

But don't worry, because …

(Getty Images)

I probed Jo for any football stories of note that she had, and who would have believed it, for the second game in succession, this involved someone with a false leg. What are the chances of that? This chap (not Ian Warvill from the Blackburn chapter), happened to work at the same employer as Jo, and had something of penchant for obtaining freebies from various suppliers, his work drawers were full of the stuff. Jo, thinking she was being funny, one early morning rooted through a drawer and picked out what she thought was a hat. Placing said 'hat' on her head, she sat in the chaps chair awaiting his arrival, fully expecting laughter from him. This did not quite happen, as when he did turn up, he revealed it was not a hat after all, his immediate response being, *"Why are you wearing my stump sock on your head?"* Jo just looked sheepish, there being no real answer, quickly removed the garment, replaced it in the drawer from where it came, and slid back to her own chair.

She also later witnessed the same chap, having a kick about with his son one day in the park, only to be shocked to see his false leg fly off in mid action.

There was a little more excitement in the second half, but little is the operative word. Much of the half was spent concentrating on food and drink purchases, sweets, meat pies and hot chocolate. It was almost as if we were at the pictures, the football widow precariously balancing a tray of goodies on her knees. It was just that the film was far from a blockbuster.

In amongst the troughing, numerous games of crowd spotting took place, where you try and look for someone sat in another stand, think you've found them, and then end up waving inanely at them. They clearly can't see you!

On the pitch, Huddlestone shot straight at the keeper and Hernandez blazed over. Brighton nearly snatched it late on when Louis Dunk was allowed to run unchallenged all the way from his own half. With McGregor stood rooted to the spot, we gave a sigh of relief when his curled shot went only inches wide. The best City chance was saved until right at the death when Clucas was denied with a rasping shot, that David Stockdale got his fingertips to, pushing the ball onto the crossbar. We could have snatched it, but in truth, we hadn't done enough to merit a win.

Elsewhere, in the general arena of football, a groundswell of activity is taking place in an attempt to reduce ticket prices. The main focus of attention in the media has been surrounding The Premier League and a campaign entitled 'Twenty's Plenty', an attempt to get all away tickets for all Premier League games capped at £20. They are currently miles away from this (and not only in The Premier League I may add).

For years the admission prices at football matches has always been on the increase. Occasionally you hear of clubs reducing prices for particular matches, preferring to fill empty seats than see swathes of barren areas, but these are fleeting.

If you are a football fan who regularly attends matches of your team, you will comprehend that it's not an easy thing to simply stop going. Your team is in your system, it's almost become part of your DNA, to some it can be like an addiction, a hard habit to break. And in the main, I believe that football clubs play on this.

Prices have continued to rise, despite the ever increasing influx of money into the game. In the next three seasons, as a result of a new sale of broadcasting rights to Sky, BT Sports and overseas revenue, no club in the top flight will receive less than £100 million per season. That's £300 million per club over the three seasons at least, and in total £8.3 billion will be shared amongst clubs in The Premier League.

Clubs have continually trotted out the lines that ticket prices need to rise, to ensure they can 'compete on the pitch'. This is simply not true. The actual revenue received from ticket sales is becoming a smaller and smaller percentage of clubs overall income. So naturally a reduction in ticket prices has only minimal effect on them. For a club say having an average attendance of 20,000, nineteen home games a season, a £5 reduction for all fans, amounts to £1.9million. That is less than 2% of their TV income, or maybe a years wages for a 'half decent' player, or in City's terms, less than half the fee we paid for Jimmy Bullard, probably the amount we equated to his dodgy knee. You can do your own maths pro-rata'ing this figure up or down, but either way it is not much.

With ever increasing prices, families will soon not be able to keep attending games together like Thomas and I are this season. The likelihood of your children falling in love with the game, the way most of us did when we first walked into a ground may be lost forever. The sights, the floodlights, the smells and sounds, the whole sensory experience could skip generations, instead being replaced by a corporate tourist repackaged version.

We've kept note of what it has cost us this season and I've included this somewhere towards the back of the book. As I write this, I've just paid £32.50 for a Tuesday night game coming up away at Ipswich. Coupled with the travel, it's a costly affair. Ipswich's ground Portman Road, is allegedly located near a red light area. When I tweeted the cost of my ticket, I did receive some replies that I could probably get more entertainment for half the price nearby! For those of you wondering, I'll be attending the football match.

You'll see from our cost summary, that by the time you add in travel, programmes and a couple of drinks, it's not cheap. Obviously not everyone attends every game but I'm fortunate that I can do so, although I'm sure this season will be a 'one off'. If we are not careful, football fans are in danger of being priced out of the game, the cost will simply be beyond the average working class supporter, if it isn't already. Maybe it is no longer a working class game already.

Surely there is enough money swilling around football for some of it to be filtered down to the spectator. The spectator for me, is the mainstay of a football match, they should be the lifeblood of a team, without supporters the game would be nothing, it would be passionless.

All of the above are the principles behind the Twenty's Plenty campaign. Historically for every supporter that decided they'd had enough, there was another ready to take their place. Further still, for years there has been an assumption that fans would never abandon their team, certainly not in large numbers.

Well maybe times are changing? The Twenty's Plenty campaign has helped to bring spectators together, and rather than act in isolation, to act as a collective. As if to say, football take note.

One of the forerunners of this is Liverpool Football Club.

Last season they had a dabble at making a statement, when many fans boycotted their away fixture at the KC, a stance against the £50 entrance fee. This was nothing directed specifically towards Hull City, we just happened to be their next away fixture. So many bought the cheapest possible ticket, juvenile priced ones, and simply didn't turn up. It was noted in the media. Earlier this month, at a home game against Sunderland they acted with significantly more intent.

The whole thing was a bit of a PR nightmare for the owners of Liverpool, and until recently, their website showed a mission statement of 'transforming fans into customers'. Firstly, how horrible does that sound? I rarely feel like a customer at a football match, often feeling to be in the wrong, despite having paid for the privilege of being there. I am a fan and will remain so.

As part of the plans to redevelop Anfield, news had been released that some tickets for next season were planned to rise to £77. That is an astronomical sum for one person to watch a game of football. Outraged by this, the Liverpool fans planned to stage a walkout of the ground, on the 77th minute to co-incide with the proposed new ticket price.

Now these things have been muted before at grounds but rarely do they amount to anything (as L**ds United demonstrated over the Pie Tax affair earlier in the season). At Anfield, it did amount to something.

At the time during the game, Liverpool were leading 2-0, and seemingly cruising to victory. Cue mass walk out and around 10,000 fans streamed out of the stadium. This was on an unprecedented scale to ever before and was a sight to behold. Watching it later that day on Match of the Day, I applauded those that took the stance.

And did it have an effect?

Well Liverpool then went on to concede two late goals and only draw the game, so you could argue that it affected the players. And furthermore, the club then backtracked on its plans to impose the £77 new ticket price and also changed its mission statement. So yes, it must have had an effect.

As a post script, since then all Premier League clubs have now agreed to place an upper limit of £30 for an away ticket. Exactly how this all pans out, we'll have to wait and see, but at least it's a start?

I totally understand that a club should be run on a sound economic basis, and that these problems are probably accentuated as you go down the football pyramid where the TV monies received are simply not there in such excess. However, all us fans are saying is think of us before splashing the cash on some overrated player. We are as much a part of the game as they are. Within a few years, they'll have all departed, hopefully us fans won't.

In summary tonight, the football, in terms of the league, left us no better off, but no worse off. Had I been a 'customer' though, I might have demanded a refund.

"...WE ONLY WANT ONE MORE, SO COME ON CITY SCORE..."

CHAPTER 46

ARSENAL (A) FA CUP 5TH ROUND – SATURDAY 20TH FEBRUARY 2016

"BORING BORING ARSENAL"

In the last round of the FA Cup, we had a thoroughly enjoyable away day at Bury, which felt as far removed from Premier League football as you could imagine. A small ground, City fans comprising a large part of the crowd, sensible ticket prices, crowd atmosphere and tension, and old fashioned muddy pitch in wintery conditions and several goals thrown in.

Today we went to the other end of the spectrum. We had been drawn away to one of the supposed 'elite' teams in the Premier League, Arsenal. This was the FA Cup after all, and ever since that 'glorious defeat' in the final a few years ago, we have been paired with them every season since. It has become a bit boring? In fact, the question is which team other than Arsenal, were the last team to beat City in the FA Cup? (Answer : Barnsley).

So a trip down to London again it was for us. Were we taking it seriously? Too right us fans were. The demands of television airing meant a lunchtime kick off at 12.45, so an early start of seven am for us. (Tiger Travel set off at 5.15am!). So yes, us fans were taken it seriously, after all this was the fifth round of the FA Cup, so why wouldn't we?

Call me old fashioned, and I am, but I used to love FA Cup Final day. Getting up early to see all the interviews with players, old games, the following of particular team(s) from the earliest qualifying rounds right through to the final itself, the whole build up to the main attraction itself.

However, the gloss seems to have been taken off this old competition now. All the riches on offer for the Premier League have resulted in clubs not taking it seriously. And this isn't just reserved for Premier League teams. Today, Arsenal made nine changes to their starting line up from their previous Premier League game. City, a Championship team with aspirations to get back into the Premier League, made ten. You could say it was Arsenal reserves versus Hull City reserves?

To me this is just another indictment of how the soul and history is being lost from the game down to money. The top teams in the Premier League have sponsors coming out of their ears to help bring more and more money in. Why do Manchester United need a car tyre sponsor? Why do Liverpool need an official skincare partner? Surely a new centre forward or defender would be of more use to them? No, it's so they can generate as much money as possible to become even richer and pay players even higher wages, as if they weren't staggering enough. It certainly doesn't seem to be getting thrown in the direction of the supporters, as ticket prices are not falling. Now there's a whole other story, as briefly touched upon already.

So many team changes did take the shine off this fixture a little. A really congested fixture list for both teams, fixtures that were clearly deemed to be of higher importance, almost implied that neither team would want a replay, in fact, would they be that bothered if they lost? Surely that can't be the right mentality can it? Yes, the usual lines will be trotted out, '*I fielded a team that I thought could win the game*' or '*We will use the full squad*', but did both teams really today?

As it turned out, City put in a stellar defensive display and we 'thrashed' them nil nil! More of the actual game a bit later in this chapter. So neither team got what they wanted. Another game, a replay at the KC, I forever seem to be going to football at the moment.

Despite all of what I've said so far, it must be said that Arsenal do have a fantastic stadium. Yes, it may be a little sanitised in atmosphere (stewards insisting on fans remaining in seats), and more like a theatre than football stadia, but it is always a good experience for an away fan. This is still Arsenal though, so we were clearly travelling with hope more than expectation.

And today, we spiced things up a little with our guests. We were joined by Colin and Cavan McGee (12), good friends and neighbours of ours. You've guessed it, they are Arsenal fans who were sitting in the City seats with us! I agreed to drive there and back on the firm understanding that they didn't jump up and celebrate when Arsenal scored. I say, 'when', as being the eternal pessimist, I did fully expect Arsenal to score. They agreed and I hope you'll agree when you've finished this chapter, that they shared a few great stories with us on the journey.

Colin's parents who were Irish, was born and raised on the doorsteps of Loftus Road in Shepherds Bush, the home of QPR. Naturally his father used to take Colin along to QPR home games often only paying for one ticket, his dad stating that '*the boy will sit on my knee, so I only want one seat*'. It always seemed to work apparently, although Colin didn't actually confess as to what age this practice carried on until.

Naturally then, Colin assumed that they both supported QPR, and that his father had 'taught him the ways'. It was only after a few years when one day, whilst perched on his dad's knee at a match, as Colin cheered for QPR, his dad told him to keep quiet. '*Why dad?*' he asked. '*We don't actually support this lot son, we just come because they are near. We support the Arsenal!*'

This obviously confused Colin, but he started to then take an interest in Arsenal Football Club, to understand why. The reason as informed by his father was mainly due to the large Irish connection at Highbury. This was during an era with Liam Brady, Frank Stapleton, David O'Leary, Pat Jennings, to name a few. And so, as duly informed by his father, and even though Colin is by his own admission, 'a plastic paddy', his team of choice from then on became Arsenal. After all, his dad was only doing exactly what I am, indoctrinating his son into '*their*' team. Mind you, at least I'm taking Thomas to watch the correct team!

As Colin got older, and many jobs later (he's had more jobs than some people have had hot dinners, including the obligatory White Van Man), he eventually met up with his now wife, Jackie. Family reasons ultimately resulted in a relocation, 'Up North' to Beverley, now having four children (should keep it in your pants Colin!).

Always keen to talk anything to do with football, Colin and I often discuss how City are doing, Arsenal's progress (or lack of it), and generally discuss anything round ball related. When the cup draw was made, they seemed a natural choice of guest.

The family are practising Christians, although this is not 'rammed down your throat'. Colin is currently playing, at the tender age of 44, in a Christian football league that covers most of Yorkshire. The general loose rules are that each team should have at least four or five practising Christians playing. There is no evidence of this, it's just understood that no team surely would be lying! I did also ask, but no, there was no swearing at the matches, certainly not taking the Lord's name in vain. I wondered how I would get on (not very well), and whether this would be a bookable offence.

He told me a little story of a previous week's fixture that certainly amused me. Or maybe I was mocking Colin a little. In this fixture, Colin was playing up front and scored a hat trick in a comfortable victory. However he seemed to have a gripe about a fourth goal that was never given. One of Colin's shots apparently had clearly gone over the line by several yards, after only being half saved by the keeper. We were talking a real Roy Carroll moment. Instead of admitting this and owning up, the keeper quickly dragged the ball back in front of the line, claiming a genuine save. No goal was given. Of course the goalie wasn't lying, and he wasn't confessing today.

Colin and Cavan's next few stories really are some to be proud of. These involve Cavan's Sunday football team, Beverley Town Dynamo's.

Somehow they had been invited to play and attend a weekend training session and mini football tournament at Barcelona. That's right, they actually played a couple of games at the Nou Camp, on the same pitch where Messi, Neymar and Suarez are currently ripping up La Liga.

At the time, they were an under 11's team playing against an under 12's opposition. The first match, all teams actually running out the tunnel to the fanfare of The Champions League music. Real childhood dream stuff.

Just before the first game kicked off, one of Cavan's team mates, Jack, decided to leave his mark on the sacred turf. Before jetting off to Barcelona, one of Jack's teeth had fallen out. Rather than wait for the usual £1 from the tooth fairy, Jack decided he had alternative plans for it, mindful of his ensuing trip. Tooth carefully hidden in his sock, he swiftly headed over to the centre circle of the Nou Camp pitch. A quick bend down, pretending to fasten his boot laces, (do they even have laces anymore?) and he quickly scooped a handful of turf out of the centre spot. Tooth was then carefully removed from sock, placed in newly dug hole, and lump of turf replaced. No one would ever know! Just a great story I thought, and I'll chuckle every time I see Barcelona kick off in future. I hope Luis '..*his teeth are offside..*' Suarez never has the same idea mind, there would be a mound in the pitch!

Colin at the time having to watch the action in the stands, was also desperate to get onto the hallowed turf. Clearly too old to come on as a substitute for a cameo appearance, (he'd never fit in the shirt anyway) he did eventually manage to blag his way on, suggesting that the boys needed some more water bottles. He therefore became the Didier Deschamps of the under 11's team – the water carrier.

Once the game started for the Dynamo's though, things did get a little worse. Cavan went on to score an own goal. At least he can say he has scored at the Nou Camp.

The final story of the day, before I actually mention the City showing, came from Colin's wife Jackie.

In her far flung youth, Jackie was a talented up and coming gymnast. This must have been many years ago as I'm sure all gymnasts retire once they get past about fifteen years old. Anyway, she managed to reach the top few girls in the North of England.

However, time after time, competition after competition, she felt like being the perennial bridesmaid, always finishing second to the same girl. Always magnanimous in defeat in the runners up spot, on every single occasion, Jackie went over to her competitor and congratulated her, shaking her hand and saying something along the lines of 'Well done, you deserved to win'.

At one rare competition though, the tables were turned, and Jackie emerged victorious – the usual winner this time in second place. It was the day Jackie had yearned for. Fully expecting to now have praise proffered to her, she waited in anticipation. Instead, her rival frogmarched in her direction, and once face to face, just said 'Fuck Off', turned and frogmarched back again. Clearly this took the shine off for Jackie. The story takes more appeal when the identity of the uncourteous girl is known. It is no other than.......................................
For obvious reasons, I'm not going to state the name. All I will say is that she now can be seen hosting or taking part in various sporting programmes on television.

By chance, within days of hearing that story, all four of the football widow, Thomas, Charlotte and I happened to be watching a particular television programme when said 'girl' appeared on the screen. And the next thing really did happen. None of us spoke, but almost in unison, all four of us flicked the v's at the screen as if to return the compliment paid to Jackie all those years ago.

So umpteen stories later, we duly parked up at Cockfosters tube station and took the short trip to Arsenal. Colin and Cavan requested if they could have a quick look in the Arsenal club shop. I agreed only on the proviso that if they bought anything, it had to be removed from the Arsenal carrier bag and placed in a Sainsbury's carrier bag.

Whilst in there, I couldn't help myself. Most of the customers were purring over the Arsenal paraphernalia, but I was more intent on looking at my phone. One of the overkeen shop assistants approached me and asked, "*Can I help you, are you looking for anything?*" I replied, "*Have you got any trophies?*" He gave a wry smile and I ended the conversation with "*Nothing in here of any interest for me*", and returned to my phone to see if any team news was yet out, had I heard of any of the names, and who would have the most ridiculous squad number. I think number 54 for Arsenal won it on the day.

I then forced the other three to sneak a quick drink in The Drayton Arms, located near the away end. This isn't the most attractive pub but for some reason I like it. Many City fans were already there, and it was amusing to listen to the back bar singing "*We're the left side, we're the left side, we're the left side Hull City*". The front bar then responding with "*We're the right side, we're the right side, we're the right side Hull City*".

Due to the fact that I was driving, and it was £4.50 a pint, we didn't stay long and then entered the stadium. As I said earlier, you can't help but be impressed. We quickly got a vantage point for our flag (which was actually picked up later on Match of the Day) and left it with a chap called Mike to look after, as our seats were miles away. There were lots of Arsenal ones on display from every far flung corner of the globe, although my favourite was simply the words '*It's up for grabs now – Anfield 89*', a reference to the iconic commentary line when Arsenal won the title over Liverpool on goal difference with practically the last kick of the season through a Michael Thomas goal (sorry any Liverpool fans reading!)

There seemed to be lots of unfamiliar faces in the City corner today, several of them being what I would refer to as football tourists, all taking selfies on their mobile phones, and also boyfriends and girlfriends holding hands, all at their 'one a season' football match. To be fair, I'm being a bit hypocritical here, as all season, I've been taking photos on my phone. My excuse is that I'm trying to get some decent photos either for this book or to post on Twitter.

A battling draw keeps the FA Cup run alive.
We thrashed Arsenal 0-0 thanks to the Jak.

There were some familiar faces too though. I bumped into an old school friend Paul Bell and son John (7). Whilst we probably had loads to catch up on having barely seen each other for twenty plus years, the only topic of conversation was Hull City.

Mark Tomlinson, Tommo, Cottingham's very own answer to Frankie Goes To Hollywood, was also in attendance, and we often bump into him at City matches. I always remember Tommo as in our Sunday league footy days, he always used to roll the top of his shorts over, in Gareth Roberts fashion. He claimed it made his legs look longer.

We also bumped into Nick, Adele and Harry West, who had travelled down on the train. Adele later told me that she was looking forward to a good drink on the way home to celebrate City's result. She was denied as the 'gestapo' train stewards were refusing to serve alcohol, as there were too many football supporters on the train!

The match finally kicked off in a fairly subdued atmosphere, the Arsenal fans couldn't be bothered. An early rendition of *"Two nil and you facked it up"* (obvious reference to the recent FA Cup final) was all they offered. The City fans retorted with "*You're just a small team in Tottenham*".

The full ninety minutes followed in a fairly predictable pattern, but possibly not the final outcome or matchday City hero.

Arsenal dominated possession, typically overplaying at times. It wasn't a bad performance by Arsenal, but it was distinctly average, in the main, unthreatening and lacking cutting edge. There was creativity, but actual danger was noticeably absent. As the minutes ticked by, I felt more and more confident that they wouldn't score.

That is not to diminish the sterling City rearguard effort though. Man to man, they all put in a good shift. And when Arsenal did work a way through, today they found Eldin Jakupovic on great form. On a number of occasions he produced fine saves, most notably from a Joel Campbell free kick, doing just enough to touch the ball onto the post, and then later tipping a deflected shot with his wrong hand around the post.

On a rare foray up front, Maguire gave a Cryuff like turn in the Arsenal box and then rather than shooting, he chose to dive and rightly received a yellow card. Welbeck did similar at the other end, but surprisingly did not see a card brandished. Or should I say *un*surprisingly, due to the usual 'big team bias'.

Arsenal did have a couple more genuine penalty appeals. Alex Bruce appeared to handball and a Meyler tackle on Chambers could have been given. It wouldn't have mattered though as on today's showing, 'The Yak' would have saved them both anyway!

By now the weather had changed to lots of rain. Phil Brown, commentating for BT Sports, must have been worried that his tan may have run, when having to carry out half time analysis pitchside. The Arsenal fans just watched silently in frustration, those in the lower seats dressed in plastic macs looking, well just ridiculous and glum. And wet.

So City held on for a nil nil draw and 'It's all back to ours' for a replay. More indication of the 'football tourists' as I heard a conversation between two Arsenal fans just behind us as we walked out. A big American chap saying to his colleague in a thick yank accent, "*Gee, and the referee blew, and no overtime?*" What is the game coming too?

We descended into the wet London streets and Thomas refuelled at a catering van. The owner was clearly more enthusiastic that the Arsenal fans with loud shouts of "*Alright darling*", "*Alright Big Man*"(to *Thomas*), "*Look at them luverly burgers*", "*Any chips with that, cheese, onions…*", "*Luverly, Jubberly*". This amused us all the way back to Finsbury Park tube station and before we knew it, we were heading back home. Colin and Cavan enquired if we could get some tickets for the replay. Are you sure you're not becoming City fans I asked.

Upon returning through our door, the football widow was getting a bit of revenge. She was hosting a girly curry night in, and so we were banished upstairs. She quickly had time to say that she'd listened to the game on '4 Live' (actually 5 Live!). Years ago, we might have watched it on Ceefax, waiting for the pages to turn over with anticipation of whether your team had scored or not, sitting with fingers crossed. Or even before that ringing the City scoreline service up, where a bloke would read out the score, and it would then get updated every two minutes or so. Nothing like actually being there I say.

However, stuck in our bedroom, with girly laughter emanating from downstairs, we thought what the hell, let's watch the highlights on Match of the Day anyway. Both managers bemoaned a fixture pile up, and concerns over when the replay would be.

Brucey even suggested that replays be scrapped and we just go to penalties after the first game. Nah said Thomas, let's try something different. Let's have Rock, Paper, Scissors, best of three.

Thomas to replace Sepp Blatter.

"…YOU'LL NEVER BEAT THE YAK…"

CHAPTER 47

IPSWICH TOWN (A) –
TUESDAY 23RD FEBRUARY 2016

"FATHER AND SON"

When the fixture list was released, this was one I wasn't looking forward to. Ipswich away on a Tuesday night, a round drive of just over four hundred miles and a guaranteed late finish. Fingers were crossed that Thomas would manage to get up for school the following day. As it turned out, it was one of my favourite trips so far, a real bonding session between Father and Son.

The day before the fixture, I read that the team were flying down the day before. How rude of them not to invite us to join them, surely there would have been room for two more? So I thought stuff it, if you can't beat them join them. A quick scour of the internet and I found a hotel room for us to stay at the night before, within walking distance of Portman Road, the Penta Hotel in Ipswich.

So the new plan was to drive down just after school chucking out time on the Monday evening. This prevented me driving there and back in the same day, but also offered me the luxury of having a few beers on the evening. We would then just see what Ipswich had to offer during the day, before heading off to the match on the evening and then drive back home straight after full time.

Now I'm sure our hotel won't have been to the same standard that the team were staying in, but it suited us just fine. It was one of those cheap hotels, the ones that have coat hangers but no actual wardrobe. However, we are males after all, so who needs a wardrobe when we just throw our clothes on the floor anyway or don't even take them out the suitcase.

Upon arrival the hotel was ideal for father and son on a football expedition. Not only did it have a twenty four hour bar (if you wanted it), there was live football on multiple screens, it had a free pool table, and even had a PlayStation and screen in one corner of the bar, for the little 'uns. And no stupid early check out so we were okay to hang around all of the following day as well if we wanted. It was like an enormous man cave and suited us down to a tee.

Several beers were supped and Thomas even drew a small crowd when re-enacting a game of Hull City V Ipswich Town on FIFA. Unfortunately, the 'dry run' ended in City losing 2-0 to a 10 man Ipswich. Hopefully, this was not to be repeated in real life the following night. Clearly Thomas was not playing against me. I've only just mastered one finger texting on a mobile so there was no chance of me sussing out a PlayStation controller. Not content with that, Thomas then went on an FA Cup run, getting all the way to the final, which certainly occupied his time until just gone midnight. Unfortunately he had changed his team to Arsenal and there was some serious cheating going on in his semi-final, when finding himself 2-1 down with a couple of minutes left, he changed the settings, basically making the opposition into statues, with no ability to run or pass. Surprise, surprise, he scored two late goals and won 3-2. How great would it be to do that in real life!

Me, having spent a few hours with a friend of mine, first name Stella, second name Artois, we actually found ourselves cheering at the screen. Think that was our sign to depart to bed.

The following day saw us try to see the sights of Ipswich Town centre, a short walk away. Either we were in the wrong place, or there isn't any. So this mainly involved Thomas trying to extract money out of me to get a new pair of trainers. It didn't work!

So instead, I suggested seeing if we could get a look in the ground and a couple of photos. Portman Road is full of memorable names, some from my youth. Bobby Robson, Alf Ramsey, Arnold Muhren and Frans Thijssen to name a few, along with a UEFA Cup Final. Whilst the tickets for the game were not cheap, the staff at the ground were very accommodating and after blagging our way into the ground mid-afternoon to get a cheeky photo with our City flag, we descended back to the hotel for a spot of lunch and pool marathon. The afternoon felt long as I was gagging for a beer, but a two hundred mile drive home clearly prevented many of these.

Sneaking in early doors at Ipswich away on a Tuesday night.

As kick off time got nearer, we decided to have a lucky pint. Understandably, the turnout was going to be low (it ended up being 393) but we saw familiar faces in the Station Hotel pub with black and amber on show.

Refuelled again we returned to the ground. On the way we found out that whilst City had not lost against Ipswich in the last seven games, winning five of them, Ipswich had something of a remarkable record when playing at home on a Tuesday night – they had won their last sixteen games on the trot, very impressive indeed.

We were surrounded by Farmer Giles accents on our short walk but soon we were in the upper corner of the The Cobhold Stand, flag hung up and hearing the familiar 'ull accent of *"five and nines"*, all in a fairly confident mood despite that Tuesday night home record of our hosts.

Overall City put on a solid, at times, inspiring performance, especially just after half time, and in the end this yielded a comfortable 1-0 victory (if there is such a thing)? Job done. This was an impressive result against a team just on the edge of the playoffs, but the guile shown in our victory, suggested, what was that Tuesday night record all about?

Having made umpteen changes for the Arsenal FA Cup matches we changed them all back again, pretty much.

The match took the familiar City pattern which we were now getting used to, if not always totally to our liking. The first half was a cagey affair but I always felt we were the better team. We looked more comfortable on the ball and it felt like it would only be a matter of time until a chance came our way.

The first actually came due to a defensive error by Ipswich. Hernandez robbed a defender, who then fouled him just outside the box. Snodgrass, not liked by the home fans due to his previous Norwich connections, struck a fine free kick which the keeper did well to tip over the bar.

Ipswich's best chance came just before half time when Daryl Murphy struck a post but other than that, I can't recall them having a shot on target all night. They were at best workmanlike and one dimensional and as such McGregor could have smoked a cigar.

The half time entertainment treated us to the Ipswich Town City 'Singing the Blues'. They certainly were by full time.

City came to life immediately after the restart and blew away Ipswich, if not in score line. Diame was at times fantastic, troubling their defenders each time he was in possession. In that kind of mood, he is a great player in the Championships; he just needs to be in that mood more often!

After only three minutes of the second half, City had taken the lead. Andy Robertson went on one of his now trademark runs, cutting in from the left all the way to the edge of the box. He played in Diame, whose well timed run was expertly matched with a delicate chip over the advancing keeper.

Chants of "Super, Super Mo, Super, Super Mo, Super, Super Mo, Super Mo Diame"

and

'Stevie Bruce went down South with the British Army,

He came back with a fucking tank

Super Mo Diame'

For the next twenty minutes we had numerous other chances and could've been three or four up. Diame, Meyler and Clucas all came close and Livermore hit a post. On another night, we might have been concerned that we'd let a late equaliser in, but I never thought that would be the case, that's how comfortable it felt.

Even when we made the usual substitutions and finished the game with no recognised strikers on the pitch, it all still felt too easy. I'd even forgotten how bloody cold it was and the full time whistle was greeted with joyous smiles and cheers. Hopefully three points nearer to promotion. Next up, Wednesday on a Friday…if you get my drift.

We descended back to our car park, now noticeably feeling the cold. We quickly turned the heaters up to full and turned on the sat nav. I gave an audible groan as it told us there was two hundred and eight miles until we reached our destination, and then we proceeded to go.. err nowhere! The traffic was extremely slow for thirty minutes or so but eventually it freed up and I put my lead boots on. One good thing about a midweek away game is that there is much less traffic on the road and little sign of any constabulary. Thomas was soon giving it big ZZZ' s but with victory in hand, our mood was good, and we rolled in the front door just gone 1.30am.

A great trip overall, thank you Thomas, thank you City.

"…SUPER MO DIAME…"

CHAPTER 48

SHEFFIELD WEDNESDAY (H)

"WEDNESDAY ON A FRIDAY"

Fresh from the euphoria of the away win at Ipswich, a home game soon followed with yet another Sky televised fixture. Wednesday at home on a Friday, if that makes sense.

This was a big game as Wednesday were still going well and in the playoff spots. However, we were at home and our record so far this season, has been fantastic at the KC.

There should be nothing quite like a local Yorkshire Derby under the lights to generate some atmosphere with two teams going at each other hell for leather. Whilst the ingredients were there for tonight's game, it sadly didn't quite deliver. Don't get me wrong, it wasn't a bad game, always on a knife edge in which either team could have nicked all three points. In the end, both teams had to settle for a 0-0 draw, our second at home on the trot.

Again, it was disappointing that the crowd wasn't slightly higher. Suppose the fact that it was cold (yet again!), the game was on the TV, and the ticket prices are what they are doesn't help. However, you can't help think that there should be ways around this. We were pulling higher attendances when we were playing in the bottom two divisions, yet, here we are on the edge of another great chance to get back into the Premier League. The words apathy and disharmony spring to mind. To some extent I can understand those sentiments. On the walk to the ground tonight, Thomas asked me if I'd prefer City to win the league or get promoted by winning a playoff final at Wembley (assuming you could guarantee the latter that is).

Without hesitation I said, "*Win the league*".

"*Why?*" He asked.

Firstly because I have never seen City actually win anything. The small list of Champions listed in the programme, all relate to my pre-City days. And secondly, because I'm not sure if a playoff final win would ever quite match that day when Deano scored the winner. That year was so unexpected, we just rode the crest of a wave. This season, for some, there is almost an assumption, an expectation that we should go up.

I'm repeating myself now as we are back to this hope and expectation thing. Thirty plus years of City has taught me, never to expect anything (other than to be disappointed at some stage).

I'd lost a few more brownie points for this fixture as we were all supposed to be away for the weekend. So rather than all set off as a family, we left the football widow to pack the car up with suitcases, food, and the dog, and she set off on her own. The three of us just simply rocked up later after the match in what we were standing in. By this time, she had unpacked everything, had her tea and gone to bed. Very understanding she is, but still, a bit of making up to do I fear.

Previous home games against Wednesday usually resulted in some sort of entertainment and talking points. John Parkin's delightful volley on the turn for one. He was a strange and frustrating player. He could certainly play, and as they say, 'had a good touch for a big lad'. However, I think he also liked a pint or two, just to wash down the odd pie or two.

I also recall a Wednesday win recently when Jakupovic inadvertently handed (literally) the lead in a 3-1 loss. For some reason, to my eyes unchallenged, he caught a cross and then carried it over the line. A goal was rightly given and probably due to his acute embarrassment, Eldin stayed down 'as if' injured. He ended up being stretchered off. Now I know for a fact that he wasn't really injured as he was taken next door to Hull Royal Infirmary, where the football widow happened to be working. Something along the lines of 'stop cluttering up A and E' were her words as she came home the following morning.

Tonight, I'd done it again. From somewhere I'd found some supporters of the opposition to join us at the game, in Jon Marris and daughter Faye. Instructions were given again not to declare their allegiances should Wednesday score. I had no worries about Jon doing this, he's not an oike like me!

After the usual quick pint, we took our seats just before kick-off. At this point I noticed that one of the City mascots for the day was Guy Franks, the son of friends and work colleagues Matt and Hannah. Looking splendid in his immaculate pristine City kit, socks 'fashionably' rolled up over his knees (stockings almost in the true sense of the word) he took his position for the pre-match photos.

This took me back to when Thomas was a mascot, an infuriating home match against Watford when Troy Deeney scored a winner right in front of us in a 0-1 home loss. He had been on the waiting list for what felt like ages but eventually his turn arrived. At this point it was time to start negotiating ! I can't recall what the opening price of the 'event' started at, but it was high, and attempted to include the cost of four match tickets, a full new City kit, and even a pre-match meal. Upon stating that we already had season tickets so did not require anymore, that Thomas had already fleeced me for every home, away and third kit that season, and that we'd all prefer to have a meat pie, we eventually managed to get the price reduced a little.

So we were set. Only one adult was allowed to accompany on the pre match ground tour so Charlotte and I remained in the bar whilst Thomas and the football widow were shown around, autograph books in hand. This was followed by a mini training session on the pitch with a youth team coach, during which Thomas got drenched as one of the pitch sprinklers went off. Undeterred and professional as ever, Thomas soldiered on looking like a drowned rat.

He then went on to cheekily ask Robbie Brady if he could possibly have his boots after the game. Courteous as ever, Robbie gave Thomas a polite reply in a brogue Irish accent.

"*What did he say*?" I enquired of Thomas.

"*Dunno, I couldn't understand a word he said!*" was his reply.

And so we were finally dispatched to our seats in the South stand where Thomas then spent the first twenty minutes or so of the game trying to get changed out of his kit and into his clothes. If he'd have had a towel he'd have tried that 'get undressed on the beach thing without anyone seeing you naked'. Deeney then scored to rub salt into the wound and the poor lad then burnt his lip on his meat pie. Not quite the idyllic dream he'd been looking forward to.

It was also another sign of how football has changed over the years. I remember the mascot having a quick knock about with the keeper, playing a few tame back passes to one another in a mud bath of a goalmouth. At some point the goalie might let one in 'accidently' as if to say to the mascot, look you've just scored against me. Really what the mascot wanted to do was smash it into the goal and see the net ripple, and then celebrate in front of the home fans (more of this at half time tonight).

It was also a far cry from a story another work colleague told me, going back to 1988. On this day, the mascot was even allowed to keep the coin that was used for the toss up and actually ended up outside the changing room door for the pre-match team talk. Asked what was discussed the impressionable youngster repeated word for word the managers pep talk.

"Get in their fucking half from the word fucking go and fucking get stuck into the fuckers."

The mascot was eight years old!

The game has moved on from then somewhat, fewer hard men exist, (although it's difficult in a modern day game when you can't actually tackle) and too many players seem to be wrapped up in cotton wool, so far removed from the real world to be true. Try watching from the terraces.

Nostalgia aside, the match started with both teams playing some nice football. Snodgrass had our best chance of the first half, forcing a good save from a volley at the far post but whilst City were lively, they were slightly let down by the quality of final ball and crossing. Wednesday played some neat incisive passing in midfield and looked dangerous going forward. I could feel myself moving nearer to the edge of my seat.

Wednesday came the closest in the first half. Forrestieri, who, the previous match had been sent off for receiving two yellow cards, both for diving, was constantly in the action. First he forced a good save from McGregor from a free kick, and soon after he smashed the crossbar from about thirty yards.

I could see Jon rise slightly in his seat with a quiet murmur of "*ooohh!*"

I uttered "*Fucking hell, we got lucky there!*"

The chance raised the decibels in the away corner with chants of '*Hi Ho Sheffield Wednesday*' and they even had the audacity to sing their own version of '*Steve Bruce had a dream*'. (How very dare they!)

So as we entered the break at 0-0, I felt a little relieved. A young chap came on the pitch at half time to compete in a crossbar challenge, basically trying to strike a ball from near the half way line onto the crossbar. A modern day 'kerbie' if you like. The guy was clearly prepared as he had tracksuit bottoms on and his football boots. I wondered if he'd tiptoed up Anlaby Road in them. Anyway, third time lucky he struck the bar and milked his celebrations. Good on him. I would have done the same.

City improved in the second half and were the better team. Wednesday seemed intent to sit deeper and let us have the ball, whilst retaining men behind it asking us to break them down. This can be City's downfall at times as it is not always that easy. Lots of probing, left to right, sometimes almost overplaying. That's not to say that we didn't create chances and two gilt edged ones fell to Sam Clucas.

Firstly Robertson played him in behind the Owls defence, only for Sam to lift the ball over the advancing keeper but unfortunately into the side netting. Later in the game, Clucas came even closer, when after a one two with Livermore, saw his shot hit the post.

City were definitely in the ascendancy but could not quite do enough to carve out a winner. So for the second home game running we had to settle for a 0-0 draw.

There was still time for a talking point when in injury time, Forrestieri saw red, for his second game running. Having already been booked for a pull on Robertson, he rather unfortunately saw a second yellow for an alleged dive. He had been at it most of the game (Snodgrass also joined in mind) to much derision from the home crowd, so *what comes around, goes around?* However, he was a tad unfortunate on this occasion after a strong challenge on him by Michael Dawson, which saw Forrestieri jump out of the way, immediately prompting me to think that Dawson was in trouble. We waited with bated breath only to laugh when the referee reached in his pocket and brandished a card to the Wednesday player. *Cheerio, Cheerio* rang out.

Fernando was distraught, thumping the turf, almost in tears, like the boy who cried wolf. If he had been one of our players, I'd have been a bit gutted. But he isn't, so *Tatty Bye*. Hey, just don't start diving in the first place and you wouldn't have got a reputation.

This was a better offering than the Brighton game though, and if we can just regain that bit of composure in front of goal then I'm still optimistic. Make no mistake, both Brighton and Wednesday will be in and around the mix come May. Let's just hope it's them fighting it out in the playoffs and not us.

"WE'RE GONNA SCORE IN A MINUTE, SCORE IN A MINUTE..." (OR MAYBE NOT).

CHAPTER 49

BIRMINGHAM CITY (A) – THURSDAY 3RD MARCH 2016

"FOOTBALL ON A THURSDAY, WHATEVER NEXT?"

What is happening to the beautiful game? The only days I ever knew that football was played on was on the odd occasion a Tuesday night, but more often at 3pm on a Saturday afternoon. Not anymore. Sky in their infinite wisdom are determined to try and get live football on our screens every single night of the week, just in case we can't get enough of it.

Tonight it was City's turn to again be selected. Getting a bit fed up of this now as I could, in a normal season, have taken the easy option of either sitting on my sofa at home with a chilled four pack, pausing the action whenever I needed to, or go down the pub to watch and chant at a TV screen. Not this season though.

Not only that, our habitual habit of not getting a result when "on the telly" continued to haunt us as somehow we managed to, lose a game 1-0 when we created enough chances to win about four games.

Now I can't recall other than a Boxing Day or New Year's Day fixture, ever playing a league game on a Thursday night. It just doesn't sound right. Being Birmingham away and to be on the safe side, it also necessitated an early afternoon eye appointment being made for Thomas. Following this, it meant we could set off slightly earlier and make it in good time.

So off to the country's second capital we headed, Thomas entertaining me on the way with an 80's music quiz on his iPhone. I have never had many memorable trips watching City in Birmingham, either at the hosts ground tonight, or at their local rivals Aston Villa. As we pulled off the motorway passing Villa Park, both Thomas and I agreed that we hoped we would not be visiting that place next season. To ensure that, we need to get promoted as Villa have been woeful in the Premier League and are definitely going down, thus losing their ever present Premier League status. Tonight would present a difficult task. Both sides came into the game with a reputation as clean sheet specialists, so a cagey and defence dominated encounter was to be expected. It ended up being anything but.

We had agreed to meet up with Bri Lee who had travelled with Danny Pullen, being the beneficiaries of some St Andrew's corporate hospitality. I'm not sure if Bri was actually invited into this, but he claimed *"nah, it's not for me"*, so he left leaving us to find him in some pub nearby.

We parked up near a school on a council estate near the ground with a distinct aroma of curry filling the night air. A quick phone call to Bri, a short walk through some side streets and we found him propping up the bar in the Royal George Inn, looking like some 'Billy-no-mates' or should I say 'Bri-no-mates'.

The pub was busy, already filled with that Brummy accent, mixed with an apparent strong hint of Irish Brogue (for some reason they seem to have a strong Irish following). As you travel around the country, you notice the various accents. 'Ull is not a very clever sounding one and you notice your twang when surrounded in alien territory. However, the Brummy one has to be the worst surely?! You can't help but catch yourself saying *'we wanna be together'*. Hearing a bit of Irish in the pub, persuaded me to have a pint of Guinness, but we soon decided to go into the ground and converse with some more like minded Hullensians.

As it was, we ended up talking to some ex-Hullites and their quest in following City certainly impressed me. It so happened that Bri knew them both having bumped into them during City's pre-season tour of Austria.

First up was a chap called Julian who now lives on the edge of the River Thames. Practically an ever present at City missing only one game home and away in the previous two seasons. He wasn't too impressed mind with the change of tonight's fixture to a Thursday, as every week he had a 7.30am meeting on a Friday morning!

Then we chatted with the Bayliss family including Janet and Chloe, and Tom, now residing in Berlin. He had flown in for the game on some allegedly cheap budget airline. It didn't end up being quite so cheap as he originally booked it before the date of the fixture had been moved, thus requiring him to change his flight at extra cost. Once again, Sky no thought of anyone actually attending the game. Tom was also busy finding places to apply his City stickers, so leaving his personal mark on St Andrew's. These basically adorning the slogan 'From Boothferry to Germany'. He found suitable places around the concourse to apply these, often also found by visiting fans in the Gent's bogs. His sister shook her head, saying 'he's had a few and often embarrasses me'. This was most notable at Spurs away last season when going up and down the carriages on the tube asking total strangers to sign his shirt. "He likes to call his game Amuse The Drunk" she added. We agreed to take possession of a few of his stickers and 'carry on his mission' at the remaining away games this season.

Thomas was loving all this, feeling like he was now part of some sort of hard-core City following. His wings were clipped a little though, when at the food counter asking for some chips, a young girl attendant called Melissa said "Aw, isn't he cute!" Hardly the description he was looking for thinking he was the up and coming next generation of football casual. He was also gazing a little at a group of noisy younger City fans who had just arrived, lots of Stone Island on show. They were later to be stood near us singing an amusing ditty or two.

We filtered into the seats and Thomas and I tied up our flag just behind the goal. A light mist of rain had started to descend so we adjourned to the back of the away seating section in front of a row of executive boxes where Bri had also taken occupation.

The match kicked off and far from being a tight cagey affair, it was end to end stuff in the early exchanges. However, lady luck was not on our side early on as Birmingham soon took the lead. Robertson, who can have the capacity to either create goals for us, or give away costly errors, did the latter, losing possession just outside our box. The ball fell to Birmingham striker Toral, who saw his shot deflect off Curtis Davis and just out of the grasp of McGregor. Despite getting a hand to the ball he could not prevent it hitting the back of the net. Shit!! One down!

This was the first league goal we had conceded in about six and a half hours. Not to be deterred though we produced a quick response with Jake Livermore thundering a long range shot onto a post. Not long after Michael Dawson saw a header clip the top of the bar from a Snodgrass in-swinging free kick, when perhaps he should have scored. Clucas then shot straight at Kuszack in the Birmingham goal when well placed. I wasn't panicking yet as it felt like a City goal was coming.

The Stone Island mob must have felt the same as they constantly sang the following number:

"Oh what a night, Oh what a night,
Mo Diame is Dynamite,
City away on a Thursday,
Oh what a night!"

Half time came and it was a surprise that we were still behind, albeit McGregor had been called into action, brilliantly saving from a Clayton Donaldson overhead kick.

The second half continued, pretty much in the same vein with the addition of now heavy rain. City had lots and lots of possession and in total ended up with twenty four attempts on goal. Just a shame that most were straight at the keeper or not on target at all. Kuszack saved well from both Snodgrass and Clucas, penalty appeals for a hand ball were unsuccessful and some valiant Birmingham defending kept us at bay. This was all typically summed up when Clucas had a shot deflected over from only about three or four yards – it seemed easier to score. The impression that it just wasn't our night suddenly seemed to dawn on us.

Despite lots of chances, it just wasn't meant to be. As the referee blew for full time, the home fans' relief was palpable. Thomas just turned to the executive boxes behind us and flicked lots of 'V's' in their direction. I understood his sentiment but clearly being his father I reprimanded him, uttering the words "wankers" under my breath.

It was by now to coin a phrase "pissing it down" and upon collecting our flag, found it extremely sodden, enough to wring out. We had not thought that one through properly. It had to remain on the back seat of my car for a few days, as the football widow did not want it on the bannister at home.

Upon returning to the car the smell of curry had gone. Shame that as I could've just eaten one. Instead we blasted the car heater up to full in an attempt to dry out. This only proceeded to send Thomas to sleep, giving it big ZZZ's and be no company whatsoever.

It continued to rain all the way home making it an even more depressing drive. Never mind, no need to panic just yet. Time to worry when we are *not* creating chances *and* losing. We have got two home games coming up against MK Dons and Forest. They're rubbish so surely we'll pick up wins there? Surely? It's all still in our hands albeit as the phrase goes "squeaky bum time is just around the corner".

Still couldn't help thinking though, if we had scored one, we'd have gone onto win. If, if, if…….

"ATTACK, ATTACK……ATTACK, ATTACK, ATTACK".

(WE DID, JUST COULDN'T FINISH).

CHAPTER 50

ARSENAL (H) FA CUP 5TH ROUND REPLAY – TUESDAY 8TH MARCH 2016

"WHAT IFS AND MAYBE'S..."

And so a possible FA Cup dream is over. We've had one almost turn to reality in recent years, so it was always a tall task to expect it to be repeated.

None the less, we've enjoyed our cup games this season, even if they have resulted in making our task even longer. The matches against Accrington, Swansea, Leicester and Bury have so far, been some of the most enjoyable of the season. Proper football, tension, and a bit of old fashioned nostalgia thrown in for good measure. Imagine what we could do if we took the cups seriously and fielded full strength teams.

However, I despise Arsenal and Arsene *'I did not see it'* Wenger, so would have loved it if we could have knocked them out. My loathing of them was confirmed at the infamous *'spit gate affair'*, when they knocked us out of the quarter finals of the FA Cup back in 2009 at The Emirates.

Leading 1-0 through a Nick Barmby goal, for long periods of the game, we succumbed to two late goals, the last looking distinctly offside. Cesc Fabregas, not even playing, then came onto the pitch at the full time whistle, and allegedly spat at certain members of the City team.

However, he plays for a 'big team', so more or less got away with it, and it was all 'swept under the carpet'. In true Arsene style, no-one saw it.

Tonight also included loads of other pointers that, for me, are all wrong about football nowadays.

We had just played a league game on a Thursday and now had shenanigans this time with the kick off time. Due to the need for a replay, and both teams already having a congested fixture list, the powers that be decided that City needed to cancel their original scheduled home Championship fixture against Brentford. This would allow this replay to be squeezed in before the following weekends Quarter Finals day.

Ok, no problem with that.

However, it also happened to be on the same evening as that of two Champions League fixtures, involving no English teams whatsoever. Why that had a bearing on a City v Arsenal, I have no idea. Still, the bigwigs at UEFA announced that our kick off time had to be brought forward to seven pm, so as not to clash with the Champions League games. Oh, the power of TV.

How utterly ridiculous. The second half would still clash anyway, not to mention if extra time and penalties were needed (it actually turned out that the requirement for such was never in question, but that's not the point).

Why would Neil from Noddle Hill or Bruce from Beverley be remotely interested? If they genuinely wanted to watch City play Arsenal in the fifth round of the FA Cup, they'd get off their backside and get there. If not, well, they are just armchair fans anyway so who cares.

This brought forward kick off was enough to confuse many of the eventual crowd. Many only took their seats well after the seven pm start, but this was primarily due to long queues outside, with no real effort to speed things up. To be fair, they didn't miss much, but to some, it will have meant less time to go all 'gooey eyed' over Arsenal.

Now I hate this. To me, I'm not really interested in the opposition at all and nor should I be. It's my team that I'm interested in and want to see play well, stuffing the opposition. At half time, fans were clamouring to get their photos with Ian Wright who was pitch side commentating for BT Sports. I even saw one 'fan' climb down from the West Stand seats, take their coat off to reveal an Arsenal top, and then have a selfie with Mr Wright. Prat. Probably owns some half and half scarves as well.

After the game, many fans also surrounded the Arsenal team bus, all happy for a glimpse of a big time Charlie. Bloody football tourists the lot of them!

Once City had battled to a draw at The Emirates in the initial fixture, there had been talk of the fixture being a sell out. It ended up far from it, with just over twenty thousand in attendance.

Colin who had attended the original fixture with us, had told us previously of his cousin who used to be a ticket tout when living in London. He'd often get up from the tea table, and state that he was 'off out' particularly if there was a big team in town at Loftus Road. A couple of occasions saw him not roll back in until breakfast the following morning, after having all his money taken off him, and being forced to spend an evening at the pleasure of the local constabulary. He now runs a legitimate ticketing company in County Donegal.

No such need for ticket touts at the KC. We can't even sell out a fifth round home FA Cup match against Arsenal. I can recall not so long ago, there being a clamour for a ground extension and / or a new, larger ground.

The pre match light show was in full force (no doubt for the benefit of the BT Sport cameras) with Insomnia being pumped out over the tannoy, and then 'We Will Rock You' by Queen. Maybe we should carry on the discotheque theme say for the first twenty minutes or so playing with an illuminous ball, just so we can add a bit more razzamatazz?!

The teams were, as usual, annoyingly announced in number order (which are now meaningless), rather than position order (goalkeeper to striker). Bring back numbers one to eleven I say. You know where everyone should be playing then.

Another thing that typified modern day football for me was evident tonight. In the first fixture, there were over 50,000 Gooners in situ, but other than the odd strain of '*Arsenal, Arsenal..*', you could hardly hear them. They were just going through the motions. Tonight, there was only just over 2,600 away fans, but they made more noise in the first two minutes, than the whole ninety at The Emirates.

The irony was not lost on them as each time there was a lull in the atmosphere, they sang, '*Is this the Emirates..Is this The Emirates..?*'

Other amusing ditty's heard them sing the usual '*Hull is a shithole, I wanna go home*' (not sure where Hull is, as there's no H in 'Ull).

This was met with the obvious, '*City of Culture, we know what we are*'

My favourite though had to be the reference to their giant defender Per Mertesacker, *'We've got a big facking German, a big facking German..'*

What then made this even more amusing was when he eventually got substituted through injury following a collision with the mighty Nick Powell. His trudge off the pitch was then met with chants from the North Stand of *'You're soft, you're a southerner..'*

Powell himself didn't come off unscathed, wearing a bandage on his head. He was clearly trying his best to look a bit like John Wile from some old WBA days, or from slightly more recent years, a blood stained Terry Butcher. Powell just didn't look anywhere near as hard.

He made it look worse when, as Mertesacker sloped off, he actually went over to him to shake hands. Where is the 'in your face' mentality?

Now don't get me wrong, Arsenal are a bloody good team. You rarely get two chances to beat them but somehow, it just felt like City, as a team, gave them too much respect. We stood off and admired them. I can barely remember a proper old school tackle.

This didn't stop Arsenal dropping like flies every time anyone went near them, rolling around as if they'd been shot by a sniper. Monreal being especially guilty of this in the second half, following a challenge from Diame. As soon as he'd noticed Diame had been shown a yellow card, he immediately sprang to his feet. Play acting and gamesmanship at its best.

City held their own for the majority of the first half without really troubling Ospina in the Arsenal goal but keeping them at arms length. However, just before half time, David Meyler had an inexplicable brainstorm and handed Arsenal the opening goal on a plate for Olivier Giroud, with a shocking attempted pass to Jakupovic.

From then on, it was pretty much one way traffic.

Arsenal continued to hit the deck and later in the game, Gabriel also went off injured, as did Aaron Ramsey, only sixteen minutes after coming on as a substitute. Even against a makeshift Arsenal defence though, City struggled to create too many goal scoring opportunities

Elmo had a goal chalked off for offside and Diame headed wide, but in the end we failed to score. At only 1-0 down, we were in theory, still in it, but late in the game, Arsenal pulled away at ease. A second goal from Giroud, soon followed by a Walcott goal made it 3-0. Game over.

Walcott added a fourth late on as fans streamed to the exits. Not sure why they were in such a rush, they'd got there forty five minutes earlier than usual.

Four nil was slightly flattering to Arsenal, but that's the difference between a Premier League team and Premier League wannabees. Who wants to go up anyway?!

The worry though is that we have now only scored one goal in the last six games, a cause for concern.

MK Dons and Forest up at home in the league next. Time to hopefully find our goalscoring boots, return to winning ways and push for a promotion place.

Hey, this was only the FA Cup. If City can't take it seriously, why should I?

The saving grace was that Arsenal were ceremonially dumped out in the next round at home to Watford. They would only have beaten us anyway!

The 'Big Facking German' is not so hard after all. But Arsenal end our FA cup run in a QF replay.

(Getty Images)

One good thing about the evening was that most of our league rivals dropped points. Derby, Middlesbrough both lost, Sheffield Wednesday and Brighton drew.

Oh, and Harry Maguire managed to hit the roof of the East Stand with a clearance!

"...QUE SERA, SERA, WE'RE (NOT) OFF TO WEMBERLEE..."

(NOT IN THE CUP ANYWAY)

CHAPTER 51

MK DONS (H) – SATURDAY 12TH MARCH 2016

"THIS COULD BE ROTTERDAM OR ANYWHERE"

Back to league action after our season's cup exploits had finally finished, and resulted in an extra nine games having been attended. As already touched on in previous chapters, several players had been 'rested' for the FA Cup fixtures to ensure that they were fully fit and refreshed for our 'bread and butter', the holy grail of trying to achieve promotion to the Premier League.

Well guess what? This didn't quite go to plan as three players who didn't even take part in the Arsenal game got injured in training! As a result, Livermore, Snodgrass and Maloney were unavailable for the fixture. To me, this just firmly endorsed that you should just go out and pick your best team available for every game. And to make matters worse, having rested players who did play today, we couldn't even beat MK Dons, having to eventually settle for a 1-1 draw at home. And they were crap!

I can only recall one previous home match against MK Dons, back in October 2004, but it was an exciting one. An evening fixture saw City, striving for successive promotions, pitted against a team in the bottom four – a home banker surely. This certainly seemed to be the case when Stuart Green put City ahead after only twenty seconds, following a partially saved Delroy Facey shot. However, it didn't turn out to be quite that simple.

City failed to press home their early advantage though and somehow, with only a few minutes left, we found ourselves 2-1 down, despite a penalty save by Boaz 'In The Middle Of Our Goal' Myhill. It looked like the best we could settle for was a draw and we thought we'd got lucky when Michael Keane equalised with a deflected shot from the edge of the box with only two minutes to go. But no, we managed to still have time to snatch an unlikely winner when Stuart Green volleyed into the bottom corner.

I always quite liked Stuart Green and thought he would have gone on to be a better player but this never proved to be the case. The fact he allegedly got 'involved' with the managers daughter, probably didn't help his cause.

No such problem today I thought, an easy home win and back to winning ways. Not so. I should have known the day's events wouldn't quite go to plan when upon entering the usual turnstiles, we hit a language barrier with one of the stewards. Without actually speaking any words, I could tell that he wanted to know the contents of our bag. At this point, I duly opened the bag, showed him the contents and told him that it just contained our flag that we hang up every home game.

Now I'm not sure he could totally understand my 'Ull accent, but I'm sure as hell couldn't understand his. He repeated some sentence or other, in what I believed to be in some Eastern European language, possibly Polish, about eight times and I was none the wiser. I looked at him, shrugged my shoulders, and told him I didn't have a Scooby Doo what he was on about, and walked off. This was to be the first, but certainly not the last sign of the day and night, that maybe Hull is trying to live up to its billing of City of Culture.

The game itself was as frustrating as hell. There was no atmosphere at all, you could hear the players shouting at each other quite clearly and the lack of MK Dons supporters (a colossal 298) didn't help matters.

City had an unfamiliar central midfield pairing of Clucas and Hayden with Diame on the left. But the team as a whole, struggled to stamp any authority on the contest, and as half time approached, I can't recall either keeper being required to make a single save of note. No surprise then that a cacophony of boos rang out as the players descended down the tunnel.

Thomas had brought his mate Will along today and having by now, turned into a hardened seasoned City supporter, is becoming a little tired of the lack of atmosphere in the South Stand. He is constantly asking if we can go and sit in the North Stand instead. I'm fine with this, particularly with so many empty seats currently, but Charlotte is not so keen, so I'm a little stuck between a rock and a hard place. Today though, having been bored rigid in the first half, Thomas and Will decided that they would try and spice their afternoon up a little, and ventured off to watch the second half in the far end. This felt weird for me, as it was one of the first times that he wasn't actually watching the game with me. It felt almost as if my use is coming to an end, and his apprenticeship is done. No longer does he want to be in the family section with the anoraks and kiddies, but with the 'wannabies'!

Whilst City couldn't muster up a win, the second half was a much more lively affair. This was partially thanks to MK actually taking the lead when a rare foray into City's box won them a corner. This was duly headed home by the centre back, Anthony Kay, evading our defenders on the line and posts, for a 1-0 lead.

This actually seemed to jolt City into life, and maybe the crowd too. Had they not scored, we may have continued to amble our way through the match.

A quick response was needed, and a quick response we got.

Within two minutes of going behind, Hernandez was subjected to a crude looking challenge just outside their box and Clucas stepped up to curl an excellent free kick into the top corner, keeper motionless. 1-1.

MK now seemed content to try and play for a draw, time wasting at every opportunity, their players needing no encouragement to go down at the mere hint of a tackle, the goalkeeper in particular. Every decision was contested, Lewington the prime suspect, in an attempt to break the game up. This caused great frustration both on the pitch and in the stands, and whilst the ascendancy was certainly with City, a second and winning goal simply wouldn't come.

Diame stood a cross up for Akpom who somehow headed over from six yards. Clucas forced a save from distance, as did Aluko. The eight minutes of added time brought no joy and more jeers followed at full time to echo the huge sense of disappointment and frustration.

This really was two points dropped. MK Dons are shit and a certainty to get relegated. Promotion teams simply should not drop points against them. Instead of us really going for it from the very first whistle, and totally taking the game by the scruff of the neck, we are contributing substandard and lethargic performances.

So what to do when you are down in the dumps. That's right go and have a few beers and do something that is enjoyable. Fortunate that we had already agreed to meet up with a few others to go and watch the excellent Paul Heaton and Jacqui Abbott at Hull City Hall.

A quick trip back home from the KC, drop the kids off, splash of aftershave, and the football widow and I were taxi bound for a night out in Hull. It's been a while since I've said that! And this is where the diverse cultural tour really took place.

Deciding to give some early food a miss, a few steady beers in Bar 82 were shared with Rich and Diane Hewson, before meeting up with Bri Lee and entourage, who had lined their stomachs at 'Pizza Not So Express'.

After ordering a pint, from what I believe was a Russian at the bar in the City Hall, we took our position towards the back of the standing area, and were soon singing along with Bri et al, including '*He's one of our own*' Nick Barmby.

Also in attendance was Ed Faulkner of The Beautiful Couch and Tribfest. Somehow he seemed to know every word of every song, strange that being the lead singer of a Tribute band!

The football widow did also join him in a rendition of Wembleyphant (City's 2014 FA Cup Final song) on which all of our family sang. Amazingly, she still knew every word, despite the fact that half the players don't even play for us anymore. Ed also kindly agreed to come and sing a few numbers for us if we ever finish this book and have some sort of book launch.

So after much bad singing (by me mainly), some bad dancing (legs and arms not always in co-ordination with each other, again mostly by me), the consensus was to have several more pints in The Empress. For me, this really was winding the clock back, but needless to say, there was no argument.

In here, we also met Kylie, a young girl from 'Ull, who was, shall we say, displaying lots of flesh, most of which was adorning artwork from a needle. This, she informed us, depicted her life story. She must have led a full and interesting life as she was only in her late twenties, although actually try to make the story out just made me look like a dirty old man.

Discussions took place about the possibility of going to Sugar Mill (or Waterfront as we still know it). This never came off though and as we descended into the early hours of Sunday, the football widow and I decided that our alcohol levels were now reading full. Basically she told me I'd had enough, and she was probably right.

With there already being a lengthy taxi queue, we decided to take a stroll through the City Centre and catch one somewhere else, to see the sights, shall we say. It wasn't that pretty, albeit others were probably thinking the same looking at me.

For some godforsaken reason we both decided that we were a bit peckish and in particular, I had designs on a donor kebab. The server, not looking like a Dave from East Hull, or a Barry from Beverley, first introduced himself as Ali, when I asked him his name. As we waited for the meat to be shaved from the rotating spit, Ali refused to have his photo taken with me. Upon asking for clarification of his name, he then informed me it was actually Muhammad, Muhammed Ali. I wasn't buying it! Then again, he probably had to serve hundreds of lairy buggers like me every Friday and Saturday night.

The football widow had sensibly (she always is) ordered a pizza and carefully carried it closed in its box to take home and eat. I, on the other hand, attempted to drop the donor meat shavings into my mouth from a great height. In principle, a donor kebab is a good idea. In practice, it is not. After a few mouthfuls, the football widow, shaking her head, convinced me to resign it to the bin, I could have a few slices of her pizza when we got home.

We eventually took our place in a taxi queue just outside Hull train station and engaged in conversation with Kelly and Tracey, a married lesbian couple from Hull, about their plans to adopt a child. As nice as they were, if not a tad on the defensive side (very much like Steve Bruce I hear you think), they were not like the lesbians in the films.

It was finally our turn to board our carriage and return from whence we came. Very out of character, the football widow immediately attempted to barter her fare. This was not initially successful, and doubting that we had sufficient fare, the taxi driver went in full circle and suggested we disembark (or words to that effect). I promptly threw the contents of my pockets onto the floor of the taxi to dispel his belief, and eventually, Callum from Bangladesh, drove us back home.

In the morning, limbs slightly aching and head fuzzy, I decided that some fresh air was the order of the day, so I took the dog for a walk. As we circled Beverley racecourse, I reflected on the previous night's events, having thankfully totally forgotten (even if only temporarily) about City, and it all came crystal clear to me.

"...CITY OF CULTURE, WE KNOW WHAT WE ARE..."

(Just hope 2016 can be City's year (not 2017), although still to be convinced)

CHAPTER 52

NOTTINGHAM FOREST (H) – TUESDAY 15TH MARCH 2016

"HOW FOOTBALL CAN SO QUICKLY CHANGE"

By the time my head hit the pillow and my eyelids shut after tonight's game, I really didn't know whether I was coming or going, or whether I still cared for our club or not. An awful lot had gone through my mind in the few hours of 'nothing but football is important' thought process. It certainly resulted in a restless sleep.

Before we get into that, any book predominantly about the 15/16 season, would not be worth the paper it's written on, without mentioning the words, Leicester City. Cue my Hull City link.

Prior to tonight's game, my mind was cast back to practically the same time just twelve months ago. On the 14th March 2015, the 'magnificent' Hull City had an away game at the King Power Stadium against the 'oh-so-unmagnificent' Leicester City. In case you had forgotten, and it can so easily be done, Leicester sat bottom of The Premier League. They'd played twenty seven games, had won only four of them and only had eleven games left of the season. They sat a colossus of nine points behind City, and bearing in mind that they had only chalked up nineteen points on the board, most 'experts' had discounted them. They were 'relegation fodder'. Even us City fans had assumed they would finish below us.

To add further doubt to any Foxes fan, their ever charming manager at the time, once of Hull City, Nigel Pearson, seemed to have lost the plot. He was confronting journalists suggesting that they were albatross' with their heads stuck in the ground, and uttering all sorts of incomprehensible nonsense. Memories of Eric and 'the seagulls' abounded.

So as we set off that day, for the relatively short drive (in Premier League terms) to Leicester, I talked myself into believing that they were a shit football team, we'd turn up and nick a 1-0 win, and we would have for definite, consigned at least one team into the bottom three, just another two needed for Premier League safety.

Whilst my thought process, even if not a bit 'Amber and Black' blinkered, was not a million miles off, the end was not quite as we thought it would be. On that day, Leicester were shit. Unfortunately, City were only a notch above shit ourselves. Also hovering around the bottom three, were QPR, Sunderland, Villa and Bloody Burnley, all of equal shiteness that season.

That day at Leicester, City toiled, almost with a foremost attempt to certainly not lose the game, and we achieved just that. A game which saw six centre halves on display said it all about the 'desperateness' to stay in The Premier League. Six centre halves surely means there will not be many goals in the game, and that is what we got. Exactly, a round sum none! Once again City thrashed them nil –nil. It was a game with 'not an awful lot in it'. What there was it was City that played it. From what I can recall, nigh on a full twelve months later, I distinctly remember two great chances for City.

In the first half, Huddlestone chipped a ball over the backline of the blue shirted Leicester defence to Elmo, who had timed his run to perfection to beat the offside trap. As I uttered the words, '*put your fucking foot through it*', rising from my seat in anticipation of the net bulging, Elmo instead decided to play the Arsenal way, and opted instead to square to Jelavic. He in turn, got himself in an awful tangle and produced a fantastic air shot and the chance was gone.

Leicester were still utter shite, and despite Huddlestone harshly seeing a second yellow card late on for a foul on some unheard of striker called, err, Jamie Vardy, I never felt in danger of us actually conceding.

And then practically in the last minute, a quick free kick by N'Doye played in Abel and a winner was beckoning. Go on City, three points and condemn them to the Championship. Only Schwarzer had different ideas and he expertly stopped Abel's shot and a 0-0 thrashing it was.

No worries, still nine points above them, with only ten games to go. Leicester were doomed so I thought. I wasn't on my own.

Twelve months on, I shall quote a selection of the comments made immediately after the game.

"The Leicester crowd willed the ball in for the final few minutes, but boo's greeted the final whistle. This felt like a fatal opportunity missed."

"Allen McGregor in Hull's goal had not one shot to save and as the clock ticked down, had Hernadez's shot gone in, the obituaries on Leicester's Premier League life could have been signed off"

"A goalless draw for Leicester does not do a huge amount to avert their likely narrative"

"Martin O'Neill was at the King Power Stadium as a guest of the club he served so well in two League Cup triumphs. This season is heading to a sombre conclusion of those heady days."

Go on, read those comments again. At that stage of the season, Leicester were condemned. City weren't. Until eventually, the early chapter of this book entitled 'Bloody Burnley' came along.

Hindsight is a great thing, but ask yourself this question now. 'Have Leicester really got any 'great' players?'. If you're honest, the answer is probably no. So how the fuck can we have been nine points clear of them with nine games to go, yet still contrive to finish six points behind them when the fat lady was singing and in full voice?

The answer is almost impossible in a Premier League era awash with money, but two things had a massive impact. TOGETHERNESS (and I mean of an entire club here), and TEAM SPIRIT. Remember those words well, as I'm sure I'll repeat them at some stage.

I have already emphasized the phrase that as long as I see a player giving 100% of their ability, I will never complain. The same must apply to supporters of the team, it's management and it's hierarchy. It is essential that the team, it's supporters, and club in general, all pull in the same direction. Only then can there be any hope of achieving the best possible results. And even if they are not actually achieved, you will never be asking yourself, 'What if..?'

From that home game with Hull City on the 14th March 2015, Leicester have showed that togetherness in swathes. Their story will ultimately be of Hollywood dreams.

Don't get me wrong, I don't particularly like Leicester. Had they not gone on that incredible run at the end of the 14/15 Premier League season, then Hull City would never have got relegated. And I would never have uttered the fateful words, *'Let's go to every game next season. Tell you what, let's write a book about it.'* It's you Leicester I blame!

However, whilst I don't like them, I cannot do anything but also admire them. For what they have achieved, since scrambling to that nil nil draw with 'Ull, is nothing short of, well, unbelievable. If someone had stopped you in the street and suggested it to you at the time, you'd have asked for the straight jacket and carted them off to the sanatorium.

31,456 watched that Leicester v Hull match at The King Power, along with a few million on Match of The Day that night. It was no doubt the last game so probably most would have either nodded off by then or pressed the off button.

Leicester proceeded to finish the season off, playing their last ten games, winnng seven of them and drawing one. They finished it off with aplomb, despatching the doomed QPR 5-1. QPR were relegated. As we watched in Spain with some pissed up 'cock-a-hoop' Geordies, so were we. My thoughts at the time. Fuck Off Newcastle. Fuck Off Leicester. Football is horrible.

Whilst that was, from a blue (and not amber and black) point of view, pretty surreal, the next thirty eight games for Leicester were most certainly off the 'Am I out of my mind, really seeing this, is this really happening, no it can't be' spectrum of football.

This is obviously post script, but Leicester have played thirty eight games, won twenty three, drawn twelve and lost only three Premier League games. They have only gone and won the Premier League! In total, after they'd sneaked a nil nil draw with City that day, read this record for all games, League and Cup.

Played 53, Won 32, Drawn 14, Lost 7, Goals scored 99 Goals Against 54.

I can't help getting a City fact in here. Seven games lost in a total of fifty three. I'll narrate the names of the teams Leicester lost to in that lot.

Chelski (not too bad), Spurs twice (on the up, even if they did ultimately manage to finish third in a two horse race in the 15/16 Premier League), Liverpool (once a force), Arsenal twice (always good for a top four spot) and oh, Hull City, in this year's League Cup.

The bookies and press were full of 'lording up' people who had put bets on them winning the Premier League at odds of 5000-1. Let's put this into context, there weren't that many. Surely. It would have been like lighting a tenner! Yet that's all we could hear. Some of the few that had put bets on said they were hating it and had cashed out, saying they weren't enjoying watching it. Yeah righto! Put it this way, I reckon I'd pay great sums of money to see Hull City win the Premier League, never mind have the chance of winning money on it. As good old 'Honest Dave' kept telling me, the press and bookies were all good at telling us about the massive payouts there were going to have to make. They conveniently never mentioned the millions of lost bets that had probably been staked on Chelski, Man City etc etc. Never trust a bookie. There is only one winner ultimately. I'm sure they won't be out of pocket for long, even if they were anyway.

As part of the ever inquisitive, maybe half drunk, mind, I can't help thinking, what if Abel's shot had gone in that day back in March 2015 and City had won. Surely they would have been relegated then? Maybe the mighty Hull would have gone on to win the 15/16 Premier League instead? Whilst we have the sceptre of Gary Lineker hosting Match of The Day in his underpants, what could have been in its place? Maybe we could have seen Gareth Roberts in his rolled up shorts, or Big Billy in a mankini?!

Then the serious part of your mind kicks in, and the words of Jim Royle come to the fore, 'My Arse'! Hull City winning the Premier League. Pffff!

Seriously though, massive credit to Leicester. They have shown what can be achieved despite all the odds. True team spirit in swathes, showing the alleged 'big boys' for what they are. Money obsessed 'Champagne Charlies'. Leicester have given us something for us all to aspire to. For the sake of repeating myself, don't expect, but believe in hope. If you expect to fail, no doubt you will.

So much East Midlands glorifying aside, on a mid March Tuesday, tonight we welcomed their close neighbours, not Notts, but Nottingham Forest to the KC. As ever, and I can't remember a game since very early in the season when it wasn't, it was bloody freezing. I recall turning to Charlotte mid second half to see her teeth chattering. This was either down to a teenage girl not getting dressed appropriately, or on field attractions not creating enough glow, or a combination of both.

Following a run of three relatively disappointing home draws, I honestly believed that a win was on the cards tonight. After all, Forest had lost five of their previous six games, which had led to the sacking of their manager Dougie Freedman. Maybe I'd been over thinking the Leicester thing, and my not very often (it's the Hull City way) over optimistic thoughts soon drained away.

My thoughts second, but first and in true style for this book, some words from the opposition corner, this time from a good friend of the football widow, Andy Wright, a lifelong Forest fan, now living in Hull.

The banter had been increasing at work all week leading up to the game. After Derby, this is the one we want to win. A match against your home town club can sometimes feel like it's a match against your friends, workmates, and to some degree, your family. Forest had started the week by getting rid of our manager and our form had been of relegation material. Meanwhile, Hull were having somewhat problems of their own, having seen their form dip over recent weeks, to the point where some quarters were now asking if Steve Bruce was the right man for the job. Could this mean that City were for the taking?

We arrived at the ground early and went in The Walton Club and met up with a few of my pals from The City Ground who sit around me. This was a bit of a shock as the place was empty barring a hand full in the snooker room. So we had no manager, no players other than loanees due to some recent injuries and a bloody transfer embargo, and now no fans. Things were looking grim for us too.

We finally got in to the ground and took our seats in the corner of the North Stand. I say 'take our seats' although we stand up as is the norm for away fans at most grounds these days. The atmosphere was pretty good, with the Forest fans in full voice, all 749 of us, singing about our days in Europe and our neighbours over in Derby and what they do to sheep.

The game was quite open in the first twenty minutes with both sides coming close and the home fans started to become a bit restless with their teams lack of finishing in front of goal. Meanwhile we were quite happy as this was probably the best we had played for a few weeks. And then Goaaaallll! Wow, where did that come from? A sublime strike from Gary Gardiner from fully thirty yards. Now we were bouncing, we'd finally scored a goal and were leading one of the league's top sides who have an immediate return to the Premier League on their minds.

We headed towards the half time break with us all milking the score line for all its worth. My half time pint tasted so much nicer, although we knew that Hull were going to come at us in the second half.

They did but we cheered every tackle and every missed pass that Hull made. The shots came thick and fast but we started to believe that a win was on the cards. And then a cruel ricochet and the ball fell to Aluko who equalised. Cue the light show. I'm glad I don't suffer from photosensitive epilepsy, those lights are bloody bright. Hull came forward in what felt like a constant wave of attacks on our goal. It felt like we are a boxer hanging on for the final bell, get that clock to ninety minutes. Despite City's best efforts, Forest held on for a draw and given our current situation, it actually felt like a win. I've avoided a serious amount of banter at work tomorrow but I'm not sure the City fans will feel the same way. All in all, a good night at the KC, and I'm looking forward to coming back next season, although I think City will be somewhere else somehow.

It's funny how fans of different teams can view the same game in different ways. I appreciated Andy's comments but after witnessing tonight's game, I'm not sure I totally agree with his thoughts about City being somewhere other than the Championship next season!

My observations of the nights affairs deepened my recent belief that a top two spot was looking a long way off.

Snodgrass and Huddlestone were back at the expense of Arsenal rookies and out of favour loanees, Akpom and Hayden. The fixture was a rearranged one, due to City's exploits in the FA Cup. When it had been due to have been played, we topped the Championship by two points. Tonight, we weren't, and looked far from a top of the table team destined for automatic promotion. The rearranged date, came just in advance of what could be arguably the biggest and most important game of the season, an away fixture the following Friday against Middlesbrough. As such a win would have boosted a waning run of form, but unfortunately it wasn't to come.

Unlike the lacklustre start to the MK Dons game, at least City started in a lively fashion. They were quicker to the ball, and imposed themselves on the game early on, and came close to taking the lead on fifteen minutes. Snoddy led a counter attack, fed Hernandez, whose shot unfortunately hit the post and Dorius De Vries kept out Diame with the follow up. It looked encouraging but the anxiety soon followed. The diminutive Vaughan began to run the midfield (as he had done at The City Ground earlier in the season), and after Dawson had thwarted Ryan Mendes on the edge of the box, and McGregor, following an earlier flap when he'd nearly punched the ball into his own net, denied Federico Macheda, Forest took the lead.

A patient move of twenty plus passes resulted in a thirty yard thunderous strike from on loan Villa player, Gardner, which left McGregor helpless. It was a truly wonderful shot, one of which City seldom score, and one to which you just have to say, well done.

Going a goal down doesn't normally suit City. Whilst we have, and can come from behind, the instances have become more and more fleeting. So the feeling in the crowd dipped and you could sense the tension. A woman sat behind us was full of '*Oooh's*' and '*Ahhh's*' and as the game dragged on, they got louder and more exasperated. For a moment I almost thought Meg Ryan was sat behind us re-enacting a scene from 'When Harry Met Sally'!

Chances came and went. Elmo had a couple, Curtis headed wide, Huddlestone had a shot deflected wide, Diame had a shot saved and it all started feeling like the inevitable, a disastrous result.

However, perseverance finally paid off, and as the clock was ticking away, finally a stroke of luck fell our way.

The 'Thudd' had a shot from the edge of the box partially blocked, but the ball squirmed its way to Aluko, City's sub, who calmly poked it home for an equaliser.

Despite there being another twenty minutes or so left, no winner could be found and a fourth consecutive home draw resulted. More jeers followed the full time whistle and we dropped to fourth in the league. The natives were growing restless.

Worse was to follow when they all got home.

During the second half, I'd noticed several adverts on the flashing electronic advertising boards displaying the slogan '*Earn Your Stripes*'

Oblivious to its meaning at the time, I assumed naively, it was some sort of PR scheme to reward fans for their loyalty in following City. Being far too dedicated this season, clearly Thomas and I would reap some gargantuan reward?

I didn't quite get what I'd bargained for!

When climbing into bed later on and updating the football widow of the night's events at the KC, (not quite pillow talk I know but she always shows interest at least) I was somewhat stopped in my tracks, whilst scrolling through posts on Twitter. You couldn't beat the timing of the PR machine at the KC.

Following a disappointing result, in what was becoming an increasing lacklustre season, it was announced (or 'leaked') exactly what the 'Earn Your Stripes' meant. As I stopped talking to the football widow in mid flow, she asked 'What's wrong?', as if something terrible had happened. It had!

Apparently, whilst exact details were to be formally announced, there would be no more season tickets at Hull City. Instead a Membership Scheme was to be introduced, whereby everybody paid the same price.

Yes. OAP's, children and adults were all to pay the same price as one another.

How absolutely ridiculous?

How is that 'earning your stripes'?

I tried to divulge the 'part informed' messages and assuming it was all gossip and scaremongering, decided to initially park my thoughts until I knew all the full facts. Never one to shout from the roof top, nor make instant reaction, I would wait to see the detail, before making my calculated assessment.

Needless to say, a night of restless sleep resulted. It didn't take long and I, like many others, was far from happy with the news. Social media went into meltdown.

The following few days, in advance of Boro away, were weary ones. More of this will no doubt follow in the ensuing chapters.

It all seems a far cry from the TOGETHERNESS that Leicester had displayed and were displaying.

"STEVE BRUCE / JAMIE VARDY IS HAVING A PARTY, BRING YOUR VODKA / WKD AND YOU'RE..."

CHAPTER 53

MIDDLESBOROUGH (A) – FRIDAY 18TH MARCH 2016.

"TOP TWO SLIPPING AWAY"

The morning after the night before.

As I awoke from my slumber, my initial thoughts were of a disappointing home result against Forest. It had led to City slipping down to fourth place in the league and more importantly out of the magic top two places that would guarantee return to the alleged 'promised land'.

Whether that phrase is actually true in my mind, I'm yet to be convinced. In an ideal (albeit unrealistic world) I'd probably settle for winning the Championship title at a canter, collecting the gazillions of pounds on offer, and then electing to stay in the Championship and play proper football (with a few tackles here and there) in front of 'proper fans'. Or maybe I'm just a romanticist stuck in the dark ages. This new-fangled 'Football' thing is yet to be fully sold to me, despite the machine continually trying to do so. Maybe I'm just a miserable old git refusing to move with the times?

What the previous night's results had told me was that automatic promotion was now far from a surety. In fact it was effectively out of our hands. So just in case, I felt it was time for our emergency backup plan to swing into action. The football calendar had already told me that May 28th 2016 was the date for the Championship play-off final at Wembley. This wasn't the greatest date in my diary as it coincided with a pre-arranged surprise 80th birthday weekend for my Mother in Cheltenham. Sorry Mum, but we may have to arrive fashionably late!

So a couple of web pages and clicks later, the reservations were made for a room in a hotel in Ruislip. One of those you can cancel at short notice without having to pay. Just in case….you know.

Recent Wembley experiences (yes, really!) with Hull City, have told me that anybody will seize the opportunity to fleece a few extra pounds out of a football supporter. Anytime a major game comes along, the prices go up. It's not just the clubs themselves, the trains, hotels, beer prices, you name it, it all only goes one way. Plus booking the room also made me, glass always half empty, feel kind of better and in control.

As if.

Despite attempting to write this book, I will never claim to be a writer. However, my few words of advice for anyone considering writing a book would be to make sure you write about something where *you* can decide the ending. My choice has not been the wisest. It is all totally out of my control.

And those words seem so apt at this moment in time.

I'll say them again, out of control.

On the pitch, whilst we were still chalking up points, it was hardly convincing. Firstly, we are not chalking up points at the same speed as Burnley or Brighton. More worryingly, we are not scoring enough goals. Only six goals in the last nine matches tells its own story.

I love a good cliché and there is not one better than 'goals win matches'. Whilst we are not letting many in, we simply are not scoring enough. That's not through lack of creating chances, as the stats always show we have lots of attempts on goal. Just that not enough tend to be on target. As Steve Bruce often puts it "It's wor Achilles heel!"

Tonight's opponents Middlesboro' were experiencing something similar. Great at keeping clean sheets, not great at putting teams out of site and winning emphatically. They too were experiencing some sort of mini crisis. The previous weekend saw their manager, Aitor Karanka, walk out of a stormy team meeting. It looked like he wasn't going to return. To see a rival team in crisis is welcoming news, so it was with great pleasure that we saw Boro' lose the previous weekend, at Charlton away. Who'd be crap enough to lose there?!

Now Charlton is probably a whole other book to be written by somebody else, as to how not to run a football club.

So tonight's game at the Riverside felt like a pivotal moment in the season for both teams. A win for either would kick-start their season and provide the springboard to achieve a top two spot. Come on City, seize the moment.

Off the pitch in recent years, Hull City has never been easy viewing.

A relegation from the Premier League in the 2009/10 season had us heading for financial disaster. The fire sale of players ensued and administration loomed. It was worrying times as a supporter.

And from the background emerged the current owners.

It must first be said, what an initial achievement they made. Yes, I know more recent events may not have you in agreement but they and their money/financial guarantees must have saved the club from the impending administration. That would have led to a points deduction and the subsequent promotion would probably have been unachievable. Other investors might have come forward, but they didn't.

They acquired the club and have injected millions into it, when, had they let it go into administration first, they could have bought it for £1 and written existing debts off.

They didn't and for that I am grateful.

My gratitude has waned though.

By their own admission, the owners are not football people. Maybe they should have put in place someone who was? Or at least, a decent PR department. Hull City's PR seems lamentable at times.

I am foremost a football supporter. And like anybody else will always have my own opinions. I may not shout them from the rooftops, but I have them just the same. Unfortunately, in the business of football, unlike most others, I simply cannot change my allegiances. If I shop at say Tesco, and don't like what they are offering, I can simply drive to Morrisons, or Asda or even Aldi!

I cannot just go and support some other team. It's like asking you to swap your kids with someone else's. Hell, you can even break up with your wife and get another one (no, I'm not going to football widow!)

The owners of football clubs know this.

So season after season most put their fans, no 'customers', down their pecking order. This is certainly how it feels to us.

Since that extremely grateful day, we, as Hull City supporters, have had to put up with a lot.

First off was a proposed name change.

This was well documented and almost laughable. If it wasn't so painstakingly drawn out. I'm not saying I agree with this name change but I was perhaps a bit less emotive than most. You can call us what you like. To me, I'm still off to watch City, and will still also refer to us now and then as the Tigers.

Second up, was, ohh, the same name change again!. Having not been granted to do so by the football authorities, we thought we'd have round two. Another knock back. No. No. No.

Hopefully that was the end of it?

In the real world it wasn't, and ever since, those that be, have ensured they smother us with Hull City Tigers nonsense.

Even the official company name was changed at Companies House.

Every bit of promotional material /propaganda referred to us as the Tigers or Hull City Tigers, not just Hull City AFC. Include here a club badge change no longer bearing the club's name.

Time for another cliché, *"Cutting off your nose to spite your face"*.

This just simply eroded merchandise sales.

But worse still, the malaise, distrust and disharmony between owners and fans just grew. And grew. And grew.

To put it simply, eight thousand or so empty seats this season tells you that.

So whilst the above is not great reading. For me personally, it was still not enough to distract me from going to watch **MY** team, with **MY** son and **MY** daughter. Oh and occasionally **MY** football widow. It does however feel like at times, I'm in a hopelessly one sided relationship with Hull City.

Lots of other shit has taken place since, including but not limited to the closure of the ticket office, the spending of £250,000 of funds on away fans at the KC (when every other club was spending it on its own fans travelling to away games), all of which have been well dialogued and discussed.

What we must remember and I'm sure I've referred to this already, is that us football supporters are, deep down, simple folk. We don't like change. History and tradition, no matter how crap, is something to be proud of.

You can call us customers if you like, but if you choose to do so, it is essential that you <u>know</u> your customers.

I'm allegedly a customer.

All I want to do is watch Hull City. Enjoy it and talk about football. Ideally the stuff on the pitch. These are and should be great times as a Hull City supporter. Unprecedented success on the pitch over a relatively lengthy period.

Yet here I am, rambling on about non-football related issues.

The aftermath of Forest at home just took things to a new level with the proposed new Membership scheme. And all on the eve of possibly our biggest game of the season (yes, I know every match feels like the biggest game of the season, but this really was!)

The new membership scheme sounded only half thought through.

I'm not going to bore you with all the technicalities. By the time this book is finished and gathering dust on your shelves it will all have been well documented. Hell, there has been nothing else to talk about!

Yes it probably has some merits but it clearly needs more considered devil in the detail. The rhetoric said "*savings of up to....*". The scheme when digested didn't feel like it. The club appeared to have held a fans working group to discuss its merits and proposals. All attendees allegedly had to sign a confidentiality agreement not to discuss in public. And then appeared to ignore most of the concern expressed.

Every supporter will have their own opinions. None will be totally right, none will be totally wrong. Opinions may well differ due to individual circumstances. Some people may gain financially, some it will cost more. Every individual will have their own idiosyncrasies that affect them. In the ensuring days, weeks and months, I have no doubt that someone, or some 'body' will raise their head above the parapet, as a spokesperson and speak out about the membership scheme. If, and more likely when they do, they will whole heartedly have my support.

Obviously I can only speak of my own experiences. For what it's worth, and the paper it's typed on, here are my initial thoughts and how it could effect us.

I first got into City regularly as a school kid. It was initially free, for managing to get into the school football team, just! I just wanted to watch football, professional football at that. At times, you could have argued if it was actually professional, but it didn't take long for me to be hooked. I was in.

That's when football starts, at a tender age. Get them early, look after them, and they will be there for life. They may flit in and out, (you don't have to watch all 46 league games every season), but they are still there.

The last thing you should be doing is to disincentivise the young. The next generation of supporters. I would say that obviously, as a dad and observing Thomas this season. But once upon a time, I was that Thomas.

Also in the immediate build up to this game, the Premier league and it's clubs all agreed to a £30 cap on the price of tickets for away fans. The owners claimed this was *"not in the interests of football"*, fearing the prospect of tickets being 'oversubscribed', and leading to an allocation process having to be set up. I just can't see this being the case for City.

There are 8,000 empty seats at the KC, fixture in, fixture out. Fill the bloody thing and atmosphere <u>will</u> be improved. Do not close parts of the ground. It doesn't matter if not a single penny more is earned by gate receipts. That will come eventually in some shape or form.

When I started watching as a kid, nobody wore City shirts around the town, it was awash with Liverpool, Man United etc etc. This is not the case nowadays. So let's not take the risk of going back to that (much to the joy of Mike Ashley and Sports Direct). Rather than quell the feeling, build on it. Do not lose the next generation of fans. The whole way the scheme appears to be written, seems to do exactly that.

Likewise, do not 'price out' senior citizens, many of which have watched City for years, and years and years. There is room for us all.

Do not make them move seats by imposing seat changes upon us. If someone wants to move seats, they will do so of their own violation. Friends are made at football. Friends you only need to see every other Saturday or occasional Tuesday. You don't even need to know their names, but they are friends just the same. You have a bond with them, a kinship. Why would anyone want to dismiss that?!

As a last parting comment for now, how does it affect me? I currently have one adult pass and three child ones. Charlotte and Thomas alternate taking a friend to each home fixture so I can concentrate on agonising on the edge of my seat through each 90 minutes.

We already sit in the now entitled *'naughty corner'*. I don't care, I'd watch City from a park bench if needs be. However, it will cost us approximately £300 extra per season for the privilege. It's not necessarily the money for me. I can afford it, although it certainly leaves a sour taste. But even I am contemplating whether I should be signing up to such a membership scheme. I never thought I'd question myself of this or feel in such a dilemma. If I'm feeling it, I'm certain that thousands of others are too.

The scheme is abhorrent.

It's the feeling of not being wanted.

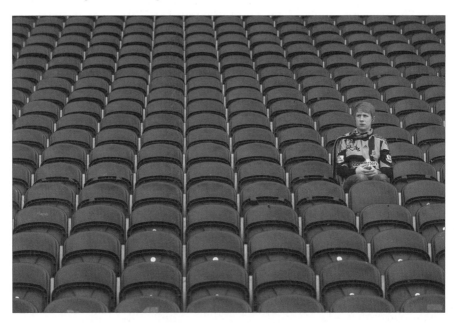

A poor run in February through to April makes us all feel a bit like this. Sad, lonely and unwanted.

(Getty Images)

Not once this season has the club made me feel important. I should. As should Thomas and Charlotte and everybody else who supports Hull City AFC and takes a seat at the KC or travels up and down the country to cheer on 'The Amber and Black.'

Believe it or not, without supporters, football really is nothing.

The immediate information coming from the club is silence. Sweet FA.

This, for me personally, is exactly the experience I have so far this season endured from the club. On repeated occasions, I have tried to engage them in this book idea. On repeated occasions my voice has fallen on deaf ears. Or ignorant ones?

So you know what? Despite wanting them to be involved, I have decided to just plod on in my own little merry way. I'll try and refuse letting the peripheral shit temper my enjoyment of following a team I love. And at the same time enjoy time with the family I love.

I love Hull City and always will. It would just be nice to feel a bit of love back now and then!

And as if by magic, football day came along again.

Amidst all the negativity and disillusionment came 'the most important' game of the season. The timing from the hierarchy could not have been worse, leaked or not. Instead of a sense of togetherness, almost ironically as tweeted by the official Club site on the day of the fixture, it felt far from it. It feels like 'them and us!' Yet still, we all really want to see the same end result, a Hull City winning team. Weird. It's almost as if a self-destruct button keeps getting pressed.

I feel sorry for the players, the management and particularly Steve Bruce too. They must feel trapped in the middle somewhat. Desperate to appease the fans, who in the main adore those who don the black and amber, but also careful not to distance themselves from the paymaster.

Poor old Steve Bruce has to play the middle ground, 'fronting up' post match interviews, in the absence of any words from up above. As if securing promotion isn't hard enough, let's just make it that much harder.

So, as we jumped in the car with the Clines immediately after school chuck out time, the conversation on the way up was not of formations, players and tactics, but of membership schemes and whether or not our future attendance supporting the club we love would continue.

It was a sickening feeling, and pre match pints in the aptly named Dr Browns pub and The Medicine Bar adjacent to the stadium, only temporarily provided a cure.

The same feeling could be felt on the concourse and terraces in the away corner of the Riverside. Whist the home side, the vast majority of the 26,791 crowd tried to create a carnival type atmosphere, flag waving, drum beating, pyro filled, almost Italian style, the small following from Hull, in the main, just felt sorry for ourselves.

Why should we care, if we are not cared for?

The Riverside, or its predecessor, Ayresome Park, is not a happy hunting ground for City. We have lost fifteen times in our last seventeen visits. This game was again on Sky, so the omens were not good. But we again travelled in hope rather than expectation. A win would lift the doom and gloom. It was a chance to put our destiny back in our own hands, and serve a large dent into a promotion rivals hopes at the same time.

Inevitably, with all that was at stake, and two teams that both pride themselves on defensive solidity, it was always going to be a tight affair. But for me, City were the better team. Huddlestone showed a calmness and level of assured passing which dictated the game in our favour. The defence, led by Curtis Davies in particular, more than capably marshalled any threat from Boro's, recent big money signing Jordan Rhodes et al. Well almost!

The first half involved few real chances of note, although Stuani had a header for Boro inside the six yard box, cleared off the line by Robertson. City's best when a Clucas cross, having evaded Aluko, playing up front on his own, found Snodgrass at the back post. His instinctive first time shot though unfortunately flew into the side netting, rather than the back of it.

We continued to dictate play in the second half. Snoddy headed wide, Diame had a shot deflected into the hands of Dimi Konstantopoulas, and Aluko then made him palm one over the bar.

And then came the chance of the match late on with only eight minutes of normal time left. Substitute Hernandez had a shot deflected into the path of Elmo. From a full six yards out, he fired the ball wildly over the crossbar. Flaying arms and cries of *"Shit!"*

That seemed about it. The fourth official put the board up to show two minutes stoppage time. Ah well, a nil-nil draw away wasn't too bad. Maybe we can win most of our remaining fixtures against mid to lower teams, hope those above slip up and we could still sneak into the top two. At least we hadn't actually lost to a rival.

Still time though for the hosts to launch one last attack. No worries, I couldn't recall McGregor having a shot to save all night.

Adomah swung a deep cross and Nugent, having come on as a substitute for the ineffective Rhodes, rose above our defence and steered a header into the net. Nugent slid on his knees as a sign for pandemonium to start in the home crowd. And so it did. And then almost immediately, the referee blew his whistle to end the proceedings.

Angst in the away corner. The run at Boro' was to go to sixteen defeats in the last eighteen. A flare was thrown in the direction of the nearby Boro' fans which only raised their decibels. Thomas' face said a thousand words, that all City fans present were feeling. It was a heart breaking end to the night. City hadn't deserved to lose, but lose we had. Our inability to convert good chances cost us again. A case of déjà vu.

The overriding feeling on the journey home was that this felt like a fatal blow to our automatic promotion chances. Not only will it have dented the team confidence, but the result will no doubt revitalise and re-unite a previously faltering Boro' side.

The game followed the pattern of many others, loads of possession, relatively few clear cut chances, wasting those that do come along, and then getting caught out by the opposition.

It is difficult to explain why results in recent weeks have taken such a dip. Other than the obvious of not hitting the back of the net often enough. These are the same players. How has it happened and more importantly, how do we fix it? And quickly.

There is a collective backlash from the supporters against the Membership Scheme, and things are starting to turn very sour.

The consequences of not going up this season, well, do not want contemplating.

"...(JUST LIKE BURNLEY), BORO'S A SHIT HOLE, I WANNA GO HOME.."

CHAPTER 54

BRISTOL CITY (H) – SATURDAY 2ND APRIL 2016

"BACK TO WINNING WAYS, AT LAST"

Following our last gasp defeat at Middlesbrough, we fortunately had a two week break due to international fixtures. In Steve Bruce's words, maybe this gave us enough chance to *'Dust worselves down'*.

Quite why an international break was organised for the Easter weekend, I'm not sure, as this clearly resulted in none of the traditional Good Friday or Easter Monday fixtures. The end product of this meant that the football widow and I actually spent all of Good Friday in the pub. At least a football fixture would have punctuated this for a few hours.

The defeat at the Riverside had felt like a near fatal blow to our chances of automatic promotion, with the ascendancy now clearly with Burnley, Middlesbrough and Brighton. We were certainly playing catch up, so this fixture was definitely one of those 'must win', 'shit or bust' games as they say, particularly as Middlesbrough had won at QPR on the Friday night.

Thankfully we were not disappointed as City ran out emphatic 4-0 winners, to just about leave us an outside chance of automatic promotion. A first win in six games, which had seen us score only twice. Maybe we had ended our wretched run and turned the corner again?

The weekend had started well as we were joined up at Filey by our good friends, the Lees family, Ged, Janine, Matthew and Adam.

Firstly a massive thank you must go out to Janine who is working tirelessly on a design for this book. As I write this, I am still to know the outcome, but have 100% faith in her remarkable artistic abilities. Ged meanwhile, the Bolton fan referred to earlier in the season, said he's a bit fed up of having to look at

Michael Dawson's face dominating their living room. Never mind Ged, he'll soon have moved out and onto one of these pages.

Friday night saw copious amounts of alcohol consumed and stories exchanged. We purchased our holiday let at Filey just over a year ago, and really enjoy going up there to break the sometimes monotonous day to day routine. It's a great place to unwind and take the dog for a stroll on the beach, and the bar of the nearest pub is only 123 steps from our front door.

So, with both families owning dogs, naturally a couple of stories about them wouldn't go amiss.

Our dog, a Golden Retriever called Fudge, can often be seen around Beverley Westwood, sometimes taking a passing interest in the would be Rory McIlroy's having a round of golf. One particular day, as Fudge and I strolled round the back of the fouteenth green, this chap hit probably the shot of his life. A fantastic iron shot from some two hundred yards away, which landed about three foot from the hole. Fudge, inquisitive as ever, decided the ball was for him, and promptly ducked under the wire fencing around the green, trotted on and picked the ball up in his mouth. He then trotted off and dropped the ball back on the fairway and then walked off. The golfer was far from happy, flaying his arms around, almost in tears. I felt for him, but decided a quick get away was the best course of action.

Ged topped this one easily. Whilst living at home with his parents many years ago, they used to have a very lively dog, a Beagle – Spaniel cross called Bramble. One weekend, Ged had ended up on a bit of a boys day out at Scarborough. Several sherberts in and he decided it would be a good idea to take a little gift home for his mum and dad. So he bought them one of those see through plastic walking sticks full of smarties that all good sea front candy stores stock.

Having then consumed several more beers, carefully carrying said walking stick from alehouse to alehouse, the early hours descended and it was time to go home. It being late, Ged decided to enter the house very quietly, via the conservatory, so as not to wake his parents. Sober, this is an easy task. Pissed, it's not. The quieter you try to be, the more noise you make.

So within seconds, Bramble was barking with excitement to see Ged, and upstairs lights were being turned on, by half awake, eye rubbing parents. Ged, already slightly uneasy on his feet was then knocked totally off them by an excitable Bramble. Still in his hand, was the plastic walking stick, having been carefully nurtured all day. Unfortunately, it had been released from Ged's grasp, done a double somersault in the air and now crashed onto the floor along with Ged, instantly dispensing all of it's smartie contents onto the floor. This was to the great delight of Bramble, who promptly 'hoovered up' all of them, licking both his own mush in the process, along with Ged's face as he lay poleaxed on the floor, inanely grinning. By this time, his stern looking father was stood over him, hands on his hips in his night attire, scowling and shaking his head. Worse was to follow.

The fact that Bramble had devoured practically every one of the smarties in a nano second soon had its effects as the dog then promptly chundered the contents of its stomach everywhere. The contents being a multi coloured fountain of spew. Let's just say, Ged wasn't in the good books.

One more story to sneak in came from Ged's cricketing days. Ged, by his own admission, was a half decent batsman, but certainly met his match when once playing for Osbaldwick. On this particular day, they were up against Dunnington, who had roped in an overseas player called James Grant. Grant was a very tall West Indian fast bowler with an extremely long run up, so as you can expect, nobody was chomping at the bit to open the batting. Ged got the short straw.

Walking to the crease, he wore all the body protection that the kit bag had to offer, such that he could barely move. There was a sense of trepidation. The bowler looked straight into Ged's eyes and walked back to the start of his long run up. The first couple of balls, Ged can't remember seeing, other than hearing the whizzing noise as the ball passed perilously close to the grill of his helmet.

The next ball came closer as it struck him just below the shoulder blade. Ged winced. A few more body blows followed until eventually they managed a single – Ged thinks it was a bye! He politely suggested to his batting partner that he wasn't moving from the non strikers end, he'd happily face the other bowler. Unfortunately for Ged, he somehow did end up facing Mr Grant again in his next over.

Remarkably, Ged managed to get bat on ball on a legside delivery, and with the speed it was being bowled at, the merest of edges saw the ball fly to the boundary. Fatal mistake. The bowler was not too pleased. He now had even more spring in his step and the next ball was Ged's downfall. As he lunged forward trying a forward defensive shot, all he could hear was the clatter of timber behind him.

Mr Grant ambled down the wicket, put his hand on Ged's shoulder, and in a deep but laid back, West Indian accent, said, *'I put ya out of ya misery'* and pointed Ged in the direction of the pavilion.

Ged trudged off and before he'd managed to finish removing all his protective clothing, another couple of batsmen had entered the fray, and returned again. Ged meanwhile, was examining his bruises, which were already ripening.

The story re-emphasized for me why I never really played cricket, much more enjoying to watch it from the stands with a cold beer in hand. We agreed to schedule in a visit to Headingley for the Yorkshire v Lancashire Twenty Twenty match later in the year. Hopefully, I'll be looking forward to an ensuing Premier League season for City, but I won't be banking on it.

So Saturday morning came around, us all nursing a few sore heads, Janine in particular. The ladies decided to stay in Filey, Janine needed some fresh air and a walk along the beach. The football widow sensed a few more glasses of wine.

I was a little anxious knowing we had to win to keep alive our promotion hopes. Ged just laughed and said, *'Relax, try being a bloody Bolton fan'*. He had a point but nevertheless, if this squad of City players don't get promoted, there will be some very disappointed members of our household.

There had been an announcement that the first eight hundred people through the turnstiles would be entitled to a free Hull Pie. The race was on! In fact, the race never really started for us, as last minute changes meant Charlotte's friend Izzy was again joining us. Not having a ticket, and being unable to pay cash on the day (despite umpteen seats being empty), this necessitated talking her through how to order online and print the ticket off. The bar code didn't eventually scan at the turnstile anyway, and the steward had to override it.

In fact, collectively, we were so slow that the six of us attending the game, rolled in with about sixty seconds to spare before kick off. No chance of a free pie. Disappointing, as you know how us Yorkshiremen like a freebie.

As we were larger in contingent than we would usually be, we moved to a row of empty seats on the very back row about ten seats or so to the right of our usual spot. This technically meant that today we were in the West Stand, not the South Stand. Being on the back row though, I even stood up for the first ten minutes or so. You don't see that from many West Standers!

We started with no natural striker again, Hernandez on the bench, having travelled half way round the world to be part of the Uruguay squad in a couple of matches and had, err, warmed the bench there too. Aluko took his place and delivered.

A spate of home draws in our previous home games meant a good early start was a must, no chance to allow the visitors to settle into the game, and to ensure nerves weren't jangling. This is exactly what we got as City started well, winning a flurry of corners on the right hand side, Moses and Snodgrass working well. Just as I uttered the words, 'we never score from corners', after the fourth of fifth had sailed aimlessly over the back post, City took the lead, when Davies got on the end of the next corner to steer the ball home. 1-0.

I've said it before, but it's worth repeating. The first goal is so so important for City. If we score first, we very rarely lose. It just gets confidence flowing through the team, and with a usually reliable defensive unit, we always feel like we are in control. Concede first however, and we really struggle to break teams down, who then have something to defend. Conversely, we do not 'come from behind' to win games very often.

So today that first goal seemed to allow City to play with much more swagger, rather than caution, and we looked to get forward quicker and with much more incision.

Bristol did have chances mind. Robertson had an off day defensively, twice letting his winger beat him. The first was blazed over, the second he had McGregor's outstretched boot to thank for keeping it out. They later had a goal chalked off for offside, a shot from just outside the box was only partly parried by McGregor, with the rebound being tucked home. Fortunately the linesman's flag was up.

Aluko was proving to be particularly lively, popping up all over the pitch, twisting and turning, as Aluko does. And when Bristol gave away possession, City broke up the other end. A nice interchange of passes eventually saw Aluko tee up a neat cross for Snoddy to head home for an unassailable 2-0 lead before half time. A third almost came just before the break, but Snodgrass' effort somehow was kept out by a fine reflex save by their keeper.

The newly introduced half time crossbar challenge, successfully achieved at the Sheffield Wednesday game, was something of an epic fail. Firstly, a 'big lad' from the crowd had a go, but was nowhere near. Reckon he'd taken advantage of the free pies on offer, and not in the singular.

Luke Campbell, Hull's very own, then got roped in to have a go. He should stick to boxing as his winkle picker pointy shoes only produced a toe poke effort that didn't even get off the floor or reach the goal. Maybe he should have punched it instead of kicking it?

City resumed where they'd left off in the first half. Both Aluko and for once, Diame, being very effective and influential.

A great move down the left saw Diame play in Robbo, who got to the byline, pulled it back to Clucas, who unfortunately fluffed his shot from six yards. Diame tried an audacious chip from his own half which had the goalkeeper back peddling, and it was certainly much better than any of the half time efforts. It was pretty much one way traffic now.

Bristol tried to change things and Odemwingie, sporting some sort of Keith Lemon bandage on his arm was subbed. Maybe he needed to leave early to drive down to QPR to get a transfer again.

A lull went from our game for a short while in the middle of the second half, but this was soon forgotten when Diame scored a great third goal. A patient passage of about thirty or so passes, just when you thought we we're going nowhere and small sections of the crowd were urging us to lump it forward (to whom I'm not quite sure), eventually resulted in the ball finding Diame just outside the box. A little shimmy to his left to open space and he rifled a shot into the bottom far corner.

He is just so unpredictable. Sometimes, stumbling over his own feet, looking off the pace. Other times, absolutely fantastic at this level. My usual 'next seat partner' Richard, turned round towards us in our new seats for the day, and we gave each other a wry nod of the head. West Stand to South Stand, enough said.

Bristol still had a couple of chances to get on the score sheet. Dawson made a good goal line clearance, and McGregor pulled off another couple of good saves to ensure a clean sheet. Ged, an impartial guest commented that our strength was certainly our defence. His team Bolton could score goals, but hell, they also know how to let them in.

In the previous game, Bristol City had beaten Bolton 6-0. We were about to beat Bristol City 4-0, so by that schoolboy logic, surely we'll be on for a 10-0 win when we play Bolton in our penultimate game?

Diame and Snodgrass both got substituted to well received applause, and Elmo and Maloney came on in their place. It was left to Elmo to play a pivotal role in eventually setting up Aluko for a deserved goal (if not without a bit of assistance from some iffy goalkeeping), before he too went off to a standing ovation.

Steve Bruce summed up at the end by stating, '*Look, there's been nothing really wrong with our recent performances. We've had more attempts, more shots, more crosses, more final third entries than any other team in this division. The one statistic which is the stand out one, is that we haven't been able to score for whatever reason, and that's been frustrating. Once we scored, then there was a calmness about us which was good to see*'

Let's hope we keep scoring then, and we'll all remain calm.

As we left to return to Filey, I was beginning to feel a bit peckish. Now then, where are all those pies?

"...WHO ATE ALL THE PIES, WHO ATE ALL THE PIES, YOU FAT...!"

CHAPTER 55

"DEBACLE AT DERBY"

After a horrible March which saw no wins, two draws and three defeats, we are glad to see the back of it. City have slipped from top spot and are now clinging on to the forlorn hope of an automatic promotion slot.

Burnley haven't lost since Boxing Day, since guess what, City had put them to the sword. Middlesbrough meanwhile are no doubt rejuvenated after that last minute Nugent goal against us at the Riverside. Brighton, despite all the experts predictions, simple won't go away. City meanwhile, well it feels like we are in freefall.

An emphatic 4-0 win the previous Saturday against Bristol City, had done that thing to me again. Yes, I had begun to believe again. I'd look at the tables again and started trying to do the mathematics. I'd looked into our fixtures, and blindly assumed we'd win the vast majority of our remaining ones. If we could just eek out a win at the I-Pro against Derby. Surely some of the teams above us would slip up. Surely?

A win may have put into the background (albeit temporarily) the distractions behind and off the pitch. There we are, I'd talked myself into it. Blind faith.

I shouldn't have bothered!

Derby are by far the best team I'd seen us play this season so far. The only one to beat us at home, and convincingly at that. It was something of a surprise that they themselves were still only clinging on to a play off spot. Mind you, they have got history of bottling it.

This whole night was embarrassing. From a personal point of view. From a Hull City point of view. And from a Hull City Supporters point of view.

It was by far, our worst experience of the season. In fact I was struggling to think of when I have been more disappointed. We entered the day hoping for a win to elevate ourselves back towards the leading three teams. We ended it closer to seventh. After the full time whistle, we'll have seven more shots at redemption, although we are now seven points off an automatic spot. Our form does not bode well.

To say that Derby completely dominated, is an insult to the very word dominance. They owned us tonight and obliterated what little remaining chances of an automatic spot we still harbour. Worse still, assuming we can stay in the play off places, we may yet have to play Derby again. Can't wait!

As soon as the fixtures had been announced back in June, we'd picked this one out to hopefully enjoy. The I-Pro is practically on the doorstep of the football widows cousin, Honest Dave, herein already mentioned. We would therefore all be coming to visit, with Dave also attending the fixture. Dave now resides in Belper, close to Derby and also used to be one of my partners in crime during our Cross Keys, Cottingham drinking days.

Very much akin to how I am now indoctrinating Thomas into 'The Hull City Way', 'Like Father Like Son', Dave's own father, Dennis, had followed the same path, albeit opting for Sunderland, not Hull City. As such, Dave is a Black Cat, and follows a Sunderland team, who are well and truly experiencing having nine lives. They somehow seem to avoid relegation from the Premier League every season, despite being crap for the vast majority of them. They must be close to using up all nine lives by now?

His visits 'up north' to see his team have diminished slightly since his move to Belper, and of latter years, certain games were more frequented in the Riflemans Arms, an old fashioned boozer in the cobbled streets of Belper. He soon became a regular face, leading him to be part of the RAGS – Riflemans Arms Golf Society. Whilst golf was certainly on the agenda, from time to time, it also co-incided with lock ins.

The landlord at the time, a fellow Mackem, also a member of the RAGS, used to welcome these lock ins, and in addition would lay on a selection of nibbles. Often the first to bed, he'd leave the 'would be golfers' to their own devices just asking that the last man standing, shut the door on his way out. Blokes being blokes, drink mixed in, this often led to an element of tomfoolery. This led to the challenge, never officially named by anyone, but I shall, called *'Who can hide the food in the best place which will take the longest to find?!'*

Cue mini scotch eggs in the ladies and prawns in curtain poles.

One particular evening, this prank went a little too far.

A certain member of the party, who for obvious reasons shall remain nameless, and, after having consumed an unfeasibly large quantity of alcohol, had the brilliant thought that they may be able to hide a mini party style pork pie in the light socket above the dart board. So, to task, they carefully removed the light bulb. Imagine the Tuesday night darts team surprise. Needless to say, they never found out.

As pork pie, jelly and all, was inserted into said light socket, it became apparent that pork pies also conduct electricity. The prankster was catapulted across the room, feeling the full force. The pub was engulfed in darkness, as the Melton Mowbray miniature caused a serious failure in the electrics. Rapid 'sober-up-id-ness' soon happened and all parties vacated the establishment. The landlord would only find the damage later in the morning, as he looked forward to his early morning cuppa.

The lights were out. Almost a metaphor for City's story tonight?

Since then, Dave has now become husband to Jo, and more recently, the 'responsible' father of Bertie. His part in drunken antics are less frequent. In addition, the last couple of weeks, his feelings towards Sunderland have taken a turn for the worse, much is his disdain for the whole Adam Johnson affair.

This recently resulted in his first visit with Bertie to Belper Town to watch 'The Nailers'. The ground is literally at the end of his street and then down a lane. Other than the sign at the top of the lane, displaying the next impending fixture, you wouldn't know it was there.

Only five days earlier, aptly on April Fools Day, the sign had been tweaked to show the next fixture as Belper Town versus Real Madrid. According to the Belper Bugle (or whatever it is called), about thirty people actually rang the club, asking how they could get tickets for the big game. The club caterer even rang, asking *'What shall we cook for this Spanish lot that are coming? Maybe paella?'*

She didn't need to worry. The actual fixture ended up being against Kidsgrove Athletic in the Evo Stick Northern Premier First Division South. It ended in a 1-1 draw, the narrative according to their website describing it as, '...*Belper's failure to turn possession into goals forced them to settle for a draw...'*

Sound familiar?

The report failed to add if any mini pork pies were on the menu for the 221 crowd. The manager of Belper that day, a certain Charlie Palmer. Centre back, Gerome Palmer, son thereof.

A day off work, and half term, meant an early departure for Belper. A few pre match beers and Dave had been busy in his diminutive kitchen, rustling up a chilli for tea. All good so far.

Over tea, Dave informed us that he'd managed to book us on the 'Ram Express'. This is basically a coach that stops off and picks up Derby supporters en route and back to the I-Pro, and save the hassle of parking your car, and experiencing road rage after the game trying to get out. Great idea and it stops just at the end of Dave's street for the princely sum of £3.

No need for apprehension, good idea I thought. It'll be great to get on the coach on the way back after a City win, with that smug feeling inside. As if we needed strength in numbers, Dave's father in law, Paul, also joined us for the evening. Paul is a Nottingham Forest fan so added to our small contingent of 'non Rams.' Charlotte and the football widow elected to stay in Belper with Jo and Bertie. Fucking wise choice in hindsight.

So we boarded the Ram Express at around 6.30ish. All aboard the I-Pro. Dave had let the cat out of the bag that there were City fans on board.

At this point, the evening started to turn sour. Or to use a better and in this case, far more appropriate phrase, Shit!

No sooner was I aboard the Ram Express, then my body, being of delicate preposition, decided to tell me that chilli doesn't suit me. It needed an escape route. So did I. Off the coach and to a toilet.

I did a bit of squirming and tried to concentrate on something else. I can't remember what, but something. We rolled around, corner after corner until we were eventually despatched outside the ground. *'Can we go in?'* I asked / pleaded / begged of Dave and Paul, as they looked up and down the statue of Brian Clough outside. An impressive ground as it is, I needed to see the worst bit and quick, the bogs.

Dave ordered two pints of gassy lager. I said I'll see you in a minute. It took less than a minute as eventually I levitated above the 'seat' (there wasn't one) in one of the two traps, to, well, fresh relief. Good, at least that's out of the way I thought, so returned to Dave. Maybe another pint would sort me out? I'd barely blown the froff off. Dave looked at me and said, *'You look shit'*. *'Never mind looking shit'*, I replied, *'I think I need another one.'* And so I departed again to trap two.

With kick off time soon emerging, Dave proceeded to slide down my pint, and we ascended to our seats. Surely the night would improve?

For the first twenty or twenty five minutes it was all okay. I was tip toeing from one foot to another, to keep my body together, and so was City's defensive line. We were looking okay.

And then much like earlier, it all went to shit. This time, not me!

In the twenty ninth minute, a slip by Curtis Davies, totally unchallenged, was pounced upon by Craig Bryson down the Derby right. The midfielders cross was turned onto the post by Chris Martin (who I have been thoroughly impressed by) and Bradley Johnson smashed the loose ball home. 1-0 down.

The goal turned the game upside down. We panicked. The hosts, suddenly had an infectious energy. It was going to be a long night. The away following no longer stood. We sat, as if anticipating our fate.

Diame did have a good chance for City when we were gifted an opening. The Derby defence let him in 'Davies-esque' and he was clean through. A couple of shifts from one foot to another, tippy tappy style, only failing to get a shot in at all and running the ball out of play altogether, without troubling the keeper. Diame, one game unplayable, the next he shouldn't be played, still unplayable, if you get what I mean.

'You're fucking shit, you're fucking shit, you're fucking shit...' mocked the Rams crowd. Exactly, I thought to myself.

A second Derby goal arrived shortly before half time. A swift quick interchange of passing, first time stuff, none of that 'I'll control it first, then look up for a pass' stuff, and we were opened up. Ping pong, ping pong and the ball was squared by Ince to Johnson to double his tally with a powerful finish past McGregor.

Derby simply had a stranglehold on the game. They were stronger than us in every department and our defence looked as tight as, well, my arse!

If we'd had a mountain to climb, it was now an Everest.

Half time came and we all looked glum. The tannoy tried to cheer me up, playing some of my favourite tunes including Bon Jovi and AC/DC. It then broke out into The Buzzcocks, 'Ever Fallen In Love With Someone'. I wondered if I was falling out of love with City. Guns and Roses then told me I was apparently in Paradise City. I think not. This was a world away from Paradise.

No changes were made at half time. The idea of continuing with Aluko up front to try and hold the ball up, alongside an erratic Diame, whilst two goals down seemed non logical. A tactical ploy maybe of, 'I'll cross my fingers and something might happen?'

It did.

Ten minutes into the second half, City lost possession on the halfway line. A pass from Bryson sent Ince galloping clear beyond Odubajo. Moses gave a little tug knowing he was beaten. Ince, not for the first time in his career, or in fact the night, fell to the floor. To his credit, it was a foul. A clear goal scoring opportunity, albeit the Ince I know, probably wouldn't have scored anyway.

Red card, Moses off and down to ten men. Only a full thirty five minutes to go.

The home crowd urged on their team to exert humiliation upon us. City displayed a bit of resilience, and at least kept possession for a while. Maybe Derby were just taking a breather.

Chris Martin was displaying good hold up play. He'd be great alongside Hernandez, the goal poacher, I thought.

As the clock ticked down with ten man City looking jaded, my thoughts turned to Steve Bruce. It may have been the home crowd diverting my sub-conscience, the shouts of '*He's got a face like an arse*' may have awoken me. I'm no body language expert, but tonight he looked like a beaten man. He has been very unequivocal about his future at City and his enthusiasm must be on the wane. At two down, there was no pacing around the technical area bellowing orders. Just a fantastic ex professional footballer, and expert Championship manager, stood with hands in his tracksuit bottoms.

I recalled the day I was at Old Trafford (don't ask me why I was there, but I was, honest) watching him head two late goals against Sheffield Wednesday, and wheeling away in delight. Tonight I clearly didn't see the same man, I just saw a broken man.

To be fair, as already said, who can blame him? He's had to face the press and fans angst, at the owners nonsensical running of Hull City AFC. He's been the sounding block and had to face a barrage of questions, mostly not about football. Surely that is all he should have to answer questions about. After all, that is his job.

His relationship with both owners and fans must be wearing thin with the fiasco going on in the background. I contemplated life at Hull City without him. I didn't want to, but his body language said he didn't want to be here anymore. At this precise time, neither did I.

We entered the last ten minutes. Ten man City knackered, Derby rampant.

They stepped up a gear. We went down one, into reverse.

No sooner had Clucas had a rasping volley saved, Derby went into our half and the ever impressive Martin put a crisp shot past Allan for a third from the edge of the box. Thomas and I collected our flag. It no longer needed to be on display.

As we untied it, McGregor made a fantastic double save to keep out Ince and then Bryson. As we trapsed back up the steps to rejoin Dave and Paul, many City supporters were heading for the exits. Those that remained sang in defiance,

'We're gonna win 4-3' followed by *'How shit must you be, it's only three nil'*

Not for long.

Bryson completed the rout in the last minute, tapping in for 4-0.

For a split moment, I hated football. I wanted the season to end now.

As only five Hull City players dared to venture over and applaud the travelling fans, (Snoddy first in particular, soon followed by captain Dawson, Davies, then Huddlestone and Maloney), I wondered where were the others, they'd quickly already sneaked down the tunnel. To those five in particular, we thank you. We are part of this, as much as you are.

We trudged out speechless. Dave and Paul tried to utter some words of encouragement. They were wasted words. Oh joy, let's climb aboard the Ram Express on our way home. As Thomas and I slumped into our seats trying not to make eye contact with anyone, Radio Derby started bellowing out. With joy, it replayed all four goals, several times over. Each one cutting deeper.

We both slunk in our seats even deeper, as if to vanish. It didn't work. The Derby contingent, The Rams, all had hard ons, even the women! Christ, you'd have thought we'd have just played Real Madrid! Their confidence was overflowing. Ours had disappeared into thin air.

We finally arrived back at Dave's house. Whilst I felt shit, the shits had gone.

Post match reviews and comments from Brucey did not install me with uber confidence.

'Our performance was bordering on the ridiculous' followed by 'We'll dust worselves down, and go again'

Never mind dusting, a full fucking spring clean would be in order.

I was reminded of a quote from yesteryear about Steve Bruce from his playing days I believe, 'I've seen milk turn quicker'. Steve will have to achieve something to turn our season around following tonight's display.

Enough of football for one night we thought, and agreed to have one more nightcap.

And with that, Dave and Jo's cat, Finnegan, shot in front of me. It's now nineteen years old, and now looks like something out of Mad Max, having just had an eye removed, with what's left having been all stitched up.

Hell, I nearly shit myself!

"...HOW SHIT MUST WE BE?.. FULL STOP..."

CHAPTER 56

HUDDERSFIELD TOWN (A) – SATURDAY 9TH APRIL 2016

"GOING THROUGH AN AWFUL SPELL"

Only four days after the mullering at Derby, next up for City was a short trip to Huddersfield. The Derby debacle still felt raw, and had felt like a knife to the heart for any lingering promotion aspirations. The sceptre of the membership scheme still looms, the club apparently still to confirm the minutia of the detail that had been released a few weeks ago.

More rumours were abound re Steve Bruce's ongoing tenure at the club. Links to Aston Villa were being reported, and Steve himself was fairly ambiguous and unequivocal when asked any questions about the subject. With all the malaise and toxicity starting to engulf anything to do with City, who could blame him if he is beginning to lose his enthusiasm?

Personally, I hope he sees the job out. This squad should be getting promotion automatically, and we have one of the best managers in this league.

So I did what all football fans do.

I somehow conveniently put to the back of my mind the 4-0 drubbing at Derby and deluded myself that, whilst it was still mathematically possible, City could still do it. Ridiculous I know, but Thomas and I travelled to Huddersfield with the male contingent of the Lee family, believing that this would be the start of 'the Magnificent seven'. Seven games left, seven wins and we'd just squeak into the top two.

I didn't voice this opinion mind, just kept it to myself!

The fact that we were allowed to actually drive to an away game at Huddersfield was in itself, something of a victory anyway.

Back on Saturday 30th March 2013, Hull City had an away fixture against Huddersfield. As is often the case, Sky selected to screen the game live and requested to change the kick off time to 5.20pm. Hey, if Sky ask?

Eventually, West Yorkshire Police agreed to this, but only if certain conditions were met, to apparently mitigate risks associated with the fixture and the new kick off time. Two of these conditions were, to limit the number of tickets available to Hull City fans, (only 1,500 were made available despite the away end holding 4,000) and to insist that **all** Hull City fans travelled on official coaches to the match.

Obviously the official coaches all left from Hull. So a Hull City supporter living in say Leeds (yes there are some) was being asked to travel from Leeds to Hull, board an official coach, on which they would be issued with their match ticket, travel to Huddersfield, and back, and then make the return leg back home. How ridiculous.

West Yorkshire Police claimed this was based on their intelligence sources, which indicated a strong likelihood of disorder and alcohol consumption. Basically, the insinuation was to treat us all like hooligans, and assume we were all going to cause trouble. How preposterous.

Supporters complained, but to no avail. Who are we after all?

The match went ahead, and City won 1-0, courtesy of a George Boyd goal. I didn't bother going. It all seemed far too complicated. I opted instead for a North Ferriby home game, with Sky on pause allowing me time to get home without missing anything, and obviously without the radio on for fear of accidently hearing anything. Needless to say, no trouble whatsoever happened.

Eventually, West Yorkshire Police were forced to be investigated over the affair. Guess what, a peer review was held by Northumbria Police over the whole episode; the police policing the police! This is all available to see on the internet but for me the over-riding factor that stood out was, West Yorkshire Police had no records or minutes whatsoever, of any such 'intelligence', and were recommended to review their policy on policing football matches and major events.

It was also suggested that West Yorkshire Police urgently address the public concern the match generated through a transparent explanation of events (ie contact the Hull City supporters). I'm not sure if this ever happened, but let's hope the whole ridiculous affair will never be repeated ever again.

Today's fixture at Huddersfield took place in the same week that the jury started to consider its verdict on the long overdue Hillsborough hearing. In this case, involving the ineptitude of the South Yorkshire Police, at a football match. Almost two years of evidence and documents surrounding that fateful day when 96 Liverpool fans ultimately lost their lives, after just going to watch a football match. Quite why it's taken almost two years is beyond me, but I suppose it's taken over twenty years for a proper hearing, so it's only right that it is done correctly. I'm sure at some point in the ensuing few weeks, 'the truth' will emerge for the whole world to see.

As we set off it was pouring down in Hull. Bri had as ever, planned things to precision, including locating his exact parking spot down a dead end street, within walking distance of the John Smiths Stadium. Upon arrival, the sun was shining, and for the first time since I can't remember when, it was actually warm at a City match. Even warm enough to sink a couple of pre match pints in the open air at the rear of the away end.

As the unusual prospect of a Saturday afternoon three pm kick off loomed, Bri, planning as ever, instructed his dad to go to the toilet and drain off the John Smith's he'd drunk. He then informed him that he needed to leave just prior to the full time whistle, go to the toilet, and get back to the car pronto. He wouldn't be stopping on the way home, as he was going out!

This ultimately resulted in his old man missing City's 93rd minute equaliser. He had been a bit naughty though and stayed long enough to witness Harry Maguire's 91st minute own goal!

My idyllic dream of a 'magnificent seven' was soon to be shattered. In the end, City scrambled a 2-2 draw, but in all, it was an apathetic performance. Diomande's injury time equaliser merely papered over the cracks, and our poor run of form stretched to only one win in our last eight league games, yielding only seven points. This is relegation form, not promotion form, and it seemed like a lifetime away since the heady heights of our table topping trip to Ipswich. A harsh dose of reality pill kicked in again.

In the wake of the horror show at Derby, Steve Bruce rang the changes. Elmo, Hernandez, Bruce and Maguire came in for the suspended Odubajo, Aluko, Davies and Clucas, the latter three of whom dropped to the bench.

They didn't make an awful lot of difference.

The play was again far too one paced and predictable.

To be fair, the first fifteen minutes or so were okay, and Hernandez should have scored with a header from six yards out following a cross from Elmo. It went straight to the keeper, and from that moment on, Huddersfield grew into the game. And we let them, looking very open at the back.

The away following sensed it. A mixture of irritation and frustration was in no uncertain terms, aired at the apparent disintegration of a season that had promised so much. It was not lost on the 2,000 or so visiting supporters, that the week heralded the second anniversary since the FA said no to the idea of City changing their name. This clearly was a sign for a robust 'City Till I Die' on 19' 04". Closely followed by many other chants, all of which were absolutely nothing to do with events <u>on</u> the pitch. The faithful were definitely waning.

For me, whilst those stood around questioned what was going on, I just commented, *'It feels like I'm stuck in a rut. I seem to have watched this match already several times this season'*. It was all getting a bit soul destroying.

And no sooner had the conversation taken place, then the City defence inexplicably backed off the opposition down our right hand side, allowing their winger to pass into the box to Jamie Patterson, who in turn, simply passed it into the net, giving the hosts a 1-0 lead. It all looked too easy, a total lack of heart and desire.

I'm not sure where Elmo was with his positioning, but Alex Bruce was certainly telling him what he thought of it. Elmo has been a great servant to City during the last three seasons but based on his performances so far this season, it seems clear that he is looking to be elsewhere. Quite where else, I'm not sure. Odubajo will certainly be replacing him once his suspension is over.

Worse was to follow, as Dawson was then forced off with an injury. Davies, initially stripped and ready to come on, was then told to sit back down again, and Maloney finally came on, thus changing the formation.

Alex Bruce missed a glorious chance to equalise, blazing over from only six yards out, before the players trudged off for half time one goal down. This was the fourteenth consecutive Championship away game City had played since we'd last scored in the first half. Not the statistic of a team aiming for automatic promotion.

We trudged off to the bar for another beer in the sun, to try and talk about anything other than football.

The second half didn't start much better and Huddersfield went close a couple of times with McGregor sparing our blushes.

Eventually though, around the hour mark, we started coming to life. Huddlestone, one of the few brighter sparks of the day, crashed a shot against the crossbar. Bruce rang some more changes, with Diomande replacing the enigma that is Diame. One week unplayable, the next three weeks, a passenger. Aluko also replaced Snodgrass.

And it was Aluko that re-invigorated us. Almost immediately he twisted and turned out wide, and set up Hernandez, who neatly struck a low volley to bulge the net, 1-1. A timely end to something of a goal scoring drought for the striker, even if his run has been punctuated by not actually starting some games. The decibel level in the away end raised as a sense of '*we can nick this*' came to the fore.

Aluko had a good chance four minutes from the end, but he only proceeded to put the ball into the crowd. The fourth official put up his board, and Bri Lee Senior, probably contemplated carrying out his son's orders to leave early.

And then calamity.

Once again, City stood off, and a cross was inadvertently turned into his own net by Big Harry. Shit, shit and more shit!

But if we can take anything from this performance, it was at least that we showed some character, to come from behind for a second time. Somehow, Alex Bruce found himself in some space in the Huddersfield penalty area and his cross, slightly deflected, found substitute Diomande, who powered an excellent header into the bottom corner. 2-2 and a point was retrieved.

The other teams at the top continued to win and it was almost certain that a top two dream was gone. In fact this point may yet prove invaluable, as a play off spot is far from certain the way we are playing. Surely City couldn't cock that up, could they?

A seven point cushion is now in place, with a likely play off against Derby. Oh joy, I can't wait to play them twice!

After the match, Steve Bruce once again looked empty, saying, *'There's no doubt about it, at the moment we're going through one of those awful spells and you can see a little bit of confidence has drained away.'* No shit Sherlock!

It's about time that some of these players now turned up. And quickly, before this season evaporates into nothing. Next up is Wolves at home on Friday. It's hardly getting me excited!

"...C'MON CITY, C'MON CITY, C'MON CITY, C'MON..." (PLEASE!)

CHAPTER 57

WOLVES (H) – FRIDAY 15TH APRIL 2016

"TOIL, TOIL AND TOIL SOME MORE"

Right, I'd talked myself into a 'magnificent seven' just prior to the Huddersfield away game. It didn't quite get off to the right start, so now I'm hoping for a 'super six'. Six games left that, on paper, should yield six relatively easy wins. Surely?!

First of the six was a home game against Wolves, who were mid table with nothing to play for, so surely a stroll in the park for the multi talented boys in black and amber. The match was again being screened on Sky, having been moved to the Friday night.

I'd got all enthusiastic again after watching the previous night a fantastic game in the Europa League, between Liverpool and Borussia Dortmund. Both sets of fans were fantastic, creating a great atmosphere. Liverpool in particular demonstrated a team together, a crowd together, and a club together. The proverbial twelfth man really lifted the team, most notably including their enigmatic manager Jurgen Klopp. A real 'team' effort eventually saw Liverpool score a last minute winner to come out on the right side of a 4-3 scoreline. Stirring stuff and I felt genuinely pleased for my pal Ady. I could picture him going mental as the winner went in. Oh for a dose of that at City. Something to rejuvenate a flagging season and inject some interest. It doesn't have to be at exactly the same level, but something to put the enjoyment back into it.

It feels so different to the current mood around City at the moment. In contrast to Liverpool, we seem to have disaffected owners, a confused manager, dismayed fans, and a set of players who have lost the art of playing together as a team anymore. Other than that, everything is just fine!

Whilst we are still in the upper reaches of the table, it somehow just feels so different to the spirit of our Championship promotion seasons in 07/08 and

12/13. Those saw a real collective spirit with no one player or thing bigger than the team. There was an enduring team spirit that helped City through spells of adversity, the whole was definitely greater than the sum of its parts. 'Dare to dream' was one of the motto's at the time.

This season, and in particular with the advent of the proposed Membership scheme, it doesn't feel the same, it doesn't feel like a dream at the moment.

Tonight the attendance dipped again to a league season low. A total of 15,504 'crammed' into the KC, and 365 of those were Wolves supporters. It feels like the lifeblood is being sucked out of City. For the first time in years, I have contemplated doing something else. Could I go and watch some 'football with soul' at North Ferriby as an alternative. They are currently performing extremely well this season and on the cusp of a remarkable promotion to the Conference. Sky, by moving this fixture to the Friday night, had presented me an opportunity to test this out, as I made a point of visiting Church Road the following day to watch The Villagers against AFC Telford.

I wasn't the only one contemplating a life without Hull City.

As an example and sign of the general mood around the club, I hereby enclose contributions from two well respected City fans. Between them, they have over 100 seasons of following City, regardless of whether those seasons were good, bad, or just indifferent.

First up, Ian Puckering, a genuine sports enthusiast and City 'diehard', and his own personal current thoughts on all things City.

I have been following Hull City all my life. It started in the late 50's and I went with my dad on the crossbar of his bike. We stood with his mates from work in the East Stand. The earliest match I remember clearly was against Bradford City in the FA Cup second round in 1960/61. I was nine years old and we went into the town and had lunch at the 'pick a dish' in Hammonds. From there by train from Paragon to Boothferry Halt, hauled by a grimy freight loco from Dairycoates shed. City lost 2-0. The Cup was special in those days, not a reason to play your reserve team. I had been to Darlington the previous season to see the start of the five game marathon and was at the memorable 5-4 win against Cook Town the following year. In the league, City held their own with a number of local lads who loved and understood the club (Greenwood, Petit, Beardsley, Lord et al).

Over the subsequent years there have been highs (Waggy and Chillo) and lows (administration twice), memorable games (Chelsea in the Cup home and away) and ones to forget (too many to mention). Good managers (Brittain) and bad (Hateley), good owners (Needler) and bad (Buchanan / Lloyd – take your choice!). But throughout it all, there have been the fans. Unwavering in their devotion and love of the club. Often down to a hard core, when it was easier to get on the train to go and watch Leeds or Liverpool, or just wear a Man United shirt around the town because it was 'cool'.

*I took my son as soon as he could walk and lifted him over the turnstiles until he became too heavy. I missed three goals in a five goal drubbing of Brighton because he kept wanting to go to the toilet. He once wandered off behind the East Stand and I did not notice he was missing. Panic ensued until he was found gathering brambles on the railway embankment 'for mummy'. She never did find out the full story. But that is as it should be. Fathers should take their sons and daughters to watch **their** team. It is as important as their mother's milk.*

And so onwards through the 80's and 90's until a seminal moment. The Great Escape season with as great a team of battlers as you will ever see. Beating Scarborough in a genuine six pointer. Little did we know then what the next ten years or so would bring. If you had predicted it at the time, then the men in white coats would have been round for you. But a golden era was about to dawn under Pearson, Taylor, Brown and Ashbee. And a brand new ground to boot to replace the tired and dilapidated Boothferry Park. Three promotions, an FA Cup final and a foray into Europe. Amazing stuff.

*So why am I falling out of love with City? After a season in which we are looking like gaining our highest number of points ever in the league, only lost one home league game, and gone further in the League Cup than ever before. The emotional bond will always be there (I **will** be 'City 'till I die') but I think I have finally had enough of been taken for granted by the club (with its attitude to ticket prices despite the TV riches) and the Premier League (with its stupid kick off times and date changes). Money rules these days. The name change and the 'go away and die' stuff indicated the current owner's attitude to us, their customers. And finally the membership scheme which sees me turfed out of the seat I have occupied since the KC Stadium opened. All without my consultation. A step too far for this fan. Its off to North Ferriby for me next season.*

Strong and stirring stuff which is then only echoed by another long standing City fan. As you read this, I'm sure many of you will be able to deduce who it is. He has had many pseudonyms and is currently going under the name 'The Outlaw Josey Wales', and he entitled his words as 'Disillusion Blues'.

The whole membership scheme is a dog's dinner, plain and simple.

Yet I can see why they have brought it in. No one should tolerate free loaders, which is fair enough and understandable, but this is a ten tonne weight dropped from a great height to crack a peanut.

I can't accept for one moment that this scheme has been thought up to save the fans money. It has been devised to stop people stealing and to stop supporters getting in on concessionary tickets that they are not entitled to.

These are old problems relevant at every club in the land. So why haven't they all thought of a Membership scheme first? Remembering that all of football fought against ID Cards / Membership schemes when Maggie Thatcher tried to force them upon us. Because it doesn't work. People still decided on the morning of a game if they are going to go or not, more so today with work patterns and such, not to mention fixture changes.

As for the 'Earn Your Stripes' slogan? I find it insulting. I'm coming up to the age soon when I will actually qualify for a concessionary pass. Fifty two years of solid support earning my stripes, now they want to take it away from me!

Also how can it be fair to ask schoolkids to pay the same as an adult? When I first starting going to City, it was with my dad. In those days, if he had to pay the same price for me, then I wouldn't have been taken and I probably would have never caught the bug. I'm no different to anyone else, its how we started. It is a seriously flawed scheme which will decimate the support. My grandson has a seat two blocks from me because he likes to be with me at half time. For him to sit there next season, his pass will cost him another £250. How is that encouraging support? I also don't want to pay for anything else monthly. I'm already loaded up against my will with gas, electric, rates and so on, and I don't want football on there as well.

On top of this, you are expected to move seats to the cheaper seats which again is insulting. I've spoken to loads of mainly elderly people, all of whom have made friends with the people who sit near them. City is the only time they meet, the only time many of them leave the house, yet they are now expected to up sticks and sit elsewhere, and for what reason? None of them are going to renew their passes if they have to move and in every case the OAP's will be paying considerably more.

Then add the 'small time' thinking of moving fans from the West Stand Upper (if we don't go up) and for what reason? To save on stewarding costs. That is all. It has to be fully staffed if two or ten thousand fans are up there, so they don't think of ways of filling it, they think of ways of closing it. Madness.

Then there's the football. It has been like a relegation season since the New Year. A sterile atmosphere with the life seemingly to having been throttled out of the club by the owners. On a slow drip by drip basis, no pre match build up in the week, not talking to the media, not daring to utter the dreaded words 'Hull City' and all our very identity diluted so it means nothing. I hate it. I don't feel as though it is my club anymore.

I've only been to two away games this season. Boro and Derby, and in both cases, the pre match socialising was far better than the game itself. The match used to be the highlight, now it just gets in the way of a good day out. An hour and a half to sober up and be quiet.

The club is in free fall.

Having said that, we still have an outstanding chance of a grandstand finish, another Wembley final and a real chance of promotion back to the Premier League. But it doesn't feel like that does it? Which shows the magnitude of the hatchet job the owners have done on our club, our fan base and our identity.

I could walk away, seriously and never come back.

Listening to and reading those words certainly made me feel glum. In a weird way, I was kind of glad that we had decided to attempt this book and the 46 thing. Its given us something to focus on and distract ourselves, even if only temporarily, away from the current malaise around the place.

Maybe a stirring home win against Wolves might lift the mood?

A rediscovery of the spark that only a few weeks ago saw City climb to the summit of the Championship, was the pre match rallying call from Steve Bruce. Along with a demand to build up some much needed momentum, ahead of a likely play off campaign.

It didn't feel like this would be the case during the build up to the match itself. Nobody seemed to be interested in the 'girls on stilts' outside the stands, nor the lightshow prior to kick off. Nobody was watching. What a waste of time, and money. Even the marketing ploy of another free food incentive, previously meat pies, had now been reduced to only two hundred hot dogs. The only apt word I can think of in the build up to the game to describe my thoughts is 'bored'. It felt like I was going through the motions.

A bloke behind us tried to get us all enthusiastic with cries of "*Meat pie, sausage roll, come on City, score a goal*" but they failed to stir us. And if I was going through the motions, it sure as hell felt like the team was as well.

The play was laboured, but also on occasions far too hurried in possession. It lacked any real rhythm or fluidity for long periods, and certainly without much goal threat.

And this was all after being gifted a goal through calamitous defending inside the first five minutes. A flick on by Elmo from a long punt forward should have been dealt with by the Wolves defence. Instead, Ikeme in the Wolves goal, made a total cock up of it, dropped the ball, gifting it to '*Diomande, City's 25*', to tap into an empty net. Added to his 'gift' at QPR, that must be two of the easiest goals a City striker will ever score in a season. It almost feels rude to claim them, but claim them we will.

Thomas immediately added that maybe that was some kind of divine retribution for McGregor's cock up at Molineux earlier in the season (or words to that effect anyway). Bloody good memory that boy!

Such a fortunate start should have been capitalised on. It wasn't and we began to struggle. The Wolves left back, Jeremy Helan, on loan from Sheffield Wednesday, was giving Moses a tough game, and started putting in some telling crosses.

One of them saw a header nestle on the top netting. I certainly thought it was in at the time.

We continued to struggle, epitomised by Elmo, 'facing' a Wolves corner out, rather than heading it. Simple you would have thought.

The previous miss though was only a temporary reprieve, as soon after, a very heavy touch by Alex Bruce, presented possession back to our opponents. Another good cross from Helan, and an unmarked Dave Edwards headed in for 1-1.

We'd been handed the lead, were complacent with it, lost it, and then never really looked like regaining it.

Our play was predictable. Constant goal kicks out to Elmo every time, throw ins that usually resulted in lost possession, poor hold up play, and an overall lack of energy, even in appealing decisions. Obviously, McGregor and his Tourette's syndrome aside!

We needed a lift. Elmo almost got it, when it looked like he'd been hauled down for a penalty, but the referee instead, rather theatrically, pointed for a corner instead. Hey, it was Elmo, and much like Forristieri in an earlier game, he has got previous, which may well have counted against him.

Half time came, with us struggling to muster any enthusiasm. I spent much of it on my phone, and was amused by one tweet which read, *'No longer going to KC. First time watching from the sofa. Same atmosphere but not having to listen to miserable twats'*

Maybe it was me, he or she was referring to. I'd drifted into a lull.

The Wolves fans suggested that *'You're support is fucking shit'*. Maybe they had a point. A rallying cry of *'Everywhere we go, everyone will know…'* was the response in the hope of an upturn in the standard of fayre on the pitch. It soon followed with Livermore having a shot that went for a throw in!

Things did start to pick up as we entered the latter stages. Ikeme thwarted a deflected Hernandez drive and followed it up, preventing Aluko, but in all that seemed to be that. Another flat and disappointing home draw.

One last fling perhaps as City were awarded a free kick just outside the box deep into stoppage time. In my doldrums, I conversed with those sat around us, and we took guesses at which row of the South Stand it would be sent into – *'we never score from free kicks'*, was, as usual uttered, admittedly by yours truly.

What an expert I am. Not. I had not banked on the sheer brilliance that can be Robert Snodgrass.

Steve Bruce, and the rest of us patient souls, finally got the spark we were looking for, as Snoddy struck a quite sublime free kick that struck the underside of the bar, and went in off the goalkeeper.

It was a goal worthy of winning any game, probably worthy of our goal of the season, even if technically it was an own goal!

Ninety minutes of a turgid affair, spiced up by a screamer. A poor game, but in the end, a result. Only winning games can restore buoyancy ahead of a seemingly inevitable involvement in the play offs, but drastic improvements are needed if we are to be truly competitive in these.

Steve Bruce commented after the game,

'We're lacking that spark at the minute. I think that's pretty evident to everyone. Let's hope this goal gives it back, because confidence is an unbelievable thing.'

'We're fourth in the league, but it feels as though we're fourth bottom doesn't it?'

'We've got to try and lift things and perform to the levels we were at six weeks ago'

'A jumping KC stadium could make all the difference. We need them to come in their thousands like they've done. They're a fantastically loyal bunch of supporters and they can play their part.'

We'll try Steve, but fans won't blindly rally. Optimism needs to be ushered back and something needs to change. Just look at the words of Ian and the outlaw Josey Wales.

"...I CAN'T HELP, FALLING IN / OUT OF LOVE WITH YOU..."

CHAPTER 58

"A TRIP TO THE ROYALS ON 19.04"

The last gasp win at home to Wolves was soon followed up by a midweek trip to Reading. Another nonsensical fixture involving long distance travel on a school night, but thankfully the last of the season. After this trip we could see the finishing line in site, we'd broken *'through the wall'* in our personal marathon.

The fixture itself was not that important. City were now too far behind the leading three clubs to mount a serious challenge for automatic promotion, yet too far clear of the team in seventh, thus meaning a play off berth was just about guaranteed. Reading sat in fifteenth place, but were in no danger of getting relegated, as the bottom three, were well, just crap.

As it turned out, we actually really enjoyed the trip, and the match itself was quite entertaining, and even produced a City win. The fixture was being played on the 19ᵗʰ April, or 19.04, a fact that was certainly not lost on the travelling 504 contingent.

The intensity and toxicity levels for City fans had gone up a notch also following recent events. Immediately after the Wolves fixture, the club announced their final version of the Membership Scheme details.

There were a few welcome minor tweaks such as South Standers not having a child in their party no longer having to move seats, and supporters in part of the West Upper could stay there, albeit only on the assumption that promotion is achieved. In addition, a Family Stand Guarantee was introduced. This basically meant that, if you have kids in your group, you will not have to pay more in total next season, than you did for 15/16. The caveat to this, is that it only applies for one season, so is only delaying the inevitable. However, a welcome change all the same. For us personally, currently having Zone 1 seats ('the naughty corner'), this at least would save us from a collective and potential hefty price increase for the 16/17 season, should we decide to sign up.

I decided to test this out just prior to setting off for Reading and rang the Membership Hotline. I initially apologised to the girl on the other end of the phone, not for if, but when, I *'had a go at her'*, emphasizing, *'It's not you I'm having a go at, it's the whole idea in principle, I appreciate you are only doing you're job'*. *'Don't worry'*, she replied. *'You won't be the first, nor the last!'*

After much too-ing and froo-ing, the girl confirmed that our total price for next season would effectively be £1,008, for our four tickets. I then proceeded to ask her how much our tickets were this year. Whilst knowing our exact seat numbers, she couldn't tell me, 'computer said no!' Obviously knowing the answer, I informed her that the cost was £684, and as such, surely that is how much I should be paying next year? *'I'll have to ask my manager'* was the reply. At least the correct answer came back, *'Yes we'll do them for the same price of £684'*. As if she was doing me a favour, despite not offering me this first time round.

She then naturally assumed I would be signing up there and then, to which I declined the offer, adding that I'd need to think about it, as in principle I can't agree with the Scheme. We'd call back before the early May deadline if we wished to take them up on their offer.

Whilst I cannot agree with the Scheme, I'm struggling to contemplate how we would fill the void. We'd tried North Ferriby, and whilst I'd give it a go, Thomas was yet to be convinced. A very welcoming place as it is, clearly the football is not of the same standard, nor do I suspect they have anywhere near sufficient finances to survive a possible season in the Conference. And if Thomas isn't 'in', then somehow it wouldn't be quite the same. I've loved the whole experience of sharing this season with him, and whilst he might be getting his own football independence now, I'm not sure I'm ready to end it just yet.

If we were still undecided about 'becoming a member', we certainly weren't on our own. We'd watched the excellent Amber Nectar periscope discussion on the Monday night, and again, talk was of nothing else other than this hastily thought through membership bollocks. Actual football had become something of an irrelevance. Ironic really, when the owners have previously referred to the supporters as being *'irrelevant'* anyway. How rude.

The owners are currently not attending any home fixtures, but only selected away ones. Maybe the plan is to piss off every single supporter so no one actually comes. They can then have the whole ground to themselves to watch, without the inconvenience of fans! Sounds ridiculous, but by now, little would surprise us City fans as to what the next gem is to be served upon us.

So with heavy heart, and many question marks still in the air, we set off for Reading just after lunchtime. We had agreed to meet our next door neighbour Sue at The Holiday Inn, very near to The Madjeski Stadium.

Sue's husband Peter very conveniently works for a company that has its head offices in Reading, down the same road as the ground. So surprise, surprise, he'd arranged to be in the office for two days, and Sue had also co-ordinated her timetable to involve a work meeting in London the following day.

So upon our eventual arrival at 5.30ish, we agreed to have a bite to eat and a couple of drinks at their hotel, then simply walk to the ground, only about five minutes away. Despite arriving two and a half hours before kick off, the fluorescent jacketed car parking attendants were all out in full force, not missing the opportunity to extort an £8 fee from us.

The lure of Reading v Hull City was not enough for Peter to join us for the evening's entertainment. No sooner had he arrived at the hotel reception from a hard days graft behind a desk and in meetings, he was changed and out again, to trip the light fantastic of Readings nightlife. Sue clearly saw this as fair game, and tea and pre match drinks were firmly lodged against Peter's room bill, no need for cash to change hands.

Tea scoffed, beer supped and we took the short stroll to tick off another new ground, only ever having visited Reading's old ground, Elm Park before, to witness a 1-1 draw way back in September 1993, 'Knees Up Linton Brown' scoring for City.

Peter wasn't the only one not tempted by the fixture, as it drew Readings lowest home attendance of the season, just under 13,000. This did not stop the PA system pumping out tunes at increasing decibel levels, akin to a disco. Like at many grounds this season, Insomnia by Faithless was being boomed out pre kick off. I'm sure this song gets played more at footy grounds nowadays than when it was actually released as a CD.

Numerous changes were made by City. Livermore, Bruce, Elmo and Clucas were dropped and in came Maguire, Huddlestone, Snodgrass and Maloney. Our start was terrible.

Reading almost took the lead twice in the first minute, Simon Cox being denied. They were only to be deprived for a further three minutes.

Quinniesta, now in the blue and white hoops of Reading, was clumsily pushed to the ground by Meyler (however else would he be!), conceding a needless free kick. Oliver Norwood sent over a good delivery and the City defence decided not to bother marking the tallest Reading player, Jake Cooper, who unchallenged, nodded home with alarming ease. 1-0 down and time for the PA to pump out the anthemic tune of Chase The Sun by Planet Funk. If you don't recognise the title or artist, you'll know it as the tune played at the darts on television.

'Da, da, da da.......' sang and danced the Reading fans in the corner to our right hand side. Knobs! Thomas gave some sort of hand gesture, which as his father, I clearly reprimanded him for, if not actually finding it mildly amusing.

To their credit, City responded fairly well, and the opening fifteen minutes was incredibly open, both sides happy to commit players forward. And in the eighteenth minute, City equalised, ending a barren run of not scoring during the first half of an away league fixture since October, six months ago. Huddlestone picked out the run of Hernandez, who outpaced the home defence and cooly slotted past Ali Al-Habsi for 1-1. Game on again.

Most of the chanting from the away section was of a toxic nature and directed at those other than the players, if you catch my drift. No sooner had we caught our breath from our equaliser, then a rousing rendition of 'City Till I Die...' and 'Since 1904...' was voiced at the 19 minutes and 4 second mark on the 19th of the 4th month. The Membership Scheme also bore the brunt, and has clearly incensed the majority.

As the game continued, I observed the eclectic mix of City supporters. It's probably no different to any other clubs, but certainly reminded me of various descriptive terms made by Dougie Brimson in his book called "The Geezers' Guide to Football", an excellent read.

You've got the **'old gits'**, who are always at pains to tell you about the great team of 1951 or some year from a time long ago that you are clearly not old enough to have witnessed (and so cannot argue against). Then you've got the '**anoraks**' or '**scarfers**' (made even worse by those new fangled wretched half and half things) who can tell you the result of every game, who scored and in what minute.

This moves onto the '**geezers**' and '**casuals**', who decked out in their designer labels, strut around like Liam Gallagher, chest pumped, shoulders thrown back. At the upper spectrum are the '**hooligans**', intent on creating animosity with the opposition fans (see below), although very rarely ever engaging in physical activity unless the numbers swell to say ten to on in their favour.

At the lower end of the spectrum are the '**kids**', the next generation of loyal supporters, who at times, are more interested in the sweets on offer and making umpteen trips to the toilet, than watching the actual game itself.

And somewhere in between, are the '**singers**'. The fulcrum of 'the team' that try and bond all the different facets together in common purpose.

There is a place for all of these mixes at a football club, it helps to make it diverse. In fact, supporters move through the categories during their supporting lives. I'm not quite sure where I currently fit in, probably heading for the anorak stage! This book is certainly making me feel this way. Thomas is certainly aiming for the casual bracket.

I wondered just what this mix of supporters would look like next season and thereafter. I doubt it will ever look quite the same. Only time will tell.

Oh, and it's probably worth mentioning just a few more categories, although in reality, they should not be worth a mention. There are the '**armchairs**', the '**plastics**', the '**corporates**' and the '**sads**'. Not proper football fans as they either are no longer part of the scene, never have been, or just roll up if there is a big club in town. As such, they have no real claim to be able to comment.

Then you have the '**opposition**', who generally should all be classed the same. For the very reason that they don't support the same team as us, to some, they should be of no real interest, apart from maybe twice a season, when they play City.

Observing over, City continued to play with purpose and Diomande was thwarted by a last ditch Anton Ferdinand tackle, and then Snoddy shot just wide. At the other end, McGregor produced a fine save pushing an Oliver Norwood thirty yarder out for a corner.

The early frenetic exchanges and pace of the game had by now died down, and we were thankful of a let off just before the hour mark.

A through ball saw a Maguire tackle inside the box. The referee immediately pointed at the spot for a Reading penalty. City players swarmed the man in black, who then went to consult his linesman, and ultimately changed his mind, awarding only a corner. Extreme frustration for the home fans, amusement to us.

The game then picked up its pace again, both teams going end to end, although one of City's did only result in a Chuba Akpom shot flying into the rows of empty blue seats, taking about a minute for the ball to be found.

City continued to press and Hernandez came close. It was all too much for Sue who decided that a visit to the loo was in order. Much to our amusement, with just over ten minutes to go, and Sue on the loo, legs akimbo probably, City took the lead. Robertson charged forward into acres of space in front of the box, and smashed home a twenty yard piledriver into the bottom corner and beyond Al-Habsi's outstretched left arm.

He may not score many, but he knows how to celebrate does Andy, as he jumped and punched the air in delight, right in front of the away section. We reciprocated by doing exactly the same, We caught a glimpse of Sue running up the steps from the concourse beneath us, as if to catch a real life replay.

The final minutes were seen out and victory was ours. The win provided, if only for the three and a half hour drive home, a moment of escapism.

Whilst not being scintillating during the last two games, we had managed back to back league wins for the first time since, well, what felt like ages. Maybe we might just be turning a corner in this topsy turvy season? Maybe there might be a happy ever after ending after all?

"... ANDY, ANDY, ANDY.....ANDY, ANDY, ANDY, ANDY ROBERTSON..."

CHAPTER 59

"IT'S ONLY A GAME"

Today marked the day that any remote dream of an automatic promotion spot was finally put to bed. We all knew it had been over for a while, but somehow when it's actually confirmed as a mathematic impossibility, it just finish's off that last bit of hope. As had so often been the case over the last few months, most things about the game felt half-hearted and a bit of an anti-climax.

We'd thoroughly enjoyed the away win at Reading earlier in the week, and I attempted to get psyched up for the weekend's game against L**ds, by enjoying a night out at The Bar and Grill in their home town the night before. I was accompanied by the football widow and some work colleagues. However, my attempts to try and teach them some football ditty's and terrace chants on the journey back fell on deaf ears. Instead we had to succumb to a Jamie Cullum CD. How very depressing. It wasn't quite the same as listening to Thomas' DJ skills, which had been ever present at the majority of the games this season.

Today's game was once again symbolic of the season as a whole.

A home game against allegedly 'our' biggest rival still saw around 5,000 empty seats. I'm not even sure the away section sold out, such seems the draw of Hull City at the moment.

A game which for the most part, saw the away fans create more atmosphere than the home ones.

A game which City start brightly yet concede the first goal.

A game in which City had 61% possession, twenty one shots (as against only five from L**ds), albeit only six were on target, yet still only yielded one point.

A game which ultimately saw the 'best squad in the division' condemned to a crack at the play offs at best, now trailing the top three teams by an unassailable ten points. At least a chance to turn our season of underachievement into, ultimately the same desired end result.

None of the above should come as much of a surprise to us.

When a fanbase is treated with contempt, it is no wonder that a hint of apathy exists. I can't help but feel the early chapters of this book were sounding more upbeat, but now full of the grim doom and despair that only being a Hull City fan can entail.

Our approach to the ground and West Park today saw us witness a number of supporters burning their recently received Membership packs as a sign that they had endured enough. No more for them. One fan even took out a full page advert in The Hull Daily Mail expressing their displeasure at the scheme. Social media was the same. Talk seemed of little else.

The ground swell of feeling was building and it seemed that a body was raising its head from above the parapet. This was the Hull City Supporters Trust, who had eloquently expressed the views of many on the Thursday. Little were we to know it yet, but this body was to grow in size and strength.

The game itself suggested to me that my days of nurturing Thomas' early supporting days were at an end. With so many empty seats today, he and his pal Will, decided to spend the entire match in the North Stand. I was no longer required. I was redundant. It felt like his training was over.

Akpom and Livermore returned in place of Meyler and Diomande and City attacked from the off. Akpom was looking lively and twice tested Silvestri. Huddlestone had a shot wide met by the opposition fans with the usual derisory arms held wide, as if to say that was nowhere near the goal. All in all though, I was feeling fairly confident. For me anyway.

And then with their first foray up front, the White Shite took the lead. A quick free kick was taken, and with the City defenders backpedalling, Lewis Cook found Chris Wood, who fed the winger. He then returned the compliment by crossing back to Wood to score unmarked from close range. It all looked too easy, and we all sighed and sank a bit deeper into our seats.

This was obviously met with great delight to the travelling L**ds fans who very kindly gave us renditions of *'Marching On Together...'* and *'YRA, we're*

Yorkshire's Republican Army..' They are clearly still dining on days long since gone!

Snoddy was also being given a reception by the L**ds supporters. Whenever he was anywhere near the North East corner, he was met with chants of *'You're L**ds and you know you are.'*

This was fondly met by the North Stand with *'We all hate L**ds, and L**ds, and L**ds..'* I'm sure I could hear Thomas bellowing it out, finger pointing wearing his Lyall and Scott. He's definitely moving out of the 'kids' category, and into the 'wannabee casual' category. Not sure either are currently wanted at Hull City mind. I, meanwhile, seem destined to stay in the naughty corner.

Far from looking happy at his team taking the lead, the rotund L**ds manager, was still 'effing and jeffing' on the touchline, gesticulating at every decision, contentious or not.

City continued to probe, without actually creating a host of clear cut chances (sound familiar?). Maguire shot wide and Odubajo had a shot deflected onto the roof of the net. And just when it seemed we'd go into the break trailing to L**ds' only meaningful effort of the half, City scored in the first minute of first half injury time.

Some nice hold up play by Akpom, allowed him to slide a pass to Snoddy, who squared for 'Johnny on the Spot' Hernandez to finish from close range for his twentieth goal of the season.

Incredibly, there was still time for City to take the lead, as the third minute of injury time saw Akpom tee up Huddlestone, who drove a low shot into the bottom corner from outside the box.

The referee blew for half time and L**ds looked shell shocked. Not fucking 'Marching On Together' now are you?

'E-i-e-i-o, up the football league we go' rang around the KC. I suspect many had missed the two City goals, departing early for a half time pint or pie. Thomas later told me his mate had, as he went for a hot dog. He also added that the concourse on the North Stand was excellent, much better that the boring South and West!

Not content to see the City supporters joyous, there was a needless half time announcement about the clubs controversial and unpopular Membership scheme. It was soon drowned out by jeering.

We'd probably just about deserved to be leading, but nearly contrived to throw it away early in the second half when, after fifty three minutes, Odubajo clumsily tripped a L**ds player to concede a penalty. However, McGregor expertly produced a fine save to his left, to deny Chris Wood to keep the score at 2-1.

The game then became a bit scrappy, and it appeared we'd see the game out and hold on for a win. Predictably we dropped a bit deeper, seemingly happy to concede possession. It ultimately cost us.

With just two minutes of normal time remaining, and despite City having many men behind the ball, substitute Jordan Botaka cut in from the right before finding Stuart Dallas. Dallas struck home a sweet shot right into the bottom corner from the edge of the box, giving Allan no chance, 2-2.

Clucas had a last gasp shot beaten away by Silvestri so a draw it was. It was a game we could and should have won really, but like on many occasions this season we didn't. We should have won at Rotherham, Charlton, Preston or L**ds. But we didn't.

Goalless draws at home to Brighton and Wednesday, along with dropped points at home to Forest and MK Dons also cost us dearly. The recent losses at Middlesbrough and Derby just simply seemed to knock the stuffing out of us and devoid us of much needed confidence. When the pressure was on, we'd been found wanting. Too many times, we'd made slow starts to games, playing at a slow tempo, apparently more determined not to concede the first goal and to not lose, than to go for it, ensuring a win.

So the play offs it is and a likely double header with Derby, the only team to do the double over us this season so far.

A full stadium with more atmosphere wouldn't have gone a miss, but we can understand why this hasn't been the case, certainly of late. The club has made no effort to unite the fans.

Easy game from a plastic seat eh?!

The final few regular games of the season will probably now be a non-event with the only thing to decide being if we play at home or away first in the play offs. Brentford, Bolton and Rotherham hardly raise the excitement levels. And at least two, hopefully three more games, for our never ending season to attend. The '46 and counting' will ultimately become 57 or 58.

So with a lack of any meaningful football for the ensuing few weeks, it would be remiss of me not to mention a highly notable event a few days after the L**ds fixture.

I've already referred to Hillsborough on a number of occasions, but on the 26th April 2016, just a 'mere' twenty seven years and eleven days after the events at Sheffield, a jury returned its verdict on the long overdue inquest. It told us all what we'd known for years.

The jury rightly concluded that 96 Liverpool fans were **unlawfully killed** at Hillsborough in 1989.

As the verdicts were read, they prompted sobbing and cries of hallelujah, amongst those of justice.

That day I read about the catalogue of errors and catastrophic errors made by police and rescue services. I read the heart rendering story of Margaret Aspinall denied a final cuddle with her dead son.

As a football supporter, it could have been anyone. Football fans out for an afternoon doing what we do, what we love to do. Never to come home.

We all knew it, but at least the truth is now out there.

"JUSTICE FOR THE 96"

CHAPTER 60

"A SEA OF RED"

As touched upon in the previous chapter, today was the day that the Hillsborough verdict was announced. We could therefore almost use the words that football doesn't matter, it's not important in the grand scheme of things.

Whilst there is an element of truth in this, we all know that deep down it's not true.

Football clubs are so important. They should represent an identity, the area and the people that surround it.

Unfortunately it has become too frequent recently, that the ownership of football clubs seem to be forgetting this, being run without a proper understanding of the traditions, their history and the community, as a whole.

Personally, I do believe the tide is changing, even if only very slowly. Supporters are now beginning to say enough is enough. They should always be the biggest and most important part of any football club; without them a club simply cannot operate. They are trying to stand up to those in authority, to spread the message, *'we are here you know'*.

Just look at Liverpool today, and the well overdue verdict. A city that stood together, shoulder to shoulder and said no. As I once read, *'If you don't fight for what you want, don't get upset for what you've lost.'*

This sentiment was all so prevalent at Hull City during tonight's fixture at home to Brentford.

Back in February, an away midweek win at Ipswich saw City go top of the Championship. Everything looked reasonably healthy and a quick return to the Premier League seemed on the cards. Hell, most of my writing seemed relatively jovial! And then the wheels fell off.

A dismal run of only three wins from the next eleven has seen us fall away from the genuine automatic promotion chasers. Such a run would be enough to make any supporter feel a bit 'miffed off'. So god knows why our club decided to try and implement this Membership scheme in the middle of this poor run. Talk about kicking you while you're down. The objections to the scheme are well documented.

Hundreds, no thousands, of season ticket holders are likely to be evicted from their seats, despite the fact that many of us still cling to the social side of the game. Football doesn't just start at ten to three on a Saturday afternoon, and end just before five. We socialise together before and after the match. We sit and talk together. Hell, the football sometimes isn't even that good, so we don't even pay that much attention to it.

And as for the no concession prices. Not for over 65's, not for children, not for the unemployed. Not for anyone. It's a joke.

Premier League football is no guarantee for a club like Hull City. We should not therefore be effectively telling inconvenient supporters that they are irrelevant, instead relying on the lovely Sky loot.

Yes we may well actually achieve promotion somehow. The KC may well be filled with happy clappers, half and half scarf wearers and day trippers. However, relegation will inevitably follow at some point soon and the plastics will be get bored and leave. We'll wish we'd looked after the loyal supporters, the oldies and the youngsters. They may well all have pissed off and found something else to do on a Saturday afternoon.

I'm certainly not the only one thinking these thoughts. That full page supporter's advert in the Hull Daily Mail, emblazoned with the words,

'Over 65 and old enough to have earnt my stripes'

'Too young to have earned my stripes. Please give me the chance. Concessions please'

Tonight was the opportunity for the supporters of Hull City to voice their opinions, collectively whilst not speaking, but certainly saying a lot.

The Hull City Supporters Trust, chaired by Geoff Bielby, had organised something of a protest. Keen to not overly distract the team, and possibly their performance, what they came up with was simple, but oh so effective.

Basically it was a red card protest against the Membership Scheme; red cards to be held aloft just prior to kick off.

A dedicated band of fans positioned themselves around various entrance points to West Park, armed with packs of A4 cards, around eight thousand in total. It wasn't obligatory to take one, but as we walked past, most were. We were certainly glad recipients of our three.

Previous recent events in particular the proposed name change have seen something of a split between the City fanbase. The Membership Scheme certainly seems to have 'united' them. The clubs apparent ability to alienate us supporters has riled us into action. And it now seems difficult to find any support for the owners, from any quarters.

As Steve Jordan took to the pitch to commence the usual KC introductions, there was an eerie silence. Each introduction was met with resounding boo's, from the West, South and North stands. He sloped off without bothering to try with the East Stand.

There was no applause or cheers for the team as they took to the field, as the vast majority of the smallest home league crowd of the season were busy holding aloft their 'red card'. It wasn't just pockets of the ground holding them up. It was all of it. It was a 'sea of red'.

The silence was temporarily broken with audible and tangible renditions, starting with *'We want...'* and ending with *'Out'*, followed by *'Membership, you're having a laugh.'*

The message was clear. The protest proved as much and it certainly feels better to know that we are now all in it together.

Nobody is necessarily saying that the Membership Scheme does not have some merit, just that in its current form, it is unacceptable. Unfortunately though, the club has persistently failed to meaningfully consult with its supporters, instead trying to railroad us into it.

Trust chairman Geoff Bielby had previously said, 'We want real consultation and debate on this. We feel the club has made a massive error. We want the club to come back to the table.'

The Trust had certainly got our vote of confidence after tonight.

Oh, and if you were interested, there was actually a match played tonight as well. Well, sort of.

With a play off spot guaranteed, we didn't really take the game too seriously. Seven changes were made. To me, this did not seem to imply that we were trying to get a settled team and build up a continued run of momentum into the play offs. The match was just something of an inconvenience.

Fortunately Brentford, in something of mid table obscurity, didn't seem to be taking it too seriously either. They weren't very good, which enabled City to rather cruise through the game, eventually coming out 2-0 victors.

Harry Maguire was one of the seven changes, and he certainly came out of the match, a winner. Harry has assumed the title of cult hero that once belonged to Paul McShane. He wears his heart on his sleeve and supporters love it. I certainly do. And he can play a bit!

Tonight he sprayed cross field balls to our wingers with aplomb. One of those was expertly brought under control by Robertson, and his cross was blasted into his own net by Brentford defender, Harlee Dean for an early 1-0 City lead.

Five minutes later and Harry's centre back partner, Alex Bruce, rather fortuitously won a penalty for a shirt pull. Diomande, after a stuttering run up, saw his spot kick saved.

No worry though as Harry, on the stroke of half time, somehow found himself on the right wing showing Elmo just how to do it, crossing for Diame to finish at the second attempt.

The second half was played at ease, and every touch by Maguire was met with cheers and chants of 'Ha-rry, Ha-rry'. The only thing that was missing was a goal to cap his performance.

The victory saw City go past the eighty point mark for the season, a record for the team at this level. We've only lost one league game at home all season.

To Derby. Oh shit, that's who we are likely to meet in the play offs. Two games played. No goals scored. Six against.

However, any records, tonight felt a little hollow.

Tonight will be remembered, not for the football, but for the resounding show of red cards towards the Membership Scheme. A turning point perhaps? A resounding and united rallying call from the supporters of Hull City.

Well done Geoff. Well done HCST.

"MEMBERSHIP, YOU'RE HAVING A LAUGH"

CHAPTER 61

"MOROSE AT THE MACRON"

When the season's fixtures were announced back in July, we'd earmarked this one. It was the day after my birthday. No longer forty six, but now the grand old age of forty seven. It was also due to be our last away game of the season. We'd also be joined again by our good friends, The Bolton supporting Lees family.

So months ago, in my mind, I'd planned a celebratory day out. A pat on the back to ourselves for managing to attend every City away game, watching them march onto the title in emphatic style. We'd be travelling to and from the game in a limo, and watching the City team being presented with the league winner's trophy in glorious sunshine, in awe of the viewing public. And we'd have been there to witness every single kick, every single tackle.

The reality was far from it!

The 'best squad in the division' had, to be honest, since late February in particular, underachieved. Automatic promotion gone, the play offs a consolation for not quite being good enough.

Janine Lees had also double booked the weekend, clearly not appreciating the importance of the football calendar, nor my birthday. Instead of spending a glorious afternoon at the Macron Stadium, she had instead, arranged to be on a short break to Italy, no longer tucking into half time meat pies, but chomping on pizza in a piazza in Pisa! She chose wisely.

Janine's absence also gave both Charlotte and the football widow the perfect excuse to dip out, and it was left to the foolish male counterparts of both family's to turn out at Bolton.

It was not the celebration I believed it could have been.

The match itself was a nothing game, yet it had been chosen again to be screened live on Sky. Perhaps too, they had originally expected us to be crowned as champions on the last day of April 2016.

Having said that, if you think things had recently been a bit grim for City, spare a thought for our opponents today, Bolton. Apparently, almost ten years to the day, they had just beaten Aston Villa 4-0 to qualify for the Europa League. Today, this was one of the worst seasons in their club's history. Administration narrowly avoided, they had won just four, yes four, of their previous forty four league games, letting in eighty goals, and collected just three points from their previous fourteen fixtures. Most of their supporters were probably just happy to have a club to support. If nothing else, they were an advert to any club being massively indebted to a single owner / investor. Sound familiar?

Their relegation fate had been sealed as far back as April 9th, so fodder to the mighty Hull City today surely? Roll them over, and continue the recent momentum into a play-off campaign. So Thomas and I, along with another 1,211 foolhardy travelling City supporters thought.

It didn't work out that way and City succumbed to a 1-0 defeat. And deservedly so. In manager Steve Bruce's words, 'It was an embarrassment.'

Previous trips to Charlton, L**ds, Rotherham and Preston had all ended with sobering defeats, but the worst was saved until last. The away form has ultimately cost us. Today was our tenth defeat on our travels, more than we have managed to win. We have also conceded more goals than we have scored. Again, another sobering thought ahead of a likely play off leg against Derby, having recently lost 4-0 there.

The Sky screening meant an early Saturday lunchtime kick off and during our outbound journey, via York to meet the Lees, we should have seen it coming. Rather than be a picturesque sunny end to the season, it was pissing it down. Even a shower of hailstones bouncing off the tarmac hinted at things to come.

The eternal optimist Thomas tried to pick up my spirits as we exited the recently sold Bolton car park (to help pay funds towards the list of creditors). 'We're gonna win dad, this lot are shit!' Even the rain stopped (momentarily) and rays of sunshine broke through. Maybe you're right I thought.

Why, at this time of the season, were we playing Clucas at left back, introducing Brain Lenihan, suggesting that Shaun Maloney is going to play a part, or asking Akpom to plane alone up front? I could see the thought process in resting the near ever present Odubajo and Robertson, but six changes, following the seven made in the previous fixture, told me we were going through the motions. It would be claimed that these players were staking a claim for a starting place. None of them did so this afternoon. We'll need to go back to the 'tried and tested'.

We took up our seats in a sparsely populated away end. Here we were met by a school pal of Thomas. This lad is a year above Thomas at school, and for the purposes of this book, we'll call him Jamie Bolton (obviously this is not his real name but we've changed it for fear of his mum finding out what he gets up to on a Saturday afternoon.) Being a school year older, this clearly gave Thomas some serious 'street cred', particularly after their discussions revealed that this was Thomas' twenty third away league game of the season.

Now I may be sounding old here, but are kids growing up younger these days?

Jamie must have been no older than fourteen, but rolled up to our seats with all the confidence and swagger of one of the Gallagher brothers, pigeon chest pumped out, shoulders rocked back. Wearing enough designed label to fill up a gondola at Prem down Anlaby Road, including the obligatory Stone Island but one stop short of a goggle jacket, this lad was certainly part of the next generation of football casual. Bearing in mind that some of this is still the type of gear I don myself in, I wondered if I should grow up and stop wearing clothes that the now 'fourteen going on twenty year olds' are dressing themselves up in. After a while, I thought, stuff that, never lose sight of your youth. Otherwise, next I'll be thinking of taking a blanket and flask to football. Jamie departed to adorn some seats with some like minded teenagers, Thomas stuck with his old man.

Not long after Jamie had left, and with the gloom of the team news in my mind, the short period of sunshine disappeared to be replaced by a downpour. As a result, we and the few around us, now getting soaked, retracted several rows back to a dry haven. If nothing else, this created something more of an atmosphere as the City contingent 'packed' themselves in closer together. In fact, as kick off time approached, we were soon joined by a coach load of City fans, fuelled I suspect with a serious amount of 'amber nectar', so much so, that the one third full away end, resulted in two standing spectators to every one seat.

On the pitch not a lot happened. The end of season fixture had all the feel of a pre-season friendly, much like the Brentford match the Tuesday prior. The fact that our already relegated opponents were comfortable against a predictable City, spoke volumes about our performance.

Lenihan actually played well on his debut and Elmo looked a bit more like his old self. On a couple of occasions, the latter set up Akpom, but unfortunately, he flattered to deceive. Snodgrass curled a free kick onto the top of the bar on the stroke of half time, but in truth, Bolton showed a much greater desire in the first half than those wearing the no name badge shirts from East Yorkshire.

They flew into tackles, sometimes recklessly, although big Harry did try to return this compliment when sending old timer Emile Heskey crashing to the floor. Maguire is exactly what a football supporter wants to see. Yes, maybe he is a yellow card waiting to happen, but he will always give total commitment and passion.

In reality, the first half, and then all of the second half, was not about what happened on the pitch, but more about the antics off it.

There was another peaceful red card protest but once this was over, the chants turned somewhat less peaceful. No sooner had a homemade bedsheet banner adorning the words, 'Scrap the Scheme' been held aloft, then the chants around us turned something slightly more vitriolic.

The usual chants (I can no longer bring myself to type the words) were vociferously bellowed out. These were later followed by 'Grandads and children, they're coming for you'. An obvious reference to the scrapping of concessionary prices for next season. How this will manifest itself against Premier League rules, should we achieve success in the play-offs, will be a discussion for another day.

In fairness, this outpouring of anger from the fans, has nothing to do with the players, but all to do with the club itself. It's constant jibs towards us 'irrelevant' fans, with ridiculous ideas and PR (or lack of it), just merely stirring ill feeling. As soon as you think things might be okay, something else is revealed, or imposed upon us.

The end of the first half saw one of the coachload around us, release what I would refer to as a smoke bomb, obviously amber in colour. Being an old 'fuddy duddy', Thomas soon corrected me and told me that is was actually a 'pyro' (apparently short for pyrotechnic and not just for use on November the fifth).

The amber smoke now surrounded us and for a few seconds, we could have been at the San Siro. When it cleared, we again realised we weren't, but were actually on the edge of Chorley FM land, although it certainly distracted us from the non entity of a football match.

The teams trudged off, all square at 0-0. We'd done well to get nil. The coach load now befriending us adjourned for a half time pint whereas the designated driver (ie me!) took to his seat. Thomas extracted a fiver from me and asked if he could go and get a pie. I couldn't be arsed, and so off he trotted.

It wasn't until early into the second half until he returned, full of stories about half time concourse frivolity. Apparently, as a number of spectators queued for their half time refreshments, some City supporter decided it would be mildly amusing to release a second amber 'pyro' into the public domain.

Well, I say public domain, but in reality it was dispensed over the counter and into the pie stand. This brought much humour to the Cod Army, with plenty of jumping up and down and beer throwing on the concourse. However, the minimum wage 'pie stand' attendants were not amused, and the roller shutter was promptly pulled down. No more pies, no more pints! It would turn out to be the highlight of the day.

If the first half was drab, the second half, certainly from a City point of view, was just dreadful.

Again, loads of possession, sideways, backwards, sideways etc with no end product. Akpom did smash a shot against the bar from good play by both Hayden and Maloney, but other than that, I can't recall any real goal threat.

So to me, it came as no real surprise when Bolton took the lead. Substitute Scott Dobbie was allowed all the time in the world to stroke home at the far post, past the Jak. City had no answer.

Whilst previous second half chanting had been mildly amusing, including one of my all time favourites, *'Pies from Fletchers, feed me till I want no more...'* (to the tune of Bread from Heaven), the songs once again turned. Chorus' of *'This is embarrasing'* and *'Top of the league, and we fucked it up'* echoed out.

Never a truer word spoken.

The full time whistle went and we'd been outdone by a team whose season had finished weeks ago. Was ours about to do the same?

Yes, the match in itself changed nothing. We are still in the play offs, but it certainly did nothing for confidence. To me, it looked like the players didn't care, they were going through the motions. We felt the same, but we certainly do care.

As we exited the stadium, we witnessed young Jamie Bolton, in frustration, angrily kicking at the roller shutter of the pie kiosk, which forty five minutes earlier was hastily shut. Tell me, he didn't care. Tell me he wasn't displaying some form of passion that appeared to be lacking elsewhere. Yet our club seem to be trying to keep the likes of Thomas and Jamie away. Why?

We rejoined the Lees. Obviously they were delighted to see a rare win.

On the short drive home, I just contemplated whether I was getting tired of this modern day football. Tired of it's inflated sense of self importance. Tired of the way football continues to take, and we all still hand over our cash anyway. Tired of grown men play acting. Tired of teams defending a one nil lead and time wasting. Just tired. None of it needs to happen really. I don't think it ever used to.

Has my football and Hull City apathy started to kick in?! Or have I just watched too many games, this season in particular?

Would a promotion to the Premier League be all that? Or maybe just a means to avoid a financial disaster like Bolton, rather than a wish to play all the 'big clubs'? It's weird as most of my years of being a Hull City fan, has involved scrapping for our very survival near the bottom of the football pyramid playing the likes of Torquay or Rochdale. But on that journey home, I asked myself did I enjoy it more?

What was Thomas' take on it?

'Stop being a miserable old git' was his response.

'I'll try son' I replied. 'I just want to go to watch football, our team, Hull City, and feel a part of it, but most of all, enjoy it. Is that too much to ask?'

Only time will tell.

"TOP OF THE LEAGUE AND WE FUCKED IT UP"

CHAPTER 62

ROTHERHAM (A) – SATURDAY 7TH MAY 2016

"WE FINISH ON A HIGH, THE END OF THE 46"

And so here we are. The chapter that should really be the last one in the book. Matchday forty six, the last regular league game of the season. But City being City, there will be at least two more chapters to be encountered, hopefully three, as beyond today, the lottery that is the play-offs beckons.

Like those immediately previous, this fixture seemed academic. Academic, but not totally irrelevant, as dependent upon Derby's result today against Ipswich, and ours, this would dictate who played at home in the second leg – a theoretical advantage.

As has been the custom in the last few seasons, and for the benefit of the Sky armchair viewers, all of the last day Championship fixtures kicked off at lunchtime. This was good news for us as we'd been invited out to a party in the afternoon, thus ensuring an early football finish, and no more 'hurumphing' from the football widow, and mutterings of *'You always put football first you do!'* Today was the best of both worlds, a few hours football, and then several hours of drinking!

Last day of the season matches are not something City specialise in. Certainly not in recent seasons anyway. Not since a home game against Bristol Rovers, twelve years ago, have we managed to muster a win. Today changed that, as eventually, on the hallowed KC turf, the boys in black and amber, cruised to an emphatic 5-1 victory, and restored a bit of my confidence back. More of that in a bit.

The day before saw the first deadline of the membership renewal. Personally, I had been in two minds what to do here. Part of me said do not sign up, purely on the basis that I wholeheartedly believe the scheme is wrong. We simply should not be penalising senior citizens, the disabled or kids. As a paying adult, I am more than happy to pay a few extra quid a season if it helps subsidise these categories. Part of me said if I do sign up, surely I'm just agreeing to it?

However, the other part of me, and that includes both Charlotte and Thomas, told me I'm not ready to give up City just yet. I've thoroughly enjoyed spending time with both of them this season, and the slight worry was that if we didn't renew, then they'd both find something else to do on a Saturday, and I'd be left high and dry. No doubt just spend the afternoon down the pub. Mmm...actually, now you mention it...!

We also currently occupy some of the 'cheap' seats in the corners so I was a little concerned that we would lose these, with a possible clamour for them amongst those being evicted from their existing seats. Added to the fact that for one season only, our prices were fixed at the 15/16 rates, I reluctantly agreed and signed up. Albeit with a heavy heart.

My logic also said that we could just stop our direct debit anyway and give notice at any time. I've got this sneaky feeling that we may end up doing this anyway, particularly if we do achieve play-off success and then get a few early Premier league hammerings against a backdrop of supporter disenchantment.

The weekend saw many long standing season ticket holders though not renewing. This cannot be good for the club and worrying if there are even more empty seats next season, regardless of which league we are in. Imaging opening up a possible Premier League campaign to a less than half full stadium. World's best league eh..?

Social media was full of '*this is our last City game*' stuff and it was sad and thoroughly depressing to read. It didn't need to be this way, but unfortunately the constant drip, drip of one off field saga after another, has been too much for a significant number of City fans to take. Reports of around only 6,000 renewals were being muted. Embarrassing for a team currently in fourth place in the league.

Compare and contrast that to a rumoured 21,000 renewals at Derby, or 15,000 at Huddersfield. The atmosphere and feeling amongst so many fans is so wholly incongruous with a season that could yet still end in a promotion. Not so much a case of 'dare to dream', but 'dare to hope'.

Having committed to a renewal, even if only temporarily, I decided to try and take my mind off City and the night before the Rotherham game, took myself off to get an alternative footie fix.

Our local amateur team, Walkington FC, had reached the final of the Whiteheads Fish and Chip Cup Final and were pitted against Wawne United down Inglemire Lane. First off, I can't believe I had to pay to gain entrance to watch some players, who were normally propping up the bar of The Barrel, but my £2 was well spent. Wawne had won the Humber Premier League, Walkington third in the league below. An end to end game eventually saw Walkington emerge 4-3 winners after extra time, with both teams giving it 100%. Having watched some of the stuff this season, it makes you wonder whether paying the modern day prima donna footballers thousands in wages, actually makes them try any harder. I certainly enjoyed the match, and for some reason, it re-invigorated my belief that City's season would end on a high also.

We arrived at the KC early doors and I once again rolled my eyes at the attempted new age matchday experience. Razzamatazz including girls on stilts, happy clappers under seats and popcorn on sale. After the match we were 'treated' to a 'lap of appreciation', not a 'lap of honour', such was the sense of underachievement and anti-climax. We even had Pharrell Williams, being blurted out, playing '*I'm happy*'. How fucking ironic I thought. We are not, but should be. I, however, with the optimism of Charlotte in particular behind me, refused to be too downbeat (even if the words here suggest otherwise) and still felt somewhat confident of play-off success.

By the time the full time whistle had been blown, we would be playing Derby away first, home leg to follow. Mmm, the self confidence ebbed away a little, with memories of our previous encounters against them. The other play off would see Brighton take on Sheffield Wednesday.

Once inside the ground, the match itself was actually very enjoyable. It always is if you end up winning 5-1. This was down to a combination of City, our starting formation being restored to something more akin to a best eleven rather than the makeshift reserves fielded recently, playing very well, and Rotherham, well playing in the proverbial flip flops. They were, after the first fifteen to twenty minutes, piss poor. City in contrast, played with an arrogance that had in recent weeks been missing.

A very open game saw chances at both ends almost from the off with Diame, playing further up front alongside Hernandez, forcing a fine save from Lee Camp at his near post.

Then Diame turned provider, with a cross that somehow eluded Snodgrass, but saw Abel thwarted twice from his usual predatory three yard range, by an exceptional block and save. A goal was coming I thought.

And it duly did. Just at the wrong bloody end!

A swift move upfield by the men in red, ended up seeing Lee Frecklington afforded too much time to hook in a precise finish over the helpless McGregor. The travelling 2,500 Rotherham fans lapped it all up as they chanted, *"Who are ya, who are ya…?"*

Good question I thought, most of us City fans haven't got a bloody clue anymore. It sure doesn't feel like the Hull City we know.

Rotherham's temporary manager, the one loads of fans love to hate, Neil Warnock, was giving it large in his technical area. No worries, City soon had him cowering back into hiding in his dugout.

Despite trailing, City continued to pile forward and Hernandez again spurned the next opportunity, when having been played clean through, Camp once again denied him. It didn't take too much longer though.

Elmo, looking more like his City days of old, (nothing to do with hoping for a new contract since this season's performances had failed to find any other clubs clamouring for his services) linked up well with Diame, and the Thud, and Snoddy expertly volleyed home. 1-1 and well deserved. *"Who is this new right winger?"* we questioned.

It took a full ninety eight seconds for us to take the lead, and what a goal it was. Hernandez became only the second City player in twenty two seasons to score twenty league goals in one season with a sublime overhead kick into the bottom corner.

As they say, Abel was on fire, and the Rotherham defence, minds obviously on their summer holidays, were definitely 'all at sea'. Twice he came close and whilst he eventually had to settle for just one goal, he could easily have taken the match ball home with a hat trick.

Huddlestone fired an effort wide before his midfield counterpart Livermore made it 3-1, somehow beating the flatfooted defence and goalkeeper to a through ball, and slotting home from a tight angle. It is no surprise that if Livermore plays well, then so do City as a team generally. He can certainly be something of a talisman.

Elmo soon after set up Diame to poke home a fourth and all before half time. Four goals in seventeen minutes and something more like what we should be expecting from City. More of this and there would have been no need for the stress, tension and anxiety of the play offs.

A rousing send off greeted the City team as they left the field of play at half time. The 'red cards' were now being used as paper aeroplanes as overdue smiles and light heartedness breezed over the terraces at the KC.

The second half didn't quite match up to the first, but the display was enough to see Livermore net his second and City's fifth after Snoddy showed great awareness to play Jake in, following a needlessly conceded corner. Clucas, Huddlestone and Livermore again could have added more, but the 5-1 scoreline remained.

Overall it was an enriching afternoon, and sent us away thinking that if we can repeat something like that against Derby, we might be in with another Wembley experience. That being said, Derby are a different proposition to Rotherham and they will certainly feel like they have the upper hand over us.

During the short drive home, we contemplated the season, and wondered why we should still be feeling a tad glum.

The forty six league games had seen us finish with a record points haul, albeit still not sufficient to gain an automatic promotion berth. This is partly down to our underachievement but high fives should also be given to Burnley. A twenty game unbeaten run since we tonked them 3-0 at the KC, saw them finish champions. Had we signed Andre Gray, this could have been a different story. Ifs and buts….

Middlesbrough edged past the unfortunate Brighton, albeit you can't help but feel that our last minute loss to them at The Riverside in March, surely gave them the impetus to achieve this.

We also recorded nineteen clean sheets in the league and boasted one of the best defensive records in the entire league. A twenty goal a season striker also appeared in Hernandez. Not since the likes of Stuart Elliott, or going even further back to Keith Edwards, had we been treated to such.

We lost only one home league game, albeit the away form ultimately saw us finish six points short.

A maiden voyage into the quarter finals of the League Cup was even achieved.

Yet somehow, it doesn't feel that great. Few City supporters appear to be enjoying the ride as it nears a potentially glorious conclusion. But at least the mood today, shifted ever so slightly.

"...46 AND <u>STILL</u> COUNTING..."

CHAPTER 63

DERBY COUNTY (A) – PLAY OFF SEMI FINAL FIRST LEG, SATURDAY 14TH MAY 2016

"A SEASON'S HIGHLIGHT – PURE POETRY"

So this was it. League campaign over and we were away first to our 'nemesis' team of the season, Derby. The only team to have done the double over us all season, and the only team to have beaten us at the KC.

I was being my usual pessimistic self. I'd tried to avoid reading about the game during the week and actually had trouble sleeping the night before. It wasn't just the thought that we might actually lose and fail to get Wembley and have a shot at promotion, it was more the fact that 'our' season journey would be over. Whilst some of the matches may have been disappointing, even a little turgid at times, I simply didn't want it to end. And certainly not in a damp squib and abject failure.

Thomas must have felt the same.

Whilst the football widow was giving it serious zzz's the night before (as if she didn't have a care in the world), I could hear Thomas shuffling about in his room come the early hours of Saturday 14th May 2016. He soon trotted through wearing his obligatory Hull City shorts and said. *"I can't sleep dad, I'm too nervous, I'm excited about tomorrow's game but just got a bad feeling that it's all going to be over. In fact, I'm bricking it!"*

It was a bit of a surreal moment. One of those when we must have both been thinking exactly the same thing at the same time. Like father like son I suppose. We briefly chatted about the seasons journey we'd just been on. We both easily agreed that our favourite game at home had been the 3-0 win against Middlesbrough, but by far the most enjoyable game overall, was the

2-0 win away at Brentford. Not only had he got a full day off school, but it was a proper football day out, open terracing, peering for a vantage point and going ape shit when Andy Robertson slotted home the first goal. I'm not 100% certain, but the fact that both results saw us go top of the league clearly helped!

As I listened to Thomas' enthusiasm, I so wanted the season to end with a Wembley win. Obviously partly for my own selfish reasons, not to mention this book's, but also for Thomas. He was only five when we beat Bristol City in 2007/08 so was too young and 'football raw' to understand the enormity of it. I wanted him to have another experience, one to remember for the rest of his life. Hell, he may even tell his own kids when he was older.

After some discussion, and for fear of waking the sleeping football widow, we decided to adjourn to our own beds. We made a pact that, at the I-Pro tomorrow, we would both sing our heads off, just in case it was our last away game of the season, our last hurrah. We both retreated to try and get some sleep, anticipation and fear mixed in our minds.

Whilst I had those wishes for Thomas in mind, I also couldn't forget the recent 4-0 drubbing at Derby, when in addition, I was, well, off colour! I closed my eyes and hoped for a bit of divine intervention, just to help our cause.

As we closed our eyes again, little were we to know exactly what Saturday 14th May 2016 would bring us.

There are certain moments in every season that stay with you. They just don't go away, they refuse to shift from your mind. They could be good, they could be bad. Even when the whole season has finished and the goals, games, events, hope and despair, start to blur, some moments remain. They are still there, as clear as the day they happened. Deano's goal in 2008 is one of those moments. I can still close my eyes and see Frazier Campbell chipping the ball to the edge of the box, and then, as if in slow motion, see the white boot of Windass thump the ball into the net. Still sends a shiver down your spine as none of us ever thought we'd see the day.

Sometimes, the moment can be personal. For me, and probably most of the 3,009 travelling City fans, Derby away on Saturday 14th May, was my / our moment of the 15/16 season.

The specific event was City's final and crucial third goal. It came in the eighth minute of second half injury time. The whole moment probably only lasted about ten to fifteen seconds in total. A rapid break from the edge of our own box saw our two full backs, Odubajo and Robertson rampaging up the field into the Derby half. Right back found left back with a sublime pass. Left back drilled a low shot past Scott Carson and into the bottom corner of the net. To us, it was a moment of beauty, pure poetry.

The Derby players were crestfallen, and crumpled to their knees.

The City faithful went beserk.

In that moment of hysteria, I took a momentary glance to my left to see Thomas, my son Thomas, fist pumping the air, screaming *"Go on City, get in there."*

I instantly knew what this game we call football, now meant to him. And what this team we call Hull City meant to him.

His apprenticeship was done. City is now in his blood, in his DNA. The City 'boy' had become a City 'man'!

In that split second, I felt so proud of him, having spent all that time this season with his old man, showing all that patience and loyalty to his team, even during times when they hadn't been so good. I gave him a quick bear hug, an embrace that said more than words and kissed him on the top of his head. I'll remember that moment for many a season to come.

And then, I turned and started fist pumping myself, joining in the rest of the delusion. *"You fucking beauty"* I screamed.

Several hours earlier, we'd set off in the May sunshine, Thomas, his mate Will, Sue and I, with a sense of trepidation. On the journey there, we'd discussed how happy we'd be to settle for a 0-0 draw and fully expected the team to set up that way. Stay in the tie and try and clinch it back at home at the KC.

Today we should also have been joined by Adrian McAndrew, a friend from our village who had texted earlier in the week asking if he could have a lift. Adrian has joined us for a few away matches in previous seasons and his quirk of always buying a mug from the club shop of whichever ground City were playing at, always amused me. I'm glad we hadn't adopted that idea this season as our 'cup cupboard' wouldn't have been able to cope! Instead, we'd just settled for keeping all of our away ticket stubs as a momento, and buying a programme at each away game.

My ineptitude at replying to Adrian in a timely fashion, meant that by the time I did reply, he'd already booked himself on Tiger Travel. As it turned out, he had a full journey ahead. He cycled from Walkington to Beverley train station, then took a train into Hull, walked to the KC and boarded his coach, to repeat the whole feat on the way back. There's some dedication for you in the name of Hull City.

As we approached the I-Pro for the lunchtime kick off, Sue was in confident mood, stating that we'd be fine today. After all, she was wearing her lucky pants. They'd worked at Forest and Brentford away, her previous two forays this season.

With that and my polite request for divine intervention, what could possibly go wrong? I even managed to return to the scene and exercise a ghost in managing to finish a pint, one that I simply couldn't do back in March. The away concourse had a buzz about it. Had the doom and gloom of recent weeks lifted? Or had the win in style against Rotherham simply given us a false expectation? All was soon to be revealed.

Even the news re the omission of Allan McGregor, due to a pulled muscle (concourse rumour being that he'd done it *'shagging the ten birds a night'*), didn't seem to dampen the spirits.

Ian Ashbee, who eight years earlier had led City to the Premier League, had been quoted as saying, *"These are the games that define your career. Heroes can be made. I'm sure the City players understand the magnitude of the game. They know what's at stake. These aren't just normal games. A loss during the season and there's always next week to put it right. If you don't perform in these two games, then you can't put it right. There's nowhere else to go and it's a long, long summer of disappointment."*

His words resonated in my mind as we climbed the steps to take our seats right near the back in the away corner. If there was a buzz on the away concourse, then there was certainly one amongst the home fans. The Rams were up for it.

There was plenty of black and white flag furling and as the teams took to the field, Derby were greeted to a tickertape reception. Not quite on a Mario Kempes 1978 Argentina scale, but a tickertape reception all the same.

This just cranked the atmosphere up a few notches and the City fans were giving their all right from the off.

City started with a 4-5-1 system and were content to defend deep and counter attack at pace to render Derby impotent. And throughout the match that is exactly what they were.

Derby were dispirited, disjointed, dismal and outdone. Not until the eightieth minute did they have a shot on target, and that went tamely straight at Jakupovic. Steve Bruce later claimed that even he could have played in goal. Hell, maybe I could, if only I could reach the crossbar. Derby were a shadow of the team that had turned us over so comprehensively in the previous two encounters this season.

That though, shouldn't take anything away from City. We made them look like that with a thoroughly professional and polished performance. As disappointing as we may have been on occasions this season, today we were unequivocally good.

Derby pressed early as you'd expect, a run of a few early corners and set pieces. But City were resolute and rock solid, both in defence and in midfield, Livermore again being inspirational.

And it was he who pounced on sloppy play by Bradley Johnson on the half hour. Winning a loose ball, he found Hernandez. A quick look up and shot, perhaps caught Scott Carson by surprise. Abel fired in a low shot into a bulging net from twenty five yards. 1-0 City.

The previous noise from the home crowd stopped. Abel raced to the corner flag in front of the away section giving his customary fingers pointed to the heavens. Maybe he too had asked for some divine intervention?

The corner of the ground was awash with a sea of amber excitement and mayhem. Grown men were lurching five rows forward from their seats in joy. The whole City team amassed in the corner in equal joy. They, and we, knew what scoring first in such an encounter meant.

From that moment on, any confidence that Derby possessed simply drained. Their crowd too quietened down and the black and amber army assumed control of the I-Pro Stadium

Even better was to follow soon after.

Odubajo, who had been marauding up and down the right flank, intent on covering every blade of grass, took a pot shot five minutes before half time. Not renowned for his goal scoring exploits (but how he deserved one on his performance today), his shot cannoned off Derby defender Jason Shackell, and we once again saw the net ripple. 2-0 City. Dreamland.

If the Derby fans were quiet before, this practically silenced them and sent them looking for solace in a half time pint. Not to worry though, the City lot made up for it. Total City strangers were hugging each other in celebration, this was our highlight of the season. This is what we'd been waiting for.

Half time was joyous, although many City fans were simply just wishing the next forty five minutes of their lives away, myself included. A 2-0 away win will do very nicely thank you.

The team ensured this was eminently achievable with an accomplished second half display, nullifying what little Derby had to offer.

Diame came close to scoring another, and Elmo hit the side netting, but not to worry, let's not be greedy and expect a third?

And then, as we awaited the referee to blow the full time whistle, a Derby corner was cleared to Odubajo. And that 'moment'.

3-0 City. Full time. Thank you and goodnight. Wembley beckoned, I could almost see it, all the way from DE24. Even we can't cock this up?!

The usual chants of *"Don't wanna go home, don't wanna go ho-oome, this is the best trip, don't wanna go home"* echoed out. I say echoed, as the Derby faithful had all filtered out, some long before Robertson's decisive third strike.

We were practically the last ones to leave the ground. We were in no real rush. We were savouring the moment, this is what an away day is all about.

I did have a few minor pangs of guilt upon our exit. The floor was strewn with discarded black and white flags, which only two hours earlier had been expectantly waved. We witnessed several young Derby supporters, probably around seven to eight years old, tears rolling down their cheeks, dads trying to offer some words of comfort and a conciliatory arm around the shoulder. Their day will come, maybe next season? Today was our day. It was all about Hull City AFC I'm afraid.

A special mention today must be given to both City full backs, Robertson and Odubajo in particular. Their overlapping, forward play and energy levels were exceptional.

Odubajo was quality personified. Whilst a deserved goal eluded him, he was fantastic at both ends of the pitch. He outplayed his opponents, be that defenders or attackers, with skill and trickery, so much so that Chris Martin had to resort to throwing him to the ground in the closing minutes, in an off the ball incident. Moses, after a bit of tactical time wasting, then got up, and beamed a broad smile. He'd won the day.

The drive home was a car full of smiles. Leicester had been crowned Premier League champions, ten points clear with only three losses all season. As we approached Gods own county, this was followed up by listening on the radio to North Ferriby edge their own play off final match to secure promotion to the Vauxhall Conference. Two remarkable and 'against all odds' achievements.

Adrian was probably pulling wheelies on his cycle home from Beverley train station.

Their seasons were over.

It felt like City's was just about to begin again.

"HE'S MAGIC, YOU KNOW, MO-SES ODU-BA-JO…."

CHAPTER 64

DERBY COUNTY (H) – PLAY OFF SEMI FINAL SECOND LEG, TUESDAY 17TH MAY 2016

"TYPICAL CITY, A DEATH BY A THOUSAND CUTS... ALMOST"

Three days after the magnificent display at Derby, we rocked up to the KC for the return leg. Some were no doubt expecting a carnival like atmosphere. An atmosphere that would maybe push to one side all the negativity surrounding the off field antics and mis-management. An evening, dare I say it, to enjoy.

Even by City standards, and those of us who have clocked enough miles up on the City milometer have witnessed many an occasion that have seen us fall near the final hurdle, any inability to proceed to a Wembley final would have been an unprecedented first. No team in play-off history, had ever lost from a two goal first leg advantage. Some bookies even had City at odds of 1/200 to reach Wembley after the first leg. I wasn't tempted to put a bet on.

And by god, how close we came to messing it all up. In the end we sneaked through, after somehow scrambling to a 2-0 home defeat, coming out 3-2 winners on aggregate. Oh, for that 98th minute Robertson goal the previous Saturday

For every inch as good as we had been on the Saturday prior, the exact same starting eleven, were as equally bad tonight. The polar opposite could be said for Derby, who on the night, were excellent.

It was a true reminder of how fickle football can be. How it has to sometimes be endured and not enjoyed. Games won and lost by fine margins, not just with the body, but with the mind as well. Oh, and how it fucks with your head as well! (a real need for blasphemy there!)

In the few days build up to the second leg, I could think of nothing else. It dominated my entire thought process. I'm sure it did for Thomas as well and I envisaged him staring out of the school window at lessons, only to be awoken from his City Wembley visions, with a shout of *"Bunton, you boy!!"*

Surely we couldn't cock this up? Just keep it tight for the first twenty minutes or so, allow them no space, knock it into row Z if needs be. Hell, even kick the opposition if needs be. Again, an easy game from your plastic seat. Doesn't stop you trying to kick every ball, head every cross, or win every tackle though does it?

We'd watched Sheffield Wednesday edge past a desperately unlucky Brighton the previous night in the other play-off semi-final, so we knew what lie in store underneath the Wembley arch, towards the back end of May.

I'd also been in touch with Geoff Bielby, chairman of the Hull City Supporters Trust, in between the fixtures, to discuss my book ideas. Unsurprisingly, being avid City fans just like us all, the Trust were incredibly supportive and proffered any kind of assistance that they could provide. A true gent, to whom I am extremely grateful.

It was also Steve Bruce's two hundreth game as manager of Hull City, and two years to the day since our FA Cup Final against Arsenal. So despite my 'in bred' Hull City fears gnawing away at the back of my mind, holding a seemingly unassailable three goal cushion, we meandered our way to the KC with hopes and expectations high.

"Enjoy the game" the football widow said, as we closed the front door behind us.

"It's not about enjoyment", I replied.

Poor girl was off for a night shift at Hull Royal, or 'Hell Royal' as it's more affectionately known. I knew she'd try to spend most of the evening on the tenth or eleventh floor, where she could gain a vantage point of the KC, all lit up. If she couldn't be there in person with us, she'd at least be there in spirit. I'd already instructed her to carry out some 'cosmic ordering' for a favourable City result. Anything to help the cause.

As we got nearer to the ground, the doubt levels increased.

Surprisingly there were hardly any queues at the turnstiles. Even a play-off semi-final couldn't sell out this season, a crowd of 20,470 only, such is the current malaise and distaste about 'most things City'. It was also later suggested to us that the turnstile stewards had been advised to just override any potential ticketing issues. *'Just get them in as quick as possible'*, being the instructions. How typically hypocritical of the club, when previously stating that the whole absurd membership scheme had come about as a result of concession tickets being used by adults.

The majority of seats were adorned by 'Hull City flags', probably about 15,000 of them. I say 'Hull City flags' in the loosest of terms, as not one of them bore the name Hull City. We just shoved ours under our seat for some poor soul to tidy up later.

A quick photo of Ian and Callum, the expert custodians of our flag at home games towards the back of the South Stand temporarily quelled our fears – the boys were confident.

The custodians of the flag at home games. They were confident ahead of Derby at home. Me? Mmmm …

The Derby fans had dubbed the game *'Istanhull'* in a bid to inspire their team – an obvious reference to Liverpool's Champions League Final comeback against AC Milan in 2005. If Liverpool could overcome a three goal half time deficit, why not Derby? And we are no AC Milan.

The game kicked off and any confidence levels I did have simply drained away in an instant.

We should have been prepared for Derby to fly out of the traps and surge forwards. It didn't seem as though we were. We were like 'rabbits caught in the headlights'.

Less than five minutes had gone, and I'd checked the clock three times already. It was most definitely going to be a long night.

Just as we had been on Saturday, the Derby fans were in great voice, urging their team forwards. The City fans in contrast, were already perching forward to the edge of their seats, head in hands. You could feel the tension all around, an air of anxiety. Each of us soon to be lost in our own private grief, yet all as one at the same time.

It didn't take long for this feeling to get worse.

Derby, firmly on the front foot, had City back pedalling. They'd just see Johnny Russell narrowly fire over, but seconds later, the dreaded early goal arrived.

Christie made a surging run down the right and crossed for Chris Martin. He smartly headed the ball back across goal for Russell, and after his first attempt was only partially blocked by Curtis Davies on the line, Russell gleefully tapped in from close range. No wild celebrations by the Derby players. Russell promptly collected the ball from the net, plonked it on the centre spot, as if to say, "Game On."

The goal could have been avoided and as sloppy as it looked, it would be symptomatic of the night as a whole.

Only six minutes gone. The Derby fans were ecstatic. The home sections, almost as one, after an initial collective intake of breath, all let out an audible groan.

The Derby lot were enjoying themselves, they sensed an unlikely turnaround, buoyed by their teams start to the game. "We're gonna bounce in a minute" they claimed. And then they all did in unison. This was repeated in amongst jovial taunts directed at the City dug out, "Steve Bruce, he's got a face like his arse, he's got a face like his arse."

Steve wasn't the only one, as we were all being put through our emotions.

The nervousness in the crowd was matched by erratic City play on the pitch. Stray passes were made, clumsy fouls committed and yellow cards littered. Shots were peppered at the City South Stand goal, but somehow we managed to hold out for a bit longer.

That was until about ten minutes before half time when Derby doubled their lead. If the first goal was sloppy, this was even worse.

Martin Olsson was allowed space on the left, and he sent in a dangerous looking low cross. A Curtis Davies deflection saw the ball spin into the direction of our left back, and goal scoring hero of Saturday. This time though, the unfortunate Andy Robertson merely proceeded to hack the ball into the back of his own net.

Any re-assurance about a comfortable Wembley passage that the KC crowd had been looking for had evaporated. We'd barely laid a glove on them, but were now like the proverbial boxer on the ropes, just waiting for a mighty right hook to finish us off.

Two nil down and still fifty five minutes to go. I felt numb, unable to come up with any words to explain what we'd just witnessed. It felt like a death by a thousand cuts, and it was bloody hurting.

So I did what any sane human being would do at that point. For the first time in the entire season, I got up and left my seat. Why, I'm not entirely sure. I wasn't going to leave the ground and I didn't need the toilet. Nor was I hungry. If anything I felt sick. But somehow, I need a momentary reprise from what I was watching on the pitch. I didn't want to see any more.

A full season was crumbling away, right here, right now.

I wandered aimlessly for a few minutes on the concourse, not really knowing what to do. I wasn't on my own.

And then a cheer from the home crowd went up and awoke me from my haze. My senses kicked in and I returned to my seat. I'd missed Odubajo burst into the Derby penalty box going down under a possible shove. The shouts were claiming for a City penalty. Go on ref, give it, give us a lifeline back into the game. The shouts were forlorn, as referee Michael Oliver had correctly pointed only for a goal kick.

The half time whistle blew and it was a relief. We needed a Curtis Davies half time team talk a la Sheffield United in that FA Cup Semi Final. Or a 'Steve Bruce managerial team talk of his career'. Otherwise we were staring at the abyss.

I'm not really sure if we got either, as the second half initially continued in the same vain that the first half had ended, all Derby.

A great early second half chance fell to Bryson inside the six yard box, who thankfully fluffed it. It was a huge let off. Had a third Derby goal gone in, then a semi-final exit would surely have been inevitable?

What soon followed was, as it turned out to be, an inspired substitution. The ineffective Tom Huddlestone was replaced with David Meyler. For all of Tom's silky skills and passing ability, he is not renowned for 'putting his foot in'. In my eyes, that's what we needed, certainly tonight anyway. Meyler has that uncanny habit and industry to his game, a never say die attitude, which was more suited to tonight's affair.

David 'put himself about' and managed to break up the fluency of Derby's game. As a result, their midfield no longer enjoyed it quite so much. They continued to have the majority of possession but now we seemed more capable of holding them at bay. We'd fought back off the ropes. A couple of late scares kept us all on our toes, or seat edges. Chris Martin was denied by a good Jakopovic save, but the early 'edginess' and panic had disappeared and we defended resolutely.

This clearly didn't stop us from biting our fingernails and watching the final minutes through our fingers, face covered.

I thought of the football widow's comments as we'd left the door earlier. *"Enjoy the game"* she'd said. She hasn't got one iota of what we'd just been through! In the words of Jim Royle, *"Enjoy the game, my arse!"*

The clock ticked down (slowly!) and eventually the final whistle arrived.

We'd survived the emotional rollercoaster, teetered on the edge of an ugly collapse, but eventually survived. Another Wembley appearance, our fourth in just eight years was booked and assured. We were ninety (possibly one hundred and twenty) minutes away from rejoining the alleged elite of English football at the first attempt.

We felt compelled to try and celebrate this prospect.

The inevitable pitch invasion took place, and one tosser aside who chose to confront a Derby player, this was all good natured. The majority even took time to applaud the Derby fans, who had been magnificent on the night and from a supporter of a different team, those comments are not used lightly.

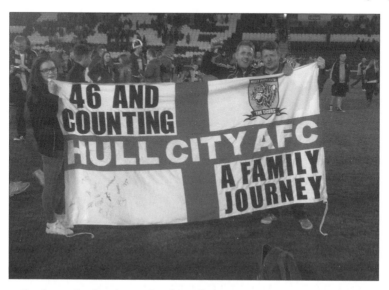

On the pitch after the Derby play off. Bri Lee seems to get everywhere.

Play Off Victory. Charlotte – 'Never in doubt'.
Me – 'Stupid bloody game. I need a drink.'

However, the feeling was very different to 2008. It was not one of euphoria, but one of utter relief. We all felt drained.

There was no re-appearance by the players. After a quick couple of photos on the pitch, we all eventually filtered our way home for a well deserved night cap. Or two.

The performance had been so Jekyll and Hyde. We'd flirted with disaster, going from arguably the best performance of the season, to one of the worst, in just three days. An insipid performance, but hopefully one that is now out of the way.

The Sheffield Wednesday manager had been in attendance. As their fans sing, *"Carlos had a dream...."*, never mind Steve Bruce.

But none the less, with just one more game to go in this seemingly never ending season, ten days time will see us converge on Wembley. This should be enough to whet the appetite of anyone connected to Hull City.

A potential hero, to emulate Dean Windass, hopefully writing this book's 'happy ever after' in the world's richest football match.

"WEMBERLEE... WEMBERLEE... WE'RE THE FAMOUS 'ULL CITY AND WE'RE OFF TO WEMBERLEE..."

CHAPTER 65

"A DIAMOND FROM THE RIGHT BOOT OF DIAME"

So here it is. A fifty seven game build up has led to this. One final game at the mecca of English football, a Championship Play Off Final in sunny May 2016. Shit or bust you could say?

Lose and serious question marks about the future of the club under its current stewardship. A club still 'languishing' in the Championship, without the income streams attached to it. A club that does not own its own ground and with one seasons parachute payments gone, is potentially a difficult proposition to sell. Particularly when you also factor in whatever the current level of debt to the owners is. It certainly makes it less attractive to a would be purchaser.

A club however in the Premier League, even if for only one season, is a different kettle of fish. Next season, the team finishing bottom is rumoured to 'win' almost £100 million. You could lose every game, let alone 'do a Derby', and still earn £100 million. And that is before any parachute payments (around £75 million), increased marketing, sponsorship, ticket sales, and merchandise sales are factored in. Experts suggest that promotion to the Premier League this season is worth somewhere between a minimum of £200 million, potentially rising to £300 million. Telephone numbers!

Now those sorts of income streams are something you can sell. Or alternatively, keep for yourselves!

No wonder they call the Championship Play Off Final, the richest game in the history of world football. It's not necessarily 'the beautiful game', but definitely, 'the bountiful game'.

Since the victory over Derby in the Semi Finals, my anticipation and thoughts about this day had immediately started. There was no way in the world that I was missing it, or not getting excited (and nervous) about it. Thirty plus years of following City have for the most part, been waiting, but never quite believing, that these occasions would happen.

However, maybe a fourth visit to Wembley in eight years might mean the novelty has worn off for some City supporters? Hell, shagging Kylie Minogue is probably exciting the first time, after that, maybe it feels routine?! (sorry, football widow for that analogy!).

Add into that the obvious current apathy and total disharmony between the club and its supporters at present, you can understand a waning lack of interest. A continuing infliction of bad news, week after week on the supporters has drained a lot of enthusiasm out of following City, particularly this season. As such, there was clearly a very different feeling to that of 2008, our last Championship play off Wembley appearance. Could anything possibly top that?

Back then, the queues snaked around the KC stadium at stupid o'clock, such was the desperation for supporters to get their hands on a ticket. Then, our allocation of thirty six thousand tickets sold out in just two days. Demand was insatiable.

Part of this could be attributed to that 'hope and expectation' thing already mentioned. Back in 2008, we 'hoped' but certainly did not 'expect'. We just rode the crest of a wave as momentum eventually took us to listening to that commentary line,

"...Quite simply, destined to be...", as the bleached hair bloke from Gypsyville scored that peach of a goal that helped secure out first ever promotion to the top flight.

This year, there was an air of expectation about going up. It just felt so different.

It all meant that City simply couldn't give their tickets away. A generous allocation of three tickets per pass couldn't get anywhere near getting rid of thirty six thousand tickets this time round. Nor did the subsequent general sale. In the end, only about twenty six thousand City seats were filled.

Thousands of supporters obviously lost since 2008, each no doubt with their own story and reason. To be fair, you can argue that many of them must have

Cruel and painful. David Nugent heads in a last gasp winner to condemn us to defeat at one of our rivals, Boro away.

(PA Images)

'How shit must we be …?' A 4-0 drubbing at the hands of Derby. Not my best night of the season.

(Getty Images)

Snoddy curls in the Goal of the Season to just about secure a play off spot (even if technically it was an own goal!)

(PA Images)

The HCST 'unite' the City fans in protest at home to Brentford.

(Getty Images)

An abhorent membership scheme is announced. No more concessions. Scenes like this may be coming to an end.

(Getty Images)

Nice tats: Abel thanks some divine intervention and celebrates the opener at the I-Pro in the play off first leg.

(PA Images)

Robertson drills home a decisive 98th minute goal to give us a 3-0 cushion. Wemberleeee beckons.

(Getty Images)

An air of expectation and dread looms around the KC. A 3-0 first leg lead. Surely even City can't cock this up?

(Getty Images)

Typical City. Death by a thousand cuts … almost. Robertson puts into his own net for 3-0 Derby. 'Squeaky Bum Time.'

(PA Images)

'No pyro, no party.' We finally edge **** Derby in the play offs. More relief than hysteria. But a play off final at Wembley is ours never the less.

(Getty Images)

A golden chance. Robertson skys over at Wembley to leave it 0-0.

(PA Images)

A Diamond from the right boot of Diame. 1-0 City.

(Getty Images)

Someone looks happy. He's not the only one.

(PA Images)

Not a bad little ground. Host again to Premier League Football.

(Getty Images)

Enough said.

(Getty Images)

been 'day trippers' anyway, since we have never averaged thirty six thousand at home games, either back in 2008 or this season. However, lost they were, which are worrying signs. All the indication is, that numbers are likely to continue falling, regardless of today's result, particularly if the current status quo is maintained.

What materialised just around kick off at Wembley today, was in reality the ultimate red card, or should we say, red seat protest. Huge swathes of empty seats in the City end and side, on a Wembley day out.

The Wednesday fans later ridiculed us by singing "*You're support is fucking shit*". There is clearly an element of truth in this, but don't discount the fact that if you are continually shat on, then things will always eventually start smelling of shit!

This was compounded by the fact that the name Hull City appeared on the Sheffield Wednesday shirts, but somehow not on our own. Symptomatic of our PR as a whole.

All in all, a constant reminder that supporters should not be taken for granted.

The feeling in the blue and white half of Sheffield was the polar opposite to that in Hull. They firmly believed that the sleeping giant was awakening, and this was their moment. Twenty plus years since they last played at Wembley, and an eternity since top flight status. The thirst for success was there for all to see. And they all wanted to see it as tickets were snapped up like gold dust. It sounded so reminiscent of City in 2008.

Days slowly ebbed by to the 28th May, and as each one passed, my predictions of what might happen constantly changed.

Our team is, man for man, even without my black and amber bias, better than Wednesday's. Play to our capabilities and we should win. However, predicting City is impossible. We have been wildly inconsistent this season. One game we can be all Championship conquering, the next simply terrible, and all within days of one another. Just look at the Derby play off games. Breath taking first leg, shite the second.

I wondered if I was beginning to want the win too much. Maybe having the dream to win was more rewarding than the actual fulfilment? I was kind of hoping that maybe all the hours spent in just getting to the games and writing this stuff up, would be rewarded for us getting some sort of City victory.

Yeah, I clearly had my own selfish reasons for wanting a win. What a perfect end to this book it would be. A perfect end to an imperfect season. Something for Thomas and I to certainly cherish and look back upon fondly in seasons to come.

To put it simply though, I couldn't call it. There had been little to choose between the teams in the two league encounters, both draws, both tight affairs. There would be no reason why Wembley, with all the added pressure, would be any different. Like everyone else, I'd simply have to cross my fingers and hope for the best.

The one thing I had decided though was that, as best I could, I was going to try and enjoy the day. It was certainly a time to forget the off field crap, and relish the day watching City at Wembley. What doesn't sound good about that?

Previous Wembley visits with City have involved me, in the main, remaining sober. Either because I've been driving, or because I've been so pent up, that drinking was not befitting with my mood levels. This season would be different. We'd already sorted out hotels back in March after the disappointing home draw with Nottingham Forest, so today, I was intent on drinking industrial quantities of alcohol. I say industrial, as much as my body might be able to take anyway.

So the day arrived.

After finally rousing Thomas out of bed, an hour later than expected, we were ready. A quick listen to

"Tiger, tiger, burning bright,
On hallowed turf, a glorious sight
What immortal hand or eye could frame, thy faithful symmetry"

We then set the clocks to 3:39, denoting the time of Deano's goal in 2008, and left Hallyink's picture of 'that goal' in our front window. An omen we hoped, for a 'new Deano' to emerge.

The football widow assumed the chauffeur's role and we all set off down south. The Yorkshire invasion had begun.

Travelling down the M62 it felt good. Many a car was draped in City colours, be that flags or scarves hanging out of windows, fluttering away. The feeling ebbed a little as we hit the M18 and M1. The gazillions of Wednesday-ites now joined us. Blue and white everywhere. It suddenly dawned on me again that there was another team playing. What if we lost, what would we all feel like then?

Our immediate destination was to ditch the car at our hotel in Ruislip, and quickly jump on the tube to partake in some pre match drinking in The Torch. We had arranged to meet Dave and Dutch Pete there, who had travelled over from Holland for the game.

Upon our arrival, the pub inside and car park outside was awash with black and amber. Even the pub sign bore the correct colours. And, so much merriment was had prior to the five pm kick off. I even seemed to be drinking 'black and amber' as my intake alternated between Guinness and lager, all with the infamous Wembley arch in view.

Determined to go and try and enjoy the day. First stop The Torch.

Many familiar faces were on show and lots of grown men had struggled to get into nostalgic City shirts from seasons gone by, clearly originally purchased when they were all a few pounds lighter in weight. The obvious favourite for me was the City green away shirt, today adorned by Andy Stannard, Cottingham's very own Tony Adams. The feeling in the pub was definitely not over confident.

'City here, City there, City every … where'

This though, had no bearing on the quantity of alcohol being consumed, which was certainly going down well.

Sir Bobby leads us to our seats.
This is it.

Eventually, after persuasion by Charlotte and Thomas in particular, we dragged ourselves away and made the short walk up Wembley Way, to see the day's main attraction. As we approached the stadium, initially I thought the steward had steered us in the wrong direction as he led us to the statue of Bobby Moore. He carefully guided us in to an extremely posh part of Wembley, no turnstiles, just an array of escalators, bars and restaurants. It felt a very long way since our first away game of the season at Accrington Stanley.

Still time to drain a £5.20 pint, the football widow instead opting for the £10 fish and chips. Wembley has to be paid for somehow I suppose.

A quick unfurling of our flag and before we knew it, kick off was imminent.

Despite the empty seats in the City end, you simply cannot do anything but be in awe at Wembley. I won't get tired of watching City play there, that's a fact. I closed my eyes and envisaged the football widow's mum pacing around her care home shouting *"Up The Tigers"*. She was certainly with us in spirit and our minds, as she had been all season.

I just kept saying to myself, *"Keep a clean sheet, keep a clean sheet"* over and over again, confident that chances would come our way at some stage. Now, Wembley and all its excitement aside, there was a football match to win. Albeit a bloody important one.

Wednesday probably started the brighter of the two teams, and had the first real opportunities.

Dawson saw an early yellow card for up ending Forestieri. The latter's free kick was 'pawed' away by Jakupovic. The same feets was repeated shortly after, this time from a Ross Wallace free kick. Not the most convincing saves, but safe enough.

From that moment on though, City began to impose themselves on the match, and I can barely remember our goal being threatened too much. It would take a full week before I watched the entire match again on a Sky re-run, and only then, did I fully realise how in control of the game City had been.

At the match that late Saturday May afternoon, whilst my face may not have portrayed it, I did actually feel reasonably confident. Yes you heard right, me, confident! Just get that all important first goal, and we'll be fine.

On the half hour a Snodgrass corner found Abel, whose header was cleared off the line. Half shouts for handball and a penalty from Dawson ensued, although they were correctly waved away.

Soon to follow, Westwood in the Owls goal, thwarted Hernandez, when played through by Diame, racing off his line to deflect his shot over the bar. Moses Odubajo then cut in from the right, to shoot just wide.

Closer still, as Diame then outmuscled the Wednesday defence, and with the aid of a few stepovers, eventually thudded a shot against the upright, Westwood motionless.

It was the closest we came to breaking the deadlock in the first half, but it was a confident display by City. As confident as you can be, still at 0-0.

Dave got the round in at half time at the ever efficient kiosks, just to keep the alcohol levels up, and we soon returned to our seats.

The Wednesday fans were in great voice and making a din. Me, I heard them, but was now edging further to the front of my seat, praying for a City goal.

An early chance for Forestieri as he tried to latch onto a Westwood punt upfield. Dawson miscued, but Curtis Davies soon made an important covering tackle to avert the danger.

The game then assumed the same pattern as that previously. Lots of City possession, probing and pushing, with chances coming along.

Dawson next to be denied by Westwood, with a low shot following a Snodgrass cross.

And then just before the hour mark, came the chance of the match. Just as they had done, away at Derby, Odubajo crossed low from the right to Andy Robertson, who had timed his run to perfection. Unfortunately this time, he ballooned the ball over the bar from about ten yards. Andy buried his head in his hands. Thousands behind the goal, myself included, did exactly the same, amidst exasperated gasps of *"Shit"*.

Maybe a goal wasn't coming?

Oh yes it was, as on seventy two minutes, the enigma that is Diame showed us a real piece of class.

A poor clearance was collected by Snodgrass. He dropped a shoulder and cut inside, and then shifted the ball right to Diame, in a few yards of space. One touch, a look up, and with a swing of his right boot, he curled a fantastic shot just beyond and over the reach of Westwood's outstretched glove.

A Wembley net rippled. 1-0

A City end erupted in joy, hands held aloft.

Diame, similarly hands aloft, was mobbed by his team mates, happy to receive the adulation. A goal fit to win any game. A goal fit to win a Wembley play off. A £200 million pound goal. And a goal fit to sign off our fifty eight game season.

I looked up to the gods and whispered a thank you, and then kissed each one of my family. My eyes felt watery and it was most definitely an emotional moment for me, in this season of all seasons.

Wednesday threw some subs on, including the big man Nuhiu. City replaced our attacking threats of Hernandez, Snodgrass and Diame for Meyler, Clucas and Maguire.

Steve Bruce was clearly confident and content to see out the remainder of the game out. Me, I could probably have done with a general anaesthetic to see out the remaining twenty minutes. Just wake me up when it's over. Unfortunately that option wasn't on the agenda, so instead, like everyone else, I had to slug it out.

Chants of *"1-0 to the empty seats"* rang out of the City end, well the occupied bits anyway.

There was no need for us to worry, as from the moment he came on, everything seemed to land on either Maguire's head or feet, and with certain aplomb, on each occasion, he alleviated any danger.

One last chance saw Helan blaze over as seventy thousand people held their breath, and with that it was all over. We were back in the Premier League.

The Wednesday players slumped to their knees. City players rejoiced and danced. After the usual handshakes, eventually Michael Dawson et al climbed the Wembley steps, emulating his brother Andy some eight years previous.

With a sense of irony, the Saturday evening Wembley clock ticked around to about 19:04. Captain Michael Dawson lifted the trophy to signal the end to a promotion winning season.

'You Beauty. Get in There.'
(PA Images)

'Caravan of Love' and 'Happy Hour' bellowed out from the PA system. I did a bit of dad dancing, the kids grimaced.

We were practically the last to leave our block, eventually being ushered out by the stewards after collecting our flag for one last time. We didn't want the day, let alone the season to end. What now?

We ambled back up Wembley Way, ducking into the Novotel Hotel for a couple more pints. This avoided the queue for the tube, and helped prolong the celebrations that bit longer. In here we bumped into the guys from Amber Nectar, who we had listened to throughout the season. Thereafter, Charlotte actually asked if we could go back to the Torch. Who were we to argue?

It was still full of City fans, set to enjoy their evening, if not quite so, the following morning.

We eventually departed Wembley around 9.45, the tube station now looking desolate, and somewhat different to several hours earlier. Hardly a soul around, just us and our Wembley thoughts.

A quick stop off at a Pizza Express for a bite to eat, much to the dismay of the staff who had looked intent on closing until our arrival. The football widow had to order for me as I could no longer read the menu. The 'amber nectar' level was almost full, and now starting to take its toll.

I began to reflect on the season as a whole.

We have certainly made some memories of our season, and am so glad we took 'the journey'.

I felt so proud of Thomas, and would not have wanted anyone else with me every step of the way.

Go on Thomas. Go on City!

"…E-I-E-I-E-I-O, UP THE FOOTBALL LEAGUE WE GO, WHEN WE GET PROMOTION, THIS IS WHAT WE'LL SING, WE ALL LOVE YOU, WE ALL LOVE YOU, BRUCEY IS OUR KING…"

A City promotion. Father and Son – A Family Journey.

(PA Images)

CHAPTER 66

"POST WEMBLEY SCRIPT"

Almost immediately after I had awoken from my Wembley slumber, I decided I didn't really want to wake up. Stuff it, let's just stay asleep and soak it all in. Unfortunately life goes on.

Fortunately for us though, the football widow had already arranged all sorts of post Wembley stuff. It was as if she'd known the outcome all along, but just kept it to herself.

First up was a night in Cheltenham, albeit a day late, to join the rest of my family in my mother's eightieth birthday celebrations. I tried to avoid being smug and tried (yes tried) to not mention that Hull City had just got promoted to the Premier League. A few passing references were made, not just by me, but I refrained, probably asking myself the question, *"has that really just happened?"*

A good night was had by all and then the football widow's surprise arrived. I knew something was in the air, but she had only booked us all a four night stay in Majorca, all inclusive. Top girl. Top wife. Top football widow. Every home should have one.

Whilst I had been panicking about what would be, she had the foresight to think ahead.

So a short drive up to East Midlands airport and Spain we were bound.

A Yorkshireman, in Spain, on an all inclusive, after a Hull City win at Wembley to gain promotion to the Premier League, after witnessing all fifty eight games of the season. Yes, the bars, all of them, were like having a tag tied to my ankle.

One particular day stands out.

A long season which involved many of these.

We'd missed breakfast, going for the teenager lie in. So feeling a bit thirsty, we went to the bar for a drink. With the full intention of having a coffee, a black one, I changed my mind at the last minute and ordered a Mahou. It was only 9.45am.

I had a couple more.

After making polite conversation, it surprisingly enough changed to football, and more importantly, Hull City. The season had finished, had it not?

Yes, but Thomas and I soon noted that next seasons fixtures were out a week on Thursday. Thomas immediately added the grounds of Bournemouth, Swansea, Watford, Crystal Palace and West Ham to his tick list. I thought of the players we could realistically sign, Robbie Brady, Ross McCormack…?

Charlotte rolled her eyes, thought, and then said to me, *"Shut up dad, you're boring!"* The football widow looked me in the eye. I knew she understood. She'd signed up for it years ago.

And with that, bored of it fifty eight times already, they left me. Alone at the bar, with yet more Mahou, all pre midday.

I sat there, gazing at the crystal blue waters beyond. Surrounded by Germans on holiday, bum bags and all. Fuck it, I ordered another one.

Needless to say, I was wearing a Hull City top. Not once had I worn one all season in attendance. But abroad, 'Brit's on the piss' style, it's obligatory?

I closed my eyes and saw Deano's volley, back in 2008, and then Diame curling a sublime shot beyond an outstretched glove to ripple a Wembley net. As a Hull City fan, does it get much better?

With my eyes still shut, I thought…

Steve Bruce had a dream. Do you know what? Back in May 2014, I had a dream. And do you know what else?

I would have signed Diame (obviously).

And I would have sent Ben Arfa back home.

I would clearly have played Daws at the back.

Oh, and definitely Abel in attack.

Why? Because….

"…..WE ARE HULL CITY…
IN AMBER AND BLACK
IN AMBER AND BLACK
IN AMBER AND BLACK.."

"ONCE, ALWAYS AND FOREVER…
AMBER AND BLACK"

But not without the help of this lot. Thank you.

HULL CITY 2015 / 16 - A SEASON IN NUMBERS AND THE COST OF FOOTBALL

Game No	Day	Date	Venue	TV	Competition	Opponents	Score City	Score Opp	Attendance	Away Following	
1	Sat	8th Aug	H		Championship	Huddersfield	2	0	19,381	2,317	Clucas 39, Akpom 71
2	Tues	11th Aug	A		League Cup 1	Accrington Stanley	2	2	2,118	1,097	Akpom 92, Luer 108
3	Sun	16th Aug	A	Sky	Championship	Wolves	1	1	20,062	1,500	Jelavic 22
4	Tues	19th Aug	H		Championship	Fulham	2	1	16,579		Elmo 34, Aluko 86
5	Sat	22nd Aug	A		Championship	Charlton	1	2	14,844	1,053	Hernandez 89
6	Tues	25th Aug	H		League Cup 2	Rochdale	1	0	10,430		Luer 9
7	Sat	29th Aug	H		Championship	Preston	2	0	16,949		Hernandez 37, Davie
8	Sat	12th Sept	A		Championship	Brighton	0	1	24,815	892	
9	Tues	15th Sept	A		Championship	Cardiff	2	0	13,763	347	Diame 8, Hernandez
10	Sat	19th Sept	H		Championship	QPR	1	1	16,651	629	Dawson 38
11	Tues	22nd Sept	H		League Cup 3	Swansea	1	0	16,286	302	Meyler 41
12	Sat	26th Sept	H		Championship	Blackburn	1	1	16,486	879	Hernandez 73
13	Sat	3rd Oct	A		Championship	Nottingham Forest	1	0	20,985	1,952	Hernandez 41
14	Sat	17th Oct	A	Sky	Championship	Sheffield Wednesday	1	1	20,389	2,074	Hernandez 51
15	Tues	20th Oct	H		Championship	Ipswich Town	3	0	15,942	456	Bruce 36, Akpom 43,
16	Sat	24th Oct	H		Championship	Birmingham City	2	0	17,436	1,444	Meyler 36, Hernande
17	Tues	27th Oct	H		League Cup 4	Leicester	1	1	16,818	2,550	Hernandez 115+1 (5
18	Sat	31st Oct	A		Championship	MK Dons	2	0	15,360	2,907	Elmo 19, Diame 90+5
19	Tues	3rd Nov	A		Championship	Brentford	2	0	9,921	943	Robertson 67, Clucas
20	Sat	7th Nov	H		Championship	Middlesbrough	3	0	20,352	2,554	Diame 44, Clucas 67,
21	Sat	21st Nov	A	Sky	Championship	Bristol City	1	1	14,590	752	Maloney 73
22	Fri	27th Nov	H	Sky	Championship	Derby County	0	2	17,410		
23	Tues	1st Dec	A		League Cup 5	Manchester City	1	4	38,246		Robertson 90+2
24	Sat	5th Dec	A		Championship	Leeds United	1	2	24,962	2,591	Elmo 51
25	Sat	12th Dec	H		Championship	Bolton	1	0	15,739		Akpom 19
26	Wed	16th Dec	H	Sky	Championship	Reading	2	1	15,139		Hernandez 62, Liverr
27	Sat	19th Dec	A		Championship	Rotherham	0	2	10,355	2,571	
28	Sat	26th Dec	H		Championship	Burnley	3	0	21,842	2,422	Livermore 57, Herna
29	Mon	28th Dec	A		Championship	Preston	0	1	13,891	1,734	
30	Fri	1st Jan	A	Sky	Championship	QPR	2	1	16,205	976	Hernandez 61, Diom
31	Sat	9th Jan	H		FA Cup 3	Brighton	1	0	10,706	390	Snodgrass 41
32	Wed	13th Jan	H		Championship	Cardiff	2	0	15,549	162	Hernandez 40, Cluca
33	Sat	16th Jan	H		Championship	Charlton	6	0	16,430	369	Hernandez 9, 16, 39, 5
34	Sat	23rd Jan	A		Championship	Fulham	1	0	16,935		Hernandez 80
35	Sat	30th Jan	H		FA Cup 4	Bury	3	1	7,064	2,746	Akpom 14,57,69
36	Sat	6th Feb	A		Championship	Burnley	0	1	17,667		
37	Sat	13th Feb	A		Championship	Blackburn Rovers	2	0	13,902	1,311	Hernandez 53, Diame
38	Tues	16th Feb	H		Championship	Brighton	0	0	17,321	407	
39	Sat	20th Feb	A	BskyB	FA Cup 5	Arsenal	0	0	59,830		
40	Tues	23rd Feb	A		Championship	Ipswich Town	1	0	17,630	393	Diame 48
41	Fri	26th Feb	H	Sky	Championship	Sheffield Wednesday	0	0	17,884		
42	Thurs	3rd Mar	A	Sky	Championship	Birmingham City	0	1	18,105	591	
43	Tues	8th Mar	H	BskyB	FA Cup 5 Replay	Arsenal	0	4	20,993	2,618	
44	Sat	12th Mar	H		Championship	MK Dons	1	1	16,183	298	Clucas 53
45	Tues	15th Mar	H		Championship	Nottingham Forest	1	1	15,663	520	Aluko 73
46	Fri	18th Mar	A	Sky	Championship	Middlesbrough	0	1	26,791	1,305	
47	Sat	2nd Apr	H		Championship	Bristol City	4	0	16,521	529	Davies 14, Snodgrass
48	Tues	5th Apr	A		Championship	Derby County	0	4	29,078	1,227	
49	Sat	9th Apr	A		Championship	Huddersfield	2	2	12,883	2,214	Hernadez 76, Dioma
50	Fri	15th Apr	H	Sky	Championship	Wolves	2	1	15,504	365	Diomande 5, Snodgra
51	Tues	19th Apr	A		Championship	Reading	2	1	12,949	504	Hernandez 18, Rober
52	Sat	23rd Apr	H		Championship	Leeds United	2	2	20,732	2,356	Hernandez 45+1, Hu
53	Tues	26th Apr	H		Championship	Brentford	2	0	15,225	214	Dean (og) 31, Diame
54	Sat	30th Apr	A	Sky	Championship	Bolton	0	1	14,366	1,213	
55	Sat	7th May	H		Championship	Rotherham	5	1	18,670	2,442	Snodgrass 25, Herna
56	Sat	14th May	A	Sky	Play Off SF	Derby County	3	0	29,969	3,009	Hernandez 30, Shake
57	Mon	17th May	H	Sky	Play Off SF	Derby County	0	2	20,470	2,309	
58	Sat	28th May		Sky	Play Off Final	Sheffield Wednesday	1	0	70,189		Diame 72
							83	49	1,099,155	62,434	

438

Result	Opponents / Scorer	League Position	Miles	Ticket Cost	Programme Cost	Train Cost	Parking	Travel	Incidentals and Subsistence
W		3	20.48	ST	£ -	£ -	£ -	£ -	£ 10.00
W	Crooks 105, Gornell 115		207.92	£ 42.60	£ 3.00	£ -	£ 3.00	£ -	£ 20.00
D	Henry 58	5	260.12	£ 39.60	£ 3.00	£ -	£ 5.00	£ 9.20	£ 20.00
W	Cairney 69	2	20.48	ST	£ -	£ -	£ -	£ -	£ 10.00
L	Makienok 52, J Gudmundsson 90+8	5	423.26	£ 33.60	£ 3.00	£ 18.00	£ -	£ 18.00	£ 20.00
W			20.48	£ -	£ -	£ -	£ -	£ -	£ 10.00
W		2	20.48	ST	£ -	£ -	£ -	£ -	£ 10.00
L	Hemed 5	6	542.74	£ 46.00	£ 3.00	£ -	£ -	£ 5.00	£ 20.00
W		4	483.80	£ 37.00	£ 3.50	£ -	£ -	£ -	£ 20.00
D	Austin 26	3	20.48	ST	£ -	£ -	£ -	£ -	£ 10.00
W			20.48	£ -	£ -	£ -	£ -	£ -	£ 10.00
D	Rhodes 90+1	4	20.48	ST	£ -	£ -	£ -	£ -	£ 10.00
W		5	168.98	£ 30.00	£ 3.00	£ -	£ 4.00	£ -	£ 20.00
D	Forristieri 28	6	123.36	£ 35.00	£ 3.00	£ -	£ -	£ -	£ 20.00
W		4	20.48	ST	£ -	£ -	£ -	£ -	£ 10.00
W		2	20.48	ST	£ -	£ -	£ -	£ -	£ 10.00
W	Mahrez 99		20.48	£ -	£ -	£ -	£ -	£ -	£ 10.00
W		2	325.90	£ 13.00	£ 3.00	£ -	£ 7.00	£ -	£ 20.00
W		1	406.50	£ 35.00	£ 3.00	£ 35.00	£ -	£ 40.00	£ 20.00
W		1	20.48	ST	£ -	£ -	£ -	£ -	£ 10.00
D	Agard 39	1	451.28	£ 131.60	£ 3.00	£ -	£ -	£ 20.00	£ 20.00
L	Butterfield 18, 34	2	20.48	ST	£ -	£ -	£ -	£ -	£ 10.00
L	Bony 12, Ineanacho 80, De Bruyne 82, 87		178.36	£ 38.60	£ 3.00	£ -	£ 10.00	£ -	£ 20.00
L	Wood 30, Adeyemi 45	4	107.96	£ 51.60	£ 3.00	£ -	£ -	£ -	£ 20.00
W		3	20.48	ST	£ -	£ -	£ -	£ -	£ 10.00
W	Blackman 29	4	20.48	ST	£ -	£ -	£ -	£ -	£ 10.00
L	Frecklington 28, Newell 57	4	110.24	£ 29.60	£ 3.00	£ -	£ -	£ -	£ 20.00
W		3	20.48	ST	£ -	£ -	£ -	£ -	£ 10.00
L	Gallagher 66	3	230.82	£ 32.60	£ 3.00	£ -	£ -	£ -	£ 20.00
W	Polter 86	3	405.74	£ 94.60	£ 3.00	£ -	£ -	£ -	£ 20.00
W			20.48	£ 15.00	£ -	£ -	£ -	£ -	£ 10.00
W		2	20.48	ST	£ -	£ -	£ -	£ -	£ 10.00
W		2	20.48	ST	£ -	£ -	£ -	£ -	£ 10.00
W		1	409.92	£ 40.00	£ 3.00	£ -	£ 2.00	£ -	£ 10.00
W	Jones 86		179.54	£ 30.60	£ 3.00	£ -	£ 5.00	£ -	£ 20.00
L	Vokes 77	1	215.20	£ 31.60	£ 3.00	£ -	£ -	£ -	£ 20.00
W		1	210.24	£ 36.60	£ 3.00	£ -	£ 5.00	£ -	£ 20.00
D		1	20.48	ST	£ -	£ -	£ -	£ -	£ 10.00
D			399.44	£ 36.60	£ 3.00	£ 35.20	£ 2.00	£ -	£ 20.00
W		1	417.20	£ 44.60	£ 3.00	£ -	£ 4.60	£ -	£ 20.00
D		1	20.48	ST	£ -	£ -	£ -	£ -	£ 10.00
L	Toral 14	2	265.36	£ 25.60	£ 3.00	£ -	£ -	£ -	£ 20.00
L	Giroud 41,71, Walcott 77, 88		20.48	£ 36.60	£ 2.00	£ -	£ -	£ -	£ 10.00
D	Kay 51	3	20.48	ST	£ -	£ -	£ -	£ -	£ 10.00
D	Gardner 28	4	20.48	ST	£ -	£ -	£ -	£ -	£ 10.00
L	Nugent 90+1	4	163.32	£ 49.60	£ 3.00	£ -	£ -	£ -	£ 20.00
W		4	20.48	ST	£ -	£ -	£ -	£ -	£ 10.00
L	Johnson 29,38, Martin 84, Bryson 90+4	4	177.96	£ 39.60	£ 3.00	£ -	£ -	£ 8.00	£ 20.00
D	Paterson 40, Maguire 90 (og)	4	129.94	£ 38.10	£ 2.00	£ -	£ -	£ -	£ 20.00
W	Edwards 19	4	20.48	ST	£ -	£ -	£ -	£ -	£ 10.00
W	Cooper 4	4	462.40	£ 32.60	£ 3.00	£ -	£ 8.00	£ -	£ 20.00
D	Wood 15, Dallas 88	4	20.48	ST	£ -	£ -	£ -	£ -	£ 10.00
W		4	20.48	ST	£ -	£ -	£ -	£ -	£ 10.00
L	Dobbie 65	4	198.96	£ 35.60	£ 3.00	£ -	£ -	£ -	£ 20.00
W	Frecklington 16	4	20.48	ST	£ -	£ -	£ -	£ -	£ 10.00
W			177.96	£ 65.00	£ 3.00	£ -	£ -	£ -	£ 20.00
L	Russell 7, Robertson og (36)		20.48	£ 60.00	£ -	£ -	£ -	£ -	£ 10.00
W			403.22	£ 240.00	£ 7.00	£ 40.00	£ -	£ -	£ 40.00
			8831.56	£ 1,548.10	£ 92.50	£ 128.20	£ 55.60	£ 100.20	£ 890.00
	Pence per mile (say 15p)		£ 1,324.73						
	Season Tickets			£ 684.00					
	Flag								£ 228.00
			£ 1,324.73	£ 2,232.10	£ 92.50	£ 128.20	£ 55.60	£ 100.20	£ 1,118.00
	Total Cost of the season	£ 5,051.33							

CHAPTER 67

"A SUMMER OF DISCONTENT"

Right this really is it, the last chapter.

The excitement and euphoria of Wembley seems a distant haze.

Rather than a pre-season filled with the speculation of possible signings and where we could finish in the Premier League, instead it's been dominated by one bad news story after another.

A refusal to sell the club and total mis-management has left us about to enter the 16/17 season labelled as the worst prepared club in Premier League history. Perhaps, it was not a promotion to savour but, in fact, the saddest promotion ever?

There will be thousands of empty seats at the KC as testimony to the highly unpopular and unjust membership scheme. Hull City fans are simply voting with their feet.

Not only that, but Steve Bruce, the most successful manager the club have had in my era, has had enough. Tired of trying to be the go between for owners and fans, he simply resigned, unable to tolerate the direction of the club, or lack of it. So no manager either at present.

A potential sale of the club, despite being 'up for sale' since April 2014, and a 'leave within 24 hours policy', the heralding of a new era of ownership, has thus far ceased to materialise. So we are stuck with what we've got.

What we've got is no fan liason, no dialogue and seemingly no hope. The bookies say so.

Not a single first team player has been bought, despite all the riches that promotion to the Premier League brings, and the squad is, to say the least, threadbare.

The goalscoring hero of Wembley has been sold, and coupled with a multitude of long term injuries to first team players like McGregor, Dawson, Bruce and Odubajo, this all meant we entered the opening day of the season with just thirteen fit first team players. Most of the bench had barely started shaving, some probably still have paper rounds!

I could go on and on, but I won't. It's all been well documented. Suffice to say, it doesn't bode well.

However, rather than leave this book on a glum note, I'd prefer to dwell on some positives. As I finally pen these last thoughts (and it's taken me too long), the Premier League season has just started. Our fit thirteen players were pitted against last season's champions Leicester.

Wow. What a performance. A 2-1 victory, against all the odds. A true team effort, epitomising the now collective and unified spirit on the terraces. Against all the odds, I had never felt so proud of a Hull City team. Hell, I'm even contemplating Swansea away. It's starting all over again?

A football club is so much more than its players, or owners. They will come and go, and perhaps, by the time the printing machines have stopped rolling, we may well have new owners. Hopefully the current fury will end. It will disappear and enjoyment will once again, be just around the corner.

The memories of 2015/16 are unique to me, yet possibly shared by all of you.

I firmly believe that, in putting together this book, I have created some memories to cherish, memories that will stay with me forever, memories of *our* club, *your* club, Hull City AFC.

I hope you enjoyed the read. If you recognise any of the characters involved, mention it them. If you recognise me, come and say hello, share a pint. I look forward to seeing you on a concourse somewhere.

We are all a family, the Hull City family.

"...WE'RE CITY TILL WE DIE, CITY TILL WE DIE..."

Picture courtesy of ©hallyink

Picture courtesy of ©hallyink